AF753831

INDONESIA

MINING, OIL AND GAS INDUSTRY EXPORT-IMPORT, BUSINESS OPPORTUNITIES HANDBOOK

VOLUME 1

STRATEGIC INFORMATION AND REGULATIONS

International Business Publications, USA
Washington DC, USA - Indonesia

INDONESIA

MINING, OIL AND GAS INDUSTRY EXPORT-IMPORT, BUSINESS OPPORTUNITIES HANDBOOK

VOLUME 1 STRATEGIC INFORMATION AND REGULATIONS

UPDATED ANNUALLY

Cover Design: **International Business Publications, USA**

We express our sincere appreciation to all government agencies and international organizations which provided information and other materials for this handbook

2014 Edition Updated Reprint International Business Publications, USA
ISBN 1-4387-2355-5

This handbook provides basic information for starting or/and conducting business in the country. The extraordinary volume of materials covering the topic, prevents us from placing all these materials in this handbook. For more detailed information on issues related to any specific investment and business activity in the country, please contact Global Investment Center, USA
Please acquire the list of our business intelligence and marketing reports and other business publications. We constantly update and expand our business intelligence and marketing materials. Please contact the center for the updated list of reports on over 200 countries.

in the USA: **Global Investment Center, USA.**
P.O.Box 15343, Washington, DC 20003
Phone: (202) 546-2103, Fax: (202) 546-3275, E-mail: rusric@erols.com

For additional analytical, marketing and other information please contact Global Investment Center, USA

Printed in the USA

INDONESIA

MINING, OIL AND GAS INDUSTRY EXPORT-IMPORT AND BUSINESS OPPORTUNITIES HANDBOOK

VOLUME 1

STRATEGIC INFORMATION AND REGULATIONS

TABLE OF CONTENTS

STRATEGIC AND DEVELOPMENT PROFILES

STRATEGIC PROFILE

Capital (and largest city)	Jakarta 6°10.5′S 106°49.7′E6.175°S 106.8283°E
Official language(s)	Indonesian
Demonym	Indonesian
Government	Unitary presidential republic
- President	Susilo Bambang Yudhoyono
- Vice President	Boediono
Independence	following Dutch colonial rule
- Declared	17 August 1945
- Acknowledged	27 December 1949
	Area
- Land	1,919,440 km^2 (16th) 735,355 sq mi
- Water (%)	4.85
	Population
- 2009 estimate	238,000,000[2] (4th)
- 2000 census	206,264,595
- Density	119.8/km^2 (84th) 312.7/sq mi
GDP (PPP)	2010 estimate
- Total	$1,027.279 billion
- Per capita	$4,379
GDP (nominal)	2010 estimate
- Total	$670.421 billion
- Per capita	$2,858
Gini (2002)	34.3
HDI (2010)	▲0.734[4] (medium) (111th)
Currency	Rupiah (IDR)
Time zone	various (UTC+7 to +9)
- Summer (DST)	not observed (UTC)
Drives on the	Left
ISO 3166 code	ID
Internet TLD	.id
Calling code	+62

Indonesia officially the **Republic of Indonesia** (Indonesian: *Republik Indonesia* Indonesian pronunciation: [r□publik □ndonesia]), is a sovereign state in Southeast Asia and Oceania. Indonesia is an archipelago comprising approximately 17,508 islands. It encompasses 34 provinces with over 238 million people, making it the world's fourth most populous country. Indonesia's republic form of government comprises an elected legislature and president. The nation's capital city is Jakarta. The country shares land borders with Papua New Guinea, East Timor, and Malaysia. Other neighboring countries include Singapore, the Philippines, Australia, Palau, and the Indian territory of the Andaman and Nicobar Islands. Indonesia is a founding member of ASEAN and a member of the G-20 major economies. The Indonesian economy is the world's 16th largest by nominal GDP.

The Indonesian archipelago has been an important trade region since at least the 7th century, when Srivijaya and then later Majapahit traded with China and India. Local rulers gradually absorbed foreign cultural, religious and political models from the early centuries CE, and Hindu and Buddhist kingdoms flourished. Indonesian history has been influenced by foreign powers drawn to its natural resources. Muslim traders brought the now-dominant Islam, while European powers brought Christianity and fought one another to monopolize trade in the Spice Islands of Maluku during the Age of Discovery. Following three and a half centuries of Dutch colonialism, Indonesia secured its independence after World War II. Indonesia's history has since been turbulent, with challenges posed by natural disasters, corruption, separatism, a democratization process, and periods of rapid economic change.

Indonesia consists of hundreds of distinct native ethnic and linguistic groups. The largest – and politically dominant – ethnic group are the Javanese. A shared identity has developed, defined by a national language, ethnic diversity, religious pluralism within a majority Muslim population, and a history of colonialism and rebellion against it. Indonesia's national motto, *"Bhinneka Tunggal Ika"* ("Unity in Diversity" *literally,* "many, yet one"), articulates the diversity that shapes the country. Despite its large population and densely populated regions, Indonesia has vast areas of wilderness that support the world's second highest level of biodiversity. The country has abundant natural resources, yet poverty remains widespread

Background: The world's largest archipelago, Indonesia achieved independence from the Netherlands in 1949. Current issues include: implementing IMF-mandated reforms of the banking sector, effecting a transition to a popularly elected government after years of rule by dictators, addressing charges of cronyism and corruption among the Chinese-dominated business class, dealing with alleged human rights violations by the military, and resolving growing pressures for some form of autonomy or independence in certain regions such as Aceh and Irian Jaya. On 30 August 1999 a provincial referendum for independence was overwhelmingly approved by the people of Timor Timur. Concurrence followed by Indonesia's national legislature, and the name East Timor was provisionally adopted. The independent status of East Timor has yet to be formally established.

Independence: Proclaimed independence on August 17, 1945. On December 27, 1949, Indonesia became independent from the Netherlands.
Population : 224.8 million
Location/Size: Southeastern Asia/735,310 sq. mi., slightly less than three times the size of Texas
Major Cities: Jakarta (capital) , Surabaya, Bandung, Medan, Semarang, Palembang, Ujung Pandang
Languages: Bahasa Indonesia (official) , English, Dutch, local dialects including Javanese
Ethnic Groups: Javanese (45%) , Sundanese (14%) , Madurese (7.5%) , coastal Malays (7.5%) , other (26%)
Religions: Muslim (88%) , Protestant (5%) , Roman Catholic (3%) , Hindu (2%) , Buddhist 1%) , other (1%)
Defense: Army (220,000) , Navy (43,000) , Air Force (21,000) , Paramilitary forces: Police (177,000) , KAMRA (People's Security) (1.5 million trainees)

ECONOMIC OVERVIEW

Currency: Rupiah
Exchange Rate: US$1 = 9,265 rupiah
Gross Domestic Product : $156.8 billion
Real GDP Growth Rate : 3.8% : 4.8%
Inflation Rate (Consumer Price Index) : 8.2% : 7.8%

Current Account Balance : $4.7 billion
Merchandise Exports : $57.1 billion
Merchandise Imports : $33.0 billion
Merchandise Trade Balance : $24.1 billion
Major Export Products: Manufactured goods, petroleum, natural gas and related products, foodstuffs, raw materials
Major Import Products: Capital equipment, raw and intermediate materials, consumer goods, petroleum products
Major Trading Partners: Japan, United States, Singapore, Hong Kong, Britain, Australia
Total External Debt : $147.6 billion

ENERGY OVERVIEW

Proven Oil Reserves: 5.0 billion barrels
Oil Production: 1.47 million barrels per day (bbl/d) , of which 1.29 million bbl/d is crude oil
Oil Production Capacity : 1.5 million bbl/d
OPEC Production Quota (since: 1.385 million bbl/d
Oil Consumption : 989,000 bbl/d
Net Oil Exports : 481,000 bbl/d
Major Oil Customers: Japan, United States, South Korea, China, Australia, Taiwan, Singapore, Thailand
Crude Oil Refining Capacity: 992,745 bbl/d
Natural Gas Reserves: 72.3 trillion cubic feet (tcf)
Natural Gas Production : 2.24 trillion cubic feet (tcf)
Natural Gas Consumption : 0.97 tcf
Net Gas Exports : 1.27 Tcf
Major LNG Customers : Japan, South Korea, Taiwan
Coal Reserve: 5.75 billion short tons of recoverable reserves of which 85% is lignite and 15% is anthracite
Coal Production : 66.5 million short tons (Mmst)
Coal Consumption : 17.1 Mmst
Net Coal Exports : 51.1 Mmst
Major Coal Customers : Japan, Taiwan, South Korea, the Philippines, and Hong Kong
Electric Generation Capacity: 19.9 gigawatts
Electricity Production : 73.1 terawatthours

ENVIRONMENTAL OVERVIEW

Total Energy Consumption : 3.6 quadrillion Btu* (1.0% of world total energy consumption)
Energy-Related Carbon Emissions : 67.8 million metric tons of carbon (1.1% of world carbon emissions)
Per Capita Energy Consumption : 17.7 million Btu (vs U.S. value of 350.7 million Btu)
Per Capita Carbon Emissions : 0.3 metric tons of carbon (vs U.S. value of 5.5 metric tons of carbon)
Energy Intensity : 22,983 Btu/ $1990 (vs. U.S. value of 13,410 Btu/ $1990)
Carbon Intensity : 0.43 metric tons of carbon/thousand $1990 (vs. U.S. value of 0.21 metric tons/thousand $1990)
Sectoral Share of Energy Consumption : Industrial (57.0%) , Transportation (22.4%) , Residential (18.8%) , Commercial (2.7%)
Sectoral Share of Carbon Emissions : Industrial (53.8%) , Transportation (24.8%) , Residential (18.8%) , Commercial (2.6%)
Fuel Share of Energy Consumption : Oil (56.0%) , Natural Gas (29.2%) , Coal (11.5%)
Fuel Share of Carbon Emissions : Oil (53.8%) , Natural Gas (26.4%) , Coal (15.3%)

Renewable Energy Consumption : 1,970 trillion Btu*
Number of People per Motor Vehicle : 45.5 (vs U.S. value of 1.3)
Status in Climate Change Negotiations: Non-Annex I country under the United Nations Framework Convention on Climate Change (ratified August 23rd, 1994) . Signatory to the Kyoto Protocol (signed July 13th, 1998- not yet ratified) .
Major Environmental Issues: Deforestation; water pollution from industrial wastes, sewage; air pollution in urban areas
Major International Environmental Agreements: A party to Conventions on Biodiversity, Climate Change, Endangered Species, Hazardous Wastes, Law of the Sea, Nuclear Test Ban, Ozone Layer Protection, Ship Pollution, Tropical Timber 83, Tropical Timber 94 and Wetlands. Has signed, but not ratified, Desertification and Marine Life Conservation

* The total energy consumption statistic includes petroleum, dry natural gas, coal, net hydro, nuclear, geothermal, solar and wind electric power. The renewable energy consumption statistic is based on International Energy Agency (IEA) data and includes hydropower, solar, wind, tide, geothermal, solid biomass and animal products, biomass gas and liquids, industrial and municipal wastes. Sectoral shares of energy consumption and carbon emissions are also based on IEA data.

OIL AND GAS INDUSTRIES

Organizations: Perusahaan Pertambangan Minyak dan Gas Bumi Negara (Pertamina) - oil exploration, production, transportation, and marketing; Perum Gas Negara (PGN) -gas distributor and transmission company
Major Producing Oil Fields: Duri, Minas, Belida, Ardjuna, Arun, KG/KRA, Widuri, Nilam, Attaka
Oil Refineries (operating capacity-bbl/d, December 1999) : Cilacap, Central Java (380,000) ; Pertamina-Balikpapan, Kalimantan (240,920) ; Musi, South Sumatra (109,155) ; EXOR-1, Balongan, Java (125,000) ; Dumai, Central Sumatra (114,000) ; Sungai Pakning, Central Sumatra (47,500) ; Pangakalan Brandan, North Sumatra (4,750) ; Cepu, Central Java (3,420)
Product Pipelines: Trans-Java (serving the Surabaya market)
Oil Tanker Terminals: Java: Cilegon, Cilacap, Surabaya, Ardjuna B (offshore) Sumatra: Pangkalan Brandan, Belawan, Dumai, Musi, Perlak, Palembang, Tanjung Uban (offshore) Kalimantan: Balikpapan Sulawesi: Ujung Pandang Irian Jaya: Sorong, Jaya Seram: Bula Natuna Sea: Ikan Pari
Major Gas Fields: Sumatra: Arun, Alur Siwah, Kuala Langsa, Musi, South Lho Sukon, Wampu East Kalimantan: Attaka, Badak, Bekapai, Handil, Mutiara, Nilam, Semberah, Tunu Natuna Sea: Natuna Java: Pagerungan, Terang/Sirasun Irian Jaya: Tangguh
Major Gas Pipelines: Sumatra: Pangkalan Brandan-Dumai
LNG Plants: Arun, Bontang

GEOGRAPHY

Location: Southeastern Asia, archipelago between the Indian Ocean and the Pacific Ocean
Geographic coordinates: 5 00 S, 120 00 E
Map references: Southeast Asia

Area:
total: 1,919,440 sq km
land: 1,826,440 sq km
water: 93,000 sq km

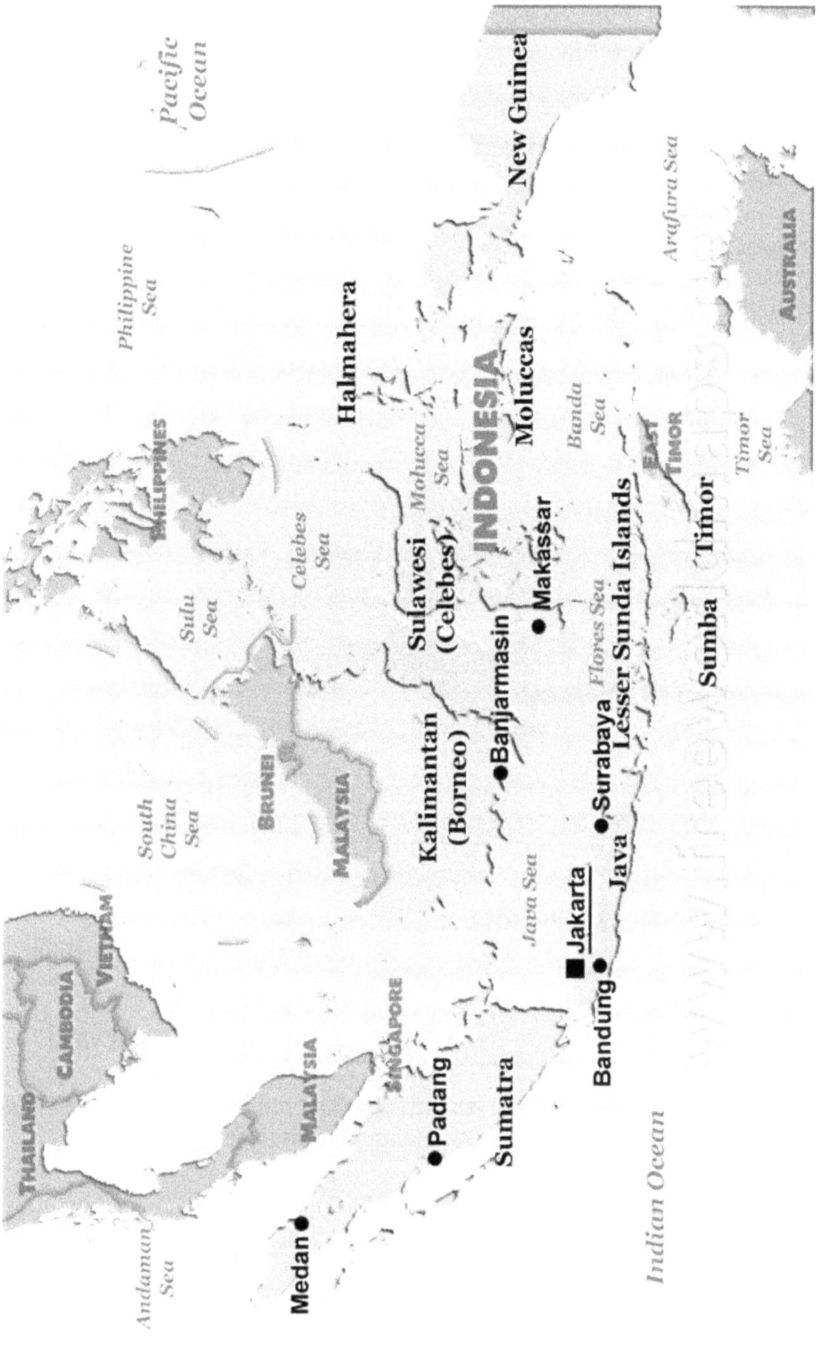

Area - comparative: slightly less than three times the size of Texas

Land boundaries:
total: 2,602 km
border countries: Malaysia 1,782 km, Papua New Guinea 820 km

Coastline: 54,716 km

Maritime claims: measured from claimed archipelagic baselines
exclusive economic zone: 200 nm
territorial sea: 12 nm

Climate: tropical; hot, humid; more moderate in highlands
Terrain: mostly coastal lowlands; larger islands have interior mountains

Elevation extremes:
lowest point: Indian Ocean 0 m
highest point: Puncak Jaya 5,030 m

Natural resources: petroleum, tin, natural gas, nickel, timber, bauxite, copper, fertile soils, coal, gold, silver

Land use:
arable land: 10%
permanent crops: 7%
permanent pastures: 7%
forests and woodland: 62%
other: 14%

Irrigated land: 45,970 sq km (1993 est.)
Natural hazards: occasional floods, severe droughts, tsunamis, earthquakes, volcanoes

Environment - current issues: deforestation; water pollution from industrial wastes, sewage; air pollution in urban areas; smoke and haze from forest fires

Environment - international agreements:
party to: Biodiversity, Climate Change, Desertification, Endangered Species, Hazardous Wastes, Law of the Sea, Nuclear Test Ban, Ozone Layer Protection, Ship Pollution, Tropical Timber 83, Tropical Timber 94, Wetlands
signed, but not ratified: Climate Change-Kyoto Protocol, Marine Life Conservation

Geography - note: archipelago of 17,000 islands (6,000 inhabited) ; straddles Equator; strategic location astride or along major sea lanes from Indian Ocean to Pacific Ocean

PEOPLE

Population: 224,784,210

Age structure:
0-14 years: 30.57% (male 34,932,102; female 33,783,603)
15-64 years: 64.96% (male 72,889,994; female 73,124,821)
65 years and over: 4.47% (male 4,413,268; female 5,640,422)

Population growth rate: 1.63%
Birth rate: 22.6 births/1,000 population
Death rate: 6.31 deaths/1,000 population
Net migration rate: 0 migrant(s) /1,000 population

Sex ratio:
at birth: 1.05 male(s) /female
under 15 years: 1.03 male(s) /female
15-64 years: 1 male(s) /female
65 years and over: 0.78 male(s) /female
total population: 1 male(s) /female

Infant mortality rate: 42.21 deaths/1,000 live births
Life expectancy at birth:
total population: 67.96 years
male: 65.61 years
female: 70.42 years
Total fertility rate: 2.61 children born/woman
Nationality:
noun: Indonesian(s)
adjective: Indonesian
Ethnic groups: Javanese 45%, Sundanese 14%, Madurese 7.5%, coastal Malays 7.5%, other 26%
Religions: Muslim 88%, Protestant 5%, Roman Catholic 3%, Hindu 2%, Buddhist 1%, other 1%

Languages: Bahasa Indonesia (official, modified form of Malay) , English, Dutch, local dialects, the most widely spoken of which is Javanese

Literacy:
definition: age 15 and over can read and write
total population: 83.8%
male: 89.6%
female: 78% (1995 est.)

GOVERNMENT

Country name:
conventional long form: Republic of Indonesia
conventional short form: Indonesia
local long form: Republik Indonesia
local short form: Indonesia
former: Netherlands East Indies; Dutch East Indies

Data code: ID
Government type: republic
Capital: Jakarta

Administrative divisions: 23 provinces (propinsi-propinsi, singular - propinsi) , 2 special regions* (daerah-daerah istimewa, singular - daerah istimewa) , and 1 special capital city district** (daerah khusus ibukota) ; Aceh*, Bali, Bengkulu, Irian Jaya, Jakarta Raya**, Jambi, Jawa Barat, Jawa Tengah, Jawa Timur, Kalimantan Barat, Kalimantan Selatan, Kalimantan Tengah, Kalimantan Timur, Lampung, Maluku, Nusa Tenggara Barat, Nusa Tenggara Timur, Riau, Sulawesi Selatan, Sulawesi Tengah, Sulawesi Tenggara, Sulawesi Utara, Sumatera Barat, Sumatera Selatan, Sumatera Utara, Yogyakarta*; note - there may be a new province named Maluku Utara
note: following the 30 August 1999 provincial referendum for independence which was overwhelmingly approved by the people of Timor Timur and the October 1999 concurrence of

Indonesia's national legislature, the name East Timor was adopted as a provisional name for the political entity formerly known as Propinsi Timor Timur until such time as the entity's independent status is formally established

Independence: 17 August 1945 (proclaimed independence; on 27 December 1949, Indonesia became legally independent from the Netherlands)
National holiday: Independence Day, 17 August (1945)
Constitution: August 1945, abrogated by Federal Constitution of 1949 and Provisional Constitution of 1950, restored 5 July 1959

Legal system: based on Roman-Dutch law, substantially modified by indigenous concepts and by new criminal procedures code; has not accepted compulsory ICJ jurisdiction

Suffrage: 17 years of age; universal and married persons regardless of age

Executive branch:

chief of state: President Susilo Bambang YUDHOYONO (since 20 October 2004) ; Vice President BOEDIONO (since 20 October 2009) ; note - the president is both the chief of state and head of government
head of government: President Susilo Bambang YUDHOYONO (since 20 October 2004) ; Vice President BOEDIONO (since 20 October 2009)
cabinet: Cabinet appointed by the president
elections: president and vice president elected for five-year terms (eligible for a second term) by direct vote of the citizenry; election last held on 8 July 2009 (next to be held in 2014)
election results: Susilo Bambang YUDHOYONO elected president; percent of vote - Susilo Bambang YUDHOYONO 60.8%, MEGAWATI Sukarnoputri 26.8%, Jusuf KALLA 12.4%

Legislative branch:
People's Consultative Assembly (Majelis Permusyawaratan Rakyat or MPR) is the upper house; it consists of members of the DPR and DPD and has role in inaugurating and impeaching the president and in amending the constitution but does not formulate national policy; House of Representatives or Dewan Perwakilan Rakyat (DPR) (560 seats, members elected to serve five-year terms) , formulates and passes legislation at the national level; House of Regional Representatives (Dewan Perwakilan Daerah or DPD) , constitutionally mandated role includes providing legislative input to DPR on issues affecting regions (132 members, four from each of Indonesia's 30 provinces, two special regions, and one special capital city district)
elections: last held on 9 April 2009 (next to be held in 2014)
election results: percent of vote by party - PD 20.9%, GOLKAR 14.5%, PDI-P 14.0%, PKS 7.9%, PAN 6.0%, PPP 5.3%, PKB 4.9%, GERINDRA 4.5%, HANURA 3.8%, others 18.2%; seats by party - PD 148, GOLKAR 107, PDI-P 94, PKS 57, PAN 46, PPP 37, PKB 28, GERINDRA 26, HANURA 17
*note:*29 other parties received less than 2.5% of the vote so did not obtain any seats; because of election rules, the number of seats won does not always follow the percentage of votes received by parties

Judicial branch: Supreme Court (Mahkamah Agung) , the judges are appointed by the president

Political parties and leaders: Crescent Moon and Star Party or PBB [Yusril Ihza MAHENDRA, chairman]; Development Unity Party or PPP (federation of former Islamic parties) [Hamzah HAZ, chairman]; Golkar [Akbar TANSUNG, general chairman]; Indonesia Democracy Party or PDI (federation of former Nationalist and Christian Parties) [Budi HARDJONO, chairman]; Indonesia Democracy Party-Struggle or PDI-P [MEGAWATI Sukarnoputri, chairperson]; National Awakening Party or PKB [Abdurrahman WAHID]; National Mandate Party or PAN [Amien RAIS, chairman]

International organization participation: APEC, AsDB, ASEAN, CCC, CP, ESCAP, FAO, G-15, G-19, G-77, IAEA, IBRD, ICAO, ICC, ICFTU, ICRM, IDA, IDB, IFAD, IFC, IFRCS, IHO, ILO, IMF, IMO, Inmarsat, Intelsat, Interpol, IOC, IOM (observer) , ISO, ITU, NAM, OIC, OPCW, OPEC, UN, UNCTAD, UNESCO, UNIDO, UNIKOM, UNMIBH, UNMOP, UNMOT, UNOMIG, UPU, WCL, WFTU, WHO, WIPO, WMO, WToO, WTrO

Diplomatic representation in the US:
chief of mission: Ambassador DORODJATUN Kuntjoro-Jakti
chancery: 2020 Massachusetts Avenue NW, Washington, DC 20036
telephone: [1] (202) 775-5200
FAX: [1] (202) 775-5365
consulate(s) general: Chicago, Houston, Los Angeles, New York, and San Francisco

Diplomatic representation from the US:
chief of mission: Ambassador Robert GELBARD
embassy: Medan Merdeka Selatan 5, Jakarta
mailing address: Unit 8129, Box 1, APO AP 96520
telephone: [62] (21) 344-2211
FAX: [62] (21) 386-2259
consulate(s) general: Surabaya

Flag description: two equal horizontal bands of red (top) and white; similar to the flag of Monaco, which is shorter; also similar to the flag of Poland, which is white (top) and red

ECONOMY

Economy - overview:
Indonesia, a vast polyglot nation, has weathered the global financial crisis relatively smoothly because of its heavy reliance on domestic consumption as the driver of economic growth. Increasing investment by both local and foreign investors is also supporting solid growth. Although the economy slowed to 4.6% growth in 2009 from the 6%-plus growth rate recorded in 2010 and 2008, by 2010 growth returned to a 6% rate and remained there in 2011. During the recession, Indonesia outperformed most of its regional neighbors. The country experienced high inflation in early 2010, mainly due to food shortages, but agencies across the government acted quickly to ensure sufficiant food stocks. The government made economic advances under the first administration of President YUDHOYONO, introducing significant reforms in the financial sector, including tax and customs reforms, the use of Treasury bills, and capital market development and supervision, and in December 2011, Fitch Ratings Agency upgraded the country's credit rating to investment grade for the first time since 1997. Indonesia's debt-to-GDP ratio in recent years has declined steadily because of increasingly robust GDP growth and sound fiscal stewardship. Indonesia still struggles with poverty and unemployment, inadequate infrastructure, corruption, a complex regulatory environment, and unequal resource distribution among regions. In 2011 the government faces the ongoing challenge of improving Indonesia's insufficient infrastructure to remove impediments to economic growth, while addressing climate change mitigation and adaptation needs, particularly with regard to conserving Indonesia's forests and peatlands.
:
GDP (purchasing power parity):
$1.121 trillion (est.)

country comparison to the world: 16
$1.054 trillion (est.)
$993 billion (est.)
note: data are in 2011 US dollars
:
GDP (official exchange rate):
$834.3 billion (est.)
:
GDP - real growth rate:
6.4% (est.)
country comparison to the world: 38
6.1% (est.)
4.6% (est.)
:
GDP - per capita (PPP):
$4,700 (est.)
country comparison to the world: 151
$4,400 (est.)
$4,300 (est.)
note: data are in 2011 US dollars
:
GDP - composition by sector:
agriculture: 14.9%
industry: 46%
services: 39.1% (est.)
:
Labor force:
117 million (est.)
country comparison to the world: 5
:
Labor force - by occupation:
agriculture: 38.3%
industry: 12.8%
services: 48.9% (est.)
:
Unemployment rate:
6.7% (est.)
country comparison to the world: 70
7.9% (est.)
:
Population below poverty line:
13.33% (2010)
:
Household income or consumption by percentage share:
lowest 10%: 3.3%
highest 10%: 29.9% (2009)
:
Distribution of family income - Gini index:
36.8 (2009)
country comparison to the world: 81
39.4 (2005)
:
Investment (gross fixed):
32% of GDP (est.)

country comparison to the world: 26
:
Budget:
revenues: $134.3 billion
expenditures: $144.1 billion (est.)
:
Taxes and other revenues:
16.1% of GDP (est.)
country comparison to the world: 181
:
Budget surplus (+) or deficit (-):
-1.2% of GDP (est.)
country comparison to the world: 58
:
Public debt:
24.5% of GDP (est.)
country comparison to the world: 105
25.7% of GDP (est.)
:
Inflation rate (consumer prices):
5.7% (est.)
country comparison to the world: 133
5.1% (est.)
:
Central bank discount rate:
6.37% (31 December 2010)
country comparison to the world: 62
6.46% (31 December 2009)
note: this figure represents the 3-month SBI rate; BI has not employed the one-month SBI since September 2010
:
Commercial bank prime lending rate:
12.2% (31 December est.)
country comparison to the world: 65
13.252% (31 December 2010 est.)
note: these figures represent the average annualized rate on working capital loans
:
Stock of narrow money:
$81.44 billion (31 December est.)
country comparison to the world: 38
$67.34 billion (31 December 2010 est.)
:
Stock of broad money:
$333.2 billion (31 December est.)
country comparison to the world: 30
$274.9 billion (31 December 2010 est.)
:
Stock of domestic credit:
$305.2 billion (31 December est.)
country comparison to the world: 35
$254.1 billion (31 December 2010 est.)
:
Market value of publicly traded shares:
$360.4 billion (31 December 2010)

country comparison to the world: 32
$178.2 billion (31 December 2009)
$98.76 billion (31 December 2008)
:
Agriculture - products:
rice, cassava (tapioca), peanuts, rubber, cocoa, coffee, palm oil, copra; poultry, beef, pork, eggs
:
Industries:
petroleum and natural gas, textiles, apparel, footwear, mining, cement, chemical fertilizers, plywood, rubber, food, tourism
:
Industrial production growth rate:
3.5% (est.)
country comparison to the world: 98
:
Electricity - production:
141.2 billion kWh (est.)
country comparison to the world: 24
:
Electricity - consumption:
126.1 billion kWh (est.)
country comparison to the world: 26
:
Electricity - exports:
0 kWh (est.)
:
Electricity - imports:
0 kWh (est.)
:
Oil - production:
1.03 million bbl/day (est.)
country comparison to the world: 23
:
Oil - consumption:
1.292 million bbl/day (est.)
country comparison to the world: 18
:
Oil - exports:
404,100 bbl/day (est.)
country comparison to the world: 32
:
Oil - imports:
767,400 bbl/day (est.)
country comparison to the world: 18
:
Natural gas - production:
82.8 billion cu m (est.)
country comparison to the world: 12
:
Natural gas - consumption:
40.47 billion cu m (est.)
country comparison to the world: 23
:
Natural gas - exports:

42.33 billion cu m (est.)
country comparison to the world: 8
:
Natural gas - imports:
0 cu m (est.)
country comparison to the world: 206
:
Natural gas - proved reserves:
3.001 trillion cu m (1 January est.)
country comparison to the world: 13
:
Current account balance:
$5.704 billion (est.)
country comparison to the world: 35
$5.654 billion (est.)
:
Exports:
$208.9 billion (est.)
country comparison to the world: 27
$158.1 billion (est.)
:
Exports - commodities:
oil and gas, electrical appliances, plywood, textiles, rubber
:
Exports - partners:
Japan 16.3%, China 10%, US 9.1%, Singapore 8.7%, South Korea 8%, India 6.3%, Malaysia 5.9% (2010)
:
Imports:
$172.1 billion (est.)
country comparison to the world: 29
$127.4 billion (est.)
:
Imports - commodities:
machinery and equipment, chemicals, fuels, foodstuffs
:
Imports - partners:
China 15.1%, Singapore 14.9%, Japan 12.5%, US 6.9%, Malaysia 6.4%, South Korea 5.7%, Thailand 5.5%
:
Reserves of foreign exchange and gold:
$136.2 billion (31 December est.)
country comparison to the world: 18
$96.21 billion (31 December 2010 est.)
:
Debt - external:
$158.8 billion (31 December est.)
country comparison to the world: 34
$196.1 billion (31 December 2010 est.)
:
Stock of direct foreign investment - at home:
$105.7 billion (31 December est.)
country comparison to the world: 33
$86.15 billion (31 December 2010 est.)

:
Stock of direct foreign investment - abroad:
$41.89 billion (31 December est.)
country comparison to the world: 35
$32.85 billion (31 December 2010 est.)
:
Exchange rates:
Indonesian rupiah (IDR) per US dollar -
8,696.1 (est.)
9,090.43 (est.)
10,389.9 (2009)
9,698.9 (2008)
9,143 (2010)

COMMUNICATIONS

Telephones - main lines in use:	12.772 million
Telephones - mobile cellular:	46.91 million
Telephone system:	*general assessment:* domestic service fair, international service good *domestic:* interisland microwave system and HF radio police net; domestic satellite communications system *international:* country code - 62; satellite earth stations - 2 Intelsat (1 Indian Ocean and 1 Pacific Ocean)
Radio broadcast stations:	AM 678, FM 43, shortwave 82 (1998)
Television broadcast stations:	54 local TV stations (11 national TV networks; each with their own group of local transmitters)
Internet country code:	.id
Internet hosts:	170,834
Internet users:	16 million

TRANSPORTATION

Railways:
total: 6,458 km
narrow gauge: 5,961 km 1.067-m gauge (101 km electrified; 101 km double track) ; 497 km 0.750-m gauge

Highways:
total: 342,700 km
paved: 158,670 km
unpaved: 184,030 km (1997 est.)

Waterways: 21,579 km total; Sumatra 5,471 km, Java and Madura 820 km, Kalimantan 10,460 km, Sulawesi (Celebes) 241 km, Irian Jaya 4,587 km
Pipelines: crude oil 2,505 km; petroleum products 456 km; natural gas 1,703 km (1989)
Ports and harbors: Cilacap, Cirebon, Jakarta, Kupang, Palembang, Semarang, Surabaya, Ujungpandang
Merchant marine:
total: 586 ships (1,000 GRT or over) totaling 2,676,875 GRT/3,700,864 DWT
ships by type: bulk 38, cargo 346, chemical tanker 9, container 19, liquified gas 5, livestock carrier 1, passenger 7, passenger/cargo 13, petroleum tanker 114, refrigerated cargo 1, roll-on/roll-off 11, short-sea passenger 8, specialized tanker 9, vehicle carrier 5
Airports: 446
Airports - with paved runways:
total: 127
over 3,047 m: 4
2,438 to 3,047 m: 12
1,524 to 2,437 m: 39 *914 to 1,523 m:* 41 *under 914 m:* 31
Airports - with unpaved runways:
total: 319
1,524 to 2,437 m: 5 *914 to 1,523 m:* 33 *under 914 m:* 281
Heliports: 4

MILITARY

Military branches: Army, Navy, Air Force, National Police
Military manpower - military age: 18 years of age
Military manpower - availability:
males age 15-49: 62,948,286
Military manpower - fit for military service:
males age 15-49: 36,826,282
Military manpower - reaching military age annually:
males: 2,273,324
Military expenditures - dollar figure: $1 billion
Military expenditures - percent of GDP: 1.3%

TRANSNATIONAL ISSUES

Disputes - international: Sipadan and Ligitan Islands in dispute with Malaysia

Illicit drugs: illicit producer of cannabis largely for domestic use; possible growing role as transshipment point for Golden Triangle heroin

IMPORTANT INFORMATION FOR UNDERSTANDING INDONESIA

Official Name: Republic of Indonesia

PROFILE

Geography
Area: 2 million sq. km. (736,000 sq. mi.), about three times the size of Texas; maritime area: 7,900,000 sq. km.
Cities: Capital--Jakarta (est. 9.7 million). Other cities--Surabaya 2.8 million, Medan 2.1 million, Bandung 2.4 million.
Terrain: More than 17,500 islands; 6,000 are inhabited; 1,000 of which are permanently settled.

Large islands consist of coastal plains with mountainous interiors.
Climate: Equatorial but cooler in the highlands.

People
Nationality: Noun and adjective--Indonesian(s).
Population (est.): 237,6 million.
Annual population growth rate (est.): 2.7%.
Ethnic groups (2000 census): Javanese 40.6%, Sundanese 15%, Madurese 3.3%, Minangkabau 2.7%, others 38.4%.
Religions (2000 census): Muslim 86.1%, Protestant 5.7%, Catholic 3%, Hindu 1.8%, others 3.4%.
Languages: Indonesian (official), local languages, the most prevalent of which is Javanese.
Education: Years compulsory--9. Enrollment--94.7% of eligible primary school-age children. Literacy--98.3% (2010).
Health: Infant mortality rate (2010)--34/1,000. Life expectancy at birth (est.)--70.76 years.
Work force: 117.4 million (2011). Agriculture—39.3%, industry—20.9%, services—47.8%.

Government
Type: Independent republic.
Independence: August 17, 1945 proclaimed.
Constitution: 1945. Embodies five principles of the state philosophy, called Pancasila, namely monotheism, humanitarianism, national unity, representative democracy by consensus, and social justice.
Branches: Executive--president (head of government and chief of state) elected by direct popular vote. Legislative--The People's Consultative Assembly (MPR), which includes the 560-member House of Representatives (DPR) and the 132-member Council of Regional Representatives (DPD), both elected to 5-year terms. Judicial--Supreme Court is the final court of appeal. Constitutional Court has power of judicial review
Suffrage: 17 years of age universal, and married persons regardless of age.

Economy
GDP (2009): $539 billion; (2010): $707 billion; (est.): $834 billion.
Annual growth rate (2009): 4.5%; (2010): 6.1%; (est.): 6.5%
Inflation, end-period (2009): 2.8%; (2010): 7%; (2011): 3.79%.
Per capita income (est., PPP): $4,668.1.
Natural resources (11.2% of GDP, 2010): Oil and gas, bauxite, silver, tin, copper, gold, coal.
Agriculture (15.3% of GDP, 2010): Products--timber, rubber, rice, palm oil, coffee. Land--17% cultivated.
Manufacturing (24.8% of GDP, 2010): Garments, footwear, electronic goods, furniture, paper products, automobiles.
Trade: Exports (2010)--$158 billion including oil, natural gas, crude palm oil, coal, appliances, textiles, and rubber. Major export partners--Japan, U.S., China, Singapore, Malaysia, and Republic of Korea. Imports (2010)--$136 billion including oil and fuel, food, chemicals, capital goods, consumer goods, iron and steel. Major import partners--Singapore, China, Japan, U.S., Malaysia, Thailand, South Korea.

PEOPLE

Indonesia's approximately 237.6 million people make it the world's fourth-most populous nation. The island of Java, roughly the size of New York State, is the most populous island in the world (136.6 million, 2010 est.) and one of the most densely populated areas in the world. Indonesia includes numerous related but distinct cultural and linguistic groups, many of which are ethnically Malay. Since independence, Bahasa Indonesia (the national language, a form of Malay) has spread throughout the archipelago and has become the language of most written communication, education, government, business, and media. Local languages are still important in many areas, however. English is the most widely spoken foreign language. Education is compulsory for children through grade 9. In primary school, more than 94% of eligible children are enrolled whereas 57% of eligible children are enrolled in secondary school.

Constitutional guarantees of religious freedom apply to the six religions recognized by the state, namely Islam (86.1%), Protestantism (5.7%), Catholicism (3%), Hinduism (1.8%), Buddhism (about 1%), and Confucianism (less than 1%). On the resort island of Bali, over 90% of the population practices Hinduism. In some remote areas, animism is still practiced.

HISTORY

By the time of the Renaissance, the islands of Java and Sumatra had already enjoyed a 1,000-year heritage of advanced civilization spanning two major empires. During the 7th-14th centuries, the Buddhist kingdom of Srivijaya flourished on Sumatra. At its peak, the Srivijaya Empire reached as far as West Java and the Malay Peninsula. Also by the 14th century, the Hindu Kingdom of Majapahit had risen in eastern Java. Gadjah Mada, the empire's chief minister from 1331 to 1364, succeeded in gaining allegiance from most of what is now modern Indonesia and much of the Malay archipelago as well. Legacies from Gadjah Mada's time include a codification of law and an epic poem. Islam arrived in Indonesia sometime during the 12th century and supplanted Hinduism by the end of the 16th century in Java and Sumatra. Bali, however, remains overwhelmingly Hindu. In the eastern archipelago, both Christian and Islamic proselytizing took place in the 16th and 17th centuries, and, currently, there are large communities of both religions on these islands.

Beginning in 1602, the Dutch slowly established themselves as rulers of Indonesia, exploiting the weakness of the small kingdoms that had replaced that of Majapahit. The only exception was East Timor, which remained under Portugal's control until 1975. During 300 years of rule, the Dutch developed the Netherlands East Indies into one of the world's richest colonial possessions, extracting natural resources through co-opted local elites but doing little to modernize Indonesia.

During the first decade of the 20th century, an Indonesian independence movement began and expanded rapidly, particularly between the two World Wars. Its leaders came from a small group of young professionals and students, some of whom had been educated in the Netherlands. Many, including Indonesia's first president, Soekarno (1945-67), were imprisoned for political activities.

During World War II, Japan invaded Indonesia (in early 1942), outclassing a combined American, British, Dutch, and Australian military command. Sizeable U.S. naval forces and smaller air and ground forces sent to defend Indonesia were defeated, with heavy losses in ships and large numbers of Americans killed or captured. The Japanese treated captured Allied troops and interned Western civilians with extreme cruelty. Because of local animosity toward Dutch colonial rule, there was no anti-Japanese guerilla movement as in the Philippines and Malaysia, and most Indonesians initially welcomed the Japanese as liberators. But increasingly harsh Japanese rule strengthened the prewar independence movement, and on August 17, 1945, 3 days after Japan's surrender to the Allies, a small group of Indonesians, led by Soekarno and Mohammad Hatta, proclaimed independence and established the Republic of Indonesia. They set up a provisional government and adopted a constitution to govern the republic until elections could be held and a new constitution written. Fighting soon broke out between Indonesian independence groups and Allied forces--mainly British, Indian, and Australian forces--sent to accept the Japanese surrender.

Dutch efforts later to reestablish complete control met resistance. Following the Philippines' independence in 1946, the U.S. was unwilling to see the Netherlands use post-war Marshall Plan support to indirectly fund the suppression of Indonesia's independence. Negotiations and on-and-off fighting in Indonesia continued until 1949. The stalemate, combined with reduced international support and a devastated economy in the Netherlands, led to the Dutch decision to withdraw from Indonesia. Colonial rule and its violent end left a legacy in Indonesia of mistrusting foreign motives, especially those of large powers. In 1950, Indonesia became the 60th member of the United Nations.

Shortly after hostilities with the Dutch ended in 1949, Indonesia adopted a new constitution, providing for a parliamentary system of government in which the executive was chosen by and accountable to parliament. Parliament was divided among many political parties before and after the country's first nationwide election in 1955, and stable governmental coalitions were difficult to achieve. The role of Islam in Indonesia was debated. Soekarno defended a secular state based on Pancasila, five principles of the state philosophy--monotheism, humanitarianism, national unity, representative democracy by consensus, and social justice--codified in the 1945 constitution, while some Muslim groups preferred either an Islamic state or a constitution that included a preambular provision requiring adherents of Islam to be subject to Islamic law. At the time of independence, the Dutch retained control over the western half of New Guinea (known as Irian Jaya in the Soekarno and Suharto eras and as Papua since 2000) and permitted steps toward self-government and independence.

Negotiations with the Dutch on the incorporation of Irian Jaya into Indonesia failed, and armed clashes broke out between Indonesian and Dutch troops in 1961. In August 1962, the two sides reached an agreement, and Indonesia assumed administrative responsibility for Irian Jaya on May 1, 1963. The Indonesian Government conducted an "Act of Free Choice" in Irian Jaya under UN supervision in 1969 in which 1,025 Papuan representatives of local councils agreed by consensus to remain a part of Indonesia. A subsequent UN General Assembly resolution confirmed the transfer of sovereignty to Indonesia. Opposition to Indonesian administration of Papua gave rise to small-scale guerrilla activity in the years following Jakarta's assumption of control. In the more open atmosphere since 1998, there have been more explicit expressions within Papua calling for independence from Indonesia.

Unsuccessful rebellions on Sumatra, Sulawesi, West Java, and other islands beginning in 1958, plus a failure by the constituent assembly to develop a new constitution, weakened the parliamentary system. Consequently, in 1959, when President Soekarno unilaterally revived the provisional 1945 constitution that provided for broad presidential powers, he met little resistance. From 1959 to 1965, President Soekarno imposed an authoritarian regime under the label of "Guided Democracy."

Soekarno favored a foreign policy of nonalignment, a stance supported by other prominent leaders of former colonies who rejected formal alliances with either the West or Soviet bloc. Under Soekarno's auspices, these leaders gathered in Bandung, West Java, in 1955 to lay the groundwork for what became known as the Non-Aligned Movement. In the late 1950s and early 1960s, President Soekarno moved closer to Asian communist states and toward the Indonesian Communist Party (PKI) in domestic affairs. The PKI represented the largest communist party outside the Soviet Union and China.

By 1965, the PKI controlled many of the mass civic and cultural organizations that Soekarno had established to mobilize support for his regime and, with Soekarno's acquiescence, embarked on a campaign to establish a "Fifth Column" by arming its supporters. Army leaders resisted this campaign. Under circumstances that have never been fully explained, on October 1, 1965, PKI sympathizers within the military, including elements from Soekarno's palace guard, occupied key locations in Jakarta and kidnapped and murdered six senior generals. Major General Suharto, the commander of the Army Strategic Reserve, rallied army troops opposed to the PKI to reestablish control over the city. Violence swept throughout Indonesia in the aftermath of the October 1 events, and unsettled conditions persisted through 1966. Right-wing groups killed tens of thousands of alleged communists in rural areas. Estimates of the number of deaths range between 160,000 and 500,000. The violence was especially brutal in Java and Bali. During this period, PKI members by the tens of thousands turned in their membership cards. The emotions and fears of instability created by this crisis persisted for many years as the communist party remains banned from Indonesia.

Throughout the 1965-66 period, President Soekarno vainly attempted to restore his political stature and shift the country back to its pre-October 1965 position. Although he remained President, in March 1966, Soekarno transferred key political and military powers to General Suharto, who by that time had become head of the armed forces. In March 1967, the Provisional People's Consultative Assembly (MPRS) named General Suharto acting President. Soekarno ceased to be a political force and lived under virtual house arrest until his death in 1970.

President Suharto proclaimed a "New Order" in Indonesian politics and dramatically shifted foreign and domestic policies away from the course set in Soekarno's final years. The New Order established economic rehabilitation and development as its primary goals and pursued its policies through an administrative structure dominated by the military but with advice from Western-educated economic experts. In 1968, the People's Consultative Assembly (MPR) formally selected Suharto to a full 5-year term as President, and he was reelected to successive 5-year terms in 1973, 1978, 1983, 1988, 1993, and 1998. In mid-1997, Indonesia suffered from the Asian financial and economic crisis, accompanied by the worst drought in 50 years and falling prices for commodity exports. As the exchange rate changed from a fixed to a managed float to fully floating, the rupiah (IDR or Rp) depreciated in value, inflation increased significantly, and capital flight accelerated. Demonstrators, initially led by students, called for Suharto's resignation. Amid widespread civil unrest, Suharto resigned on May 21, 1998, 3 months after the MPR had selected him for a seventh term. Suharto's hand-picked Vice President, B.J. Habibie, became Indonesia's third President. President Habibie reestablished International Monetary Fund (IMF) and donor community support for an economic stabilization program. He released several prominent political and labor prisoners, initiated investigations into the unrest, and lifted controls on the press, political parties, and labor unions.

In January 1999, Habibie and the Indonesian Government agreed to a process, with UN involvement, under which the people of East Timor would be allowed to choose between autonomy and independence through a direct ballot held on August 30, 1999. Some 98% of registered voters cast their ballots, and 78.5% of the voters chose independence over continued integration with Indonesia. Many people were killed by Indonesian military forces and military-backed militias in a wave of violence and destruction after the announcement of the pro-independence vote.

Indonesia's first elections in the post-Suharto period were held for the national, provincial, and sub-provincial parliaments on June 7, 1999. Forty-eight political parties participated in the elections. For the national parliament, Partai Demokrasi Indonesia Perjuangan (PDI-P, Indonesian Democratic Party of Struggle, led by Megawati Sukarnoputri) won 34% of the vote; Golkar ("Functional Groups" party) 22%; Partai Kebangkitan Bangsa (PKB, National Awakening Party, linked to the moderate Islamic organization Nadhlatul Ulama headed by former President Abdurrahman Wahid) 13%; and the conservative Islamic Partai Persatuan Pembangunan (PPP, United Development Party, led by Hamzah Haz) 11%. The MPR selected Abdurrahman Wahid as Indonesia's fourth President in November 1999 and replaced him with Megawati Sukarnoputri in July 2001.

The constitution, as amended in the post-Suharto era, now provides for the direct election by popular vote of the president and vice president. Under the 2004 amendment, only parties or coalitions of parties that gained at least 3% of the House of Representatives (DPR) seats or 5% of the vote in national legislative elections were eligible to nominate a presidential and vice presidential ticket.

The 2004 legislative elections took place on April 5 and were considered to be generally free and fair. Twenty-four parties took part in the elections. Big parties lost ground, while small parties gained larger shares of the vote. However, the two Suharto-era nationalist parties, PDI-P and Golkar, remained in the lead. PDI-P (opposition party during the Suharto era) lost its plurality in the House of Representatives, dropping from 33% to 18.5% of the total vote (and from 33% to 20% of the seats). The Golkar Party (Suharto's political party) declined slightly from 1999 levels, going from 22% to 21% of the national vote (from 26% to 23% of DPR seats). The third- and fourth-largest parties (by vote share) were two Islamic-oriented parties, the United Development Party (PPP) (8% of the votes, 10.5% of the seats) and National Awakening Party (PKB) (10.5% of the vote, 9.45% of the seats). Susilo Bambang Yudhoyono's nationalist Democratic Party (PD) won 7.45% of the national vote and 10% of the DPR seats, making it the fourth-largest party in the DPR. Seven of the 24 parties won no DPR seats; six won 1-2 seats, and the other six won between 2%-6% of the national vote (between 5-52 DPR seats).

The first direct presidential election was held on July 5, 2004, contested by five tickets. As no candidate won at least 50% of the vote, a runoff election was held on September 20, 2004, between the top two candidates, President Megawati Sukarnoputri and retired General Susilo Bambang Yudhoyono. In this final round, Yudhoyono won 60.6% of the vote. Approximately 76.6% of the eligible voters participated, a total of roughly 117 million people, making Indonesia's presidential election the largest single-day election in the world. The Carter Center, which sent a delegation of election observers, issued a statement congratulating "the people and leaders of Indonesia for the successful conduct of the presidential election and the peaceful atmosphere that has prevailed throughout the ongoing democratic transition."

In 2009, national legislative elections were held on April 9 and presidential elections were held in July. They were peaceful and considered free and fair. New electoral rules required that a party win 2.5% of the national vote in order to enter parliament. A total of thirty-eight national and six local (Aceh only) parties contested the 2009 legislative elections. At least 171 million voters registered to vote in these elections. Voter turnout was estimated to be 71% of the electorate. Nine parties won parliamentary seats in the House of Representatives (DPR). The top three winners were secular nationalist parties: President Yudhoyono's Partai Demokrat, with 20.85% of the vote; Vice President Jusuf Kalla's Golkar Party, 14.45%; and former president Megawati's opposition PDI-P party, with 14.03%. The next four largest parties were all Islamic-oriented parties: PKS, PAN (6%), PPP (5.3%), and PKB (4.9%). Only PKS maintained its 2004 vote share (7.88%); the other three declined in popularity. The smallest two parties in Parliament, Gerindra and Hanura, with 4.46 and 3.77% of the vote respectively, were headed by retired Suharto-era army generals Prabowo Subianto and Wiranto (one name only). The 2009 DPR members took their seats October 1.

Also in 2009, the threshold was revised so that only parties or coalitions of parties that gained at least 20% of the House of Representatives (DPR) seats or 25% of the vote in the 2009 national legislative elections would be eligible to nominate a presidential and vice presidential ticket. Partai Demokrat, Golkar, and PDI-P parties, the top winners in the legislative elections, nominated presidential candidates. To win in one round, a presidential candidate was required to receive more than 50% of the vote and more than 20% of the vote in 17 of Indonesia's 33 provinces. If no candidate did so, the top two candidates would have competed in a second round in September 2009.

Three tickets competed in the presidential elections. Incumbent President Yudhoyono and his running mate, non-partisan former Central Bank Chair and Economics Minister Boediono, won the election with such a significant plurality--60.6%--that it obviated the need for a second round of elections. Main challenger and former president and opposition leader Megawati Sukarnoputri and running mate Prabowo Subianto trailed with 28%. Meanwhile, Vice President Jusuf Kalla and running mate Wiranto came in last at 12.7%. Indonesia's Consultative Assembly (MPR) inaugurated President Susilo Bambang Yudhoyono for his second term as president on October 20, 2009.

Natural disasters have devastated many parts of Indonesia over the past few years. On December 26, 2004, a 9.1 to 9.3 magnitude earthquake took place in the Indian Ocean, and the resulting tsunami killed over 130,000 people in Aceh and left more than 500,000 homeless. On March 26, 2005, an 8.7 magnitude earthquake struck between Aceh and northern Sumatra, killing 905 people and displacing tens of thousands. After much media attention on the seismic activity on Mt. Merapi in April and May 2009, a 6.2 magnitude earthquake occurred 30 miles to the southwest. It killed more than 5,000 people and left an estimated 200,000 people homeless in the Yogyakarta region. An earthquake of 7.4 struck Tasikmalaya, West Java, on September 2, 2009, killing approximately 100 people. On September 30, 2009, a 7.6 magnitude earthquake struck Western Sumatra. No official statistics were released on deaths and injuries; however, press reports indicated more than 1,100 fatalities.

GOVERNMENT AND POLITICAL CONDITIONS

Indonesia is a republic based on the 1945 constitution providing for a separation of executive, legislative, and judicial power. Substantial restructuring has occurred since President Suharto's resignation in 1998 and the short, transitional Habibie administration in 1998 and 1999. The Habibie government established political reform legislation that formally set up new rules for the electoral system, the House of Representatives (DPR), the People's Consultative Assembly (MPR), and political parties without changing the 1945 Indonesian constitution. After these reforms, the constitution now limits the president to two terms in office.

Indonesia adopted a bicameral legislative system following the establishment of the DPD (Regional Representatives Council), which was first elected in 2004. The DPD is composed of four representatives from each of Indonesia's 33 provinces. Although it can make proposals and submit opinions on legislative matters concerning the regions, it does not have the power to create legislation. The MPR consists of both the DPD and the DPR. The MPR has the power to inaugurate and to impeach the president (upon the recommendation of the DPR). The current Speaker of the MPR is Taufik Kiemas (from the opposition PDI-P Party) and the Speaker of the DPR is Marzuki Alie (from the ruling Democrat Party). These speakers and four deputy speakers for the DPR and MPR took up their positions on October 5, 2009. The largest party in the DPR, now President Yudhoyono's Partai Demokrat, filled the influential DPR speaker position.

The president, elected for a 5-year term, is the top government and political figure. The president and the vice president were elected by popular vote for the first time on September 20, 2004. Previously, the MPR selected Indonesia's president. In 1999, the MPR selected Abdurrahman Wahid, also known as Gus Dur, as the fourth President. The MPR removed Gus Dur in July 2001, immediately appointing then-Vice President Megawati Sukarnoputri as the fifth President. In 2004, Susilo Bambang Yudhoyono was directly elected to succeed Megawati. He was re-elected in 2009.

The president, assisted by an appointed cabinet, has the authority to conduct the administration of the government.

President Yudhoyono's Partai Demokrat (PD) holds 148 of the 560 seats in the House of Representatives (DPR), making it the largest political party represented in the legislature. Partai

Demokrat has a coalition with Golkar and four Islam-oriented parties. The coalition holds a majority of the seats in the DPR. The People's Consultative Assembly (MPR) has 692 members, including 560 members of the DPR and the 132 representatives of the Council of Regional Representatives (DPD). Up to and through 2004, citizens elected legislators for the DPR and DPD, but their vote was based on a party list system. This ensured that the party elite, placed at the top of the party candidate lists, were voted into office. In 2009, a multi-member district "majority vote wins" system allowed voters for the first time to directly put a candidate who won a plurality of votes into office.

Prior to 2004, some legislative seats had been reserved for representatives of the armed forces. The military has been a significant political force throughout Indonesian history, though it had ceded its formal political role by 2004. The armed forces shaped the political environment and provided leadership for Suharto's New Order from the time it came to power in the wake of the abortive 1965 uprising. Military officers, especially from the army, were key advisers to Suharto and Habibie and had considerable influence on policy. Under the dual function concept ("dwifungsi"), the military asserted a role in socio-political affairs. This concept was used to justify placement of officers in the civilian bureaucracy at all government levels and in regional and national legislatures. Although the military retains influence, the wide-ranging democratic reforms instituted since 1999 abolished "dwifungsi" and ended the armed forces' formal involvement in government administration. The police were separated from the military in 1999, further reducing the military's direct role in governmental matters. Control of the military by the democratically elected government has been strengthened.

Reflecting historically independent sentiment, Hasan di Tiro established the Free Aceh Movement (Gerakan Aceh Merdeka, GAM) in December 1976 to seek independence for Aceh. Some 15,000 died in military conflict in Aceh over the following 3 decades. Through peace talks led by former Finnish President Martti Ahtisaari, a peace agreement between GAM and the Indonesian Government that provided wide-ranging autonomy for Aceh was signed on August 15, 2005. By December 2005, GAM declared that it had disbanded the military wing of its organization, and the Indonesian Government had withdrawn the bulk of its security forces down to agreed levels. On December 11, 2009, Aceh held gubernatorial and district administrative elections, the first truly democratic elections in over half a century in Aceh, resulting in the election of a former separatist leader as governor. In 2009, Aceh participated in the national legislative and presidential elections and elected its own provincial legislature.

Principal Government Officials
President--Susilo Bambang Yudhoyono
Vice President--Boediono
Minister of Foreign Affairs--Marty Natalegawa
Ambassador to the United States--Dino Patti Djalal
Ambassador to the United Nations--Hasan Kleib

The **Embassy** of Indonesia is at 2020 Massachusetts Avenue NW, Washington, DC 20036 (tel. 202-775-5200-5207; fax: 202-775-5365). Consulates General are in New York (5 East 68th Street, New York, NY 10021, tel. 212-879-0600/0615; fax: 212-570-6206); Los Angeles (3457 Wilshire Blvd., Los Angeles, CA 90010; tel. 213-383-5126; fax: 213-487-3971); Houston (10900 Richmond Ave., Houston, TX 77042; tel. 713-785-1691; fax: 713-780-9644). Consulates are in San Francisco (1111 Columbus Avenue, San Francisco, CA 94133; tel. 415-474-9571; fax: 415-441-4320); and Chicago (2 Illinois Center, Suite 1422233 N. Michigan Avenue, Chicago, IL 60601; tel. 312-938-0101/4; 312-938-0311/0312; fax: 312-938-3148).

ECONOMY

Indonesia has a market-based economy in which the government plays a significant role. There are 141 state-owned enterprises, and the government administers prices on several basic goods, including fuel, rice, and electricity.

In the mid-1980s, the government began eliminating regulatory obstacles to economic activity. The steps were aimed primarily at the external and financial sectors and were designed to stimulate employment and growth in the non-oil export sector. Annual real gross domestic product (GDP) growth averaged nearly 7% from 1987-97 and most analysts recognized Indonesia as a newly industrializing economy and emerging major market.

The Asian financial crisis of 1997 altered the region's economic landscape. With the depreciation of the Thai currency, the foreign investment community quickly reevaluated its investments in Asia. Foreign investors dumped assets and investments in Asia, leaving Indonesia the most affected in the region. In 1998, Indonesia experienced a negative GDP growth of 13.1% and unemployment rose to 15%-20%. In the aftermath of the 1997-98 financial crisis, the government took custody of a significant portion of private sector assets via debt restructuring, but subsequently sold most of these assets, averaging a 29% return. Indonesia has since recovered, albeit more slowly than some of its neighbors, by recapitalizing its banking sector, improving oversight of capital markets, and taking steps to stimulate growth and investment, particularly in infrastructure. GDP growth steadily rose in the following decade, achieving real growth of 6.3% in 2010 and 6.1% growth in 2008. Although growth slowed to 4.5% in 2009 given reduced global demand, Indonesia was the third-fastest growing G-20 member, trailing only China and India. Growth rebounded in 2010 to 6.1% and is forecast to have reached 6.2%-6.5% in 2011. Poverty and unemployment have also declined despite the global financial crisis, with the poverty rate falling to 12,5% (March 2011) from 13.3% a year earlier and the unemployment rate falling to 6.6% (February 2011) from 6.8% a year earlier.

Indonesia's improving growth prospects and sound macroeconomic policy have many analysts suggesting that it will become the newest member of the "BRIC" grouping of leading emerging markets. In December 2011, Fitch Ratings upgraded Indonesia's sovereign debt rating to investment grade. A similar upgrade to investment grade is expected from Standard and Poor's and Moody's.

In reaction to global financial turmoil and economic slowdown in late 2008, the government moved quickly to improve liquidity, secure alternative financing to fund an expansionary budget and secure passage of a fiscal stimulus program worth more than $6 billion. Key actions to stabilize financial markets included increasing the deposit insurance guarantee twentyfold, to IDR 2 billion (about U.S. $235,000); reducing bank reserve requirements; and introducing new foreign exchange regulations requiring documentation for foreign exchange purchases exceeding U.S. $100,000/month. As a G-20 member, Indonesia has taken an active role in the G-20 coordinated response to the global economic crisis.

Economic Policy: After he took office on October 20, 2004, President Yudhoyono moved quickly to implement a "pro-growth, pro-poor, pro-employment" economic program, which he has continued in his second term. The State Ministry of National Development Planning (BAPPENAS) released a Medium-Term Development Plan for 2010-2014 focused on development of a "prosperous, democratic and just" Indonesia. The Medium-Term Development Plan targets average economic growth of 6.3%-6.8% for the period, reaching 7% or above by 2014, unemployment of 5%-6% by the end of 2014, and a poverty rate of 8%-10% by the end of 2014.

President Yudhoyono's economic team in his second administration is led by Coordinating Minister for Economic Affairs Hatta Rajasa. Sri Mulyani Indrawati continued as Finance Minister until May 2010, when she resigned to take a senior position at the World Bank. She was succeeded by Agus Martowardojo, a well-respected banker who had led Indonesia's largest state-owned bank. In July 2010, Indonesia's DPR Commission XI approved the appointment of Darmin Nasution as Governor of Bank Indonesia, following a 14-month vacancy of the position after former Governor Boediono stepped down to become Yudhoyono's running mate. In May 2010, President Yudhoyono established a National Economic Committee to provide strategic recommendations to accelerate national economic development and a National Innovation Committee to provide input and recommendations to increase national productivity, create a culture of innovation, and speed up economic growth.

In May 2011, President Susilo Bambang Yudhoyono launched the Master Plan for the Acceleration and Expansion of Indonesia's Economic Development (MP3EI), to increase infrastructure and investment spending and to provide a roadmap for Indonesia to move up the value-chain and increase the level of innovation. The plan outlines Rp 4,000 trillion ($ 468.5 billion) in potential infrastructure projects in multiple sectors including hydroelectric and solar power, palm oil, new roads including toll motorways, mining , expansion of broadband internet, and nickel, cobalt and aluminum factories.

Indonesia's overall macroeconomic picture is stable. By 2004, real GDP per capita returned to pre-financial crisis levels and income levels are rising. In 2010, domestic consumption continued to account for the largest portion of GDP, at 56.7%, followed by investment at 32.2%, government consumption at 9.1%, and net exports at 1.6%. Domestic consumption has been the main growth driver from the expenditure side during the last half century while government consumption has hovered between 5-10% of GDP for most of that time.

In 2010, Indonesia has seen an increase in manufacturing output and exports, with relatively cheap labor and a complementary large and growing domestic market. Exports of natural resources, such as oil and gas, coal and crude palm oil (CPO) have made up around 50% of Indonesia's exports and have been key drivers of growth. With the share of total exports to fast-growing emerging markets increasing and demand for commodities likely sustainable, export growth is likely to remain buoyant. In contrast, imports may grow even faster with infrastructure development andstrong domestic demand growth. ,. Net exports will likely continue to diminish and, with higher net income outflows (the counterpart to large portfolio inflows), it is expected the current account will eventually shift into deficit in the medium term.

Following a significant run-up in global energy prices in 2010-2008, the Indonesian Government raised fuel prices by an average of 29% on May 24, 2008 in an effort to reduce its fuel subsidy burden. Energy subsidies had been allocated Rp 223 trillion ($23 billion) in 2008, or 5.6% of GDP. The fuel price hikes, along with rising food prices, led consumer price inflation to a peak of 12.1% in September 2008. To help its citizens cope with higher fuel and food prices, the Indonesian Government implemented a direct cash compensation package for low-income families through February 2009 and an extra range of benefits including an expanded subsidized rice program and additional subsidies aimed at increasing food production. Citing high opportunity costs and poor targeting, the government has continued to signal its intent to reform subsidies. They plan to prohibit private cars from consuming subsidized fuels in Java and Bali beginning April 1, 2012. By 2015, the policy is expected to be implemented nationwide.

Banking Sector: Indonesia has 120 commercial banks (October 2011), of which 10 are majority foreign-owned and 28 are foreign joint venture banks while the number of bank branches has continuously increased from 6,397 in 2000 to 14,510 in 2011. The top 10 banks control about 62.4% of assets in the sector. Four state-owned banks (Bank Mandiri, BNI, BRI, BTN) control about 34.8% of assets (September 2011). The Indonesian central bank, Bank Indonesia (BI), announced plans in January 2005 to strengthen the banking sector by encouraging consolidation and improving prudential banking and supervision. BI hoped to encourage small banks with less than Rp 100 billion (about U.S. $11 million) in capital to either raise more capital or merge with healthier "anchor banks" before end-2010, announcing the criteria for anchor banks in July 2005. In October 2009, BI announced a single presence policy to further prompt consolidation. The policy stipulated that a single party could own a controlling interest in only one banking organization; exceptions would be granted in controlling two banks that do business under different principles, such as commercial and sharia, or one of which is a joint venture bank. Controlling interest is defined as 25% or more of total outstanding shares or having direct or indirect control of the institution.

BI has started to move toward Basel II standards in 2011, which focus on advancing other aspects of the Indonesian Banking Architecture (IBA) and has improved operations of its credit bureau to centralize data on borrowers. The IBA is a joint effort between BI, the Capital Market and Financial Institution Supervisory Board (BAPEPAM-LK), and the Ministry of Finance that was launched in 2004. A cornerstone program of the IBA is the structural reinforcement of the national banking system, aimed at building stronger capitalization for commercial banks to underpin its expansion and accelerate the required consolidation process among Indonesia's 120+ banks. Another important banking sector reform was the decision to eliminate the blanket guarantee on bank third-party liabilities. BI and the Indonesian Government completed the process of replacing the blanket guarantee with a deposit insurance scheme run by the independent Indonesian Deposit Insurance Agency (also known by its Indonesian acronym, LPS) in March 2010. The removal of the blanket guarantee did not produce significant deposit outflows from or among Indonesian banks. Sharia banking has grown in Indonesia in recent years, but represented only 3.7% of the banking sector, about $14.4 billion in assets as of October 2011.

In October 2011, Indonesia has a new regulator to oversee a growing financial industry. The new regulator, Financial Services Supervisory Authority (OJK), will take over the supervision of banks, brokerages and insurance firms from the central bank (BI) and the capital market watchdog BAPEPAM-LK. By early 2013, OJK will have the power to supervise capital markets and non-banking institutions, while the oversight of commercial banks will start from 2014.

Exports and Trade: Indonesia's exports were $158 billion in 2010, a rise of 35% from $116.5 billion in 2009. The largest export commodities for 2010 were oil and gas (17.8%), minerals (14.9%), textile and footwear (8.9%), crude palm oil (8.54%), electrical appliances (8.2%), and rubber products (4.7%). The top destinations for exports for 2010 were Japan (16.3%), China (11.6%), the U.S. (11.1%), Singapore (8.5%), and Korea (8.3%). Meanwhile, total imports in 2010 were $136 billion, up from $96.83 billion in 2009. Indonesia is currently our 28th-largest goods trading partner with $23.4 billion in total (two-way) goods trade during 2010. The U.S. trade deficit with Indonesia totaled $9.5 billion in 2010 ($6.9 billion in exports versus $16.5 billion in imports).

Oil and Minerals Sector: Indonesia left the Organization of Petroleum Exporting Countries (OPEC) in 2008, as it had been a net petroleum importer since 2004. Crude and condensate output averaged 944,000 barrels per day (bpd) in 2010, down slightly from 948,000 in 2009. In 2010, the oil and gas sector is estimated to have contributed $23.3 billion to government revenues, or 20.9% of the total. U.S. companies have invested heavily in the petroleum sector. Indonesia ranked third in world liquefied natural gas (LNG) exports production in 2010. Indonesia's oil, oil products, and gasturned positive in 2009 with a $29.4 million surplus, but have been negative since with a 2010 oil and gas trade deficit of $627 million and a deficit of$602 million deficit Jan-Nov 2011.

Indonesia has a wide range of mineral deposits and production, including bauxite, silver, and tin, copper, nickel, gold, and coal. Although the coal sector was open to foreign investment in the 1990s through coal contracts of work, new investment was closed again after 2000. A new mining law, passed in December 2008, opened coal to foreign investment again, although it eliminated the difference between foreign and domestic ownership structures. Total coal production reached 255 million metric tons in 2010, including exports of 198 million tons. Two U.S. firms operate two copper/gold mines in Indonesia, with a Canadian and a U.K. firm holding significant investments in nickel and gold, respectively. Although coal production has increased dramatically over the past 10 years, the number of new metals mines has declined. This decline does not reflect Indonesia's mineral prospects, which are high; rather, the decline reflects earlier uncertainty over mining laws and regulations, low competitiveness in the tax and royalty system, and investor concerns over divestment policies and the sanctity of contracts.

In early 2010, the Government of Indonesia also formally decided to become a candidate country of the Extractive Industries Transparency Initiative (EITI), which will increase accountability and transparency in energy revenue transactions between the government and oil, gas, and mining firms.

Investment: President Yudhoyono and his economic ministers have stated repeatedly their intention to improve the climate for private sector investment to raise the level of GDP growth and reduce unemployment. However, in addition to general corruption and legal uncertainty, businesses have cited a number of specific factors that have reduced the competitiveness of Indonesia's investment climate, including: corrupt and inefficient customs services; non-transparent and arbitrary tax administration; inflexible labor markets that have reduced Indonesia's advantage in labor-intensive manufacturing; increasing infrastructure bottlenecks; and uncompetitive investment laws and regulations. In each of the past three years, the Government of Indonesia has announced a series of economic policy packages aimed at stimulating investment and infrastructure improvements and implementing regulatory reform.

A new investment law was enacted in 2010, which contains provisions to restrict the share of foreign ownership in a range of industries. The 2010 iteration of the negative investment list includes long-awaited legal clarifications alongside limited liberalization. The clarifications include a continuous review of closed sectors for increased market access. The decree confirms that investment restrictions do not apply retroactively unless the new provisions are more beneficial to the investor. The changes also clarify that capital investments in publicly listed companies through the stock exchange are not subject to Indonesia's negative list unless an investor is buying a controlling interest.

In 2010, the Overseas Private Investment Corporation (OPIC) updated its 1967 investment support agreement between the United States and Indonesia by adding OPIC products such as direct loans, coinsurance, and reinsurance to the means of OPIC support which U.S. companies may use to invest in Indonesia. Over its 39-year history OPIC had committed more than $2.1 billion in financing and political risk insurance to 111 projects in Indonesia. Currently, OPIC is providing more than $75 million in support to seven projects in Indonesia in the energy, manufacturing, and services sectors and is also now supporting several new renewable resources/clean tech investment funds that are privately-managed and can look to invest in commercially-attractive projects in Indonesia.

On September 2, 2008, the DPR passed long-awaited tax reform legislation. The legislation reduced corporate and personal income tax rates as of January 1, 2009. Corporate income tax rates fell from 30% to 28% in 2009 and to 25% in 2010, with additional reductions for small and medium enterprises and publicly listed companies. The legislation raises the taxable income threshold for individuals, cuts the maximum personal income tax from 35% to 30%, and provides lower marginal personal income tax rates across four income categories. Taxes on dividends also fell from a maximum of 20% to a maximum of 10%. Long-planned labor reforms have been delayed.

The passage of a new copyright law in July 2002 and accompanying optical disc regulations in

2004 greatly strengthened Indonesia's intellectual property rights (IPR) regime. Despite the government's significantly expanded efforts to improve enforcement, IPR piracy remains a major concern to U.S. intellectual property holders and foreign investors, particularly in the high-technology sector. In March 2009, President Yudhoyono issued a decree establishing a National Task Force for IPR Violation Prevention. The IPR Task Force was intended to formulate national policy to prevent IPR violations and determine additional resources needed for prevention, as well as to help educate the public through various activities and improve bilateral, regional, and multilateral cooperation to prevent IPR violations. It has yet to fully realize these aims. In 2010, Indonesia was removed from the U.S. Trade Representative's "Priority Watch" list and placed on the "Watch" list. However, Indonesia was raised back to the Priority Watch List in 2009 due to an overall deterioration of the climate for IPR protection and enforcement and some concerns over market access barriers for IP products. There have not been signs of improvement in recent years. Amendments to the copyright and patent laws are scheduled to be discussed by Parliament in 2012.

Environment: President Yudhoyono's administration has significantly increased Indonesia's global profile on environmental issues, and U.S.-Indonesia cooperation on the environment has grown substantially. Indonesia is particularly vulnerable to the effects of climate change, which include rising sea levels and erosion of coastal areas, increased frequency and intensity of extreme weather events, species extinction, and the spread of vector-borne diseases. At the same time, Indonesia faces challenges in addressing the causes of climate change. Indonesia has the world's second-largest tropical forest and the fastest deforestation rate, making it the third-largest contributor of greenhouse gas emissions, behind China and the U.S. President Yudhoyono pledged at the 2009 G-20 in Pittsburgh to reduce Indonesia's greenhouse gas emissions by up to 41% below business as usual by 2020, in addition to eliminating fossil fuel subsidies. Indonesia continues expanding its constructive engagement in Southeast Asia, within the G-20 and Major Economies Forum, and in other international bodies to encourage other developing countries to adopt and implement ambitious steps to reduce the impacts of global climate change. In June 2010, President Barack Obama pledged to support U.S.-Indonesia shared goals on climate change through a Science, Oceans, Land Use, Society and Innovation (SOLUSI) partnership and through the establishment of a climate change center. The United States is providing $6.9 million in support – with matching funds from Norway – for the new Indonesia Climate Change Center (ICCC), which will focus on mapping and monitoring of carbon-rich peat lands and tropical forests with expertise from the U.S. Forest Service, bringing the best available science and analysis to policy leaders on key strategies and decisions to mitigate and adapt to climate change.

In 2004, President Yudhoyono initiated a multi-agency drive against illegal logging that has significantly decreased illegal logging through stronger enforcement activities. The Department of Justice-sponsored Environmental Crimes Task Force supports this enforcement effort. The State Department and the U.S. Trade Representative negotiated with the Indonesian Ministries of Trade and Forestry the U.S. Government's first Memorandum of Understanding on Combating Illegal Logging and Associated Trade. Presidents George W. Bush and Yudhoyono announced the MOU during President Bush's November 2009 visit to Indonesia. Implementation of the MOU includes collaboration on sustainable forest management, improved law enforcement, and improved markets for legally harvested timber products.

This effort will strengthen the enabling conditions for avoiding deforestation, specifically addressing the trade issues that are involved. The U.S. Government also contributed to the start of the Heart of Borneo conservation initiative to conserve a high-biodiversity, transboundary area that includes parts of Indonesia, Malaysia, and Brunei. The three countries launched the Heart of Borneo initiative in February 2010. In 2009, the Governments of Indonesia and the U.S. concluded a Tropical Forest Conservation Act (TFCA1) agreement, and in 2012 are expected to finalize a new TFCA2 agreement. The agreements reduce Indonesia's debt payments to the U.S.

over the next 10 years; these funds will be redirected toward tropical forest conservation in Indonesia.

Through the recently signed Millennium Challenge Corporation (MCC) Compact for Indonesia, the Government of Indonesia will implement a Green Prosperity Project totaling $332.5 million to support environmentally sustainable economic growth through enhancing management of forests, peat lands, and other natural resources and deployment of renewable energy.

In June 2011, the U.S. Environmental Protection Agency (EPA) and Indonesia's Ministry of Environment signed an MOU, expanding environmental cooperation and formalizing cooperation on the "Breathe Easy, Jakarta" initiative to improve air quality and protect public health.

Indonesia has the world's greatest repository of marine biological resources and is one of the most important fisheries. It lies at the epicenter of the Coral Triangle, covering just 3 percent of the globe but containing more than half the world's reefs and three-quarters of all known coral species. Fisheries generate some 20 percent of Indonesia's GDP, and over 60 percent of the nation's protein comes from the sea. The number of coastal fishers in Indonesia has increased by over 40 percent in the last 10 years.
President Yudhoyono called for a Coral Triangle Initiative (CTI) in August 2010. The Coral Triangle Initiative is a regional plan of action to enhance coral conservation, promote sustainable fisheries, and ensure food security in the face of climate change. In December 2010, the U.S. Government announced its support for the six CTI nations (Indonesia, Malaysia, Philippines, Timor-Leste, Papua New Guinea, and Solomon Islands), and to date the United States is the largest bilateral donor to the CTI. Indonesia hosted the first-ever World Oceans Conference in Manado, North Sulawesi, May 11-15, 2009. The World Oceans Conference was also the venue for the Coral Triangle Initiative Summit, at which leaders from the six CTI nations launched the CTI Regional Plan of Action.

U.S. support to Indonesia's globally important marine resources includes USAID's five year $35 million Marine Resources Program, partnerships on ocean research and exploration, and maritime law enforcement capacity-building.

From June to August 2010, the National Oceanic and Atmospheric Administration (NOAA) research vessel Okeanos Explorer and the Indonesian Baruna Jaya research fleet made a pioneering joint mission to the "Coral Triangle" in the Indo-Pacific region. NOAA works actively with Indonesian marine scientists on research and capacity-building efforts, including developing tsunami early detection systems, deploying ocean instruments that allow scientists to predict long-term climate change, exploring uncharted deepwater habitats, and anticipating and monitoring outbreaks of harmful toxins affecting our food sources. The United States and Indonesia are also working with private sector partners to develop sustainable alternative business models to improve food security and increase incomes in economically disadvantaged coastal communities.

NATIONAL SECURITY

During the early 1960s under Soekarno, Indonesia pursued a policy of "Konfrontasi" toward newly independent Malaysia, characterized by small-scale but bitter fighting against forces sent to defend Malaysian Borneo. Since the late 1960s Indonesia has had peaceful relations with its neighbors. Without a credible external threat in the region, the military historically viewed its primary mission as assuring internal security.

The Indonesian National Police, which had been a branch of the armed forces for many years, was formally separated from the military in April 1999, a process that was completed in July 2000.

With 250,000 personnel, the police represent a much smaller portion of the population than in most nations. The police play a central role in responding to the internal threat posed by militant extremists and have seen considerable success in apprehending terrorist suspects.

Indonesia's armed forces (Tentara Nasional Indonesia, or TNI) total approximately 350,000 members, including the army, navy, marines, and air force. The army is the largest branch with about 280,000 active-duty personnel. Defense spending in the national budget accounts for 1.8% of GDP, but is supplemented by revenue from many military businesses and foundations. Military leaders have said that they wish to transform the military into a professional, external security force, providing domestic support to civilian security forces as necessary. However, given current levels of training, maintenance, and expertise the TNI would not prevail against a modern, determined, and even smaller opponent.

The military historically maintained a prominent role in the nation's political and social affairs. A significant number of cabinet members have had military backgrounds, while active duty and retired military personnel occupied a large number of seats in the parliament. Commanders of the various territorial commands played influential roles in the affairs of their respective regions. The October 2004 inauguration of the national parliament ended the military's formal political role but not its political influence.

FOREIGN RELATIONS

Since independence in 1945, Indonesia has espoused a "free and active" foreign policy, seeking to play a role in regional affairs commensurate with its size and location but avoiding involvement in conflicts among major powers. Indonesian foreign policy under the "New Order" government of President Suharto moved away from the stridently anti-Western, anti-American posturing that characterized the latter part of the Soekarno era. Following Suharto's ouster in 1998, Indonesia's Presidents have preserved the broad outlines of Suharto's independent, moderate foreign policy. The traumatic separation of East Timor from Indonesia after an August 1999 East Timor referendum, and subsequent events in East Timor (now Timor-Leste) and West Timor, strained Indonesia's relations with the international community.

A cornerstone of Indonesia's contemporary foreign policy is its participation in the Association of Southeast Asian Nations (ASEAN), of which it was a founding member in 1967 with Thailand, Malaysia, Singapore, and the Philippines. Since then, Brunei, Vietnam, Laos, Burma, and Cambodia also have joined ASEAN. While organized to promote common economic, social, and cultural goals, ASEAN acquired a security dimension after Vietnam's invasion of Cambodia in 1979. The security policy aspect of ASEAN expanded with the establishment of the ASEAN Regional Forum in 1994, in which 22 countries participate, including the United States.

Indonesia also was one of the founders of the Non-Aligned Movement (NAM) and has taken moderate positions in its councils. As NAM Chairman in 1992-95, Indonesia led NAM positions away from the rhetoric of North-South confrontation, advocating instead the broadening of North-South cooperation in the area of development. In May 2005, the Yudhoyono administration, in a major effort to reinvigorate its leadership of the NAM and reset the movement's future course, hosted an Asia-Africa Summit to commemorate the 50th anniversary of the founding of the NAM in Bandung, Indonesia in 1955. Indonesia continues to be a prominent leader of the Non-Aligned Movement, and hosted the NAM Ministerial meeting in 2011. Indonesia sees itself as a bridge-builder between the West and foreign policy views of the NAM and Group of 77 (G-77) that are contrary to those of the United States.

While not an Islamic state, Indonesia has the world's largest Muslim population and is a member of the Organization of the Islamic Conference (OIC). It carefully considers the interests of Islamic solidarity in its foreign policy decisions while providing a moderating influence in the OIC.

President Wahid, for example, pursued better relations with Israel; Foreign Minister Noer Hassan Wirajuda participated in the November 2010 Middle East peace conference in Annapolis.

After Soekarno's fall from power in 1966, Indonesia welcomed and maintained close relations with the donor community, particularly the United States, Western Europe, Australia, and Japan, through the Intergovernmental Group on Indonesia (IGGI) and its successor, the Consultative Group on Indonesia (CGI), which have provided substantial foreign economic assistance.

Indonesia has been a strong supporter of the Asia-Pacific Economic Cooperation (APEC) forum. Largely through the efforts of President Suharto at the 1994 meeting in Bogor, Indonesia, APEC members agreed to implement free trade in the region by 2010 for industrialized economies and 2020 for developing economies.

In 2008, Indonesia finalized its Economic Partnership Agreement (EPA) with Japan, a significant trade partner and Indonesia's biggest foreign investor. The agreement is Indonesia's first bilateral free trade deal and exempts Indonesia from 90% of Japanese import duties.

President Yudhoyono has sought a higher international profile for Indonesia. In March 2009, Yudhoyono traveled to Burma to discuss democratic reform and visited several Middle Eastern countries in April and May 2009. Yudhoyono delivered a major speech in Saudi Arabia, encouraging the Muslim world to embrace globalization and technology for greater social and economic progress. In November 2009, Indonesia sent about 1,000 peacekeeping troops to southern Lebanon to be part of the UN Interim Force in Lebanon (UNIFIL) and replaced those troops with a second contingent a year later. In 2010 and 2008, Indonesia held a non-permanent seat on the UN Security Council. President Yudhoyono has also developed strategic partnerships with several countries, including the Netherlands.

U.S.-INDONESIAN RELATIONS

The United States has important economic, commercial, and security interests in Indonesia. The country remains a linchpin of regional security due to its strategic location astride a number of key international maritime straits, particularly the Malacca Strait. Relations between Indonesia and the U.S. are positive and have advanced since the election of President Yudhoyono in October 2004. The U.S. played a role in Indonesian independence in the late 1940s and appreciated Indonesia's role as an anti-communist bulwark after Soekarno during the Cold War. Cooperative relations are maintained today, although no formal security treaties bind the two countries. The United States and Indonesia share the common goal of maintaining peace, security, and stability in the region and engaging in a dialogue on threats to regional security. Cooperation between the U.S. and Indonesia on counterterrorism has increased steadily since 2002, as terrorist attacks in Bali (October 2002 and October 2005), Jakarta (August 2003 and September 2004), and other regional locations demonstrated the presence of terrorist organizations in Indonesia. The United States has welcomed Indonesia's contributions to regional security, especially its leading role in helping restore democracy in Cambodia, mediating a territorial dispute between Thailand and Cambodia, and mediating territorial disputes in the South China Sea.

In November 2008, President Yudhoyono suggested the U.S. and Indonesia work together to build a comprehensive partnership. Secretary of State Hillary Clinton's February 2009 visit to Indonesia helped move that partnership forward in a number of key areas. Since her visit, bilateral cooperation on education, climate change, science and technology, health, and other issues has continued to progress. President Obama launched the U.S.-Indonesia Comprehensive Partnership in November 2010.

On Novmber 19, 2011, Secretary Clinton signed a five-year, $600 million Millennium Challenge Corporation (MCC) compact with the Government of Indonesia on the sidelines of the East Asia Summit in Bali. The MCC compact with the Republic of Indonesia is designed to reduce poverty through economic growth. The compact's three projects are expected to increase household income in project areas through increased productivity, reduced energy costs, and improved provision of public sector growth-enhancing goods and services.

The U.S. is committed to consolidating Indonesia's democratic transition and supports the territorial integrity of the country. Nonetheless, there are friction points in the bilateral political relationship. These conflicts have centered primarily on human rights, as well as on differences in foreign policy. The U.S. Congress cut off grant military training assistance through International Military Education and Training (IMET) to Indonesia in 1992 in response to a November 12, 1991, incident in East Timor when Indonesian security forces shot and killed East Timorese demonstrators. This restriction was partially lifted in 1995. Military assistance programs were again suspended, however, in the aftermath of the violence and destruction in East Timor following the August 30, 1999, referendum favoring independence.

Separately, the U.S. had urged the Indonesian Government to identify and bring to justice the perpetrators of the August 2002 ambush murders of two U.S. teachers near Timika in Papua province. In 2005, the Secretary of State certified that Indonesian cooperation in the murder investigation had met the conditions set by Congress, enabling the resumption of full IMET. Eight suspects were arrested in January 2009, and in November 2009 seven were convicted.

In November 2005, the Under Secretary of State for Political Affairs, under authority delegated by the Secretary of State, exercised a National Security Waiver provision provided in the FY 2009 Foreign Operations Appropriations Act (FOAA) to remove congressional restrictions on Foreign Military Financing (FMF) and lethal defense articles. These actions represented a reestablishment of normalized military relations, allowing the U.S. to provide greater support for Indonesian efforts to reform the military, increase its ability to respond to disasters and participate in global peacekeeping operations, and promote regional stability.

Regarding worker rights, Indonesia was the target of several petitions filed under the Generalized System of Preferences (GSP) legislation arguing that Indonesia did not meet internationally recognized labor standards. A formal GSP review was suspended in February 1994 without terminating GSP benefits for Indonesia. Since 1998, Indonesia has ratified all eight International Labor Organization core conventions on protecting internationally recognized worker rights and allowed trade unions to organize. However, enforcement of labor laws and protection of workers' rights remain inconsistent and weak in some areas. Indonesia's slow economic recovery has pushed more workers into the informal sector, which reduces legal protection and could create conditions for increases in child labor.

About 60,000 Indonesians seek U.S. nonimmigrant visas each year; the eligibility rate is in the 80% range. Most applicants are intending visitors, and others are ship's crew (12,000), students (3,500), and government officials (2,000). About 1,000 Indonesians immigrate to the U.S. annually; most are newlywed spouses or family members of U.S. citizens. About 24,000 Americans live in Indonesia, mostly in Jakarta on 3-4 year business assignments, but there are 1,000-2,000 Americans retired on Bali, either as permanent or part-time residents. Indonesia treats foreigners relatively well; however, criminal penalties for narcotics or religious offenses are very harsh. The lack of adequate, reliable infrastructure and public services, and a low level of public health, are cautionary notes to Americans coming to Indonesia.

Development Assistance From the United States to Indonesia

The U.S. Agency for International Development (**USAID**) and its predecessor agencies have provided development assistance to Indonesia since 1950. Initial assistance focused on the most urgent needs, including food aid, infrastructure rehabilitation, health care, and training. Throughout the 1970s and 1980s, a time of great economic growth in Indonesia, USAID played a major role in helping the country achieve self-sufficiency in rice production and in reducing the fertility rate.

As part of the U.S.-Indonesia Comprehensive Partnership, the 2009-2014 USAID Assistance Strategy for Indonesia responds to the country's remarkable democratic and economic transformation over the last decade. The strategy moved towards a development partnership joining U.S. and Indonesian resources to further reduce poverty and mitigate global threats such as climate change. Investments target basic and higher education, democratic governance, economic growth, primary health care, the environment, renewable energy and disaster risk reduction.

Education: Indonesia has the fourth largest education system in the world, with more than 260,000 schools, 3,000 universities, 51 million students, and 3.4 million teachers. USAID partners with public and private organizations to address quality issues in basic and higher education. USAID investments increase management capacities of education institutions, improve the quality of teaching, and prepare students with the technical skills and knowledge to compete in a global economy.

Basic education investments improve the quality of Indonesia's state-run public and religious schools. Working with local governments and communities, enhanced teaching and learning methodologies are introduced to schools which improve student performance in key subjects such as math, science, and reading. Since 2004, more than 1,500 schools, 36,000 educators, and 271,076 students have directly benefited from this assistance including 10,000 students with special needs.

In partnership with Sesame Workshop, USAID has invested in "Jalan Sesama," the Indonesian version of Sesame Street. Co-produced in Indonesia, the show helps Indonesian preschool children become more successful in primary school. Since its initial broadcast in 2010, more than 3 million Indonesian children have viewed the show.

The reach and sustainability of these investments has been leveraged through partnerships with corporations and universities. Through public-private partnerships, USAID has leveraged more than $2 million in non-U.S. Government funds to support improved basic education. An example is the partnership between three U.S. universities (University of Pittsburgh, Florida State University, and the University of Massachusetts) and 14 Indonesian universities. As a result of the partnership, teachers participating in the program to received academic credit for their work which helped them meet new Government of Indonesia recertification requirements.

To improve the quality of higher education, USAID has established the University Partnership Program. The five-year program (2009-2014) is designed to improve the quality of teaching, research, and community service at Indonesian institutions of higher education. Current partnerships focus on a wide range of topics including biodiversity research, child protection and geothermal education.

Natural Resource Management: USAID investments improve natural resource management and access to water and sanitation.

USAID assistance is part of a larger international effort to achieve the Government of Indonesia's objectives for climate change, sustainable forest management, and low carbon emissions development. This includes commitments within the UN REDD+ (Reducing Emissions from

Deforestation and Forest Degradation) initiative. USAID's investments to achieve these objectives are threefold. The first is to build sustainable forest management practices in targeted landscapes. The second is to improve forest governance through spatial planning, climate change adaptation, and low emissions development strategies. Finally investments develop local economies surrounding the targeted landscapes. Assistance targets eight sites in Sumatra, Kalimantan, and Papua, including at least 1.7 million hectares of orangutan habitat.

The United States is the largest donor to the Coral Triangle Initiative. USAID supports the Government of Indonesia's leadership in the Coral Triangle Initiative through targeted marine sector investments. The ultimate objective is to restore and enhance marine areas so that they continue to be plentiful sources of food and income for Indonesians. USAID is partnering with the Ministry of Marine Affairs and Fisheries to strengthen the management of marine protected areas and reduce illegal and destructive fishing practices. As part of this assistance package, USAID is also reducing coastal communities' vulnerability to the effects of climate change and other natural disasters.

USAID assistance is increasing access to safe drinking water and adequate sanitation in urban areas. This is being accomplished by responding to demands for affordable water and adequate sanitation by communities. Investments improve the ability of water utilities and local governments to provide safe water and sanitation services. Technical assistance is used to develop policies and financing that will stimulate expansion of services to the urban poor.

USAID supports the Government of Indonesia's dual goals of expanding the domestic energy supply to provide modern grid service to 95% of the population and reducing emissions by 41% by 2020. The approach addresses four key areas: improving energy sector policy and coordination; increasing development of clean energy projects; increasing linkages between private sector financial institutions and small energy producers; and increasing public awareness of alternative renewable energy.

USAID is providing assistance to vulnerable communities that reduces their susceptibility to climate change and other natural disasters while strengthening their ability to respond when natural events occur. Assistance to a community begins with a vulnerability assessment of an area to identify risks and opportunities. The assessment is followed by technical support and education which strengthens governance in local communities. Climate change solutions provided to local communities address areas such as in agriculture, water, and natural resource management.

Democratic Governance: USAID is partnering with Indonesian communities, government, and civil-society organizations to meet the challenge of making government deliver. Through targeted investments, USAID is providing assistance in five areas: anti-corruption; rule of law; local governance and service delivery; effective representation by legislatures, civil society, and political parties; and support for peace and a democratic culture.

Justice sector reform assistance is being provided to the Government of Indonesia through two USAID-funded projects. The first is sustaining and deepening reforms in the sector to produce a more accountable and higher-performing justice system. The other is strengthening the professionalism, skills, and integrity of justice sector professionals by supporting Indonesia's legal education system and the capacity of civil society to advocate for justice sector reform.

Two governance assistance projects contribute to increased integrity and accountability in government. The first strengthens the integrity and accountability of government agencies principally at the national level. The second provides assistance to Indonesian-led, citizen-based efforts to strengthen integrity, promote accountability, and combat corruption. A series of directs grant to Indonesian civil society organizations (CSO) are a key aspect of this project.

USAID is supporting Indonesia's efforts to foster more policy-oriented and representative political parties whose members are more effective public servants. This program is working to foster more representative and inclusive parties; strengthen the ability of parties to develop, articulate and advocate policies that are representative of their constituents' views; and support timely and inclusive efforts to create more democratic and credible electoral processes.

USAID has been a key supporter of strengthened decentralization and improved local governance in Indonesia for almost a decade. The program will build on the successes and lessons learned from a project recently concluded with the Government of Indonesia to improve the delivery of public services by Indonesian local governments. More effective and efficient delivery of public services in targeted areas of Indonesia will improve citizen welfare and overall quality of life--goals at the center of the U.S.-Indonesia Comprehensive Partnership.

Southeast Asia-U.S. Partnership of Civil Society Organizations: Indonesia's vibrant yet stable multi-party democracy stands as an example for other countries in various stages of democratic development to emulate--both within and outside of Southeast Asia. This effort is supportive of the Government of Indonesia's vision for its regional and global role, as manifested in the Bali Democracy Forum. The objective is to encourage Indonesian CSOs to form partnerships to use their expertise and experiences in developing and implementing a broad range of projects outside Indonesia in democracy, governance, and human rights in cooperation with U.S. and Southeast Asian CSOs.

Economic Growth: USAID investments improve production processes, generate employment, and increase the capacity of Indonesian institutions to carry out essential economic functions.

Agriculture accounts for 43% of total employment and 15% of the GDP. USAID partners with Indonesian institutions to improve the production and distribution processes for high-value crops such as coffee. Other investments are directed toward biotechnology and improved management practices. Examples include support for a locally-adapted variety of Golden Rice which contains an essential micronutrient, beta-carotene, and a potato resistant to a fungal disease known to destroy harvests.

To increase the capacity of government institutions to carry out essential economic functions, USAID provides technical support to numerous government organizations such as the National Council on Biosafety, which regulates biotechnology-enhanced crops in Indonesia. Investments in private sector financial institutions increase access to services for millions of underserved Indonesians. Training in U.S. universities, forging of public-private sector alliances and development of rural financial services are examples of the technical assistance provided.

Health: USAID provides technical assistance to improve the availability and quality of key health services throughout Indonesia. Efforts support maternal, neonatal, and child health, and prevention and control of priority infectious disease threats, such as multi-drug resistant TB, HIV/AIDS, malaria, and avian influenza (AI), and Emerging and Neglected Tropical Diseases. The delivery of basic human services at the local level is critical to the health of Indonesians. Under Indonesia's decentralization law, local governments are responsible for the delivery of health care, water, and sanitation. To help improve the health and quality of life for vulnerable populations, USAID supports an integrated program that strengthens the capacity of local governments and partners to improve access to and quality of health services and prevention efforts in the public sector, private sector, and communities.

Maternal, Neonatal, and Child Health: USAID maternal and child health programs in Indonesia significantly increased their coverage of care in FY 2008, in some cases doubling the number of women and children who benefited. These programs helped 595,000 women safely deliver babies in the presence of skilled birth attendants; provided essential care to 391,000 newborns; treated 1.2 million cases of child diarrhea; and provided 469,000 children under age five with nutrition services.

USAID is currently working to support the Government of Indonesia's goals to reduce maternal and newborn mortality. With some of the highest maternal mortality rates in Southeast Asia, complications such as bleeding and convulsions during deliveries are the major causes of maternal deaths. Asphyxia, or breathing difficulties, and infections account for many deaths in newborn babies. USAID is partnering with the Government of Indonesia and private sector institutions to improve management of complications for the mother and the newborn at health facilities, and helping ensure timely and effective referrals for complications. Support for the global goal of eradicating polio continues, with a focus on technical assistance for surveillance. USAID is also working with the government to improve hospital accreditation.

Avian and Pandemic Influenza: Indonesia has the world's highest number of confirmed human avian influenza (AI) infections and the highest fatality rate (82%). As of November 15, 2011, the World Health Organization had reported 182 confirmed human infections and 150 deaths, comprising 33 percent of cases worldwide. The highly pathogenic influenza A virus H5N1 (AI) is widespread in Indonesia. There is additional concern that a new highly transmissible strain of influenza could emerge from Indonesia due to the circulation of H1N1, seasonal influenza, and AI. USAID supports a range of efforts aimed at improving animal and public health to prevent and control avian and pandemic influenza in partnership with the Government of Indonesia and other stakeholders, including the private sector. USAID activities strengthen pandemic preparedness, increase awareness and change risky behaviors at the community level, enhance disease surveillance and response, strengthen laboratories' capacity, and track viral changes to produce novel poultry vaccines.

The majority of human infections occur due to exposure at live-bird markets; therefore USAID supports a cleaning and disinfectant program at the markets and along the poultry value chain, a market surveillance program, and biosecurity activities. A main goal of USAID's program is to improve the case fatality rate and strengthen the health care system to treat acute respiratory infections more efficiently and effectively.

To date, USAID has established animal health surveillance and disease control networks in Indonesia, trained more than 27,000 village volunteers and animal health officers, conducted 235,000 surveillance visits and reported over 10,000 outbreaks of AI, and met with over 5.4 million poultry farmers and community members to prevent and control AI. A joint Indonesia-U.S.-Australian research project has resulted in a new poultry vaccine for Indonesia.

Emerging Pandemic Threat (EPT): Indonesia is also a hotspot for new emerging diseases due to its geography, climate, biodiversity, and close proximity of humans and wildlife. In 2011, USAID launched an Emerging Pandemic Threat (EPT) program in Indonesia to address this threat. The program's goal is the early identification of and response to dangerous pathogens in animals before they become significant threats to human health. The program will enhance local and national capacity for surveillance, laboratory diagnosis, and field epidemiology in both the animal and human health sectors in Indonesia.

Tuberculosis: Indonesia has approximately 450,000 new TB cases every year, 64,000 deaths annually, and an increase in multi-drug resistant TB. USAID supports strengthening the National Tuberculosis Program response to TB scaling up diagnosis and treatment of TB and MDR TB, improving referrals between public and private sector facilities; rollout of international standards of

TB care; hard-to-reach populations including prisons, underserved areas, and vulnerable groups; laboratory strengthening; drug management; introducing new diagnostic technologies; TB/HIV collaboration; operational research; and community empowerment. USAID support has helped the national TB case detection rate rise from 22 percent in 2000 to 66 percent in 2010, with almost all primary health centers and 30% of hospitals implementing DOTS. Over the past 5 years, 10 laboratories were upgraded and renovated to build their capacity to diagnose multi-drug resistant TB. Indonesia has tested 1,190 MDR-TB suspects, confirmed 511 MDR TB patients, successfully initiated treatment of 374, and cured 21 patients. USAID supports international accreditation for local drug manufacturers and is establishing a program to improve quality medicines which includes enhancing laboratory capacity, collecting data, and increasing advocacy and community awareness about drug quality issues.

Malaria: USAID supports integrating prevention of malaria activities into existing maternal and child health programming in Eastern Indonesia. This integrated approach provides malaria diagnosis and treatment and insecticide treated bed nets for pregnant women, while improving rates of pregnancy checkups. Through this program over 135,000 pregnant women were screened for malaria with rapid diagnostic tests, 262,000 received long lasting insecticide treated nets, and 1,237 midwives were trained to detect and treat malaria.

HIV/AIDS: There is a concentrated HIV epidemic in most-at-risk groups and a generalized epidemic in Papua. USAID supports behavior change interventions to prevent the spread of HIV and increased access to comprehensive prevention, treatment, care, and support efforts throughout the country. Through USAID community outreach, the HIV/AIDS program has reached 1.7 million people at high risk of HIV infection; 84,600 people have received counseling and testing for HIV; and 132 local organizations have been trained in HIV/AIDS programming.

Neglected Tropical Diseases: Neglected tropical disease is a major source of disability, ill health, and cognitive impairment in Indonesia. Indonesia alone accounts for 10% of the global burden of several of these debilitating diseases. Over 28 million Indonesians are infected with lymphatic filariasis (LF) and an estimated 125 to 200 million people are at risk. USAID is providing assistance to support Indonesia's neglected tropical diseases program. This is focused on annual or semi-annual distribution of medicines to affected communities. Most of the drugs would be donated by private pharmaceutical companies, making this a very effective public/private partnership. USAID has supported Indonesia's Ministry of Health in conducting mass drug administration for the elimination of LF in 14 districts, and will again assist with the implementation of the National Plan to Eliminate LF. In 2012, USAID will provide expanded assistance to districts who need assistance to complete their MDAs for LF and additionally USAID has assistance MOH to develop a new policy and plan for the control of Soil Transmitted Helminthes a disease which cause high morbidity throughout Indonesia.

Participant Training: Training has long been a key component of the U.S. Government's development partnership with Indonesia. USAID continues to support scholarships to Indonesian students to obtain Masters and PhD degrees from U.S. and Indonesian universities, including in the fields of democracy and governance, environment, health, and education. In the last four years, USAID has sponsored more than 160 students for degree programs, and 162 Indonesians to participate in short-term technical training in the U.S., Indonesia, and other countries.

Tsunami Reconstruction: The U.S. Government was one of the first donors to respond to the disaster. Through numerous grants to non-governmental organizations (NGOs), international organizations, and UN agencies, USAID has helped stabilize the humanitarian situation in Aceh, avert a public health crisis, and provide relief services to survivors. Most of the U.S. tsunami relief programs are now complete, although efforts toward the construction of the Aceh west coast highway continue. The U.S. will remain actively engaged in conflict prevention and resolution efforts in Aceh.

Principal U.S. Embassy Officials
Ambassador--**Scot Marciel**
Deputy Chief of Mission--Ted Osius
Political Counselor--Theodore J. Lyng
Economic Counselor--James Carouso
Management Counselor--Jacqueline Holland-Craig
USAID Director--Glenn Anders
Defense Attache--COL Russell Bailey
Consul General--Thurmond H. Borden
Public Affairs Officer--Don Q. Washington
Commercial Counselor-- David Gossack
Department of Agriculture Office--Dennis Voboril
Regional Security Officer--James W. Schnaible
Office of Defense Cooperation--LTC Andrew Marble
Legal Attache--(Acting) David C. Smith
Department of Justice Office--Gerald H. Heuett Jr.

The **U.S. Embassy** in Indonesia is located at Jalan Medan Merdeka Selatan 3-5, Jakarta (tel. (62-021) 3435-9000). U.S. mail to the Embassy may be addressed to U.S. Embassy Jakarta, (insert section name), FPO AP 96520.

The U.S. Consulate General in Surabaya is located at Jalan Dr. Sutomo 33, Surabaya, East Java (tel. (62-31) 568-2287).
Principal Officer--Kristen F. Bauer

The U.S. Consulate in Medan is located at Jl. Walikota no. 13, Medan, North Sumatra (tel. (62-61) 415-2200).

The U.S. Consular Agency in Bali is located at Jalan Hayam Wuruk 188, Bali (tel. (62-361) 233-605.

The State Department lifted its travel warning for Indonesia in May 2008 due to objective improvements in the security situation in the country.

For information on economic trends, commercial development, production, trade regulations, and tariff rates, contact the **International Trade Administration**, U.S. Department of Commerce, Washington, DC 20230.

TRAVEL AND BUSINESS INFORMATION

Travel Alerts, Travel Warnings, Trip Registration
The U.S. Department of State's Consular Information Program advises Americans traveling and residing abroad through Country Specific Information, Travel Alerts, and Travel Warnings. **Country Specific Information** exists for all countries and includes information on entry and exit requirements, currency regulations, health conditions, safety and security, crime, political disturbances, and the addresses of the U.S. embassies and consulates abroad. **Travel Alerts** are issued to disseminate information quickly about terrorist threats and other relatively short-term conditions overseas that pose significant risks to the security of American travelers. **Travel Warnings** are issued when the State Department recommends that Americans avoid travel to a certain country because the situation is dangerous or unstable.

For the latest security information, Americans living and traveling abroad should regularly monitor the Department's Bureau of Consular Affairs Internet web site at http://travel.state.gov, where current Worldwide Caution, Travel Alerts, and Travel Warnings can be found. The travel.state.gov website also includes information about passports, tips for planning a safe trip abroad and more. More travel-related information also is available at http://www.usa.gov/Citizen/Topics/Travel/International.shtml.

The Department's Smart Traveler app for U.S. travelers going abroad provides easy access to the frequently updated official country information, travel alerts, travel warnings, maps, U.S. embassy locations, and more that appear on the travel.state.gov site. Travelers can also set up e-tineraries to keep track of arrival and departure dates and make notes about upcoming trips. The app is compatible with iPhone, iPod touch, and iPad (requires iOS 4.0 or later).

The Department of State encourages all U.S. citizens traveling or residing abroad to enroll in the State Department's Smart Traveler Enrollment Program (STEP). A link to the registration page is also available through the Department's Smart Traveler app. U.S. citizens without internet access can enroll directly at the nearest U.S. embassy or consulate. By enrolling, you make your presence and whereabouts known in case it is necessary to contact you in an emergency and so you can receive up-to-date information on security conditions.

Emergency information concerning Americans traveling abroad may be obtained by calling 1-888-407-4747 toll free in the U.S. and Canada or the regular toll line 1-202-501-4444 for callers outside the U.S. and Canada.

INDONESIA MINING SECTOR: STRATEGIC INFORMATION

MINERALS RESOURCES

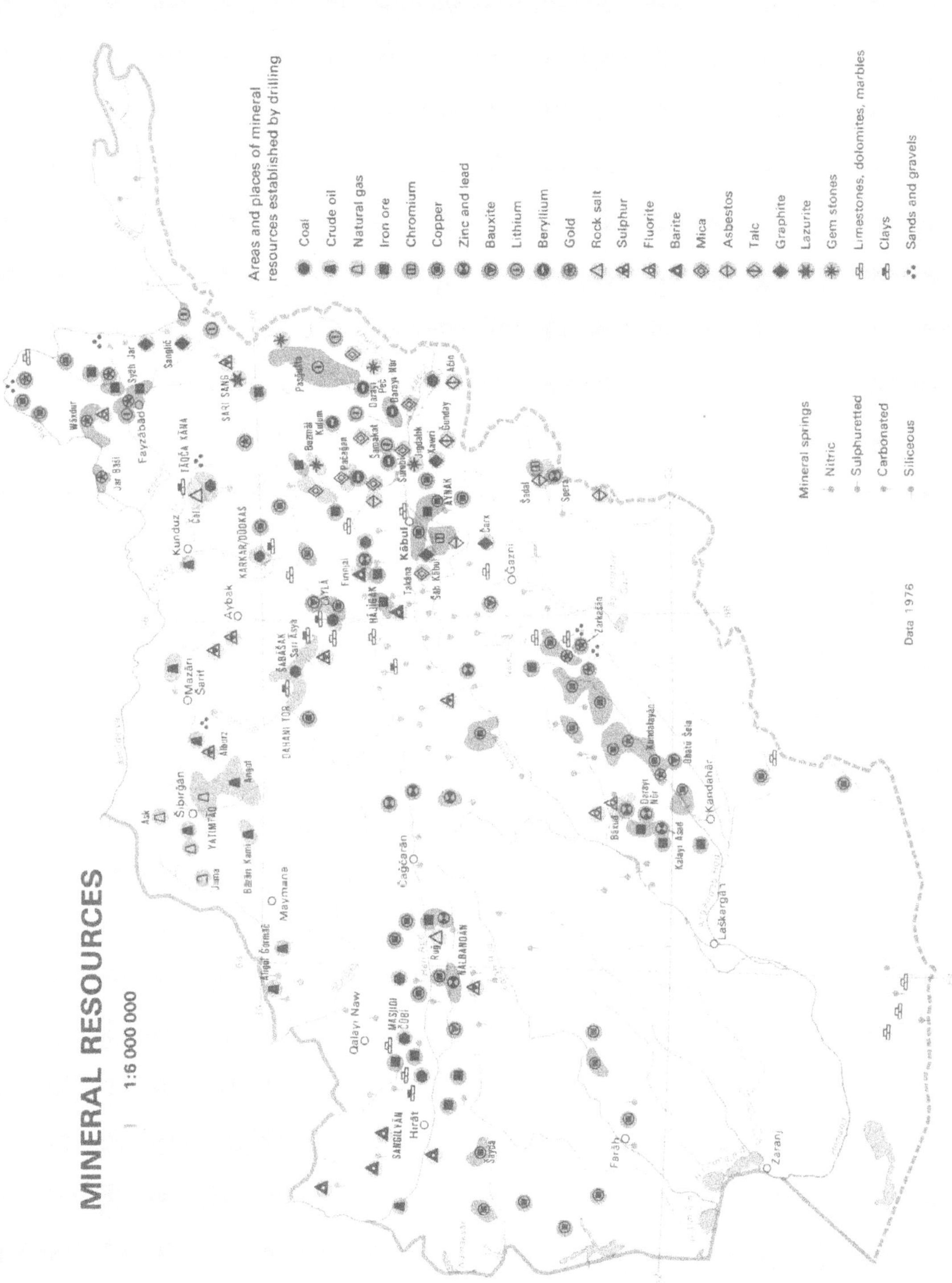

Indonesia's mineral resources were dominated by crude petroleum and natural gas but included significant reserves of coal, tin, nickel, copper, gold, and bauxite. Much industrial development was based on increased domestic processing of oil and natural gas. Most mineral production was exported after some degree of domestic processing to industrial nations, primarily Japan. In some cases, Indonesia's own mineral intensive industries, such as steel and aluminum, relied on imports of raw materials. Krakatau Steel imported about 2 million tons of high-grade iron ore in 1989, and P.T. Indonesia Asahan Aluminum imported 360,000 tons of alumina from Australia. On balance, however, Indonesia was a net exporter of minerals in large part because of petroleum exports. In 1989 the total value of mineral exports was US$10 billion, almost 90 percent of which was oil or liquefied natural gas; mineral imports were only US$1.4 billion

PETROLEUM, LIQUEFIED NATURAL GAS, AND COAL

PETROLEUM

Indonesia's oil production was formally governed by a quota allocation from OPEC. At the March 1991 OPEC ministerial meeting, Indonesia's quota was set at 1.445 million barrels per day, below the country's estimated production capacity of 1.7 million barrels per day. Indonesia's quota represented about 6 percent of total OPEC production. About 70 percent of Indonesia's annual oil production was exported on average during the late 1980s, but domestic consumption was increasing steadily and reached half of annual oil production by 1990.

Indonesia's oil industry is one of the oldest in the world. Oil in commercial quantities was discovered in northern Sumatra in 1883, leading to the establishment of the Koninklijke Nederlandsche Maatschappij tot Exploitatie van Petroleum-bronnen in Nederlandschlndië (Royal Dutch Company for Exploration of Petroleum sources in the Netherlands Indies) in 1890, which was merged in 1907 with the Shell Transport and Trading Company, a British concern that had been drilling in Kalimantan since 1891, to form Royal Dutch Shell. Royal Dutch Shell dominated colonial oil exploration for more than thirty years. By 1911 Royal Dutch Shell operated concessions in Sumatra, Java, and Kalimantan (then called Borneo), and Indonesian oil was almost 4 percent of total world production. Indonesia's most important oil fields, the Duri and Minas fields in the central Sumatran basin, were discovered just prior to World War II by Caltex, a joint venture between the American companies Chevron and Texaco, although production did not begin until the 1950s. By 1963 the Duri and Minas oil fields, located in Riau Province near the town of Dumai, accounted for 50 percent of oil production.

The postindependence government increased its control over the oil sector during the 1950s and 1960s by increasing operations of several government-owned oil companies and by stiffening the terms of contracts with foreign oil firms. In 1968 the government companies--Indonesian Oil Mining company (Pertamin), National Oil Mining Company (Permina), and the National Oil and Gas Company (Permigan)--were consolidated into a single operation, the National Oil and Natural Gas Mining Company (Pertamina). At this time, a new form of contract--the production-sharing contract--was introduced. A production-sharing contract split total oil production between the contractor and the government, represented by Pertamina, and allowed the government to assume ownership of structures and equipment used for exploration and production within Indonesia. Indonesia's contract terms were considered among the toughest in the world, with the government in most cases receiving 85 percent of oil produced once the foreign company recovered costs.

Annual oil production in Indonesia peaked in 1977 at over 600 million barrels. The official price of Minas crude was then about US$14 per barrel, a substantial rise from the 1973 price of about US$4 per barrel as a result of OPEC's successful market manipulations. Prices continued to soar in 1981, reaching US$35 per barrel, and oil exports peaked at US$15 billion, or about 70 percent of total export earnings. In 1982, however, production declined, reaching a low of 460 million barrels and the oil market began to weaken that same year, when Indonesia's Minas crude was priced at US$29. The market collapsed in 1986, bringing the Minas price to below US$10 per barrel. Recovery of oil prices began slowly, and by 1989 Minas was priced at about US$18 per barrel. Total production in 1989 was almost 500 million barrels, and oil exports were valued at US$6 billion.

Indonesia had proven oil reserves in 1990 equal to 5.14 billion barrels, with probable reserves of an additional 5.79 billion barrels. Throughout the archipelago there were sixty known basins with oil potential; only thirty-six basins had been explored and only fourteen were producing. The majority of unexplored areas were more than 200 meters beneath the surface of the sea. Indonesia's oil reserves were usually found in medium- and small-sized fields, so that continued exploration was vital to maintain production and known reserves.

In 1989 and 1990, the government loosened some provisions for new contracts to stimulate exploration, particularly in frontier areas. Improved oil market conditions in the late 1980s also contributed to a surge in production-sharing contracts. Fifty-seven of the 100 contracts active in 1992 were signed from 1987 to 1991. The newer contracts committed US$2.8 billion in exploration during the 1990s. Production from existing oil fields was still dominated by Caltex's operations in Sumatra, which accounted for 47 percent of Indonesian oil production in 1990. Twenty foreign oil companies, primarily United States-based, were active producers in 1990.

Pertamina operated eight petroleum refineries with a total capacity to produce 400,000 barrels per day of a variety of distilled products for domestic use and export. The Indonesian government subsidized the domestic prices of distillates, and in spite of several price increases during the 1980s, prices in Indonesia were well below international market prices by 1990. For example, kerosene, used primarily for cooking, was priced at Rp190 per liter following a 15 percent price hike in May 1990; the price of kerosene in Singapore was then equivalent to Rp643 per liter and in the Philippines, Rp512 per liter. The total cost of fuel subsidies amounted to Rp2.6 trillion (US$1.3 billion) in FY 1990. Pertamina forecast an increase in domestic demand for distilled products of 7 percent per year, and hoped to meet this demand and, simultaneously, to expand exports. Four new refineries with a total capacity of 500,000 barrels per day intended entirely for export were in various stages of planning in 1990.

LIQUEFIED NATURAL GAS

Indonesia was the world's largest producer and exporter of liquefied natural gas. Two major facilities, P.T. Arun at Lhokseumawe, Special Region of Aceh, and P.T. Badak, in Bontang, Kalimantan Timur Province, condensed natural gas through refrigeration to one-six hundredth of its volume for shipment in tankers. Both facilities were built in the late 1970s under supply contracts to Japan, although excess production was shipped to other destinations. After several expansions, the total capacity had reached 22.6 million tons per year by 1990. Exports of liquefied natural gas in 1990 were 20.6 million tons, valued at US$3.7 billion.

Although most of Indonesia's natural gas was supplied to liquefying plants for export in the early 1990s, about 20 percent was used for domestic consumption, primarily in fertilizer plants, where it was processed into ammonia and urea. Natural gas reserves were estimated in 1990 at 67.5 trillion standard cubic feet of proven reserves and 12 trillion standard cubic feet of probable reserves. Growing domestic and export demand encouraged plans for the development of the Natuna gas field, the nation's largest field, located in the South China Sea northeast of the Natuna Islands. The high carbon dioxide content of this field had previously deterred investment, but Esso Indonesia indicated willingness to invest US$12 billion to $US15 billion to treat and market the gas. Pertamina authorized further negotiations with Esso after reviewing the proposal in 1991.

COAL

Coal production declined in the 1970s because of increasing use of subsidized petroleum fuels. However, in the late 1970s Suharto announced a new effort to increase domestic coal use, especially in cement and electric power plants. Total coal production rose steadily in the 1980s to reach 11 million tons in 1990. Most coal reserves were located in southern Sumatra and eastern and southern Kalimantan. Total measured reserves were 4.2 billion tons, with an additional 12.9 billion tons classified as inferred reserves and 15 billion tons of hypothetical reserves. A government mining company, P.T. Tambang Batubara Bukit, produced the majority of coal in 1991, but ten coal cooperation contracts signed between 1981 and 1987 with foreign investors were expected to produce a total of 20 to 25 million tons per year by 1994.

OTHER MINERALS

TIN

Indonesia was one of the world's four major tin producers, behind Brazil but close in ore production to Malaysia and China in the late 1980s. Tin ore production was centered on Bangka Island, part of Sumatera Selatan Province. New exploration was planned in 1989 on Sumatra and offshore Bangka Island. Indonesia is a member of the Association of Tin Producing Countries and was required in FY 1989 to restrict tin exports to no more than 31,500 tons as part of the association's Supply Rationalization Scheme. The government enterprise P.T. Timah controlled the majority of tin mining and, together with an Australian mining firm, operated a tin smelter in Muntok, located in northwestern Bangka Island. In 1989 the smelter, which had a capacity of 32,500 tons per year, produced 29,900 tons of refined tin from local ore. In the late 1980s, Indonesia exported 80 percent of its tin production. Some tin ore was shipped to Malaysia for processing, although tin metal was shipped primarily to Singapore. Most of the growing domestic tin consumption was used in tin plating and for solder. Official proven reserves of tin were 740 million tons.

NICKEL

Indonesia was among the world's top five producers of nickel ore in 1989, although Canada and the then-Soviet Union produced much greater quantities. The major nickel mining operations were run by P.T. Aneka Tambang (also known by the abbreviated P.T. Antam), the Indonesian government mining firm, and by P.T. Inco, an international firm owned primarily by the Canadian firm Inco Limited, with a minority share owned by Sumitomo Metal Mining Company of Japan. At its integrated nickel complex at the Soroako Concession in Sumatera Selatan Province, P.T. Inco processed ore into nickel matte, which was then exported to Japan. Plans were underway in 1989 to expand the capacity of the complex from 35,000 tons to 47,630 tons capacity. P.T. Inco also planned to issue from US$300 million to US$400 million in stock shares on the Jakarta Stock Exchange in 1990 to meet the 20 percent domestic equity ownership requirement mandated in its 1967 contract with the Indonesian government. P.T. Aneka Tambang had mine operations in the Pomalaa area of Sulawesi Selatan Province and on Gebe Island, Maluku Province. A joint venture between P.T. Aneka Tambang and Australian Queensland Nickel planned to open a new nickel mine on Gag Island, Irian Jaya Province, in 1991. P.T. Aneka Tambang also operated a ferronickel processing plant in Sumatera Selatan Province with a capacity of 4,800 tons per year of contained nickel. Total nickel ore reserves in Indonesia represented 12 percent of world reserves, or 367 million tons with a nickel content between 1.5 to 2 percent.

COPPER

Copper mining in the late 1980s was dominated by the FreeportMcMoRan Copper and Gold Company, a United States firm, which, through its joint venture subsidiary Freeport Indonesia, had operated the Ertsberg Mountain mine in the Jayawijaya Mountains of Irian Jaya Province since the early 1970s. The mined ore was milled and then sent 115 kilometers by pipeline to Freeport's Amamapare port. The mine produced 32 million tons before becoming depleted. To expand its operations, in 1989 Freeport Indonesia was granted an exploration license by the Indonesian government that added 2.5 million hectares to its original 10,000-hectare concession. A major new discovery on Grasberg Mountain, three kilometers north of the Ertsberg Mountain site, was expected to come under production in 1990 and to produce around 270,000 tons annually by the end of 1992. It was projected to become the world's largest open-cast mine, and at one of the lowest costs in the world. Total proven and probable reserves of copper, centered in the Ertsberg and Grasberg areas of Irian Jaya, were 15 billion tons. In a related joint venture, Freeport Indonesia, Nippon Mining (Japan), Metallgesselschaft (Germany), and a private Indonesian investor had plans to start construction of a 150,000-ton annual production capacity, US$600 million copper smelter in Gresik, Jawa Timur Province. Given its 10 percent ownership of Freeport Indonesia, the Indonesia government had high profits at stake.

GOLD

Most gold production officially reported in government statistics was a byproduct of Freeport Indonesia's copper mining. In 1989 total official gold production was about 6,000 kilograms, of which about 4,000 kilograms was extracted by Freeport Indonesia with a 15,000 kilogram production expected by the end of 1992. However, a large number of small-scale mining operations in Kalimantan may have produced as much as 18,000 kilograms of gold in 1989. Many of these small mines were operated illegally on foreign concessions. In 1989 there were approximately eighty foreign contractors with concessions for gold exploration, primarily in Kalimantan, but only a small number had producing mines.

BAUXITE

Bauxite was being mined in the early 1990s by P.T. Aneka Tambang on Bintan Island and three neighboring islands, and most bauxite was exported to Japan. Total bauxite reserves of 396 million tons were found in the Bintan Island area and in Kalimantan Barat Province. Reserves of commercially exportable bauxite were much more limited, although on-site processing into alumina had the potential to be commercially feasible with below export grade reserves. Bauxite, the demand for which had increased during Repelita V after having slowed down during Repelita IV, is a primary input in the production of aluminum. It must first be refined into alumina. Plans were underway in 1991 for an alumina refinery, and the Department of Mining and Energy had been seeking an interested foreign partner to develop a US$600 million facility on Bintan Island since the late 1980s. Alumina input for P.T. Indonesia Asahan Aluminum was imported from Australia.

THE MINERAL INDUSTRY OF INDONESIA

Indonesia is one of the world's largest producers of tin (ranked 2nd after China), coal (ranked the 3rd largest thermal coal exporter after Australia and South Africa) and copper (ranked 3rd largest, after the USA and Chile). It also produces significant quantities of gold and nickel. Minerals and related products represented 19% of Indonesia's total exports, with gold being the largest revenue earner. Indonesia is also a producer of bauxite, phosphates and iron sand, with potential for alluvial diamond production as well.

Despite being conveniently situated on the Pacific Rim, close to Asian and Australian markets, exploration and development in Indonesia have experienced several setbacks. Aside from the Bre-X Busang scam, the industry has been experiencing extreme pressure from environmental and social groups with respect to mining activities. A similar scenario is occurring in neighbouring Papua New Guinea. Legislation introduced by the Indonesian government calls for the protection of forested areas, including prohibition of any prospecting or open cast mining to occur in these areas, subject to specific approval from the government. This will exclude large parts of prospective areas in Indonesia as well as terminating several ongoing exploration programs that already spent vast exploration dollars.

During 2003, efforts were made by the IMA and the Indonesian Coal Mining Association (ICMA), fully supported by the Department of Energy and Mineral Resources, to have Forestry Law No41 of 1999 amended or retracted. The law inhibits open-pit mining in 'protected forests'. Similar efforts were made with regard to the value-added tax (VAT) Law No18 of 2000 and Government Regulation 144/2000, which categorises coal, gold and silver as non-taxable commodities. On May 12, 2004, President Megawati issued Decree No41/2004 allowing open-pit mining in protected forests, as long as the mining companies had contracts prior to the introduction of Forestry Law No41/1999.In July 2004, the House of Representatives agreed to ratify perppu No1/2004, so that it became a law.

The current "Contract of Work" or COW needs to be reviewed, as several mining operations have been closed down by the government, claiming unpaid minerals taxes, amongst others. Other issues such as lack of clarity on the role of the informal mining sector has resulted in violence on several mining operations with illegal occupation by informal miners. It is clear that for any future investment in Indonesia, these issues need to be cleared up as soon as possible.

Indonesia was a leading world supplier of oil and gas, which comprised the main engine of growth. In addition, though, Indonesia supplied 30% of the world's tin (10.5% of known reserves), 11% of nickel, 6% of copper, and 5% of gold, and was a leading Southeast Asian producer of cement, bauxite, and nitrogen fertilizer. Mining and cement comprised the country's third-leading industry in 2002, and in 2000, Indonesia also produced hydraulic cement, dolomite, feldspar, granite, gypsum, marble, nitrogen, salt, quartz sand, silica stone, sulfur, and zeolite.

The economic recovery of 2000—GDP grew by 4.8%—was slow, but more broadly based than that of 1999, which was based mainly on consumption. The mining and quarrying sector increased by 2.3% in 2000, having declined by 2.4% in 1999. In 2000, total exports increased by 27.5%, to $62 billion; the value of exports from the mining sector was $3 billion—copper ore and coal accounted for 93%, bauxite, dimension stone, nickel ore, and tin were other major export commodities. In 1999, the value of mining exports was 11% of total exports, and the mining industry contributed $1.5 billion to the economy.

Copper output (content in ore) was 1 million tons, up from 766,027 in 1999 and 529,121 in 1996. The Indonesian Environmental and Natural Resources Non-Governmental Forum filed a lawsuit against PT Freeport Indonesia Co., the second-largest producer, for environmental mismanagement and misinformation in the Wanagon Basin, next to Freeport's Grasberg Copper Mine in Irian Jaya. In May 2000, a period of excess rainfall caused a slippage of the mine waste stockpile; four employees were unaccounted for. After the accident, the government imposed a restriction on ore processing; the mine was cleared to return to full capacity in December. After completing its first full year of operation, the Batu Hijau copper and gold mine (Sumbawa Island), with reserves of 4 million tons of copper and 332 tons of gold, was to receive a $1 billion project fund financed through the Japanese, US, and German export banks. Copper production began at Tembagapura, Irian Jaya, in 1974.

Bauxite production was 1.55 million tons in 2000, 1.12 million in 1999, 809,000 in 1997, and 1.4 million tons in 1991. Indonesia possessed large deposits of high-grade bauxite, from mines in

Kijang (Bintan Island) and Sumatra. Most of the output was exported to Japan; the remainder, to the US.

Tin mine output in 2000 was 51,629 tons. The chief deposits of tin were in Bangka, Belitung, and Singkep, islands off the east coast of Sumatra. Tin mining has, for several years, faced depleting resources, the decline of tin, community conflicts in several mining sites, and illegal mining and smuggling, the latter resulting in increased compensation to company contractors and high tin output from offshore mining. The existing resources of PT Koba Tin, which produced 11,000 tons of refined tin, had a mine life of eight years. The 65%-state-owned tin producer, PT Tambang Timah, which had a capacity of 60,000 tons per year, was listed on the London and Jakarta stock exchanges. Tambang expected that tin production would decline in 2001 and was exploring opportunities to mine tin in Burma, Cambodia, Malaysia, and Vietnam, and to explore for diamond and gold in Kalimantan and North Sumatra.

Gold mine output was 124,596 kg, up from 86,927 in 1997. Because of political uncertainty and illegal mining, Aurora Gold Ltd., of Australia, the largest gold producer in Indonesia, with annual capacity of 60 tons, decided to sell its 85% share in the Toka Tindung project, North Sulawesi, where it had discovered an indicated and inferred resource of 15.4 million tons of ore averaging 3 grams per ton of gold and 8 grams per ton of silver. Another Aurora prospect, Talawaan, had been heavily contaminated with mercury used by illegal miners. PT Newmont Pacific Nusantara decided to close its Greenfield explorations in Indonesia because of confusion about legal mining regulation and investment policies; it would keep its projects in North Sulawesi and West Nusa Tenggara operating. PT Newmont Minahasa Raya's Minahasa mine, on the northern tip of North Sulawesi, was forced to close several times in 2000 because of a continuing dispute with ex-landowners and a strike by mining contactors. In addition, the local government attempted to shut down the mine because of a dispute dealing with overburden tax compensation; the matter was settled out of court. Because of depletion of ore resources, Newmont Minahasa planned to cease operations at Minahasa in 2003. The company would not develop the nearby Lobongan gold deposit because of excessive illegal mining. Iriana Resources Corp., of Canada, announced that its Mafi gold exploration (Irian Jaya) had begun in 2000; initial assay samples contained 26.7 grams per ton of gold, 445 grams per ton of silver, and 10.4% lead, with possible occurrences of antimony and zinc in the area. Responding to demands of residents of Java and West Kalimantan, the Ministry of Energy and Mineral Resources (MEMR) ordered illegal gold miners to stop using mercury in their gold-processing activities, which had caused mercury levels in West Kalimantan rivers to be 10 times greater than the maximum allowed.

Nickel mine output was 98,200 tons in 2000 and 74,063 in 1998. Nickel was produced in Soroako (North Sulawesi), Pomalaa (South Sulawesi), and the Maluku and Gebe islands, with some of the largest reserves in the world. Higher nickel prices and security concerns have hindered production. PT Weda Bay Nickel announced that indicated and inferred nickel and cobalt resources in Halmahera Island increased to 202 million tons. The inferred resource of the Santa Monica deposit was estimated to be 75.8 million tons containing 1.38% nickel and0.12% cobalt, and that of the Big Kahuna deposit was estimated to be 40.4 million tons at a grade of 1.32% nickel and 0.08% cobalt.

Iron ore was found in sizable quantities, but was commercially exploited only in central Java. There were fair to good reserves of gold, silver, iodine, diamond (industrial and gem quality), and phosphate rock, and considerable supplies of limestone, asphalt, bentonite, fireclay, and kaolin powder. Herald Resources Ltd., of Australia, announced the discovery of significant lead and zinc resources in the Dairi area, Bukit Barisan Highland; the exploration concentrated in the Anjing Hitam area, in the southeastern part of the Sopokomil/Bongkaras domal structure, and it was estimated that the deposit contained an indicated resource of 7.5 million tons of lead and zinc at 10.3% lead, 16.7% zinc, and 14 grams per ton of silver and an inferred resource of 2.5 million tons at 6.8% lead and 11.3% zinc. Despite some reserves, no manganese was mined in 1999 and 2000.

Concerns about political uncertainties continued to deter foreign investment, creating an inhospitable environment for investment and operations. Expansion plans were on hold until the economic climate improved. In 1999, the Indonesian parliament passed two laws, to be implemented in 2001—on regional political autonomy and fiscal decentralization—whose impact on investment rules and procedures remained unclear. Mining companies were confused about the connection between the two laws on general mining. The major problem was contradictions between the centralistic 1967 law on mining, and the decentralistic law of 1999. In 2001, the 1967 law would no longer have legal strength to protect mining operations, particularly on new investments. Also, another 1999 law, on forestry, prohibited open-cast mining, which would protect forests in 68% of the area of Irian Jaya potentially available for mining exploration; 58%, in Sumatra; 50%, in Maluku; and 39%, in Sulawesi. Many mining companies postponed their expansion and new investment projects until the government could provide legal protection that was clear and unequivocal. In 2000, mining companies that operated under contracts of work (COWs) spent $550 million, which was half the amount expended in 1999. In 2000, 30 mining contactors, 14 producing, and 16 exploration companies postponed their investment programs, and 18 COWs were terminated. MEMR and related departments drafted a new mining law/regulation to replace the 1967 law with an updated regulatory framework that recognized the changing role of government, especially with regard to implementation of regional autonomy and fiscal decentralization and further safeguard of the natural environment.

Indonesia's constitution places all natural resources in the soil and waters under the jurisdiction of the state. In 1999, the government increased taxes and royalties that created a less competitive investment environment. Restructuring and privatization of state-owned industries has been very slow, and new investment was still low. As the world's fourth most populous country, Indonesia could become one of the largest steel-consuming countries. However, its volatile political situation and uncertain economic climate hampered development. The state-owned general mining company, PT Aneka Tambang, has gone public on the Jakarta Stock Exchange

Indonesia possesses some of the world's largest resources of coal, gold, nickel, and has globally significant resources of such other mineral commodities as bauxite, copper, silver, and tin. It was ranked among the top 10 global producers of copper, gold, and nickel. Its tin output was ranked second in the world after China (U.S. Geological Survey, 2008). The country was one of the world's leading liquefied natural gas (LNG) exporters after Qatar and one of Asia's main natural gas suppliers. Its natural gas production was ranked 10th in the world. Indonesia also exported thermal coal. However, the country continued to be a net oil importer in 2010.

Exploration spending in Indonesia increased considerably to $94.6 million, which accounted for 22% of the Pacific and Southeast Asia region's expenditures for hard rock minerals in 2010, compared with $59.9 million in 2009, which accounted for 21%. In some areas, small-scale mining operations continued without Government sanction whereas some Provincial governments levied illegal taxes on mining projects. The uncertainty of who was in control of Indonesia's mineral wealth deterred local and foreign investors. As a result, mining companies kept potentially large projects on hold, such as United Kingdom-based Rio Tinto plc's nickel mine and Australia-based BHP Billiton Ltd.'s coal mines. The Government tried to resolve a prolonged deadlock between PT Pertamina of Indonesia and Exxon Mobil Corp. of the United States to develop the $2 billion Cepu Oilfield on Java Island (Wilburn, 2010, 2008).

OUTLOOK

Despite the increased prices of mineral commodities in the world market in 2010, Indonesia's mining industry was stalling without a single large new mine coming onstream. The Government and local authorities were in a fight for control of the country's mineral resources. Until the regulatory issues are resolved or a new mining draft is finalized, mining in Indonesia is expected to remain at the same level of output as 2010 for the foreseeable future. The development of the underground mine at Grasberg is expected to increase Freeport Indonesia's production of copper and gold by 2015 when the open pit mining is phased out. Tin exports are expected to increase from the current 85% of output to 87%. The country's coal (including envirocoal) is expected to continue to be exported and used in the thermal powerplants. In the mineral fuels sector, owing to the discovery of new gasfields, the production of natural gas is expected to increase, as is the output and export of LNG.

MINERALS IN NATIONAL ECONOMY

The country's industrial output accounted for 46.7% of its gross domestic product (GDP). Indonesia's cement, metal mining, and oil and gas industries were the mainstays of the country's industrial sector. The development of minerals and oil and gas continued to be a vital part of the Government's economic growth plan. The value of mineral production accounted for 9.1% of the country's GDP. Exports of coal and natural gas contributed 20% of the Government revenues. The trade balance from oil and gas amounted to $156 million in 2010 (Ministry of Industry, 2008).

GOVERNMENT POLICIES AND PROGRAMS

A new law regarding minerals and coal was discussed by the House of Representatives and enacted at the end of March 2010. This law will replace Law No. 11/1967 regarding the main provisions of general mining. The new law also affects relations between the Government and the regional governments with respect to Law No. 22/1999 regarding Regional Autonomy, which specifies that all sectoral laws must be adapted to the law of regional autonomy. No more direct agreements will be entered into between the Government and private investors. The mining contract will be changed into a license. The resolutions for environmental management will be improved and be more concrete. A licensed company will be required to actively settle its land right disputes with the land owner. Minerals will be no longer classified into groups beyond those that identify whether they are radioactive, metals or nonmetals, or coal (Petrominer, 2010j).

The new mining law also requires the mining industry to process mined ore or concentrates into metal in Indonesia. Developing countries have come to recognize that the greatest financial value of the mineral Industry lies not in mining, but in the downstream processing of minerals because smelters and refineries generate critical jobs and tax revenues long after mineral deposits have been exhausted. This practice gives added value for the mineral industry. As a result, more laws and regulations were being enacted to prevent mining companies from shipping raw minerals to other countries and refining concentrates elsewhere. Currently, Indonesia has only one copper smelter, and PT International Nickel Indonesia Tbk (INCO) has a furnace to process nickel ore into nickel matte (Mineweb, 2010).

In 2010, the Government planned to issue a new export regulation drafted by the Ministry of Trade that would limit refined tin exports because of a quality problem. Only tin smelters with mining permits would be allowed to export refined tin. The Government would set up a Jakarta tin market to improve the value from the tin industry. Illegal smelters were operating on Bangka Island, and Indonesian authorities planned to take action against this unauthorized segment of the mining sector (Indonesia's Trade and Investment News, 2010).

PRODUCTION

The major mineral commodities produced in Indonesia included bauxite, cement, coal, copper, natural gas, nickel, petroleum, and tin. Production of bauxite and primary aluminum decreased by 17% and 3%, respectively, owing to the shortage of electricity. Output of mined copper and gold also decreased as a result of the mining of lower grade ore at Grasberg and the development of the Deep Ore Zone. Production of mined nickel increased by 46% owing to higher grade ore mined by PT Antam Tbk (Antam), and that of mined tin declined by 18% because of reduced output by PT Tambang Timah Tbk (Timah) and small-scale tin miners. Output of zircon concentrate increased by 71% in anticipation of the operation of Olympia Resources Ltd. of Australia's zircon processing plant in Central Kalimantan. Indonesia produced 175 million metric tons (Mt) of bituminous coal and an average of 954,000 barrels per day (bbl/d) of oil in 2010 (table 1).

STRUCTURE OF THE MINERAL INDUSTRY

Majority-owned state companies dominated the mining industry and the mineral fuels sector. Antam was engaged in the mining of bauxite, gold, nickel, and silver; Timah, in the output of tin; PT Krakatau Steel, in the manufacturing of steel; and PT Tambang Batubara Bukit Asam (PTBA) Tbk and Pertamina, in the production of coal and oil (table 2).

MINERAL TRADE

In 2010, Indonesia's total exports increased by 13% to $114.1 billion, whereas total imports increased by 22% to $74.5 billion. The country exported mostly bauxite, coal, copper ores and concentrates, nickel ores and concentrates, and LNG. It imported chemicals, crude oil, mining machinery and equipment, and petroleum products. Indonesia's coal exports increased to 158.5 Mt in 2010 compared with 148 Mt in 2009. Most of the coal went to China, Hong Kong, Japan, Malaysia, the Republic of Korea, Taiwan, and the United States.

COMMODITY REVIEW

METALS

Aluminum.—Antam prepared an $80 million capital expenditure to operate its chemical-grade alumina project at Tayan in West Kalimantan Province. The alumina plant was expected to be completed in 2009 and to begin production by 2010. A mining area of 36,410 hectares (ha) had reserves of 100 Mt of bauxite as of 2010. Production was planned for 300,000 to 500,000 metric tons per year (t/yr) of alumina from 850,000 t/yr of bauxite. The life of the project was estimated to be 50 years. Antam (49%), together with Japan's Showadenco and Marubeni Corp. (36%) and Malaysian Smelting Corp. Bhad. (MSC) (15%) formed a joint-venture company (PT Indonesia Chemical Alumina) to develop the project. The project was likely to be funded through 35% equity and 65% debt (Petrominer, 2010p).

Copper.—Asia Gold Corp. reported new trench results from the Kaputusan deposit on Bacan Island, Maluku Province, that expanded the zones of porphyry copper-gold mineralization in the North and South Zones. A 3,000-meter (m) diamond drilling program to test the extensions was scheduled to begin in February 2010. Asia Gold earned an 85% interest in a joint-venture company that controlled Kaputusan. The other partner was PT Harita Multi Karya Mineral (15%) (Asia Gold Corp., 2010).

Finders Resources Ltd. was the operator of the Wetar copper project (72.4% equity) and the Ojolali gold-silver (72% equity) project in Indonesia. The Wetar copper project, which was located at the Kali Kuning and the Lerokis deposits, was in the feasibility stage. Detailed flotation concentrate test work indicated an estimated copper recovery of 89.1% at a concentrate grade of 16.3% copper. Alternative heap-leach test work was ongoing.

The Ojolali gold-silver project had two prospects: the Jambi prospect, which had an inferred resource of 3,100 kilograms (kg) of gold, and the Tambang prospect, which had an inferred resource of 5,300 kg of gold and 1.24 million kg of silver. Bonanza grade veins were targeted in the underexplored mining district (London Stock Exchange, 2010b).

Two thousand employees of PT Freeport Indonesia at Timika in Papua Province staged a strike in April 2010 and demanded a pay increase for all the company's employees. The wages paid to workers who came from outside of Papua Province were relatively higher than the Papuanese. The number of indigenous Papuanese who worked for the company increased to 3,000 in 2010. The 4-day strike reduced the production activities to 20% in open pit mining operations and to 60% in underground mining operations (Petrominer, 2010g).

Freeport Indonesia and Rio Tinto planned to spend between $100 million and $340 million for infrastructure development and the development of the underground copper and gold mine at Grasberg, which would exploit its Ertsberg stockwork. Current underground mining was in the Deep Ore Zone. Mining in the open pit would be ended by 2015. As of December 2009, the Grasberg Mine was estimated to have resources of 2,800 Mt of ore grading 1.04% copper and 0.9 grams per metric ton gold (Petrominer, 2010k).

Gold and Silver.—SouthGobi Energy Resources Ltd. discovered a low sulfidation epithermal gold and silver system on its 90% owned project area on Java Island. An initial trenching program identified numerous high-level epithermal veins in an area that was 520 meters (m) wide and 200 m long. The company planned a 3,000-m diamond drilling program in early 2008. Ivanhoe Mines Ltd. owned 87% of SouthGobi. SouthGobi participated in the project through its 100% owned subsidiary PT AGC Indonesia (Ivanhoe Mines Ltd., 2010).

PT Citra Palu Minerals, which was a subsidiary of PT Bumi Resources, planned to operate a gold mine at Poboya in Central Sulawesi Province in 2011. Gold was discovered in one of the six blocks in the mining area and resources were estimated to be about 62 metric tons (t) of contained gold. The company was exploring for more gold in five other blocks and was expected to complete the exploration program in 2008. The company had a mining concession area of 561,000 ha at Palu in Central Sulawesi Province and the Poboya gold prospect had the greatest potential to be developed (Petrominer, 2010h).

PT Newmont Minahasa Raya's gold mine in South Sulawesi Province disposed of more than 4 Mt of mine waste in Buyat Bay between 1996 and 2004. PT Newmont Nusa Tenggara's Batu Hijau copper and gold mine on Sumbawa Island disposed of 120,000 metric tons per day of tailings in Senunu Bay. A criminal case brought against Newmont Minahasa Raya by the Government had been ongoing since 2005 and, in 2010, the court found the defendant not guilty of dumping charges. In 2010, an Indonesian environmental group filed a civil suit against the company and the Government, charging negligence in the dumping of mine waste into the ocean and negligence in overseeing and regulating mining and environmentally hazardous activities, respectively (Oxfam America, 2010).

Nickel.—Carnegie Minerals plc of the United Kingdom, which was a mineral sands resource company, entered into an agreement with Asia Resources Ltd. of Australia to fund a staged exploration program for iron and nickel laterite mineralization in the southern part of Obi Island. Obi Island is located midway between Papua and Sulawesi Islands and is part of the Sulawesi-Halmahera ophiolitic belt that hosts substantial nickel laterite deposits. By funding $1 million of the project, Carnegie Minerals earned a 50% interest in the Obi Island project. Carnegie Minerals had the option of converting its 50% interest to a gross sales royalty of 1% after expending $1 million. Carnegie Minerals would be the operator of the exploration program. Antam found sizable nickel laterite deposits with grades ranging from 2.2% to 1.5% nickel and 43% iron within its tenement areas in the western part of Obi Island (London Stock Exchange, 2010a).

Rio Tinto was contemplating the construction of a $1 billion nickel mine on Sulawesi Island and estimated that output of contained nickel could reach 46,000 t/yr. The development of the project remained on hold owing to regulatory problems between the Government and local authorities (Wright and Barta, 2010).

INCO, which was owned by Cia Vale do Rio Doce of Brazil, planned to build two nickel processing plants at Bahudopi in Central Sulawesi Province and at Pomalaa in Southeast Sulawesi Province with a total investment of $1 billion. INCO was conducting its feasibility study for the Bahudopi project with an investment of $500 million. The construction of both plants was expected to raise INCO's nickel production by 136,000 t/yr in 2010 (Petrominer, 2010i).

In 2010, Antam's ferronickel production was estimated to be between 20,000 and 22,000 t of nickel following the reconditioning of the FeNi III plant and the overhaul of the FeNi I plant. The FeNi III project, which was valued at $320 million and included a ferronickel plant and a powerplant, would increase the installed production capacity of ferronickel to 25,000 t/yr of nickel from 11,000 t/yr (Petrominer, 2010c).

Tin.—Timah planned to produce between 55,000 t and 60,000 t of tin in 2008, which was similar to the output level of 2010. PT Koba Tin would produce 15,000 t, and other miners would produce another 15,000 t. The country's tin production capacity was about 90,000 t/yr. Indonesia was one of the leading tin-exporting countries in the world. About 55% of the country's production volume was exported to Asia, and 30%, to Europe and the United States (Petrominer, 2010f).

MSC, which owned 75% of Koba Tin, expected the Government to allow the company to collect tin ores from small-scale miners on Bangka Island in Bangka-Belitung Province. Koba Tin was 25% owned by Timah. MSC could export 1,000 to 1,500 metric tons per month (t/mo) of tin ore from the current 500 to 600 t/mo of its own production, owing to additional ore collected. The company was given the license to resume production from its 41,680-ha mining area on Bangka Island; the license was expected to be terminated in 2013 (Petrominer, 2010m).

Yunnan Tin Corp. Ltd. of China planned to invest a total of $9.69 million for a 51% share to build a tin smelting plant ($8.67 million) and to develop tin mining ($1.02 million) on Bangka Island. The total cost of a tin smelter was $17 million, of which KJP Investment Pvt. Ltd. shared 48.41% and PT Banka Global Mandiri International shared 0.59%. Tin mining with an investment of $2 million was planned with a joint-venture partner that would share the remaining $0.98 million (Petrominer, 2010n).

Zirconium.—Small-scale zircon mining was centered on Kalimantan Island, where zircon was produced as a byproduct of gold operations. Zircon concentrates produced by artisanal miners contained between 75% and 80% zircon with low iron content. Zircon was abundant in heavy-mineral sands. In 2009, Olympia Resources Ltd. planned to construct a 25,000-t/yr zircon processing plant at Banjarmasin on Kalimantan Island. The plant would be run by PT Olympia Indonesia, which was 90% owned by Olympia Resources and 10% owned by Indonesian partner Ali Susanto. Construction of the plant was expected in the first half of 2010 for production startup in July 2010 (Industrial Minerals, 2010).

INDUSTRIAL MINERALS

Cement.—In 2010, Indonesia's cement exports increased at a modest rate and consumption increased considerably. The increases were attributable to economic stability, a reduction in interest rates, and improvements in public purchasing power. A boom in infrastructure construction would keep demand for cement high for the near future, but based on the current consumption trend, the country might face a shortage of cement supply in the next 3 to 5 years (World Cement, 2010).

MINERAL FUELS

Coal.—PT Lahai Coal, which was a subsidiary of BHP Billiton, planned to invest $50 million to develop a coal mine at Nuara Teweh in the Laung Tuhup District in Central Kalimantan Province. The mine was expected to produce coal with an initial capacity of between 720,000 t/yr and 1 million metric tons per year (Mt/yr) in late 2010. The concession area was estimated to have a coal deposit of mixed quality—coking coal (60%) and thermal coal (40%). Coal would be exported to France, Italy, Japan, the Republic of Korea, and Thailand. PT Manunggal Multi Energi discovered coal reserves of 55.32 Mt at Darmon in South Sumatra Province. The calorific value of the coal was between 4,733 kilocalories per kilogram (kcal/kg) and 6,212 kcal/kg, with an average of 5,500 kcal/kg. Initial production would be between 1 and 2 Mt/yr. Coal would be used for the $200 million, 250-megawatt (MW) Kuala Tanjung thermal powerplant in North Sumatra Province (Petrominer, 2010o).

Tata Power Co. of India acquired a 30% stake each in Bumi Resources' PT Kaltim Prima Coal (KPC) and PT Arutmin Indonesia for a total of $1.3 billion. Other bidders were Kepco of the Republic of Korea, Marubeni Corp. and Mitsubishi Corp. both of Japan, and Reliance Energy Ltd. of India. Tata Power wanted to secure the coal supply for its powerplants, which were being built at Mundra in the State of Gujarat, India. Tata Power would require 21 Mt/yr of coal for its new powerplants. By holding Arutmin Indonesia and KPC, Tata Power would be able to meet nearly 50% of its need for coal. Bumi Resources planned to use the cash fund for the development of noncoal assets and started expanding to mining ventures of copper, gold, and iron ore. Bumi Resources owned 100% of Arutmin Indonesia and 95% of KPC before Tata Power's acquisition. Bumi Resources produced 70 Mt of coal in 2010 and planned to increase output to 90 Mt in 2010 (Petrominer, 2010d).

PT Adaro Indonesia operated two open pit mines at the Paringin and the Tutupan deposits in South Kalimantan Province and produced 36 Mt of coal in 2010 compared with 34.4 Mt in 2009. The coal was ultra clean and environmentally friendly envirocoal. About 70% of coal output was exported to China, Europe, India, Japan, New Zealand, Taiwan, and the United States. Adaro Indonesia also supplied coal to the Cilacap, the Jawa-Bali, and the Paiton powerplants. Its total coal reserves were estimated to be 3,000 Mt (Petrominer, 2010a).
PTBA planned to acquire 11 coal mining companies in Central, East, and South Kalimantan Provinces. The acquisition at $176 million would be made through its subsidiary, PT Bukit Asam Prima, which sold and purchased coal. The current coal production of PTBA was 11 Mt/yr and with the acquisition of the additional coal companies, production would increase to 20 Mt/yr. PTBA also planned to develop the 4x600-MW Banko Tengah thermal powerplant (Petrominer, 2010l).

PTBA planned to supply PT Indonesia Power's Suralaya powerplant in Banten Province with 6.1 Mt of coal from its mines on Kalimantan and Sumatra Islands in 2008. The powerplant would require between 11 Mt and 14 Mt of coal, and the shortage would be met by a tender of 2.5 Mt and by buying on the spot market. Owing to the transportation problem with freight, PTBA supplied 5.5 Mt of coal in 2010. Meanwhile, Arutmin Indonesia's Asam-Asam Mine in East Kalimantan Province received an order to supply 10 Mt/yr of coal to the projects of the 10,000-MW crash program. The crash program included

11 powerplants. The mine was estimated to contain more than 200 Mt of low-calorie coal. Low-calorie coal also would be supplied from its Mulia and Satui Mines in South Kalimantan Province. Arutmin Indonesia produced 18 Mt of coal in 2010 (Petrominer, 2010b).

Kenertec Corp. of the Republic of Korea signed an agreement to invest in a coal liquefaction project worth $5.5 billion in East Kalimantan Province. The company formed a consortium made up of Posco Engineering and Construction, PT Nuansa Cipta Coal Investment, and Samsung Securities for the project. In the first stage, the consortium would invest $2 billion to produce 30,000 bbl/d of liquefied coal for 5 years. Kenertec was expected to process 1 Mt/yr of coal. In the second stage, the consortium would invest $3.5 billion to increase production by 70,000 bbl/d to 100,000 bbl/d (Petrominer, 2010e).

Natural Gas.—Total S.A. of France made two gas discoveries in the offshore Mahakam Block. The company and its partner, Inpex Corp. of Japan, planned to start production in 2012. Total supplied gas to the 22.6-Mt/yr Bontang LNG export terminal in East Kalimantan Province. Indonesia's installed capacity of LNG was 30 Mt/yr. The $5 billion Tangguh LNG export project in Papua Province was in progress, and first production was expected in late 2008. Tangguh would add 7.6 Mt/yr to the country's LNG production because two trains at the 6.8-Mt/yr Arun plant were shut down in 2000. Tangguh had a 2.6-Mt/yr LNG contract to supply China's Fujian terminal and a 3.7-Mt/yr agreement with Sempra Energy to supply a terminal in Baja California, Mexico (Petroleum Economist, 2010b).

PT Elnusa expected to begin gas production in 2008-09 from its only gasfield in the Bangkanai Block in Central Kalimantan Province. Gas output would be sold to state power company Perusahaan Listrik Negara and to the local market and, if possible, to the Bontang LNG plant. The field had a gas reserve of 28.3 billion cubic meters. Four wells had been drilled followed by two more wells in 2010. About $10 million would be needed to drill a well with a depth of 2,740 m (Rigzone.com, 2010).

Petroleum.—Pertamina and ExxonMobil planned to drill two appraisal wells at the Banyu Urip oil discovery in the Cepu Block and three exploration wells in Cepu's other fields. The Cepu Block was estimated to contain 0.6 billion barrels of oil and 48.1 billion cubic meters of gas. Pertamina expected oil production from Cepu to begin at the rate of between 10,000 bbl/d and 20,000 bbl/d in 2008 (Petroleum Economist, 2010a).

Santos Ltd. of Australia began oil production from its Oyong Field offshore Surabaya in East Java Province. Production was expected to be between 8,000 and 10,000 bbl/d. Gas production of 1.6 million cubic meters per day was expected to be delivered to the Grati powerplant in East Java Province in the first half of 2009. The partners in the project were Santos (45%) as operator, Singapore Petroleum (40%), and Cue Sampang (15%) (Petroleum Economist, 2010b).

Pertamina planned to team up with Mitsui Corp. of Japan to revamp its Citacap oil refinery in Central Java Province. The $1.8 billion upgrade would increase refining capacity by between 62,000 and 410,000 bbl/d. Equity financing of $0.5 billion would come from Pertamina and Mitsui, and the remaining $1.3 billion would come from banks (Petroleum Economist, 2010a).

REFERENCES CITED

Asia Gold Corp., 2010, Trench results continue to expand the Kaputusan porphyry copper-gold prospect: Asia Gold Corp. press release, January 29, 3 p.

Indonesia's Trade and Investment News, 2010, Limit on refined tin exports: Indonesia's Trade and Investment News. (Accessed January 8, 2010, at http://www.ekon.go.id/v3/index2.php?option=com_content&task=view&id=460.)

Industrial Minerals, 2010, Indonesian zircon on the ascent: Industrial Minerals, no. 472, January, p. 15.
Ivanhoe Mines Ltd., 2010, SouthGobi Energy Resources discovers encouraging gold and silver prospects in Java, Indonesia: Vancouver, British Columbia, Canada, Ivanhoe Mines Ltd. press release, December 17, 2 p.
London Stock Exchange, 2010a, Carnegie signs iron-nickel exploration agreement: London Stock Exchange Market News. (Accessed November 2, 2010, at http://www.londonstockexchange.com/lsecws/ifspages/marketnewspopup.aspx?id=1616247.)
London Stock Exchange, 2010b, Wetar copper project update: London Stock Exchange Market News. (Accessed April 20, 2010, at http://www.london stockexchange.com/lsecws/ifspages/marketnewspopup.aspx?id=14649467.)
Mineweb, 2010, Proposed Indonesian mining law to mandate domestic metals smelting: Mineweb. (Accessed January 5, 2010, at http://www.mineweb.net/sustainable_mining/551583.htm.)
Ministry of Industry, 2008, Fact and figures: Ministry of Industry [Indonesia]. (Accessed June 26, 2008, at http://www.depperin.go.id/English2009.)
Oxfam America, 2010, Newmont update April 2010: Oxfam America. (Accessed May 11, 2010, at http://www.oxfamamerica.org/newsandpublications/news_updates/newmont-update-april-2010.)
Petroleum Economist, 2010a, News in brief: Petroleum Economist, v. 74, no. 8, August, p. 37.
Petroleum Economist, 2010b, News in brief: Petroleum Economist, v. 74, no. 11, November, p. 45.
Petrominer, 2010a, Adaro increases production: Petrominer, v. 34, no. 11, November, p. 33.
Petrominer, 2010b, Advantageous to Arutmin Indonesia: Petrominer, v. 34, no. 10, October, p. 37.
Petrominer, 2010c, Antam increases ferronickel production: Petrominer, v. 34, no. 3, March, p. 36.
Petrominer, 2010d, At last Tata enters into KPC and Arutmin: Petrominer, v. 34, no. 4, April, p. 33.
Petrominer, 2010e, Coal liquefaction n East Kalimantan: Petrominer, v. 34, no. 8, August, p. 36.
Petrominer, 2010f, Controller of world tin: Petrominer, v. 34, no. 12, December, p. 42.
Petrominer, 2010g, Demonstrations of protests detrimental to state income: Petrominer, v. 34, no. 5, May, p. 62.
Petrominer, 2010h, Dominating domestic mines: Petrominer, v. 34, no. 9, September, p. 28.
Petrominer, 2010i, Inco to build two nickel plants: Petrominer, v. 34, no. 4, April, p. 32.
Petrominer, 2010j, Mining law principal changes: Petrominer, v. 34, no. 3, March, p. 38.
Petrominer, 2010k, More investment in underground mining: Petrominer, v. 34, no. 6, June, p. 40.
Petrominer, 2010l, PTBA to acquire 11 coal companies: Petrominer, v. 34, no. 7, July, p. 29.
Petrominer, 2010m, Small-scale miners can be useful: Petrominer, v. 34, no. 6, June, p. 37.
Petrominer, 2010n, Tommy has eyes on Koba Tin: Petrominer, v. 34, no. 7, July, p. 28.
Petrominer, 2010o, Two more companies develop coal mining: Petrominer, v. 34, no. 3, March, p. 34.
Petrominer, 2010p, US$80 million for Tayan: Petrominer, v. 34, no. 2, February, p. 35.
Rigzone.com, 2010, Indonesia's Elnusa to start producing gas: Rigzone.com. (Accessed January 5, 2010, at http://www.rigzone.com/news/article.asp?a_id=39657.)
U.S. Geological Survey, 2008, Mineral commodity summaries 2008: U.S. Geological Survey, 199 p.
Wilburn, D.R., 2010, Exploration review 2009: Mining Engineering, v. 59, no. 5, May, p. 45.
Wilburn, D.R., 2008, Exploration review 2010: Mining Engineering, v. 60, no. 5, May, p. 55.
World Cement, 2010, News in brief: World Cement, v. 38, no. 5, May, p. 12.
Wright, Tom, and Barta, Patrick, 2010, Indonesian mining stalls: The Wall Street Journal, February 7, p. A8.

INDONESIA: PRODUCTION OF MINERAL COMMODITIES[1]

(Metric tons unless otherwise specified)

Commodity		2004	2005	2009	2010
METALS					
Aluminum:					
Bauxite, wet basis, gross weight	thousand metric tons	1,331	1,442[r]	1,502	1,251
Metal, primary		[e]247,000	252,300	250,300	242,400
Chromite sand, dry basis[e]		1,000	1,000	1,000	1,000
Copper:					
Mine, Cu content		840,318	1,064,200	818,000[r]	796,900
Metal					
Smelter, primary		211,600	275,000	201,200	224,000
Refinery, primary		210,500	262,900	217,600	221,400

Gold, mine output, Au content[2]	kilograms	91,710	130,620	93,176[r]	117,851
Iron and steel:					
Iron sand, dry basis		89,664	32,203	87,970[r]	61,077
Metal:					
Ferroalloys:					
Ferronickel		39,538	36,690	32,445	34,000
Ferromanganese[e]		12,000	12,000	12,000	12,000
Silicomanganese[e]		7,000	4,000	5,000	6,000
Pig iron, direct reduced iron	thousand metric tons	1,470	1,390	1,290	1,400
Steel, crude	do.	3,682[r]	3,675	3,759[r]	3,900
Steel, semimanufactured	do.	4,238	4,859	5,150	5,400
Nickel:					
Mine output, Ni content[3]		136,000	135,000	157,200[r]	229,200
Matte, Ni content		81,120	77,471	72,782	77,928
Ferronickel, Ni content		7,945	7,003	7,572[r]	9,498
Silver, mine output, Ag content	kilograms	261,960	320,590[r]	261,398[r]	268,967
Tin:					
Mine output, Sn content		65,772	78,404	80,933	66,137
Metal[4]		49,872	65,300	65,357[r]	64,127
Zirconium concentrates, gross weight	r	500[r]	2,600[r]	65,000[r]	111,000
INDUSTRIAL MINERALS					
Cement, hydraulic	thousand metric tons	33,230	33,917	35,000[r]	36,000
Clays:[e]					
Bentonite		5,000	5,000	5,500	5,500
Fire clay	thousand metric tons	1,900	2,000	2,000	2,100
Kaolin powder		15,000	15,000	15,000	15,000
Diamond:[e]					
Industrial stones	thousand carats	23	23	23	23
Gem	do.	7	7	7	7
Total	do.	30	30	30	30
Feldspar[e]		24,000	24,000	25,000	25,000
Gypsum[e]		6,000	6,000	6,000	6,000
Iodine[e]		75	75	75	75
Nitrogen, N content of ammonia	thousand metric tons	4,120	4,400[e]	4,300[e]	4,400[e]
Phosphate rock[e]		600	600	600	600
Salt, all types[e]	thousand metric tons	680	680	700	700
Stone:					
Dolomite[e]		3,100	3,100	3,200	3,200
Granite	thousand metric tons	3,340	4,170	4,200	4,300
Limestone[e]	cubic meters	16,000	16,500	16,000	17,000
Marble[e]	do.	1,000	1,000	1,000	1,000
Quartz sand and silica stone[e]	do.	150,000	150,000	155,000	155,000
Sulfur, elemental[e]		83,500	83,000	82,000	81,000
Zeolite[e]		400	400	400	400
Commodity		2004	2005	2009	2010
MINERAL FUELS AND RELATED MATERIALS					
Coal:					
Anthracite[e]		50,000	50,000	52,000	53,000
Bituminous	thousand metric tons[e]	131,530	142,920	181,061[r]	174,833
Gas, natural:					
Gross	million cubic meters	83,740	85,830	102,300[r]	95,020
Marketed[e]	do.	52,000	53,000	52,000	53,000
Petroleum, crude including condensate	thousand 42-gallon barrels	362,000	352,000	367,000[r]	381,000

[e]Estimated; estimated data are rounded to no more than three significant digits; may not add to totals shown. [r]Revised. do. Ditto.
[1]Table includes data available through October 8, 2008.
[2]Includes Au content of copper ore and output by Government-controlled foreign contractors' operations. Gold output by operators of so-called
people's mines and illegal small-scale mines is not available but may be as much as 20 metric tons per year.
[3]Includes a small amount of cobalt that was not recovered separately.
[4]Output by Central Government-controlled foreign contractors operations. Tin output from small tin smelters is not available but may be as much as
40,000 metric tons per year.

MINING AND ENERGY IN INDONESIA

KEY POINTS

With world class reserves in leading minerals, oil, petroleum, coal and gas, Indonesia's mining and oil sector generates significant exports and foreign currency. This helps buffer the economy against downturns and makes the sector critical to Indonesia sustaining economic growth.

Four key challenges confront Indonesia's mining community: devolution, as most mines are in regional Indonesia; social stability in some regional areas; increased illegal mining; and new regulations on environmental standards. These challenges highlight the importance of strong relationships between mining firms, all three levels of government and local communities.

Foreign companies contribute significantly to mining sector activity, with their investment exceeding US$10 billion in the last three decades. Australian firms account for about one third of this foreign investment.

Australian firms are well placed to use their geographical proximity and mining expertise to help Indonesia develop its mineral resources. Opportunities include assessing resources, refining and distributing mineral output, and exporting mining related equipment, supplies and services.

As in other sectors, potential investors should undertake thorough due diligence assessments. The need to modernise, improve management and create financial transparency may be major issues.

The investment environment in the mining sector has changed rapidly since the financial crisis. Political devolution, for example, may make government more responsive to the needs of local investors, but generates uncertainty. Miners also have concerns about social stability in some regional areas, stringent new environmental requirements and illegal mining.

This chapter briefly surveys Indonesia's mineral resource endowments, outputs and exports, then analyses post crisis developments in the mining sector. After discussing the likely impact of new regulatory and fiscal measures on mining, it reviews Australian business opportunities in the sector.

Indonesia enjoys world class reserves in leading minerals, coal, oil and gas. Sizeable reserves, as yet unproven, may lie in remote and less accessible eastern Indonesia. Proven oil reserves, mainly onshore, amount to 5 billion barrels. Oil production from new, smaller fields has increased over recent years, offsetting the decline of larger, more mature oil fields. Oil exploration is concentrated in the frontier regions, particularly eastern Indonesia (Energy Information Administration, 2000). Joint offshore petroleum cooperation areas between Indonesia and

Australia offer mutually beneficial prospects. Indonesia's total proven natural gas reserves amount to 72.3 trillion cubic feet; the domestic gas market remains underdeveloped; and opportunities to provide a distribution network and pipeline infrastructure are likely to attract Australian interest (Energy Information Administration, 2000). Indonesia's significant coal reserves have a sulphur and ash content of less than 1 per cent and are close to major Asian markets. Copper and gold reserves also are substantial, and already attract significant investment.

The mining and oil sector contributes a large share of Indonesia's exports and foreign currency earnings, and provides an important buffer against economic downturns. Hence, the sector's health is critical to Indonesia's medium term economic outlook.

In 1998, the value of mining sector output declined by much less than GDP, somewhat buffering the economy from the crisis (Figure 9.1). The output value of non-oil and gas mining grew 38 per cent between 1997 and 1999, largely driven by export-oriented coal, gold, copper and silver production. Overall mining and energy sector output contracted mildly, because of a 6 per cent fall in oil and gas production, a response to low oil prices, and falling extractive quarrying due to reduced construction activity (Figure 9.2 and Appendix Table 9.1).

However, the output volume of most other minerals and precious metals has risen significantly since 1994 and continued to rise even during the crisis (Figure 9.2).

Mining Sector Largely Resists the Crisis

Since the crisis, mineral exports have remained relatively strong, underpinning mining sector output (Figure 9.3). Volumes of mineral exports rose more than their US dollar value because the US dollar prices of oil and most minerals fell during the crisis. Since commodity prices recovered in 1999 and 2000, export values also have risen.

Figure 9.3 Value of Mining, Petroleum and Other Exports, 1995-99

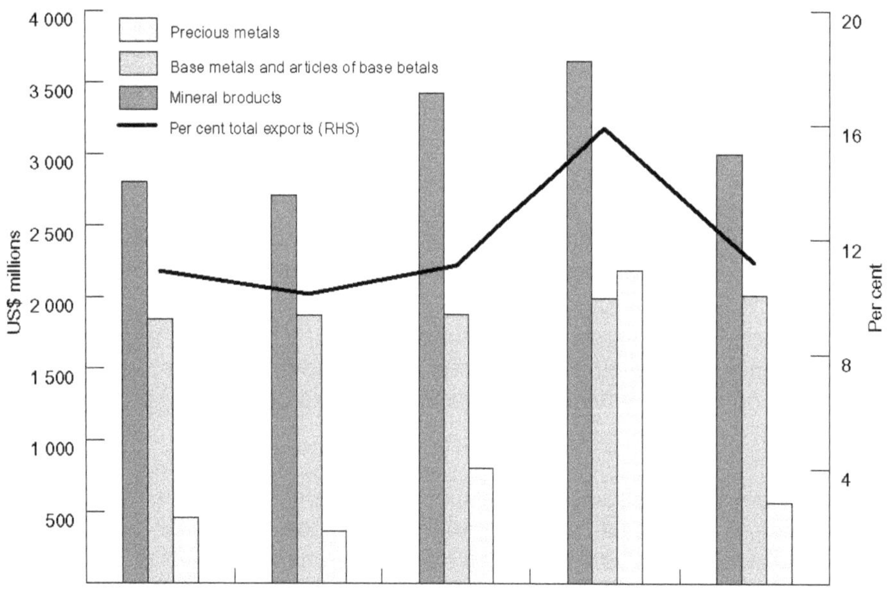

Source: PricewaterhouseCoopers, 2000.

Four new developments are challenging the mining community. First, devolution is likely to have significant effects as most mines are in regional Indonesia. Consequently, investors are encouraged to develop fresh strategies during the transition to a new, decentralised political system. Second, issues of social stability and security concern mine operators in several regions. Third, the increase in illegal mining since the crisis concerns both the Government and the mining community. Fourth, the Government has introduced stringent new regulations on environmental standards, some of which exceed international norms.

Devolution eventually may improve the investment environment for miners. It offers the regions a greater share of mining revenues, ensuring local communities benefit more directly from mining activity. In future, local governments, rather than the central government may sign miners' contracts of work, potentially strengthening local support for miners (Millane, 2000). Devolution delegates the issuing of permits for mining investment and exploration to the regions; eventually this may reduce the cost of obtaining approval. It also requires local government to conduct environmental inspections (Department of Mines and Energy, 2000). Devolution may encourage regions to compete for new foreign investment, benefiting miners.

However, the transition to a new system of government is raising some concerns amongst miners. Miners are uncertain whether contracts of work drawn up between mining companies and the central government will remain relevant.[2] Devolution may reduce coordination between neighbouring districts, increasing administrative costs for mining projects encompassing more than one district. The central government is seeking to quell these concerns. New Ministry of Mines and Energy regulations establish procedures for provinces to issue mining permits for investment, exploration and production in areas lying within two or more districts and up to 12 miles offshore from their coasts. Initially, some regions may find it difficult to meet previous standards in issuing permits and inspecting environmental performance. If some regions are unable to control the environmental degradation associated with illegal mining, this could undermine public support for the operations of legitimate miners.

Some analysts also are concerned transparency issues at the local government level may increase risk (Transparency International, 2000). As the allocation of taxation responsibilities between central and local governments is not fully clarified, concerns exist local governments may seek to impose ad hoc taxes.

During the transition phase, investors should seek to strengthen relationships with all three levels of government and local communities. New firms should seek assistance from firms with established networks of contacts and information.

[1] Unlike manufacturing and service sectors, which mainly centre on Java, oil and natural gas are concentrated in Riau and Aceh, in Sumatra, and East Kalimantan, on the island of Borneo; copper is concentrated in Irian Jaya, which has one of the world's largest copper mines, PT Freeport Indonesia.

[2] Some local interest groups are using the transition period to devolution to urge the rewriting of contracts of work with foreign mining companies.

CONTRACTS OF WORK

Indonesia's constitution stipulates the state owns all natural resources.[3] The Indonesian Government or state enterprises therefore retain exclusive authorisation rights for all stages of mining activity from survey, exploration, exploitation, production, refining, transport and marketing. Consequently, state enterprises are prominent in the mining and petroleum sectors.

Contracts of work evolved to attract private sector investment to resource development, originally for oil production, then minerals and coal mining. Like miners operating leases in other countries, private sector miners holding contracts of work can extract and sell minerals and energy resources from defined leases, and in return, pay levies including land rent and royalties. Successive generations of contracts increasingly have favoured the state and imposed more fiscal and other obligations on contractors.

CONTRACTS OF WORK FOR MINERALS

Individual contracts result from negotiations between the state and company, but ultimately are at the government's discretion. Contracts assign to the contractor full commercial and operational risks. Contractors relinquish rights to all areas examined during exploration and evaluation, and the government must receive the results of work done. Contractors must employ Indonesian nationals to the maximum extent possible and implement training programs. Companies also must include Indonesian capital as soon as production begins and commonly must transfer 51 per cent of company shares to Indonesian ownership after ten years. Contracts last 30 years but can be extended by mutual agreement. The contract defines royalties and rents payable, in addition to normal corporation and general sales taxes.

Increasing demands for greater autonomy in many provinces where mines are located has given rise to civil unrest and some instances of violence, adversely affecting mining operations and the safety of workers. Although regional devolution may reduce some of these tensions, miners need to remain sensitive to these risks.

The increase in illegal mining since the crisis is concerning the Government and the mining community alike. Illegal mining is most serious in the gold, coal and diamond sectors; estimates of its value vary widely, but in the case of gold, range from 12 to 33 per cent of output (Kuo, 1999). For example, in 1992, state mining company PT Aneka Tambang, Antam, reported large numbers of illegal miners had arrived and by 1998, they had halved output and exports from its Pongkor gold and silver mine (Millane, 2000; and Antam, 1998). BHP's subsidiary, PT Arutmin, in South Kalimantan, also suffers from large scale illegal mining.

The Government is attempting to reduce illegal mining by warning against the purchase of illegal output and banning the use of government roads to transport illegally mined material. It also has introduced tough new environmental regulations in response to the damage caused by illegal operators. Emerging regional institutions could reduce the incidence of illegal mining over the medium term. New reforms redistributing mining royalties to regions also should increase incentives for district governments and their communities to eradicate illegal mining.

Mining companies can assist the Government reduce illegal mining by working with authorities to detect and eradicate illegal mining. Some miners are pooling their surveillance and security resources. Mining companies also should maintain good relationships with local communities and authorities, so they can actively deter illegal miners.

LARGE SCALE ILLEGAL MINING DEVALUES COAL RESOURCE

Illegal mining often is large scale. BHP's subsidiary, PT Arutmin, in South Kalimantan, is subject to illegal miners who use a fleet of 200 trucks and 16 excavators. They transport their output using a road and a jetty built across environmentally sensitive coastal marshlands.

Illegal miners account for as much as 4 million of the 22 million tonnes of coal mined in South Kalimantan annually; this represents a loss of output worth A$92 million at current prices.

Much of the province's illegal coal comes from the mine area PT Arutmin owns. Industry sources report an environment of intimidation and threats of violence.

The Government is negotiating several important mining sector laws, including new environmental and contract laws. Mining companies should watch closely these developments.

Public reaction to the damage caused by illegal miners has prompted tighter environmental legislation (Department of Mines and Energy, 2000). The Environmental Protection Agency, BAPEDAL, issued Decree PP18 in February 1999, imposing stricter standards on waste discharge. The 1999 forest law reserves large areas for water catchment and limits new mining activity in these areas. These new standards in some cases exceed international norms. The Government has provided assurances the law does not seek to restrict established exploration or mining agreements. Mining companies should improve contact with local environmental bodies, including non-government organisations, to reassure these groups about the firm's environmental credentials, and share information on environmental strategies.[4]

[4] In Indonesia, often mining occurs in rainforests with up to 180 cm of rainfall per year, so soil erosion, sediment, contamination of offsite water bodies and land reclamation for post-mining uses are important issues. Another environmental issue in coal mining is the loss of fine coal particulates; here loss of coal revenue and royalties can be up to 20 per cent of production, and mining can pollute water supplies (Hamilton, 1998).

ENVIRONMENTAL GOVERNANCE IN INDONESIA

The Ministry of Environment requires firms to prepare environmental impact assessments for activities which may affect the environment, and enforces environmental quality standards (Millane, 2000). However, under devolution, these responsibilities will be delegated to regional governments. The Bureau of Environment and Technology reviews, develops and coordinates environmental polices and regulations within the Ministry of Mines and Energy. The Directorate of Technical Mining, also within the ministry, inspects and enforces environmental policy. Both agencies will retain their roles after regional devolution.

Contracts of work signed since the financial crisis include higher royalty rates on key minerals, although in most cases, these continue to be offset by the lower costs of exploration and corporate tax rate in Indonesia (Figure 9.4 and Table 9.1). For example, under Regulation No. 13 of 2000, gold royalties rose to 3.75 per cent from between 1 and 1.5 per cent, and copper royalties rose to 4 per cent from 2 per cent. Indonesian investment guidelines provide a refund of the 10 per cent value added tax, VAT, paid on imported mining capital equipment. The Government is aware that some mining firms have expressed concern about difficulties in obtaining this refund (Aurora Gold, 1999). As devolution occurs, potential investors should watch carefully developments in taxation and royalties applied to mining revenues.

Effective Tax Rates Rise

Factor	Indonesia	Australia	Philippines	Chile	United States
Royalties on gold and copper	3.75 per cent (gold) 4 per cent (copper)	2.50 per cent	2.00 per cent	Nil	Nil
Exploration dead rent US$/ha/yr	0.35	0.30	1.30	2.90	Nil

Mining dead rent US$/ha/yr	1.50	10.00	1.30	2.90	Nil
Corporate tax rate	30 per cent	36 per cent	35 per cent	15 per cent	15 to 35 per cent

Source: *Jakarta Post*, 22 May 2000.

Foreign companies contribute significantly to mining sector activity, investing a cumulative US$10.8 billion over the last 30 years. Of this, US companies account for US$6.4 billion while Australian mining investment approvals to 31 May 2000 account for US$3.2 billion (34 per cent of total applications). US mining company, PT Freeport Indonesia, one of the largest foreign investors in Indonesia, accounts for the bulk of US investment in the mining sector (Millane, 2000).

Applications to invest in the mining sector, excluding oil and gas, have declined significantly since 1996 (Table 9.2). If this trend continues over the medium term, replacement investment may be insufficient to maintain current production levels. The Department of Mines and Energy reports foreign and domestic mining investment intentions falling sharply in 1999. Imports of surface mining equipment fell from US$815.4 million in 1997 to US$650.3 million in 1998, corroborating this. In 1999, oil and gas sector investments improved slightly, reflecting higher oil prices. However, foreign oil producers, who produce 95 per cent of petroleum output, increased their total investment to an estimated US$5.3 billion from US$4.3 billion in 1998 (Millane, 2000).

Mining Investment Approvals Declining

Domestic and Foreign Investment in Mining, 1995-99

1995		1996	1997	1998	1999
Domestic investment					
Non-metallic 9 009 mining investment, Rp. billion		7 965	11 639	3 469	Less than 1 000
Mining share of domestic approvals	12.9 per cent	7.9 per cent	9.8 per cent	5.7 per cent	Less than 2 per cent
Foreign investment					
Mining approvals US$ million	Less than 415	2 487	1 457	237	200
Mining share of foreign investment approvals	Less than 1 per cent	8.3 per cent	4.3 per cent	1.7 per cent	1.5 per cent

Note: Capital Investment Coordinating Board investment data exclude the oil and gas and financial sectors. Source: Capital Investment Coordinating Board, as quoted in Millane, 2000.

Opportunities exist across the archipelago, particularly in the rugged eastern reaches. Australian expertise in identifying resources, mapping geology and collecting geophysical data, particularly in remote areas, suits these conditions.

Providing contracting and support services to other mining companies reduces exposure to risks associated with mining. Services include the design and construction of mines, materials handling, environmental engineering, infrastructure provision, and supply of mineral transport systems and mining equipment. Major Australian companies, including Theiss and Clough, have large contracts to operate mines, although they face stiff competition from US firms.

Local partners and bureaucracies have rising human resource needs; these generate opportunities for providing training in mining technologies, mine operation and environmental monitoring.

The abolition of Pertamina's monopoly on oil production and liberalisation of oil refining and distribution offer substantial opportunities for Australia.[5] New arrangements proposed in 1999 allow the Department of Mines and Energy to award private companies oil production contracts which Pertamina currently undertakes.

In January 2000, after initial delays, the Government initiated a panel to oversee the reform of Pertamina, including installing new management. In September 2000, the Government reaffirmed its strong commitment to reform comprehensively the energy sector, submitting to the legislature two new laws to privatise and reform the electric power and the oil and natural gas sectors (Energy Information Administration, 2000; and International Monetary Fund, 2000).

Privatisation may offer opportunities for Australians to acquire established mining enterprises. Australian mining investors could assist these firms with business management, technical and accountancy expertise.

Two state mining enterprises will be sold in 2000 or early 2001. PT Aneka Tambang, specialising in gold and nickel mining, currently is 65 per cent government owned. A further small share will be sold in 2000 or 2001, and eventually the balance will be sold. PT Tambang Batubara Bukit Asam, specialising in coal mining, currently is 100 per cent government owned, with a minority share earmarked for privatisation. Shares in both enterprises will be sold either through initial public offerings or by attracting a strategic partner. In addition, the remainder of mining company, Antam, partially floated on the Sydney stock exchange in August 1999, eventually will be sold under commitments to privatise the majority share of all state enterprises. A standby list of state mining enterprises for sale includes PT Tambang Timah (tin mining), currently 65 per cent government owned.

However, as in other state enterprise privatisations, potential investors should undertake thorough due diligence assessments of enterprises offered for privatisation. Minority ownership may constrain efforts to modernise and improve management, and financial transparency may be lacking. Investors may need to convert current exploration and mining titles to contracts of work, especially if they acquire majority foreign ownership.

Pertamina, the state company responsible for distributing oil and gas throughout Indonesia, also is involved in crude oil production.

Newcrest Mining Ltd set up a small office in Jakarta in 1991 and explored the Halmehera region in cooperation with local firm, PT Aneka Tambang. Newcrest holds 82.5 per cent of the joint venture. They discovered the Gosowong gold deposit in September 1993, and the Government approved a sixth generation contract of work in April 1997. Between September 1997 and November 1998, with a sound understanding of the application process and good communications with relevant government agencies, the venture acquired the necessary permits. Construction started late in 1998 and the plant was commissioned in July 1999.

The project achieved its targets despite the financial crisis of 1997-99, and exceptionally heavy rainfall during construction. The firm gave priority to recruiting and training local people, fostering local business development, and carefully managing environmental issues.

The Gosowong project's success demonstrates maintaining effective communication with all levels of government, as well as local community representatives, is invaluable.

Austrade maintains a directory of Australian companies able to provide equipment and services to Indonesia's mining, quarrying and construction industries. Australian export promotion groups, Austmine and Austenergy, support firms seeking to export mining equipment, related supplies and services to Indonesia.

Austrade assigns a high priority to assisting export companies, visiting major mines, identifying new opportunities, and promoting Australian companies and expertise in the mining sector. Austrade and a range of mining companies participate in Indonesia's annual Mining Indonesia exhibition. The Australian Embassy in Jakarta also facilitates high level contact with relevant ministers and officials.

Mining is likely to remain an important sector in the Indonesian economy. New developments in governance and politics may promise a better environment for harnessing Indonesia's substantial mineral wealth. However, the transition to political devolution raises taxation, legal and governance issues for miners, creating uncertainty, and illegal mining problems are increasing. Investors need to remain alert to local developments and the interests of stakeholders.

Appendix Table 9.1 Coal, Gold, Copper and Silver Dominate Output Advance Production Growth and Volumes of Selected Minerals and Petroleum, '000s tons

	1994	1995	1996	1997	1998	1999
Petroleuma	15992.9	15992.6	16179.5	15963.5	15843.8	14513.4
Tin ore concentrate	30.6	38.4	51.0	55.2	53.9	47.8
Copper ore concentrate	1095.8	1516.6	1758.9	1840.7	2640.0	2645.2
Nickel ore	2302.0	2513.3	3426.9	2829.9	2734.0	3245.3
Bauxite	1342.4	904.5	841.9	808.7	1055.6	1142.5
Coal	31238.5	41516.7	47338.6	52074.3	60320.8	69357.6
Iron sand concentrate	334.9	348.4	425.1	487.4	561.0	562.3
Goldb	42.6	62.8	83.6	90.0	124.0	129.0
Silverb	107.2	265.2	254.9	270.4	349.9	292.3

Note: a Thousands of barrels.
b Thousands of kilograms.

OIL AND GAS SECTOR: STRATEGIC INFORMATION

BASIC INFORMATION

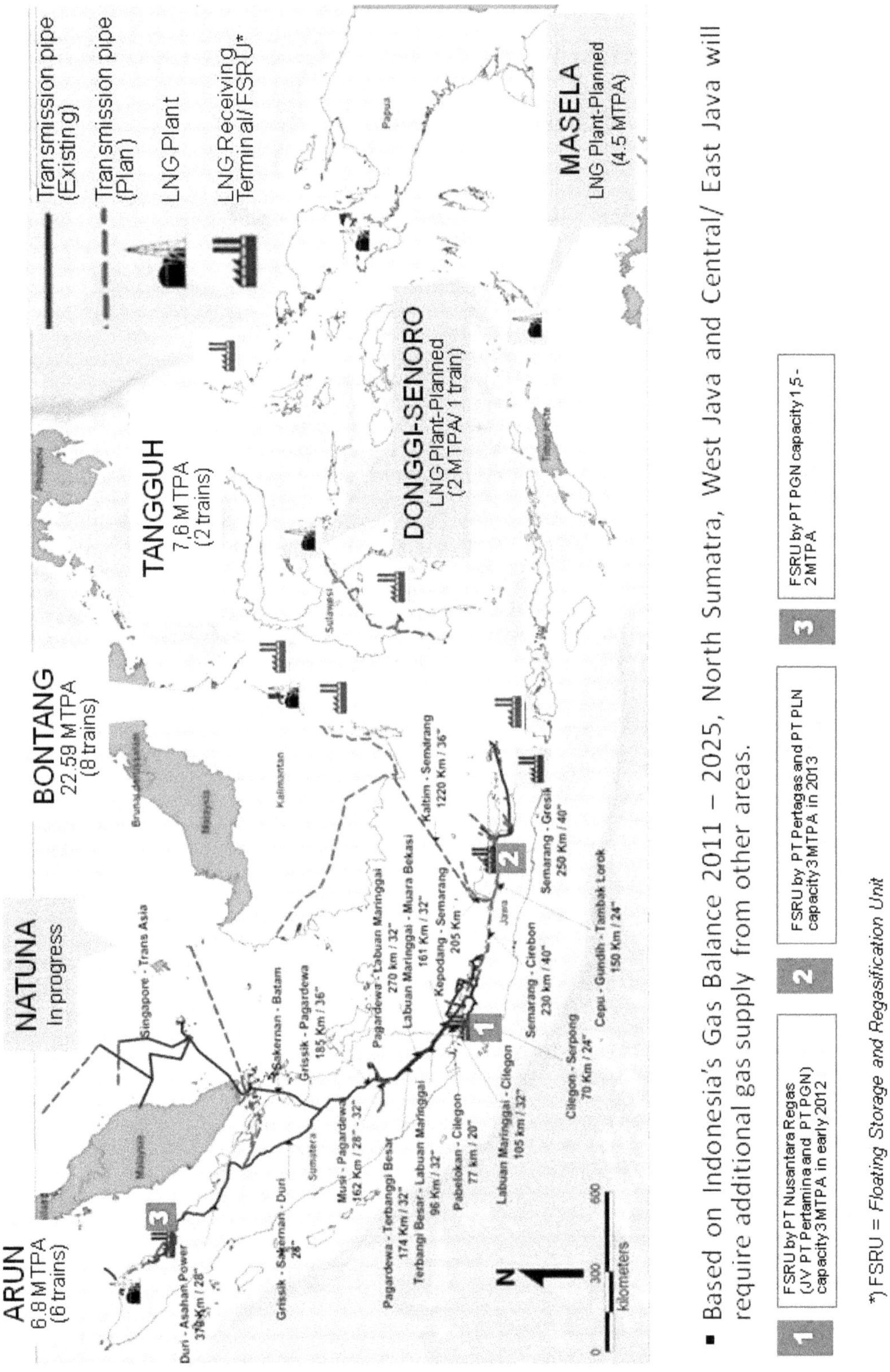

Indonesia has the largest population in Southeast Asia and the fourth largest population in the world (behind China, India, and the United States). It is also the world's third-fastest growing economy. Although Indonesia has been a net importer of oil since 2004, it is the sixth largest net exporter of natural gas, and the second largest net exporter of coal. However, as a result of inadequate infrastructure and Indonesia's complex business environment, Indonesia has struggled to attract investment sufficient to meet its energy development goals.

Indonesia's total primary energy consumption grew by nearly 50 percent between 1999 and 2008. Oil continues to account for the most significant share of Indonesia's energy mix, at 44 percent in 2009. Coal consumption has tripled over the decade, accounting for 29 percent of total energy consumption in 2008, surpassing gas as the second most consumed fuel.

Indonesia is also a significant consumer of traditional biomass in its residential sector, particularly in the more remote areas that lack connection to Indonesia's energy transmission networks (power grids and pipelines, for example). The International Energy Agency estimates that combustible renewables and waste account for about a quarter of total primary energy supply.

OIL

Indonesia's oil production has declined in recent years, as older fields decline and new projects fail to replace them. Indonesia is currently a net importer of both crude oil and refined products. Indonesia's crude oil production has been declining since 1998, due to the maturation of the country's largest oil fields and failure to develop new, comparable resources. Indonesia was a member of the Organization of Petroleum Exporting Countries (OPEC) from 1962 to 2009. In 2004, the country became a net oil importer and in January 2009, suspended its OPEC membership.

SECTOR ORGANIZATION

Indonesia's upstream oil sector is dominated by several international oil companies - in particular Chevron, Total, Conoco Phillips, Exxon, and BP. Chevron is the largest single oil producer in Indonesia, accounting for more than 40 percent of the country's total crude production. PT Pertamina, Indonesia's state-owned integrated energy supply company, accounted for approximately 15 percent of 2009 crude and condensate production, making it the second largest producer in the country.

The Indonesia Ministry of Energy and Mineral Resources is responsible for entering into production sharing contracts (PSCs), while the state-owned legal entity BPMigas serves as the upstream regulator that manages and implements these agreements. Indonesia's 2001 Oil and Gas Law significantly restructured Indonesia's upstream oil and gas sector - most notably transferring the upstream regulatory role from PT Pertamina to BPMigas. Although PT Pertamina continues to be wholly state owned, the 2001 law also led to its establishment as a limited liability corporation in 2003. Senior Pertamina officials have indicated plans to divest two of its subsidiaries by about 20 percent in an initial public offering, but details and timing have not been confirmed.

In addition to its upstream activities, PT Pertamina operates nearly all of Indonesia's refinery capacity, procures crude and products imports, and supplies products to the domestic market. While Pertamina's monopoly in the retail market ended in 2004, the company continued to be the sole distributor for subsidized fuels until early 2010.

Indonesia Oil Supply and Consumption,1999-2009

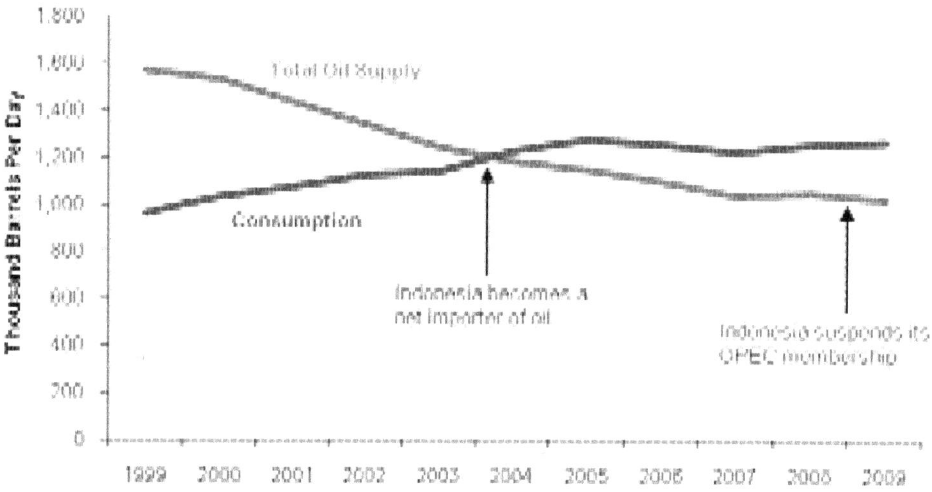

Source: EIA International Energy Statistics

Exploration and Production

According to Oil & Gas Journal, Indonesia had 3.9 billion barrels of proven oil reserves as of January 2011. In 2010, total oil supply averaged just over one million barrels per day (bbl/d). Of this total, about 943,000 bbl/d was crude oil and lease condensate production. Crude and condensate production has declined at an annual average rate of 4.1 percent between 2000 and 2010.

Indonesia's two largest producing oil fields are the Minas and Duri fields, located on the eastern coast of Sumatra. Chevron operates both fields with a 100 percent working interest under the Rokan Production Sharing Agreement. Producing since 1952 and 1955 respectively, production at both fields is in decline, even with the employment of enhanced oil recovery techniques at both fields to bolster production. Chevron uses steam injection enhanced oil recovery for 80 percent of the Duri field, one of the largest steamflood projects in the world.

The most significant recent discovery with the potential to counteract some of Indonesia's production decline is the Cepu Block of East and Central Java. Exxon Mobil is the operator of the Cepu PSC (45 percent interest), in a joint venture with PT Pertamina's E&P unit (45 percent working interest) and four local government companies (10 percent interest). Cepu is estimated to contain 600 million barrels of recoverable liquids, and to have a peak production of 165,000 bbl/d. Although discovered in 2001, the project has encountered several delays in the development process, and Exxon recently revised its goal for peak production from 2012 to 2014. Banyu Urip is currently the only producing field in the Cepu PSC, and as of January 2010, had reached a production level of about 18,000 bbl/d.

BPMigas and the Indonesian government have introduced policies aimed at increasing investment in the country's upstream sector - in particular via investment incentives and improving the flexibility of the PSC bidding process. However, the upstream investment environment is still considered to be risky, and 2009 and 2010 licensing rounds were disappointing. Recent events that caused particular concern were Parliament's attempts to mandate cost recovery caps for PSCs, as well as the government's cabotage rule - a shipping regulation requiring all marine vessels to carry the Indonesian flag. The government has since announced that cost recovery caps would be removed, and that implementation of the cabotage rule will except oil and gas vessels. However, Indonesia failed to meet its 2010 production goal of 965,000 bbl/d of crude and condensate production, and signed only 21 new oil and gas PSCs in 2010, relative to 34 in 2008.

REFINING

Indonesia has a refinery capacity of just over one million bbl/d, according to Oil & Gas Journal. Spread across eight refineries owned by PT Pertamina, the majority of the country's refinery capacity is located on Java and Sumatra. The three largest refineries are Cilacap (348,000 bbl/d) in Central Java, Balikpapan (260,000 bbl/d) in East Kalimantan, and Bolongan (125,000 bbl/d) in West Java. Refinery output goes primarily to the domestic market, but meets only about 70 percent of domestic consumption. Pertamina plans to eliminate the need for product imports by 2017, and in the last few years has announced several refinery upgrade, expansion and greenfield projects in support of this goal. However, most of these projects have been delayed, as low refining margins and lack of government financial incentives have deterred investment from international partners.

Pertamina signed an agreement with Kuwait Petroleum Corporation in August of 2010 to study an upgrade to the Bolongan refinery in West Java. The company is also in discussion with Saudi Aramco to build a new 200,000-300,000 bbl/d refinery in East Java, though Saudi Aramco indicated late in 2010 that Indonesia's government would need to provide more incentives in order to secure the company's participation. Pertamina's planned 300,000 bbl/d Banten Bay refinery in Bojanegoro is currently administered by a joint venture with Iran's Oil Refining Industries Development Company and Malaysia's Petrofield Refining - but the project was recently evaluated as being "economically infeasible" by Pertamina leadership.

The above-mentioned projects would all be supported by some level of guaranteed crude supply from Kuwait Petroleum Corporation, Saudi Aramco, and the National Iranian Oil Company respectively. These sources are vital for project viability as Indonesia's domestic crude production continues to lag. However, after years of delays and failed partnerships, there is little confidence in the mid-term completion of any of these projects, and none are expected to be online prior to 2015. Upgrades to existing refineries may continue to move forward - for example, Cilicap's 62,000 bbl/d residual fluid catalytic cracking unit still appears to be on track for 2013 or 2014 completion.

CONSUMPTION

Consumption of refined products grew at a fairly steady 4.7 percent average annual growth rate between 1995 and 2005, but declined by about two percent in both 2009 and 2010, largely as a result of the 126 percent increase in the price of subsidized fuel implemented in 2005. The 2005 price increases - and the removal of fuel subsidies for large industrial consumers - were part of President Yudhoyono's early attempts to gradually eliminate fuel subsidies. Consumption increased in both 2008 and 2009, exceeding 1.3 million bbl/d in 2009.

Fuel subsides will account for nearly ten billion dollars in 2010, or about ten percent of the government's tax revenues. In December of 2010 the Indonesian parliament approved a measure to remove fuel subsidies for all vehicles excluding motorcycles and public transportation vehicles. Cash transfers will be used to ease the impact on the economically disadvantaged. The policy was initially slated for April 2011 implementation in the greater Jakarta area, and nationwide by 2013. However, implementation was indefinitely delayed in March 2011 due to concerns over the effect on the rate of inflation.

NATURAL GAS

Natural gas production has increased by more than a quarter since 2005. Indonesia exported about half of its natural gas consumption in 2009 - but the share of domestic consumption is expected to increase. According to *Oil & Gas Journal*, Indonesia had 106 trillion cubic feet (Tcf) of proven natural gas reserves as of January 2011. Indonesia is the fourteenth largest holder of proven natural gas reserves in the world, and the third-largest in the Asia-Pacific Region. Although domestic consumption of natural gas has nearly doubled since 2004, Indonesia continues to be a major exporter of pipeline and liquefied natural gas (LNG).

Sector Organization

The regulatory structure that shapes Indonesia's upstream oil sector also forms the basis for the gas sector (see Oil: Sector Organization). BPMigas serves as the upstream regulator, and state-owned PT Pertamina - though still active in upstream exploration and production - no longer plays a regulatory role. Pertamina accounts for about 15 percent of natural gas production. International oil companies such as Total, ConocoPhillips, and ExxonMobil dominate the upstream gas sector, while natural gas transmission and distribution activities are carried out by the state-owned utility Perusahaan Gas Negara (PGN).

Production

In 2009, Indonesia produced 2.6 Tcf of dry natural gas. Production has grown at an average annual rate of about 1.5 percent over the previous two decades, and Indonesia's 2009 gas production was the eleventh-highest in the world. A little more than half of Indonesia's 2009 production came from offshore fields, although the government estimates that more than 70 percent of the country's conventional gas reserves may be located offshore. An increasingly large majority of Indonesia's natural gas production has come from non-associated fields in recent years, with associated gas accounting for about 18 percent of gross production in 2009.

Indonesia's geography presents a challenge to resource development, because the archipelago nation's most prolific blocks of conventional gas reserves are located far from its major demand markets. The most significant areas for current natural gas production are:

East Kalimantan's offshore fields, particularly the Mahakam PSCs operated by Total
South Sumatra, particularly the onshore Corridor PSC operated by Conoco Philips
Aceh and North Sumatra, including Exxon Mobil's declining offshore Arun field
South Natuna Sea, offshore Block B operated by Conoco Phillips

In 2009, East Kalimantan's offshore Mahakam PSCs accounted for about a third of gross production.

In addition to expansion of current projects, there are several major new gas projects in development for the next decade. Total and Petronas (Malaysia) recently joined ExxonMobil and Pertamina to develop the Natuna D-Alpha field in the East Natuna Sea. Pertamina expects the project to start by 2021, and has estimated that East Natuna in total holds 46 Tcf of gas. However, the field contains about 70 percent carbon dioxide, significantly tightening production margins for its developers. Chevron is pursing the deepwater Gendalo-Gehem project with partners Eni (Italy) and Sinopec (China). At its peak, the project - which spans four PSC blocks - may produce 400 Bcf per year. The project is Indonesia's first deepwater gas project. According to BPMigas, the first stage of the project will come from the Bangka field, and may commence as early as 2014. Inpex (Japan) received permission to begin development in its Masela block, which is estimated to hold about 14 Tcf of natural gas. This offshore block in the Arafura Sea will serve export markets through the planned associated LNG terminal (see LNG section), and is expected to begin production in 2016.

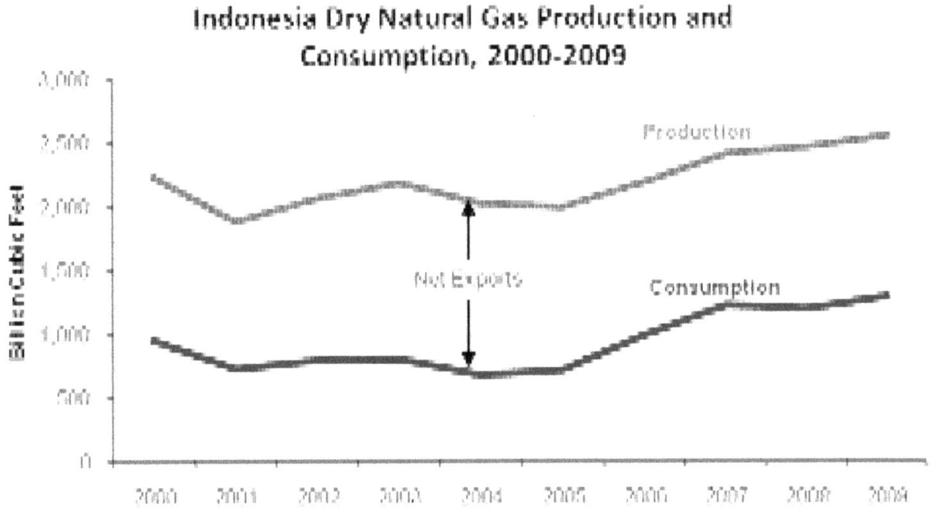

In addition to its considerable conventional gas resources, Indonesia also holds an estimated 453 Tcf of coalbed methane (CBM), a type of unconventional gas whereby methane - the primary component of natural gas - is extracted from coal beds. CBM reserves are located relatively close to Indonesia's population centers, primarily in South Sumatra and Kalimantan. The government began awarding PSC's in 2008, though all are still in exploration phase. However, first production is expected to begin in some of the PSCs held by local companies in late 2011 and 2012. Though local consortiums hold many of the existing CBM PSCs, foreign majors BP, Eni (Italy), and Dart Energy (Australia) also hold shares in Indonesia's CBM blocks.

Exports

Indonesia was the world's sixth largest net exporter of natural gas in 2009. Although the majority of Indonesia's gas exports are transported as LNG, Indonesia also exports about a quarter of its gas exports via pipeline to Singapore, with which it has two pipeline connections: one from its offshore fields in the West Natuna Sea, and the other from the Grissik gas processing plant in Sumatra. These pipelines have a combined capacity of approximately 400 Bcf/y and deliver gas to Singapore under long-term contracts, both set to expire around 2020. However, as part of its efforts to secure its own domestic supply, the Indonesian government has expressed an interest in negotiating a reduction in the volumes of these contracts.

The remaining three-quarters of Indonesia's gas exports - excluding a small amount of pipeline exports to Malaysia - are exported as LNG. Japan is the major destination for Indonesia's LNG exports, accounting for about 65 percent of total LNG exports, but South Korea and Taiwan are also significant importers (see Liquefied Natural Gas for more information).

Consumption and Distribution

Indonesian gas production initially was geared towards exports, but the country's declining oil production has driven an effort to shift increasing volumes toward domestic consumption. In 2009, Indonesia consumed 1.3 Tcf of natural gas, or about half of its total dry gas production. Although the industrial sector accounts for the largest portion of domestic consumption, the power sector is expected to be the most significant driver of future consumption growth.

Indonesia's gas distribution utility Perusahaan Gas Negara (PGN) currently operates more than 3,500 miles of natural gas transmission and distribution pipelines. However, domestic distribution infrastructure is almost non-existent outside of PGN's Java and North Sumatra strategic business units. According to PGN, in 2009 there was over 400 Bcf of unmet demand for gas among domestic industrial and electric power consumers.

PGN began operations of the South Sumatra-West Java pipeline in 2008, providing an important link between the gas producing region of South Sumatra and the densely populated market of West Java. The Grissik-Duri pipeline is another important domestic transmission pipeline, as it provides gas to Chevron's Duri (see Oil: Exploration and Production) field for its steamflooding and power generation activities. A pipeline problem in September of 2010 resulted in a production outage, which has since been cited as a contributing factor to Indonesia's failure to meet its 2010 oil production goals.

LIQUEFIED NATURAL GAS

Indonesia was the third-largest exporter of liquefied natural gas in 2009, following only Qatar and Malaysia. There are three operational liquefaction terminals in Indonesia, with a combined production capacity of about 1.6 Tcf (32 million metric tons (MMT)) per year. In 2009, Indonesia exported about 950 Bcf of LNG.

The Bontang LNG terminal in East Kalimantan is the largest in Indonesia at about 1.1 Tcf/y (22.6 MMT/y), and one of the largest in the world. Bontang delivered its first cargo in 1977, and was followed shortly thereafter (1978) by the Arun liquefaction terminal in Northern Sumatra. Due to a lack of sufficient additional gas reserves in the Arun field, LNG exports from the Arun plant have been declining in recent years, and are expected to stop altogether by 2014. The newest addition, BP-operated Tangguh in Western Papua, came online in July of 2009 and exported almost 330 Bcf in 2010. BP had originally intended to add a third train to Tangguh's first two trains, but has not yet proceeded with plans for this project.

The next anticipated addition to Indonesia's liquefaction capacity is the Donggi-Senoro LNG plant in Central Sulawesi. The project developers (Mitsubishi, Kogas, Pertamina, and Medco) signed a final investment decision in early 2011, and the 370 Bcf/y (2.5 MMT/y) plant is expected to be commercial in 2014. Inpex, a Japanese company, received government approval at the end of 2010 for the Masela liquefaction terminal in the Arafura Sea, but has delayed the expected startup date of the floating terminal until 2018.

LNG exports have been a politically charged topic in Indonesia, due to the perception of LNG exports removing much-needed gas from the domestic market. The expected growth in gas demand, in addition to the currently unmet demand, has led the government to pursue policies for securing domestic supplies for the local market. The Donggi-Senoro plans received government approval only after 30 percent of the output was designated for domestic consumption. Similarly, a third of the output from Inpex's planned Masela floating LNG liquefaction terminal will be designated for the domestic market, according to regulator BPMigas. Indonesia also plans to reorient the output from the Bontang LNG plant - which is relatively centrally located - into the domestic market over the next decade. Though the plant will remain operational, it will send LNG within Indonesia - and no longer serve export markets by 2020.

Indonesia's Liquefaction Capacity

	Location	Capacity (Bcf/y)	Commercial Operations
Operational			
Arun	Aceh	102	1978
Bontang	East Kalimantan	1101	1977
Tangguh	Papua	370	2009
Planned			
Donggi-Senoro	Sulawasi	102	2014
Masela	Arafura Sea, Maluku Province	122	2016+

Sources: FACTS Global Energy, BP, Inpex

In order to have more flexibility to secure supplies of both domestic and foreign LNG, plans for several LNG receiving terminals are underway in Indonesia. The first regasification terminal, a 143 Bcf/y (3.0 MMT/y) joint-venture between Pertamina and PGN, will supply the Jakarta market starting in the first quarter of 2012. Pertamina also plans to invite bids for an additional receiving terminal of similar size to serve East Java. In addition, Pertamina and PLN (Indonesia's state electricity firm) have announced plans to develop eight LNG receiving "mini terminals" by 2015, with a total capacity of 67 Bcf/y (1.4 MMT/y). These terminals will be scattered throughout the eastern region of the island nation, and are intended to guarantee supply of natural gas for electricity plants.

COAL

Indonesia's coal exports have more than quadrupled in the last decade, making it the second-largest coal exporter in the world, and a critical player in Asian coal markets. According to EIA estimates, Indonesia has 4.8 billion short tons of recoverable coal, of which the vast majority is located in Sumatra and East and South Kalimantan. Government and industry estimates suggest that the resource base may be considerably higher than this amount. Indonesian coal production - which is primarily bituminous or sub-bituminous in rank - has approximately quadrupled between 2000 and 2009, reaching 333 MMst in 2009. In the same year, Indonesia consumed 77 MMst of coal, which was less than a quarter of its production, but more than three times the consumption level in 2000. Power plants accounted for nearly two-thirds of 2009 total coal sales. Electricity sector demand for coal is expected to more than double by 2014 as a result of coal-fired generation capacity additions.

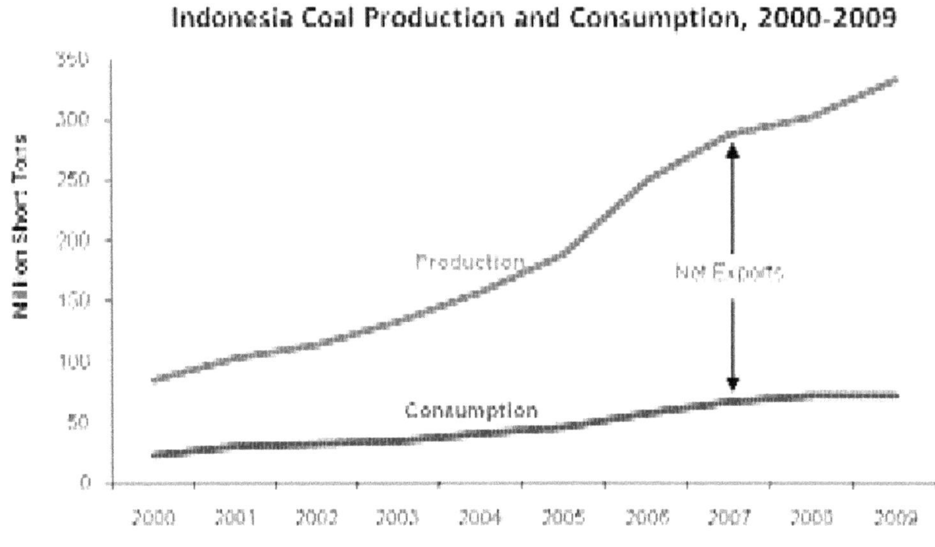

Source: EIA *International Energy Statistics*

Although coal consumption has grown significantly in the last decade, the majority of additional production has gone towards exports. In order to guarantee sufficient domestic supply, the Indonesian government has set a domestic market obligation of 24 percent for producers. Indonesia is now the second-largest exporter of coal (after Australia) on the international market, and is the largest exporter of thermal coal used for power plants. Indonesia's coal exports primarily serve Asian markets, with about 70 percent of 2009 total exports being sent to China, Japan, Taiwan, and other Asian markets. In 2010, Indonesia was the leading source of Chinese coal imports.

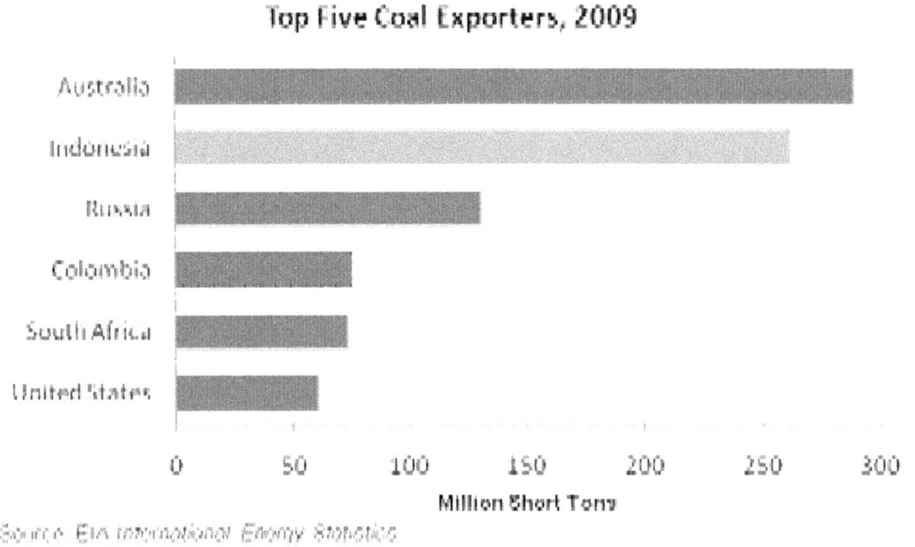

Source: EIA *International Energy Statistics*

ELECTRICITY

Although Indonesia generates 86 percent of its electricity from conventional thermal sources (coal, gas, and oil), it was the third-largest generator of geothermal power in 2009.

Indonesia had 27.8 gigawatts of installed generating capacity in 2008. Indonesia generated 122 billion kilowatthours (Bkwh) of electricity during 2008, of which 86 percent came from conventional thermal sources (oil, natural gas, and coal), eight percent from hydroelectric, and six percent came from geothermal and other renewable sources. Of the conventional thermal total, coal accounts for the largest share at 47 percent, followed by gas at 33 percent, and oil at 19 percent.

State-owned electric utility PT PLN (Perusahaan Listrik Negara) is the most significant company in the electric power sector. PLN owns and operates 86 percent of the country's generating capacity through its subsidiaries, and maintains an effective monopoly over distribution activities. Although the most recent 2009 Electricity Law ends PLN's distribution monopoly, sufficient implementing regulations to support this law have yet to come into effect.

Indonesia's generating capacity has increased by more than a quarter in the decade leading up to 2009. However, as of 2009, only 65 percent percent of Indonesia's population has access to electricity. In addition, because capacity growth has lagged behind the pace of electricity demand growth, grid-connected areas have also suffered from power shortages. Investment in Indonesia's power sector had lagged for several reasons, including inadequate supporting infrastructure, difficulty obtaining land-use permissions, subsidized tariffs, and an uncertain regulatory environment.

In order to address the capacity shortage, in 2009, the government embarked upon the first stage of its "fast track" plan, designed to add 20 additional gigawatts to the grid by 2014. The first stage, which includes 10 gigawatts of primarily coal-based generation, was initially set for completion in 2010 - though subsequent delays have led to a revised completion date of 2013. The second phase, which includes an additional 10 gigawatts to be completed by 2014, includes more cleaner sources of generation such as natural gas and renewables. Unlike in many other countries, Indonesia's government is encouraging an increased use of coal in the power sector, due to its relatively abundant domestic supply, and in order to reduce the use of expensive diesel and fuel oil.

Top Generators of Geothermal Electricity, 2008

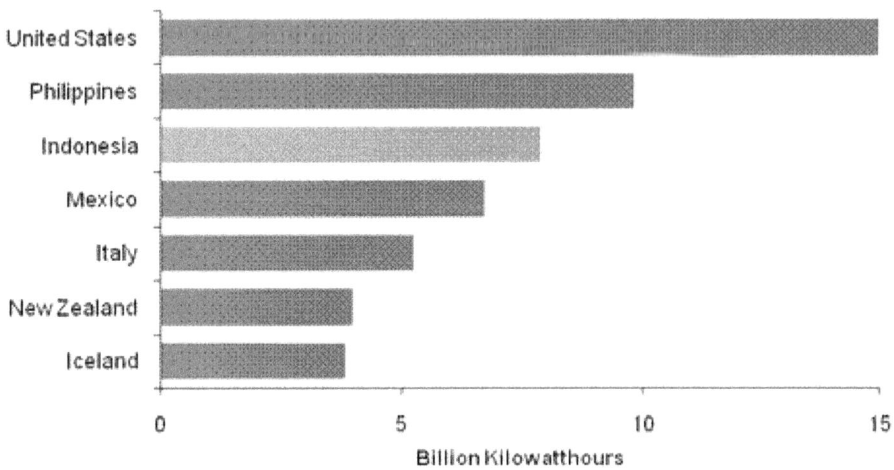

Source: EIA *International Energy Statistics*

Indonesia's power sector is notable for its significant level of geothermal power, and was the third-largest geothermal generator in the world in 2008. However, Indonesia's 2008 capacity of approximately one gigawatt falls substantially below its available resource, which the government has estimated to be sufficient to generate 28 gigawatts. Government plans to increase the use of renewable energy to 15 percent of the electricity portfolio by 2025 are centered on development of geothermal resources. The second phase of the fast track plan includes additional geothermal capacity of nearly four gigawatts by 2014, most of which will be operated by independent power producers.

OIL EXPLORATION BASICS

RESERVES AND PRODUCTION

In 2009 Indonesia ranked twenty-first among world oil producers, with approximately 1.3% of the world's daily production. The GOI places Indonesia's proven oil reserves at approximately 4.44 billion barrels, according to official data. These figures are 13% lower than in 2000. Oil exports were $10.9 billion in 2009, up from $10.04 billion in 2005. Total oil and gas exports (including LNG) were $21.41 billion in 2009, compared with $19.2 billion in 2005, and represented 22% of Indonesia's export earnings, down from 23% in 2005. In 2009 Indonesia produced an average 1,005,700 barrels per day (bpd) of petroleum crude and condensate, according to government figures. Production fell to 912,000 bpd in 2010, according to unofficial government data. Indonesia's production of crude oil and condensate continues its multi-year trend of gradual decline from 1.062 million bpd in 2005, 1.09 million bpd in 2004, 1.15 million bpd in 2003, and 1.25 million bpd in 2002. Indonesia has produced well below its OPEC crude production quota of 1.451 million bpd (without condensate), as a result of declining investment and maturing oil fields.

In 2009 Indonesia's 1,005,700 bpd of daily production consisted of 883,200 bpd of crude and 122,500 bpd of condensate. This was a 29 percent drop from 2000. Almost all oil producers reported flat or declining output in 2009. Pertamina was an exception, increasing output from 50,700 bpd in 2005 to 94,300 bpd in 2009, an increase of 46%. Continued sluggish investment and a decrease in new exploration were key factors behind the decline. PT Chevron Pacific Indonesia's production, which accounted for 48.3% of the country's crude oil production in 2009, declined 7.5% from 525,200 bpd in 2005 to 485,800 bpd in 2009. Pertamina passed Total Indonesia to become the second largest oil producer in 2009 with 9.4% of production. In 2009 the GOI renewed its commitment to increase output in its energy blueprint and set a production target of 1.3 million bpd by 2009. In May 2008 Vice President Jusuf Kalla revised the target to 1.2 million bpd by 2010. Production increased in 2008, but few industry observers believe Indonesia can achieve those production goals without significant changes to the system of incentives and regulations for production sharing contractors. **Table: Crude and Condensate Production by major producers (1,000 bpd)**

Company	2005	2009	Change (%)
Chevron (Caltex)	471.4	446.8	-5%
Chevron (Unocal)	53.8	39.0	-27%
Pertamina	50.7	94.3	86%
Total	88.0	90.9	3%
ConocoPhillips	73.0	64.1	-12%
CNOOC	65.4	57.0	-13%
Medco(Exspan)	54.2	45.2	-17%
Petrochina	42.4	43.6	3%
BP	24.8	26.6	8%

BumiSiakPusako	27.3	25.7	-6%
Others	111.2	72.5	-35%
Total	1,062.1	1,005.6	-5%

IMPORTS

Indonesia remains a significant importer of crude oil. Indonesia's crude oil imports dropped sharply in 2009 to 116.2 million barrels from 148.5 million in 2004. Saudi Arabia, Brunei, and Nigeria are the major suppliers. Fuel product imports dropped to 133.4 million barrels in 2009, down from 165.7 million barrels in 2005 and 154.4 million barrels in 2004. In term of value, oil imports in 2009 increased 5% to $17.96 million, compared with $17.08 million in 2005.

EXPLORATION AND INVESTMENT

Of an estimated 60 oil basins, approximately 22 have been extensively explored. Most oil exploration is currently being carried out in the basins of Western Indonesia under PSCs. The bulk of Indonesia's oil reserves are located onshore and offshore in Central Sumatra and Kalimantan. The GOI has placed increased emphasis on developing oil reserves in remote locations, such as Papua, where proven and potential reserves are estimated at 109.1 million barrels.

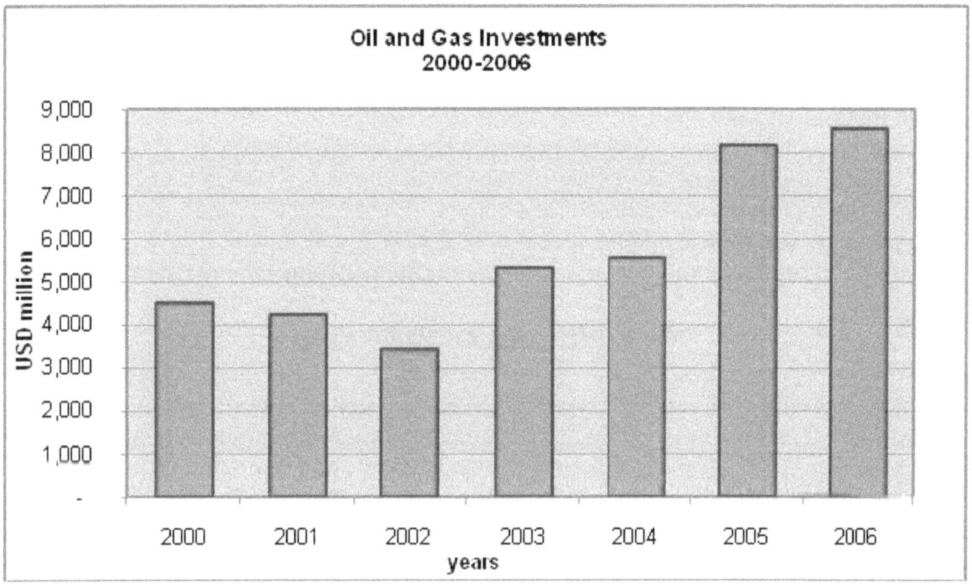

The oil and gas industry today faces several crucial problems, particularly in the upstream sector, due to aging oil and gas assets and investment climate uncertainties. Officials hope oil contractors will aggressively increase exploration activities to look for new reserves. With no significant oil discoveries in western Indonesia in the last 10 years, the government hopes eastern Indonesia's frontier and deep-sea areas may contain sizable oil reserves. The number of exploration drilling wells completed in 2009 dropped sharply to 35, compared with 68 in 2005. In 1998, explorers drilled 145 wells. The success ratio (successful wells versus wells drilled) reached 45.7% in 2009, up slightly from 43.8% percent in 2005. ***Seismic Activities*** According to MIGAS, a total of 14,962 kilometers of combined 2-D and 3-D seismic activities were carried out in 2009, continuing the steady downward trend since the 1997 peak of 469,198 kilometers.

EXPLORATION BLOCKS AWARDED

The government awarded 9 oil and gas exploration blocks in 2010, 27 blocks in 2009, 9 in 2005, 16 in 2004 and 15 in 2003.

The direct bidding round is one of the Government's revamped procedures for exploration and production contracts in a bid to increase their attractiveness. Previously, oil and gas companies could only receive a concession through an official tender.

Now, the government accepts proposals for blocks without waiting for a formal bidding session. Under this special bidding process, after a company applies to acquire a new exploration block, the government invites other bidders to participate. If no other bidder emerges within a set timeframe, the government grants the block to the sole bidder. The government also offered new, more attractive terms and conditions for new exploration blocks in 2005. Winning PSCs would get between 20 and 35 percent splits for oil and between 30 and 40 percent for gas. Under previous PSC terms, companies generally receive a 15 percent split for oil and 30 percent split for gas. The government also set first tranche petroleum (FTP) obligations at 10 percent. Indonesia's production continues to decline due to lack of investment and aging fields. At the same time, several political leaders throughout 2010 and 2008 have voiced concern regarding the escalating share of expenditures related to reimbursing contractors for their costs of exploration and production as stipulated in their PSCs. The Ministry of Energy and Mineral Resources enacted a negative list of cost recovery in June 2008, prohibiting many costs that had previously been allowed.

BP Migas chairman R. Priyono said in May 2008 that he will seek to link increases in cost recovery with increased production. A 2008 report by BPMigas said the government paid $8.33 billion to oil and gas producers in 2010 for recovery costs, a rise of 6.4%. In 2009 and 2005, the government paid $7.8 billion and $7.3 billion, respectively. Industry analysts say rising recovery costs are driven by increased competition for equipment and qualified personnel due to record petroleum prices, the significantly higher costs of maintaining production from aging wells, and new exploration and production in deepwater and remote locations.

MERGERS AND ACQUISITIONS

U.S.-based Chevron acquired Unocal in August 2005, strengthening its position as Indonesia's largest oil producer. Caltex and Unocal both assumed the Chevron name but continue to conduct operational activities under separate subsidiaries. In August 2004, Indonesia's largest oil and gas company, Medco Energi International completed acquisition of Novus Petroleum Limited, a company listed in the Australian Stock Exchange with assets in the Middle East, United States, Australia and Indonesia. The acquisition led to the change of Novus' directors as it cut its global assets. ***Mergers***

- Chevron and Unocal, Aug 2005.
- Conoco & Phillips – ConocoPhillips, Sept 2002.
- Chevron & Texaco – ChevronTexaco, Sept 2001
- Santa Fe Snyder & Devon – Devon Energy Corp, Aug 2000.
- BP Amoco & Arco – BP, Apr 2000.
- TotalFina & Elf – TotalFinaElf Sam, Feb 2000.
- Exxon & Mobil – ExxonMobil Corp, Nov 1999.
- El Paso & Sonat – El Paso Energy Corp, Oct 1999.
- Total & Fina – TotalFina, Jun 1999.
- Lasmo & Monument – Lasmo Plc, Jun 1999.

- Santa Fe & Snyder – Santa Fe Snyder Corp, May 1999.
- Nisseki & Mitsubishi Oil Co. – Nisseki Mitsubishi Abushild, Apr 1999.
- Kerr McGee & Oryx – Kerr McGee Corp, Feb 1999.
- BP & Amoco – BP Amoco Plc, Jan 1999.
- British Borneo & Hardy – British Borneo Oil & Gas Plc, Oct 1998.
- Ocean Energy & Seagull – Ocean Energy Inc, Jun 1997.

Takeovers

- Medco Energi – Novus Petroleum, August 2004
- Conoco – Gulf Indonesia Resources, July 2002
- CNOOC – YPFMaxus, Jan 2002.
- PetroChina – Devon Energy, April 2002
- Husky Oil Ltd. – Renaissance energy, Aug 2000.
- Canadian Natural Resources – Ranger Oil, July 2000.
- Fortune (Indo Pacific) – GFB Resources (Java) Ltd, Jul 2000.
- Agip – British Borneo, May 2000.
- Singapore Petroleum Company Ltd – LL&E Indonesia, Jan 2000.
- Maple/Matrix – GFB Resources (Langsa) Ltd, Jan 2000.

THE FUTURE

Pundits had forecast Indonesia's imminent shift from net oil exporter to net importer for several years. Those predictions finally were realized on a monthly basis in 2004. A steady decline in production, coupled with lower exploration investment levels, accelerated the transition to net importer earlier than forecasters has predicted. However, with substantial reserves of natural gas and coal, Indonesia remains a net energy exporter.

The March 2009 agreement between ExxonMobil and Pertamina to begin development of the Cepu bloc and the drop in domestic petroleum consumption following the 2005 and 2008 price hikes might be a step toward bringing Indonesia back into the net exporter camp, although more production is necessary. To maintain momentum, industry observers encouraged the GOI to implement legislation and policies to rationalize the use of Indonesia's energy resources. The government, however, has not made any fundamental changes to the subsidized fuel regime, despite the price hikes. A 2005 industry survey conducted by the IPA and PriceWaterhouseCoopers concluded that Indonesia's oil and gas industry is at a critical juncture. Survey participants lauded positive government efforts toward improving the investment climate in the upstream industry, such as improved fiscal incentives, the development of an overall energy blueprint, and an improving gas pipeline infrastructure. Industry representatives said, however, that Indonesia should improve its fiscal terms for oil and gas production for both mature and frontier areas. Often the balance between risk and reward is generally viewed as insufficient to attract major exploration funds. These problems are exacerbated by small reserve accumulations and high infrastructure costs. To address these concerns, the Minister of Energy and Mineral Resources issued Regulation 8/2005 in April 2005, which gave contractors developing marginal oil field an additional 20% reimbursement in cost recovery. In its 2005 bidding round the government offered also a more favorable contractor production split of up to 70/30 (government/contractor) and up to 60/40 for oil and gas respectively.

As part of its Energy Blueprint in January 2009, Indonesia renewed its intention to achieve a production target of 1.3 million bpd by 2009. Industry leaders say that five actions by the GOI are crucial to reach this production target in the medium term:

- Harmonizing conflicting laws and regulations, including the timely implementation of regulations;
- Improving teamwork, coordination and cooperation among GOI entities;
- Implementing judicial reform;
- Changing the regulatory paradigm to a "shared economic interest" model;
- Having more predictability in allowed cost recovery; and
- Protecting contract sanctity.

PSC UPDATE

Chevron Chevron Indonesia operations include former Caltex Pacific Indonesia (CPI) and Unocal assets which were consolidated after the merger of Chevron and Unocal in 2005. Chevron's operations in Indonesia are geographically dispersed and include onshore exploration & production and self-use power generation in Sumatra, offshore production in Kalimantan, and geothermal and power operations in Java. In addition to these operations, Chevron holds a 25% non-operating interest in the South Natuna Sea Block B, operated by ConocoPhillips, and interests in several other exploration blocks.

Chevron produces nearly half of Indonesia's crude oil production; in 2010, Chevron achieved a gross average daily oil-equivalent production of over 585,000 barrels of petroleum and condensate, a 20% increase compared with 485,800 bpd in the prior year. However, oil production averaged 470 MBOEPD equaling approx 172 MM barrels on an annual basis while gas averaged 336 MCFPD equaling approx 123 BSCF on an annual basis. The majority of the firm's oil production came from the Duri and Minas fields in the Rokan PSC (Production Sharing Contract) located in central Sumatra. Daily gross production from all of Sumatra operations are approximately 90 producing fields, averaged 425,000 barrels of crude oil and 54 million cubic feet of natural gas in 2010. Chevron's offshore operations are located in East Kalimantan with production from both shelf and deepwater assets. During 2010, daily gross production from Kalimantan Operations' two producing PSCs (East Kalimantan and Makassar) averaged 34,000 barrels of oil and condensate and 192 million cubic feet of gas. In addition, Chevron continues to advance the development of its deepwater natural gas projects and has submitted the final Plan of Development to the Government of Indonesia for the projects located in Kalimantan's Kutei Basin. Chevron's downstream activities include sales of paraxylene, benzene and fuel catalysts to refineries in Java, and the company enjoys a sizable domestic market share of lubricants and fuel additives.

In the electric power business, Chevron renamed Amoseas as Chevron Geothermal Indonesia in 2004. The 110 MW Darajat III project achieved commercial operation in July 2010. From the Unocal merger, Chevron acquired another geothermal facility in Gunung Salak, Central Java. In addition, the company also operates a 300 MW co-

generation facility in North Duri to support its Central Sumatra activities. Chevron says it is evaluating further expansion of its Darajat and Salak fields and is seeking opportunities to explore and develop new geothermal fields in Indonesia. ***ExxonMobil*** ExxonMobilwas created from the merger of Exxon and Mobil in November 1999, leading to the consolidation of Exxon, Esso, and Mobil operations in Indonesia. ExxonMobil (EM) celebrated 100 years of doing business in Indonesia in 1998, including 30 years as a production-sharing contractor, 20 years as a producer of liquefied natural gas and 10 years as a producer of liquefied petroleum gas. ExxonMobil has concentrated on two major projects in Indonesia since 2005: the Cepu oil and gas block in East and Central Java and the off-shore Natuna D-Alpha block.

In the first quarter of 2008, the government announced that it had terminated ExxonMobil's rights to develop the 46 TSCF off-shore Natuna D-Alpha gas field and appointed state oil company

Pertamina to run the project. The government said ExxonMobil failed to show sufficient progress in developing the field. ExxonMobil officials pointed to their expenditure of approximately $400 million for exploration activities and asserted its contract gave the firm the right to an extension until 2009. Industry analysts generally share the opinion that Pertamina has neither the financial nor technical expertise to develop the Natuna field on its own. EM executives say they remain committed to a joint partnership with the GOI on the Natuna project, according to public and media statements by the company. In March 2009, ExxonMobil and Pertamina signed a joint operating agreement (JOA) for the Cepu Banyu Urip oil and gas block. Production is likely to start in late 2008, according to company press statements. EM believes the Banyu-Urip field has an estimated resource base in excess of 300 million barrels of oil and significant volumes of gas. ExxonMobil proposes a $2.6 billion capital investment to fully develop the block. The company estimates peak crude oil production will be 171,000 bpd. Major gas supplies could be available for sale to meet existing shortfalls in East and Central Java. The company estimates the project will generate annual gross revenues between $700 million and $1.2 billion at peak production. In 2005, Pertamina and ExxonMobil signed a new cooperation contract for the Cepu block, where each holds a 45 percent interest in the block. Previously EM held a 100% participating interest under a PSC awarded by Pertamina in 1990. The March 2009 JOA resolved a disagreement over operatorship with EM securing the lead to develop the project and Pertamina executives playing key roles.

In North Sumatra, ExxonMobil's natural gas operations include the Arun, Pase, South Lhoksukon, and North Sumatra Offshore fields, which supply gas to the Arun LNG plant. Gas supplies from the field is declining and not sufficient to meet export commitments and supply the local fertilizer industry in Sumatra. The government has requested that ExxonMobil divert some of its production from elsewhere in Indonesia to supply the

fertilizer plants even at the cost of the GOI having to purchase LNG cargoes from the world spot market to meet its contractual export commitments. In April 2009, ExxonMobil divested its 50% participating interest in A-Block in the Madura Strait to a consortium of Indonesian, British, and Japanese firms. The company also sold its 68 percent interest in another Madura Strait PSC to Husky Energy in 2004. ***BP*** With more than three decades of operating history in Indonesia, BP has become one of the largest foreign investors with a cumulative capital investment to date of over US$5 billion. BP has business interests upstream, downstream, and in the chemicals sector and employs over 1,000 Indonesian nationals. BP's operating assets offshore North West Java cover 8,300 square kilometers, from north of Cirebon to the east to Kepulauan Seribu to the west. BP West Java has been the major gas supplier to state-owned electricity company PLN since 1993, enabling PLN to generate electricity for the Greater Jakarta and West Java areas. BP West Java supplies gas also to gas company PGN and fertilizer producer PT Pupuk Kujang.

The Tangguh LNG Project is a major multinational development, with a lifespan of more than 30 years, to produce the natural gas fields in the remote Bintuni Bay area of Papua Barat. The gas reserves were discovered in the mid-1990s with proved reserves of 14.4 TSCF. It is operated by BP Berau Ltd. and will begin its operation towards the end of 2008 with deliveries to customers likely to begin in early 2009.

BP is involved in VICO Indonesia through its joint venture with ENI. VICO operates the Sanga-Sanga Production Sharing Contract (PSC) and employs more than 1,000 nationals In chemical business, BP has a 50/50 joint venture with Mitsui in PT AMI which produces PTA (purified terephtalic acid), feedstocks for fiber / string and also polyesther bottling industries. BP also produces and markets lubricant under the Castrol brand. ***ConocoPhillips*** ConocoPhillips has had a presence in Indonesia for more than 40 years. It has focused in two core areas: the South Natuna Sea and onshore South Sumatra. It has 11 exploration and production licenses comprising roughly 14.5 million gross acres. The company operates nine Production Sharing

Contracts (PSCs), four of them offshore: South Natuna Sea Block B, Ketapang, Amborip VI and Kuma. The remaining five PSCs are onshore: Corridor TAC (technical assistance contract), Corridor PSC, South Jambi B, Sakakemang JOB (jointly operated) in South Sumatra and Warim PSC in Papua. ConocoPhillips holds a nonoperator interestsin the Banyumas PSC onshore Java. In 2009 and 2010, the company sold its interests in the Block A PSCs in North Sumatra and was awarded the Amborip VI PSC in the Arafura Sea and Kuma Block in Makassar Straits.

ConocoPhillips is the largest supplier of pipeline gas in Indonesia through the South Sumatra pipeline and West Natuna

pipeline. The company owns and operates 621 miles of onshore and offshore natural gas pipelines that deliver ConocoPhillips's South Sumatra natural gas to market, including the Grissik-to-Duri and Grissik-to-Singapore pipelines. Meanwhile, natural gas from Block B is sold via two long-term contracts. In the first contract, ConocoPhillips is a participant in the West Natuna Gas Supply Group (WNG). WNG jointly markets natural gas from fields in three South Natuna Sea PSCs, including Block B, to SembGas in Singapore. The second contract is solely supplied with natural gas from Block B and provides deliveries to Petronas in Malaysia. In August 2003, ConocoPhillips began supplying natural gas from its south Sumatra Corridor PSC to Singapore's PowerGas, via the Grissik-Batam-Singapore gas pipeline. The company has also supplied natural gas to Singapore's Sembawang Gas from its West Natuna gas fields since 2001 and to Petronas' Duyong Complex offshore Malaysia from South Natuna Sea Block B since August 2002. ConocoPhillips has been a major player in the pipeline gas business since 1998, when it began supplying gas from the South Sumatra Corridor Block PSC to the Chevron-operated Duri steamflood in Central Sumatra.

ConocoPhillips holds a 40 percent operating interest in the offshore Block B PSC, South Natuna Sea. The Belanak floating production, storage and offloading (FPSO) project at the Block B PSC started oil production in December 2004. The FPSO has a capacity to process 100,000 bpd of oil and 430 million cubic feet of gas per day. Natural gas production from the field is exported via pipeline to Singapore and Malaysia. In offshore East Java, ConocoPhillips has an operating interest in the Ketapang block. The company believes the block has significant oil potential and plans an additional 5 wells in 2009. Malaysia's Petronas has an equal, non-operating interest in the block. ConocoPhillips plans to drill and invest over $3 billion in projects in the Natuna Sea and Ketapang over the next 4 years. ConocoPhillips is also a major player in the $900 million South Sumatra to West Java gas development project. The project includes a 660-kilometer pipeline from ConocoPhillips Subang gas field in the Corridor Block to the state-owned electricity utility PLN gas-fired power plants in West Java. The company signed a gas sales agreement in August 2004 with state gas company PGN for 2.3 TSCF of gas to supply industrial customers in West Java and Jakarta over a 17 year period commencing 2010. Gas supply will come from the Suban gas field on Corridor Block PSC, South Sumatra and will be transported via the South Sumatra-West Java pipeline. ***Amerada Hess*** Amerada Hess consolidated its holdings in Indonesia and sold most of its Indonesian assets during 2002-2003. Amerada Hess' present assets in Indonesia are a 75 percent operating interest in Pangkah PSC and a 25 percent working interest in the Jambi Merang JOB. It produced approximately 4,000 boepd in 2009.

Amerada Hess has focused its operations in Indonesia on the development of the Ujung Pangkah gas field located in the Madura Strait, offshore East Java. The company is also constructing an offshore well head platform and an onshore gas processing facility in Gresik. Amerada

Hess plans to pipe gas from the Ujung Pangkah gas field to PLN's Gresik power plant. In December 2004, the company signed a 400 BSCF gas supply contract with PLN for 20 years starting at the end of 2009. ***Medco*** Indonesia's largest private oil company, Medco began exporting crude oil in 2000. It also formally changed its name to "PT Medco Energi Internasional

Tbk." at that time. Medco is 50.7 percent owned by Encore International Ltd, which is affiliated with the Panigoro family. On January 2005, Encore signed conditional sales purchase agreements to buy out (Thai) PTTEP's 40% share and Cumin Limited's 19.9% percent share in New Links Energy Resources. Encore is now the sole shareholder of New Links. In 2005, Medco launched a secondary public offering, which increased public investors' shareholding in Medco up to 42.6 percent. Medco, through its subsidiaries, owns 15 oil and gas blocks throughout Indonesia, 9 of which are in production, while the rest are in the exploration phase. Medco's production remained steady in 2009 at 56,367 bpd, though down from 2009. An ongoing production decline in Medco's largest fields, Kaji Semoga in Rimau PSC, South Sumatra, is the primary reason for drop off from 2000-2002. Medco plans to utilize waterflood optimization and enhanced oil recovery (EOR) to slow down the decline rate in its Sumatra fields. Medco's proven oil reserves now stand at 99 million barrels.

In late 2003, Medco assumed the sole risk in exploration drilling in Jeruk in the Sampang PSC. They struck oil in 2004. Other interest holders in the PSC, Singapore Petroleum Company and Cue Energy, decided to reinstate their rights to the Jeruk field at that time. In August 2004 Medco completed its takeover of Novus Petroleum Limited, a listed Australian oil and gas company with assets in the Middle East, Australia, U.S. and Indonesia. Through the acquisition, Medco gained interests in two Indonesian producing fields, Brantas and Kakap. Shortly thereafter, Medco began consolidation and shed some of Novus' assets. The company sold Novus' Pakistani, U.S., and Australian assets, as well as 18 percent and 6.25 percent of Brantas and Kakap PSCs in Indonesia. The company believes its future lies in natural gas development. Medco's proven gas reserves stand at 267.6 BSCF. Medco's gas production more than doubled to 192 mmcfd in the period from 2002 to 2004, before dropping back to 127.2 mmcfd during 2009. LPG sales also went from zero in 2003 to 100.1 MTD in 2009. In addition to gas blocks in south Sumatra, Medco's Exspan Tomori Sulawesi holds a 50 percent operating stake in the Senoro-Toili JOB with PT Pertamina. The block has estimated natural gas reserves of 2.5 TSCF. In January 2009, Medco shipped its first oil from the Senoro's Tiaka field to Pertamina's Plaju refinery.

In July 2005 Medco entered into an Exploration Joint Venture Agreement with the U.S.-based Anadarko Petroleum's Indonesian subsidiary. Under the agreement Anadarko will provide $80 million over three years in exchange for up to 40 percent interest in Medco's exploration assets. Medco also acquired

100% of the Sembakung Technical Assistance Contract (TAC), a mature producing field in Perkasa Equatorial Sembakung and signed a PSC agreement with Libya's National Oil Company for the Area 47 concession, Northwest Libya. In 2009, Medco plans $300 million in capital expenditures to continue with its acquisition strategy, of both domestic and international assets.

EMP Energi Mega Persada (EMP) is an active producer, developer and explorer in the upstream oil and gas sector. It was incorporated in 2001 and listed on the Jakarta Stock Exchange in 2004. The company became embroiled in controversy in May 2009 when a mudflow began from a wellhead at their Brantas PSC in East Java. The company contends that unrelated seismic activity caused the wellhead blow out, not negligent drilling practices, as some community activists and NGOs charged. Roughly 50,000 people have been displaced and 30 factories have been forced to shut down, according to government information. The mudflow has caused approximately Rp. 7.3 trillion ($797.8 million) in infrastructure damage through 2010, according to GOI estimates. In April 2010, the GOI said it set aside Rp 2.5 trillion ($273 million) in the state budget to repair infrastructure damaged by the mudflow. It said it will seek full repayment from Lapindo, although the government later relieved Lapindo from full responsibility by declaring the mudflow the result of an earthquake 300 km away from the drilling site. Geologic experts say the mudflow may continue for years or perhaps even decades. According to the company, Lapindo has been paying Rp 2.5 million per year ($273) in rental assistance to each family displaced and

Rp 300,000 per month ($33) in living costs to each person in the impact area. Lapindo announced plans to end all such payments on May 1, 2008, although they continue to some families that have not yet been resettled. In November 2009 the Capital Market Supervisory Agency disallowed EMP's proposed deal to sell its interest in Lapindo to Freehold Group, an independent company incorporated in the British Virgin Islands. In July 2010 EMP deconsolidated Lapindo Brantas Inc, Kalila Energy Limited, and Pan Asia Enterprise from EMP's consolidated financial statements. In March 2008 through a series of financial transactions approved by GOI regulators, EMP diluted its stake in Lapindo Brantas Inc to 0.01% by selling Lapindo to Lyte Ltd of Jersey, UK. By this action, EMP may no longer face significant potential liability for the mud flow.

Soon after incorporation in 2001 EMP embarked on a series of acquisitions. In 2003 EMP acquired Kondur Petroleum, operator of the Malacca Strait PSC with a 34.46% working interest. In 2004, it bought PT Imbang Tata Alam (ITA) which had a 26.03% working interest in the Malacca Strait PSC. Kondur and ITA together hold a 60.49% working interest in the PSC. In March 2004, it bought Kalila Energy Ltd. (KEL) and Pan Asia Enterprise Ltd. (PAN) which controlled 100% of Lapindo Brantas. Lapindo has a 50% working interest and is operator of the Brantas PSC. In August 2004 EMP acquired a 100% working interest in the Kangean PSC through EMP Exploration (Kangean) Ltd. and EMP Kangean Ltd. EMP Kangean Ltd is the operator of the PSC. EMP bought THP for $308.6 million. THP owned five PSCs. In May 2010 EMP concluded a $720 million deal with Japan's Mitsubishi and Japan Petroleum Exploration Co. Ltd to give the two firms an aggregate 50% working interest in the Kangean PSC. EMP retained a 50% interest in the Kangean PSC.

In June 2010 EMP established strategic alliance to cooperate on gas exploration in the Suci Block in East Java with PT Indelberg Indonesia Perkasa and Pertamina in East Java. In April 2008 EMP bought the Tonga PSC in North Sumatera for $11.8 million. The company estimates that Tonga PSC has up to 90 million boe. ***CNOOC*** The China National Offshore Oil Company (CNOOC) produced 57,000 bpd in 2009. CNOOC's holdings now include an operating 65.34% interest in the Offshore South East Sumatra PSC, a 36.72 percent interest in the Offshore Northwest Java PSC, a 25 percent interest in the West Madura PSC offshore East Java, a 50 percent interest in the Poleng TAC in East Java, and a 39.51 percent interest in the Malacca Strait PSC. CNOOC's Indonesian operation had net proved reserves of 155 million boe, accounting for approximately 7 percent of total company reserves. In 2004, the company produced and 81.5 thousand bpd of oil and 18.8 BSCF of gas.

CNOOC's Indonesia strategy is to tap into the export market as well as get more involved in the domestic natural gas industry. CNOOC entered the LNG export business when it bought a 12.5 percent stake in the $3 billion Tangguh LNG project in late 2002. Production in CNOOC's South East Sumatra PSC continued to decline over the past 4 years. Main oilfields Cinta and Widuri are already 30 years old and are steadily declining. However, the company is optimistic that it will be able to maintain production level through the development of marginal fields and new gas fields in the area. In April 2005, CNOOC received increased financial incentives from the government for its 6 marginal fields. CNOOC secured a gas sales agreement with PLN in 2004 to supply 80 billion BTU to PLN's proposed Cilegon Power plant in West Java starting in 2009 and lasting 12 years. They will supply the gas mainly from the newly developed Zelda and Banuwati fields in the Southeast Sumatra PSC.

CRUDE OIL MARKETING

Indonesia, through Pertamina, BP Migas and its foreign partners, sells crude oil using the Indonesia Crude Price (ICP) formula. Indonesian crude is generally low sulfur and waxy. Indonesia's representative Minas crude (often referred to in marketing terms as Sumatra Light Crude or SLC) produced in Central Sumatra has an American Petroleum Institute (API) gravity of

34.5 degrees at 60 degrees F and a sulfur content of between 0.06 percent and 0.10 percent by weight.

Effective October 1, 1999, Pertamina changed the ICP pricing formula for official export prices of Indonesian crude. The ICP formula has three components:

the Asian Petroleum Price Index (APPI), the Rim Intelligence Company price, and the Platts price. The APPI component is derived from twice weekly APPI price assessments adjusted by a basket of regionally traded crude oils (including Indonesian Sumatra Light Crude and Malaysian Tapis) using a 52-week moving average. Pertamina lowered the portion of the APPI panel quota from 33.3% to 20.0% and increased the portion of the spot assessments of Platt and RIM to 40.0% each. The purpose of the adjustment was to better reflect world prices through more emphasis on the spot market. The Ministry of Energy and Mineral Resources reviews the oil pricing formula semi-annually. Asian countries are the largest markets for Indonesian crude. Japan accounted for 31% of Indonesian crude oil exports in 2009, followed by South Korea (18%), Australia (13.8%), China (10%), and the United States (6.6%). Indonesia's overseas markets have exhibited declining sales volumes since 2002. Exports declined 15% by volume from 2005. **Indonesia 2009 Crude Export Destinations**

Pertamina has an office in Singapore through its wholly owned Hong Kong-basedsubsidiary Pertamina Energy Trading (ex-Perta Oil). The company promotes and facilitates trade in crude oil and fuel between Singapore and Indonesia, offers logistical services to Pertamina, and represents Pertamina's interests.

NATURAL GAS

Production Indonesia has natural gas reserves of 187.09 trillion standard cubic feet (TSCF) as of 2009 (93.95 TSCF proven and 93.14 TSCF possible), a decline of 3% from 2005. In 2009, the country produced 2.954 TSCF of gas, ranking eighth in world gas production. Production declined one percent from 2005 levels. Indonesia's largest producers in 2009 (in order) were Total, Pertamina, ConocoPhillips, ExxonMobil, VICO, BP, Petrochina, and Chevron, all of which operate under production sharing contracts and account for 90 percent of the country's total production. Gas reserves are equivalent to almost four times Indonesia's oil reserves and can supply the country for 62 years at current production rates. According to the GOI, over 71 percent of natural gas reserves are located offshore, with the largest reserves found off Natuna Island (28.8%), East Kalimantan (25.2%), South Sumatra (13%) and Papua (12.8%). However, not all of these reserves are commercially viable, due to both the quality of the gas and the distance to market. In 2009, the government announced a policy re-orienting natural gas production to serve the domestic electric power market. Government ministers said Indonesia will honor all existing contracts but not necessarily renew current ones as they expire between 2008 and 2011.

In 2009, Indonesia supplied 14% of the world's LNG, down from 26% in 2003. LNG accounts for 41% of the country's total natural gas production and is exported mainly to Japan, South Korea and Taiwan. Pipeline gas exports to Singapore began in 2001, reaching 181.3 BSCF in 2005 (the latest year for which figures are available). A new Sumatra-Singapore pipeline was inaugurated in late 2003. Revenues from gas exports are substantial -- $10.5 billion in 2009, about 10 percent of Indonesia's total export revenues. Most of Indonesia's gas comes from Natuna (53.56 TSCF in reserves), Kalimantan (47.77 TSCF in reserves) and Sumatra (33.51 TSCF in reserves), but there are large reserves in Papua (24.47 TSCF in reserves) and other areas in the archipelago (27.78 TSCF in reserves).

GROSS NATURAL GAS PRODUCTION BY MAJOR PRODUCERS (MMSCF)

Company	2004	2005	2009	%
Total	909,932	1,067,190	1,097,341	2.83
Pertamina	383,870	379,612	368,576	-2.91
ExxonMobil	507,096	379,125	322,254	-15.00
ConocoPhillips	319,317	344,886	345,070	0.05
Vico	329,511	251,876	208,371	-17.27
BP	182,209	123,668	136,799	10.62
Chevron (Unocal)	124,199	120,343	107,225	-10.90
Petrochina/Devon Energy	73,668	67,629	111,090	64.26
Others	200,330	251,012	257,372	2.53
Total	3,030,132	2,985,341	2,954,098	-1.05

Source: MIGAS Roughly 55% of Indonesia's natural gas was marketed as LNG or liquefied petroleum gas (LPG) for export, 5.6% for electricity, 6.4% for fertilizer and 3.4% for city gas. Less than 6% was flared.

Indonesia lost its title to Qatar as the world's leading exporter of LNG in 2009, according to media reports and industry analysts. Its share of world production

dropped from 18.8% in 2005 to 14% in 2009. Indonesia exported 46.1 million tons of LNG in 2009, according to government data. LNG production at Arun and Badak (Bontang) was 22.4 million metric tons (MT) in 2009, a decrease from the 2005 production level of 23.7 million MT. Japan, South Korea and Taiwan were the key markets for LNG. Indonesia began exporting 325 million cubic feet per day (mmcfd) to Singapore via a subsea pipeline from West Natuna under a 22-year contract in 2001. Deliveries of natural gas to Malaysia's Duyong gas platform began in August 2002, under a 20-year contract for 250 mmcfd. Gas sale revenues will likely total $14.2 billion over the life of both contracts. In August 2003, the South Sumatra-Singapore gas pipeline was completed. It will eventually supply 350 mmcfd over a 20-year contract. **Lower Subsidies, New Laws Stimulate Domestic Demand**

Domestically, gas demand comes primarily from fertilizer and petrochemical plants (34%) and the power industry (25%). The GOI has indicated that gas will play a significant role in meeting the country's growing electric power demands. The reduction of fuel subsidies in October 2005, and their elimination for some industrial uses, eased fuel price distortions and made natural gas increasingly competitive as a fuel alternative, stimulating gas demand. The government eliminated the subsidy for industry fuels in 2005 and phased out premium fuel and gasoil subsidies by the end of 2009. In October 2005, state gas company PGN raised industrial gas prices to $4.5 per mmbtu from $3.9 per mmbtu. In January 2009 PGN raised prices again to $5 per mmbtu, and again in 2008 to $5.60 per mmbtu. Even at that price, however, gas was still equivalent to only about 19 cents per liter of diesel oil compared to the industrial diesel oil price of $1.20 per liter or the subsidized auto diesel price of 60 cents per liter.

In May 2008, PGN agreed to increase its gas sales to PLN by 200 million cubic feet per day under a three year contract at a price of $5.60 per mmbtu. Gas will be transmitted from PGN South Sumatra to West Java via pipeline. The Oil and Gas Law of 2001 introduced other changes that encourage domestic gas use. The new law permits direct "free market" negotiations of gas contracts between buyer and seller. Previously, production sharing contractors (PSCs) had to sell their gas to the state-owned petroleum company, Pertamina, which in turn sold the gas to the final buyer. Several PSCs report that the GOI's new direct negotiation mechanism is working well and that the upstream authority BP Migas has generally stayed out of the negotiations, except in cases where either the buyer or seller requested its participation. However, MIGAS recently came out against an expansion of the program. These provisions have raised domestic demand estimates and led to a number of new gas sales agreements. BP Migas estimates that by 2018, Indonesia's domestic gas demand will increase to 2.18 TSCF per year. In 2009, domestic gas demand was 1.35 TSCF with 4% growth projected in 2010. Meanwhile, domestic gas sales reached 0.92 TSCF in 2010, a slight increased from 0.85 TSCF in 2009.

Growing Power Needs Will Drive Gas Demand Power generation needs in Java and Bali will also drive growing domestic gas demand. Over the last several years, peak power demand grew by an average of six percent annually, while power capacity did not increase. Peak loads on the Java-Bali grid (which accounts for of 80 percent of Indonesia's power demand) reached a record high of 16,251 MW in November 2010, and were projected by PLN to reach 16,995 MW in 2008. As a result, PLN acknowledged that their reserve margin declined from 28% in 2003 to 21% in 2008, and are projected to decline to 14% in 2009. (Note: desired reserve margins are normally between 25 and 30 percent. PLN's numbers are based on declared capacity, rather than reliable capacity. Maintenance on plants can bring down actual capacity and reserve margins.) PLN estimates that Indonesia needs over 23,000 MW in new capacity between 2005 and 2015 to prevent a long-term power crisis and restore its power reserve margin. Much of that new capacity will be fueled by gas and coal. PLN plans to raise natural gas use by the power sector from 17% in 2004 to 40% by 2015. By volume, this means an increase from 483 mmcfd to 1.7 billion cubic feet per day (bcfd) in 2015.

Increasing gas consumption in the energy mix makes strong economic sense, particularly with current crude oil price levels. Petroleum-based fuels are expensive – about 6.2 cents per kilowatt hour (kwH), or 2.5 times more costly than gas. PLN spends about $1.6 billion annually on oil-based fuels and estimates it can save up to $1 billion per year by switching to gas. This, however, requires a reliable gas infrastructure and a secure gas supply. The switch is an important element in restoring the financial health of Indonesia's power industry, although low electricity tariffs continue to undermine the industry. At the same time, it also has significant implications for Indonesia's export revenues derived from natural gas. **Impediments to Domestic Gas Growth** In its Energy Blueprint, the Ministry of Energy and Mineral Resources plans to increase gas's proportion in the national energy mix to 30.6% by 2025 from the current 26.5%. However despite changes spurring gas demand, impediments limit domestic gas growth. The primary obstacles include a limited transmission and distribution system, financing limitations, and continued regulatory uncertainty. To address the inadequate state of gas transmission and distribution networks, state gas utility PGN started four new transmission projects to meet rising power sector demands for gas, as follows:

Projects	Length (km)	Capacity (mmscfd)	Comp letion
Grissik – W.Java	661	400	2010
Duri – Medan	521	250	2010
E. Kalimantan -Central Java	1,219	1,100	2010/ 2010
E.Java-W.Java	680	350	2008/ 2010

Source: PGN

In addition to these projects, the GOI is proposing to build an LNG receiving terminal in West Java, to process and distribute gas from existing LNG plants (Bontang), as well as future plants in Papua (Tangguh) and South Sulawesi (Donggi). PGN is extending its distribution network and plans to ship compressed natural gas (CNG) over short to medium distances to remote areas. In addition, PGN is also investigating the feasibility of developing an integrated mini-LNG transportation system. The project will involve a mini-LNG receiving terminal located in Makassar, South Sulawesi, which will ship LNG from the Bontang LNG plant. Many producers require explicit financial guarantees to sell gas domestically. The government's reluctance to provide such guarantees poses another obstacle to domestic gas growth, according to industry observers. In the power industry, a number of PSCs have requested that PLN provide standby letters of credit (SBLC) before investing in long-term gas supply agreements. According to industry analysts, PLN's credit availability with government-linked banks is limited. PLN has asked Bank Indonesia to exclude SBLCs from the legal lending limit to get around this obstacle. Some power analysts suggest that if PLN would permit higher returns on investment, companies would be willing to assume more of this risk themselves. Another constraint to gas development is the absence of a competitive gas pricing system. Under the historic system, prices for gas supply contracts are negotiated on a field-by-field basis between Pertamina and individual producers after the discovery of the gas field. Prices are fixed for a designated supply for the duration of the contract. Hence, the producer's price for gas is different for each PSC. Consumer prices are set on a cost-plus basis.

Currently, the negotiated gas price for power generation is far below the global average, in the range of $4.50 to $6 per mmbtu, compared to current global natural gas prices, which average around $11 per mmbtu in mid-2008. The World Bank and the Asian Development Bank (ADB) have urged Indonesia to adopt a pricing regime that creates greater incentives for companies to find and produce gas. A competitive domestic gas price would allow Indonesia to realize the full value and potential of its gas reserves. Without pricing changes, the domestic gas market provides few incentives for the exploration and development of gas fields that are too small to support LNG but more than adequate for domestic gas customers. A second major constraint is the absence of a predictable basis for forecasting the future value of gas, such as an indexed price formula. A final constraint has been the subsidy provided for alternative fuels. **Regulations Require Clarification** The current regulatory environment sends mixed signals to investors which inhibits the exploration and development of potential gas reserves. Despite domestic market obligation (DMO) provisions in the 2001 Oil and Gas law promoting gas use and the issuance of downstream Regulation 36, industry players still do not see a clear set of "rules of the game." Industry players say that they want clarification of the exact DMO quantity and whether the government will honor existing PSC contracts. In addition, doubts about contract sanctity, contract extensions, security, and taxation hurt the gas investment climate.

The end result of this uncertainty, and the consequent lack of exploration, is stark. According to the American Chamber of Commerce, gas blocks signed before 1971 still account for nearly 60 percent of Indonesia's commercial reserves. Blocks

signed after 1990 account for only 14 percent of commercial reserves. **Expanding Future Production** Indonesia is blessed with abundant reserves, although there is a geographical mismatch between location of gas reserves and energy needs. The Ministry of Energy and Mineral Resources estimates total gas demand between 2008- 2018 will reach 22,200 BSCF, while supply is estimated at 13,231 BSCF. In the long-term, Java's additional gas supply will rely on the development of gas fields outside the island and the completion of pipeline and LNG projects. In addition to geographical constraints, other barriers to developing Indonesia's gas resources include the availability of financing, long project lead-time, and the lack of incentives to explore and exploit gas reserves. Private sector participants identified the following key areas to increase development in the gas sector:

- Increase incentives to find and produce natural gas;
- Harmonize conflicting laws and eliminate the lengthy bureaucratic process for project approval;

- Clarify the gas DMO obligation;
- Promote private investment and ownership, through price stability and an equitable cost recovery mechanism;
- Address gas reliability concerns for those firms that invest in major gas facilities; and
- Provide government guarantees for gas payment by state owned enterprises.

A Trans-ASEAN Gas Pipeline? ASEAN's Energy ministers signed a memorandum of understanding on July 5, 2002 to push ahead with a $7 billion natural gas pipeline project in a bid to alleviate concerns over supply shortages and to improve economic development. Minister of Energy and Mineral Resources Purnomo Yusgiantoro said the project's masterplan has been completed, and a council will soon be established to oversee the completion of the gas grid. Purnomo said more than 1,000 kilometers of the grid have already been constructed. ASEAN has identified the need for 4,500 kilometers of pipeline to complete the project, which might reach 6,000 kilometers, if the necessary new Indonesian domestic pipelines are included. Purnomo said Indonesia will be a major player in the trans-ASEAN gas pipeline project because of its enormous gas reserves. ASEAN members have previously said that a regional natural gas pipeline, as well as an electricity grid, is the most efficient way for ASEAN countries to prevent a future energy crisis. Indonesia has already developed several pipelines - from West Natuna to Singapore, West Natuna to Malaysia, and from South Sumatra to Singapore. It is also studying a possible pipeline from West Natuna to Thailand.

ASEAN members will develop regulations and frameworks for the cross-border supply, transportation and distribution of natural gas throughout the region. This will be supervised by a future ASEAN Gas Consultative Council. The key reason behind the gas grid is the need to reduce oil consumption and to provide backup energy sources for

ASEAN members. ASEAN members hope to complete the gas grid by 2020. However, recent press reports indicate that delays in developing Natuna Block D Alpha have delayed the project. **Integrated Transmission System** The South Sumatra pipeline is part of state gas company PGN's plan for an integrated gas transmission pipeline system, known as the Integrated Gas Transporation System (IGTS). The IGTS will eventually link the islands of Sumatra, Java, and Kalimantan via a 4,200-kilometer integrated gas pipeline. Reputed to be Southeast Asia's longest, the pipeline is being funded by the World Bank, ADB, other institutions, as well as PGN's own internal funding. PGN's network will flow 2.2 bcfd of natural gas after its scheduled completion in 2010. ***Project One - Grissik-Duri Pipeline*** Phase One became operational in 1998. The 544-kilometer Grissik/Duri gas transmission pipeline transports 310 mmcfd of natural gas from the Grissik gas plant in ConocoPhillips Indonesia's Corridor PSC in South Sumatra. The project will supply Caltex's Duri Steam Flood Project in Central Sumatra for 15 years. ConocoPhillips is the producer, Caltex is the buyer, and PGN is the pipeline network owner.

The Grissik/Duri pipeline project is the first part of an 850-kilometer gas transmission pipeline to link South Sumatra to Singapore. Phase Two, which covers a 530-kilometer leg from Grissik to Singapore by way of Batam Island, was completed in August 2003. Both the Grissik/Duri pipeline and the Grissik/Singapore pipeline have been included in the TransgasIndo pipeline consortium, jointly owned and operated by PGN and a joint venture among ConocoPhillips, Petronas, Talisman, and Singapore Petroleum. ***Project Two: South Sumatra–West Java Pipeline*** This 1,100-kilometer pipeline project provides gas from ConocoPhillips and Pertamina fields in Sumatra to West Java power plants and industrial users. A combination of JBIC loans and proceeds from a PGN bond and IPO offerings funded the construction, which was completed in 2010. Phase I of the project involved construction of a 450 kilometers pipeline from Pagardewa, South Sumatra to Cilegon and Serpong, West Java. Phase I provides 250 mmcfd of gas from Pertamina's Pagardewa gas field and ConocoPhillips' Grissik field to the Muara Tawar, Tanjung Priok and Muara Karang gas-fired power plants in Jakarta. Phase II connects Grissik to

Pagardewa via a 270 km pipeline, a parallel line from Pagardewa to Labuhan Maringgai and a 190 km pipeline from Labuhan Maringgai to Muara Bekasi, and Rawamaju in West Java. Phase II can provide up to 600 mmcfd. PGN completed the procurement tender for the project in 2005 and finished construction two months ahead of schedule in October 2010. This pipeline supplies natural gas from Pertamina's gas fields in Prabumulih to West Java industrial users.

In September 2010, the downstream regulator announced a tender worth $269 million for a 220 km extension of the pipeline from Muara Bekas to Cirebon. The government closed bidding for the

project in February 2008 and aims to have gas flowing by 2010. ***Project Three: East Kalimantan-Central Java*** The most ambitious of the five projects, the 1,200-kilometer East Kalimantan-Java pipeline would transport up to 1.1 bcfd of gas through a combined offshore and onshore pipeline stretching from Kuala Badak, East Kalimantan to Semarang, Central Java. PGN would partially fund the project from a bond and IPO offering. At an estimated cost of $1.2 billion, PGN will need substantial outside financing. PGN completed the feasibility study of the project and announced the tender in December 2005. PT Bakrie Brothers won the tender in July 2009 and has been seeking financing and gas commitments since that time. Consequently, PGN did not meet its original target to begin project construction in 2010. It is doubtful that they will meet their other goal of flowing first gas in 2010, according to industry analysts and media reports. ***Project Four: East/West Java Pipeline*** This proposed project will involve construction of a 730 kilometers pipeline stretching from Gresik (East Java) to Cirebon and Muara Bekasi (West Java) along with a 300-kilometer East and Central Java distribution link. The pipeline will have the capacity to transport about 700 mmcfd of natural gas and cost an estimated $540 million. Currently PGN plans for project construction to start in 2008 with completion in 2010. ***Project Five: Duri – Dumai – Medan Pipeline***

An extension of the Grissik-Duri project, the 521-kilometer pipeline will transport gas from Duri, Riau to Medan, North Sumatra. The project will be the northern extension of an integrated Sumatra transmission network and supply gas to Asahan Power. PGN, Kondur Petroleum and Asahan Power signed an MOU in October 2004 for the sale of 80-140 mmcfd gas through the pipeline. PGN plans to finance the estimated $574 million project via internal and external finance lending. In March 2008, PGN pushed back the start date for construction to sometime in 2009.

INDONESIA OIL AND GAS SECTOR STRATEGIC AND PRACTICAL INFORMATION

INSTITUTIONAL FRAMEWORK

"All natural resources in the soil and the waters of the country are under the jurisdiction of the State and shall be used for the greatest benefit and welfare of the People."

-Article 33, Indonesian Constitution

The Indonesian Parliament (Dewan Perwakilan Rakyat – DPR) passed the oil and gas bill into law on October 23, 2001. The new law replaced Oil and Gas Law No. 44/1960 and Law for Pertamina No. 8/1971. It reduces the government's power over the petroleum sector and allows for open competition in the downstream oil and gas distributing and marketing area. The new law authorizes the establishment of an implementation agency ("badan pelaksana") and regulatory agency ("badan peraturan") to assume state oil and gas company Pertamina's roles. The implementation agency has replaced Pertamina in managing Production Sharing Contract (PSCs) with private oil and gas companies, thus eliminating the conflict-of-interest inherent when upstream producer Pertamina regulated the activity of its competitors. The law also removed Pertamina's monopoly in the downstream sector with the regulatory agency assuming the responsibility for managing natural gas and domestic fuel distribution and supply.

The GOI generally met the law's stipulation that the two new agencies be established within one year of the law's enactment, and that Pertamina establish itself as a limited liability company ("persero") within two years (see below).

Pertamina will maintain its overall responsibility for domestic fuel supply and distribution until December 31, 2009. Existing PSC's will be grandfathered and in effect until expiration of the contract. By the end of 2003, the GOI had issued three of five required implementing regulations under the law covering Pertamina's transition to a limited liability company, and the establishment of the implementing and regulatory agencies. By October 2004, the government issued the remaining two implementing regulations, on the upstream and downstream sectors.

All energy activities dealing with petroleum and gas fall under the Ministry of Energy and Mineral Resources, which is charged with creating and implementing Indonesia's energy policy. The Ministry of Energy and Mineral Resources is divided into several directorates, with the Directorate General of Oil and Gas (MIGAS) responsible for all aspects of petroleum industry development, including employee training and promulgating regulations.

BP MIGAS

On July 16, 2002, President Megawati signed Government Regulation No 42/2002, establishing an implementing body for oil and gas upstream operations, Badan Pelaksana Minyak dan Gas Bumi (BP Migas), as required by Oil and Gas Law No 22/2001. This upstream implementing body has taken over Pertamina's regulatory functions and responsibilities in managing oil and gas contractors.

BP Migas has managed upstream regulatory activities since mid-2002. However it lacked implementing regulations until 2004 when the GOI issued Regulation 35 under the Oil and Gas Law 22/2001.

BP Migas' main responsibilities are to: 1) provide recommendations to the Minister in preparing and offering work areas and cooperation contracts; 2) sign cooperation contracts; 3) control upstream business operations and 4) appoint sellers of the government's share of oil and gas.

BP Migas is a non-profit state legal entity and acts on behalf of the government as party to the cooperation contract with business entities. At the same time it also controls all oil and gas business operations.

BP Migas is led by a chairman and vice chairman, assisted by five expert staff and four main operational divisions—planning, operations, finance and marketing, and general affairs. The chairman is appointed by the President, based on the recommendation of the Minister of Energy and Mineral Resources after approval by the House of Representatives (DPR). The Chairman must periodically report to the President (every six months or as requested), via the Minister of Energy and Mineral Resources. The agency must also report and gives copies of signed Production Sharing Contracts to the DPR.

BPHMIGAS

On December 30, 2002 President Megawati Sukarnoputri signed Government Regulation (PP) 67/2002 establishing a new downstream regulatory body, the Badan Pengatur Hilir Minyak dan Gas Bumi (BPH Migas), which assumed the role of Pertamina in controlling downstream activities. BPH Migas was given the responsibility to regulate, develop and supervise the downstream industry. However BPH Migas lacked implementing regulations until 2004 when the GOI issued Regulation 36 for the downstream activities laid out in Oil and Gas Law 22/2001.

BPH Migas' broad responsibilities are to: 1) regulate and determine the supply and distribution of oil-based fuel, 2) regulate the transmission and distribution of natural gas, 3) allocate fuel to meet national fuel oil reserve goals, 4) plan the use of oil and gas transportation and storage facilities, 5) set gas pipeline tariffs, 6) set natural gas prices for household and small consumers, 7) recommend pipeline levies, and 8) set the price of pipeline rights.

BPH Migas has the regulatory and development responsibilities to: 1) issue business licenses, 2) determine fuel types and standards for retail sale, 3) formulate strategic reserves policies, 4) determine price formulas for subsidized fuel, 4) protect occupational health and safety, 5) ensure environmental protection, and 6) promote community development. The agency is also charged with developing the master plan for national gas transmission and distribution. It also ensures the availability and distribution of fuel oil, and monitors reserves, market share and trading volumes.

BPH Migas is a smaller body than its upstream counterpart, BP Migas. BPH Migas consists of a committee of nine (one Chairman and eight members). Committee members are appointed by the President, based on the recommendation of the Minister of Energy and Mineral Resources after approval by the House of Representatives (DPR). The Chairman must periodically report to the President (every six months or as requested), via the Minister of Energy and Mineral Resources.

PERTAMINA

On June 18, 2003, President Megawati Sukarnoputri signed government regulation (PP) No. 31/2003 to transform the state oil and gas company Pertamina into a limited liability company (Persero). The objective of the new regulation was to establish a competitive and efficient entity, thereby increasing economic activity and the welfare of the people.

Under the new regulation, all state assets belonging to Pertamina are to serve as the capital of the new entity. The Minister of Finance based on a joint evaluation by the Minister of Energy and Mineral Resources and the Minister of Finance determined the amount of capital allocated to the new entity. The restructured Pertamina has authority from the government to supply fuel oils for domestic consumption, with compensation to be provided by the government. The regulation also gave Pertamina all the state's geothermal power assets with the proviso that they be handed over within two years to a new subsidiary. Pertamina said it plans to form a new subsidiary this year, PT Geothermal Energy, to manage those assets.

Pertamina significantly contributes to Indonesia's petroleum output. It ranks 6th in crude oil production and was Indonesia's 3rd largest producer of natural gas in 2004. Pertamina executives have expressed their determination to enhance Pertamina's position in the newly deregulated upstream sector.

In the down stream sector, Pertamina will maintain its monopoly on the distribution of subsidized fuel products throughout the archipelago until December 31, 2009. President Susilo Bambang Yudhoyono delayed full downstream fuel market deregulation by issuing Regulation 71/2005 on November 16, 2005 which extended Pertamina's public service obligation (PSO) due to the lack of interest by other qualified companies.

In 2004, Pertamina suspended its operation in Block 3, Western Desert, Iraq due to political uncertainty. The company however, says that it wishes to resume exploration activity there as soon as the contract is ratified and the environment is permissive. Pertamina also ventured into Libya, where it won two exploration contracts in October 2005 for Block 17-3 on the Mediterranean Sea and Block 123-3 on the Sahara desert. Pertamina said it targeted Libya for investment to increase its resource base and to develop professionalism and credibility in the global oil business. The company reported provisional earnings of Rp 11.3 trillion ($120 million) in 2005, almost double its annual target. The company said its upstream subsidiary, Pertamina E&P plans to invest up to $100 million and drill 120 wells in 2009 to boost its oil and gas production.

GOVERNMENT AGREEMENTS AND CONTRACTS

Indonesia has two categories of agreements and contracts for its petroleum industry. The first category refers to the bundle of rights and obligations granted to an investor to invest in cooperation with the GOI in oil and gas exploration and exploitation. These types of contracts are the Production Sharing Contract (PSC), the Technical Assistance Contract (TAC), and the Enhanced Oil Recovery (EOR) contract, defined as follows:

Production Sharing Contracts:

- A cooperation contract for oil and gas exploration between BP Migas and a private investor (which includes foreign and domestic companies, as well as PT Pertamina);
- BP Migas is the supervisor or manager of the PSC;
- Investors are participating interest holders and Contractors;
- The government take is under a production sharing arrangement whereby the GOI and the Contractors take a split of the production measure in revenue based on PSC-agreed percentages;
- Operating costs are recovered from production through Contractor cost oil formulas as defined by the PSC;
- The Contractor has the right to take and separately dispose of its share of oil and gas;
- Title of the hydrocarbons passes to the Contractor at the export or delivery point.

Technical Assistance Contracts:

- Variation of a cooperation contract, or PSC;
- Typically used for established producing areas and therefore usually covers exploitation only;
- BP Migas is the supervisor or manager of the TAC;

- Operating costs are recovered from production;
- The Contractor does not typically share in production;
- The TAC can cover both exploitation and exploration if it involves an area where the GOI has encouraged exploration;
- In accord with Oil and Gas Law 22/2001, existing TACs will not be extended.

Enhanced Oil Recovery:

- Variation of a cooperation contract, or PSC;
- Used for established producing fields with the intent of applying advanced technology to increase the recovery of hydrocarbons in the reservoirs;
- Pertamina is usually a participant, along with investors; collectively they are the Contractor;
- BP Migas is the supervisor and manager of the EOR;
- Operating costs are recovered from production and typically capped at a percentage. In some cases, the incremental oil lifted from an EOR operation may be shared on a production sharing basis;
- In many cases, the EOR may also include provisions concerning how the parties will conduct petroleum operations.

In addition to contracts that give bundles of rights to explore and exploit, the participants in the PSC, TAC or EOR may also enter into separate agreements to discuss how they are going to conduct petroleum operations. These are known as Joint Operating Agreements (JOA) and Joint Operating Bodies (JOB), defined as follows:

Joint Operating Agreements:

- A separate agreement in addition to the cooperation contract;
- Governs the relations of the participating interest holders, defining their rights and obligations, and describing the procedures the Contractors will abide by;
- The JOA typically includes: 1) the scope of operations; 2) designation, rights and obligations of the operator; 3) establishment of an Operating Committee; 4) production disposition; 5) relinquishment, withdrawal and assignment; 6) confidentiality; 7) force majeure; and 8) dispute resolution and choice of law.

Joint Operating Bodies:

- Typically part of the JOA;
- Governs the operations on behalf of the participating interest holders by establishing a non-legal entity, the JOB, to conduct petroleum operations;
- Representatives of the participating interest parties appoint representatives to the JOB;
- The JOB prepares an operating work program and budgets and carries out operations pursuant to the JOB agreement and the cooperation contract;
- Participating interest holders remain the Contractors;
- JOAs are supervised by BP Migas.

FISCAL DECENTRALIZATION LAW

With implementation of a new fiscal decentralization law in January 2001, revenue-sharing formulas came into effect that directed 15 percent of the Indonesian Government's net oil revenues and 30 percent of its net natural gas revenues to provincial and district governments. The GOI's net oil and gas revenues refer to profit after cost recovery and deduction of the PSC share. Of the 15 percent of the oil revenue flowing to the regions, 6 percentage points will go to the regency of origin (where the PSC is located), 6 percentage points will be shared among the other regencies in the province, and 3 percentage points will go to the provincial government.

The same relative shares apply to gas revenues – 12 percent to the regency of origin, 12 percent among the remaining regencies and 6 percent to the provincial government.

OPEC

Indonesia joined OPEC in 1962 as active member and hosted important OPEC conferences in 1964, 1976, 1980 and 1997. OPEC member countries meet at least twice a year to coordinate their production policies in light of market fundamental. Organization of Petroleum Exporting Countries (OPEC) produce about 38 percent of the world's oil and 50 percent of the oil traded internationally. During 2004, Indonesian Minister of Energy and Mineral Resources Purnomo Yusgiantoro held the rotating OPEC presidency.

In an effort to control oil price volatility and anticipate strengthening crude prices, the Extraordinary Consultative Meeting of the Conference of the OPEC Oil Ministers in June 2005 agreed to raise production by 500,000 barrels per day to 28 million barrels per day, effective July 1, 2005. This was due to concern of possible shortages due to shortage of effective refining capacity and based on a forecast increase in oil demand in 2005. In addition, OPEC has also called upon non-OPEC members to join efforts in maintaining market stability. OPEC, through five increases, raised production quota by 4.5 million b/d from 23.5 million b/d to 28.0 million b/d since April 2004. Indonesia received a 233,000 b/d quota increase to 1.451 million b/d, although actual output is closer to 1 million b/d.

OPEC quota

(in million b/d)

Members	Apr-04	Jul-04	Agust-04	Nop-04	Mar-05	Jul-05
Algeria	750	814	830	862	878	894
Indonesia	**1.218**	**1.322**	**1.347**	**1.399**	**1.425**	**1.451**
Iran	3.450	3.744	3.817	3.964	4.037	4.110
Iraq	-	-	-	-	-	-
Kuwait	1.886	2.046	2.087	2.167	2.207	2.247
Libya	1.258	1.365	1.392	1.446	1.473	1.500
Nigeria	1.936	2.101	2.142	2.224	2.265	2.306
Qatar	609	661	674	700	713	726
S.Arabia	7.638	8.288	8.450	8.775	8.937	9.099
UAE	2.051	2.225	2.269	2.356	2.400	2.444
Venezuela	2.704	2.934	2.992	3.107	3.165	3.223
Total	23.500	25.500	26.000	27.000	27.500	28.000

Source: OPEC

The Ministry of Energy and Mineral Resources has stated that Indonesia intends to remain an OPEC member despite its falling net oil export volumes. As Indonesia finds it increasingly difficult to maintain a net exporter status, industry observers will likely continue to question whether the country should keep its OPEC membership.

OTHER PROFESSIONAL BODIES

IPA

Indonesian and foreign oil companies operating in Indonesia established the Indonesian Petroleum Association (IPA) in 1971 in response to growing foreign interest in the Indonesian oil sector. Contractors and the government meet frequently to discuss matters such as production ventures and energy economics. The IPA's objective is to use public information to promote the exploration, production, refining and marketing aspects of Indonesia's petroleum industry.

IGA

Pertamina and key gas producers Mobil and Huffco sponsored the establishment of the Indonesian Gas Association (IGA) in 1980. The main objective of IGA is to provide a forum to discuss matters relating to natural gas and to advance knowledge, research and development in the areas of gas technology. IGA also aims to promote the development of infrastructure and cooperation among producing, transporting, consuming and regulatory segments of the gas industry.

The IGA and the IPA sponsored Indonesia's membership in the Permanent Council of the World Petroleum Congress (WPC).

CRUDE OIL

RESERVES AND PRODUCTION

In 2005 Indonesia ranked twentieth among world oil producers, with approximately 1.4 percent of the world's daily production. The GOI places Indonesia's crude oil reserves at 8.6 billion barrels, with proven reserves of
4.3 billion barrels and potential reserves of 4.3 billion barrels. These figures are 5 percent lower than in 2003. Oil exports were an unofficial $8.2 billion in 2005. Preliminary total oil and gas exports (including LNG) were $19.2 billion in 2005, compared with $16.3 billion in 2004—24.5 percent of Indonesia's export earnings, up from 23.8 percent in 2003.

In 2005, Indonesia's overall crude oil production continued to decline to an unofficial 1.06 million b/d, falling short of its 1.08 million b/d target. Indonesia produced well below its OPEC crude production quota of 1.451 million b/d (without condensate), as a result of declining investment and maturing oil fields.

In 2004 Indonesia produced 1.094 million b/d, consisting 0.966 million b/d of crude and 128,600 b/d of condensate. This was a 4.6 percent drop from the 2001 level of 1.147 million b/d (1.013 million b/d for crude and 133,800 b/d for condensate). Almost all oil producers (Chevron, CNOOC, BP, Petrochina, Pertamina, Vico, and ConocoPhillips) reported declines. Continued sluggish investment and a decrease in new exploration were key factors behind the decline. PT Chevron Pacific Indonesia's production, which accounted for 46.3 percent of the country's crude oil production in 2004, remained stable during 2003 and 2004 at almost 506,900 b/d. Total Indonesia took over from Chinese National Offshore Oil Corporation (CNOOC) as second largest oil producer in 2004 with 7.5 percent of production.

The GOI is renewing its commitment to increase output in its energy blueprint. It has set a target of 1.3 million b/d production target by 2009. BPMIGAS believes new production from several existing PSCs will reverse the decline, citing amongst others, Pertamina (Salawati), Petrochina (Jabung and Sukowati), Total Indonesie (Peciko) in the short term and ExxonMobil (Cepu) and Santos (Jeruk) in the medium term.

Table: Crude and Condensate Production by major producers (1,000 Barrels/Day)

Company 2003	2004	Change (%)
Caltex* 506.9	507.0	0.0
Total 81.1	81.8	0.8
CNOOC 94.9	81.5	-14.2
Unocal* 53.9	55.7	3.3
Exspan 66.4	54.0	-18.6
Pertamina 43.6	48.4	10.9
ConocoPhilips 51.4	44.1	-14.2
Petrochina 40.5	36.6	-9.7
BP 38.8	31.3	-19.4
Bumi Siak Pusako 32	30.0	-6.2
Vico 32.3	28.8	-10.8
ExxonMobil 25.4	21.2	-16.5
Others 79.6	74.1	-6.9
Total Indonesia 1146.8	1,094.4	-4.6

Note: *Changed to Chevron after merger.

EXPLORATION AND INVESTMENT

Of an estimated 60 oil basins, approximately 22 have been extensively explored. Most oil exploration is currently being carried out in the basins of Western Indonesia under PSCs. The bulk of Indonesia's oil reserves are located onshore and offshore in Central Sumatra and Kalimantan. The GOI has placed increased emphasis on developing oil reserves in remote locations, such as

Papua, where proven and potential reserves are estimated at 109.1 million barrels.

The oil and gas industry today faces several crucial problems, particularly in the upstream sector, due to aging oil and gas assets and investment climate uncertainties. Officials hope oil contractors will aggressively increase exploration activities to look for new reserves. With no significant oil discoveries in western Indonesia in the last 10 years, the government hopes eastern Indonesia's frontier and deep-sea areas may contain sizable oil reserves.

The number of exploration drilling wells completed in 2004 dropped sharply to 36, consisting of 12 wildcat wells and

appraisal wells. The associated success ratio (successful wells versus wells drilled) reached 61.1 percent, up from 42.4 percent in 2003 and 33 percent in 2002.

Pertamina and BP Migas reported that several oil companies shelved a number of investment plans in 2004 due to issues including contract sanctity, regional autonomy, security, manpower, taxes, and uncertainty surrounding the implementing regulations for the Oil and Gas Law. Oil companies' expenditures have slowly moved up again since 2002 owing mainly to increases in production expenditures. According to the Energy Ministry's Oil and Gas Directorate (MIGAS), oil companies spent a total of $5.6 billion in 2004, a 4.8 percent increase from the 2003 total of $5.3 billion.

Seismic Activities

According to MIGAS, a total of 15,041 kilometers of combined 2-D and 3-D seismic activities were carried out in 2004, continuing the steady downward trend since the 1997 peak.

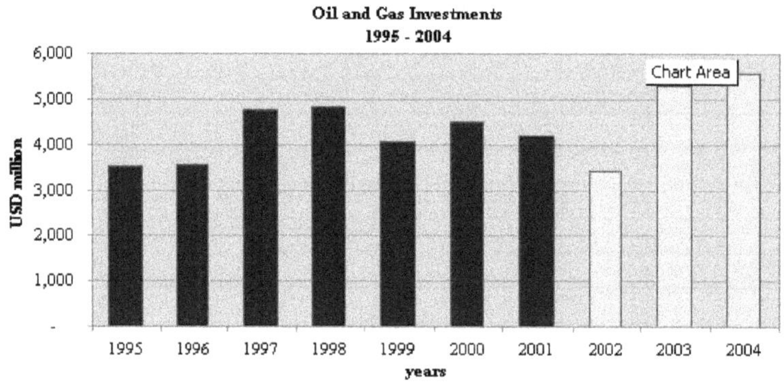

EXPLORATION BLOCKS AWARDED

The government awarded 9 oil and gas exploration blocks in 2005, compared with sixteen in 2004 and fifteen in 2003. All of the blocks awarded in August 2005 were through a direct bidding process. Four of the 13 direct offer blocks remain unsold: North East Madura V, North Bali II, Taritip and Amborip V. Winners in the direct bidding round were predominantly local oil companies, some with little previous experience.

The nine contracts in 2005 went to Lhokseumawe (Zaratex NV), West Kampar (Sumatra Persada Energi), Bungamas (Erry Guna), Bengkulu (Commissioning Services Indonesia), Citarum (Bunga Parahyangan Ranhill Energia), NE Madura IV (Energi Timur Jauh), Sebatik (Star Energy), Amborip VI (ConocoPhillips), and Wailawi (BUMD Benuo Taka). Exploration commitments by the winners totaled $102.5 million with signing bonuses to the government totaling $7.9 million.

In June 2005, the government offered 14 oil and gas blocks through regular tender and 13 through direct tender. On June 2, 2009 the GOI announced winners for seven of the 14 regular tender. The GOI said it received 15 bids for the 7 blocks, as well as three non-conforming bids on the Cakalang, Buton I and Buton II blocks. There were no bidders on the other seven blocks.

The direct bidding round is one of the Government's revamped procedures for exploration and production contracts in a bid to increase their attractiveness. Previously, oil and gas companies could only receive a concession through an official tender. Now, the government accepts proposals for blocks without waiting for a formal bidding session. Under this special bidding process, after a company applies to acquire a new exploration block, the government invites other bidders to participate. If no other bidder emerges within a set timeframe, the government grants the block to the sole bidder. The government also offered new, more attractive terms and conditions for new exploration blocks in 2005. Winning PSCs would get between 20 and 35 percent splits for oil and between 30 and 40 percent for gas. Under previous PSC terms, companies generally receive a 15 percent split for oil and 30 percent split for gas. The government also set first tranche petroleum (FTP) obligations at 10 percent.

MERGERS AND ACQUISITIONS

US based Chevron acquired Unocal in August 2005, strengthening its position as Indonesia's largest oil producer.

Caltex and Unocal both assumed the Chevron name but continue to conduct operational activities under separate subsidiaries.

In August 2004, Indonesia's largest oil and gas company, Medco Energi International completed acquisition of Novus Petroleum Limited, a company listed in the Australian Stock Exchange with assets in the Middle East, United States, Australia and Indonesia. The acquisition led to the change of Novus' directors as it cut its global assets.

Mergers:

- Chevron and Unocal, Aug 2005.
- Conoco & Phillips - ConocoPhillips, Sept 2002.
- Chevron & Texaco – ChevronTexaco, Sept 2001
- Santa Fe Snyder & Devon – Devon Energy Corp, Aug 2000.
- BP Amoco & Arco – BP, Apr 2000.
- TotalFina & Elf – TotalFinaElf Sam, Feb 2000.
- Exxon & Mobil – ExxonMobil Corp, Nov 1999.
- El Paso & Sonat – El Paso Energy Corp, Oct 1999.
- Total & Fina – TotalFina, Jun 1999.
- Lasmo & Monument – Lasmo Plc, Jun 1999.
    - Santa Fe & Snyder – Santa Fe Snyder Corp, May 1999.
    - Nisseki & Mitsubishi Oil Co. – Nisseki Mitsubishi Abushild, Apr 1999.
- Kerr McGee & Oryx – Kerr McGee Corp, Feb 1999.
- BP & Amoco – BP Amoco Plc, Jan 1999.
- British Borneo & Hardy – British Borneo Oil & Gas Plc, Oct 1998.
- Ocean Energy & Seagull – Ocean Energy Inc, Jun 1997.

Takeovers:

- Medco Energi – Novus Petroleum, August 2004
- Conoco - Gulf Indonesia Resources, July 2002
- CNOOC - YPFMaxus, Jan 2002.
- PetroChina - Devon Energy, April 2002
- Husky Oil Ltd. – Renaissance energy, Aug 2000.
- Canadian Natural Resources – Ranger Oil, July 2000.
- Fortune (Indo Pacific) – GFB Resources (Java) Ltd, Jul 2000.
- Agip – British Borneo, May 2000.
- Singapore Petroleum Company Ltd – LL&E Indonesia, Jan 2000.
- Maple/Matrix – GFB Resources (Langsa) Ltd, Jan 2000.

THE FUTURE

Pundits had forecast Indonesia's imminent shift from net oil exporter to net importer for several years. Those predictions were finally realized on a monthly basis in 2004. A steady decline in production, coupled with lower exploration investment levels, accelerated the transition ahead of consensus forecasts. However, with substantial reserves of natural gas and coal, Indonesia remains a net energy exporter. The March 2009 agreement between ExxonMobil and Pertamina to begin development of the Cepu bloc and the nine percent drop in domestic petroleum consumption following the October 2005 price hikes may bring Indonesia back into the net exporter camp when official figures for 2005-2009 are released. To maintain momentum, however, industry observers encouraged the GOI to implement legislation and policies that will rationalize use of Indonesia's energy resources.

A 2005 industry survey conducted by the IPA and PricewaterhouseCoopers concluded that Indonesia's oil and gas industry is at a critical juncture. Survey participants lauded positive government efforts toward improving the investment climate in the upstream industry, such as improved fiscal incentives, the development of an overall energy blueprint, and an improving gas pipeline infrastructure.

Industry representatives said, however, that Indonesia should improve its fiscal terms for oil and gas production for both mature and frontier areas. Often the balance between risk and reward is generally viewed as insufficient to attract major exploration funds. These problems are exacerbated by small reserve accumulations and high infrastructure costs. To address these concerns, the Minister of Energy and Mineral Resources issued Regulation 8/2005 in April 2005, which gave contractors developing marginal oil field an additional 20% reimbursement in cost recovery. In its 2005 bidding round the government offered also a more favorable contractor production split of 70/30 (government/contractor) and 60/40 for oil and gas respectively.

As part of its Energy Blueprint, Indonesia renewed its intention to achieve a production target of 1.3 million b/d by 2009. Industry leaders say that five actions by the GOI are crucial to reach this production target:

- Harmonizing conflicting laws and regulations, including the timely implementation of regulations;
- Improved teamwork, coordination and cooperation amongst GOI entities;
- Implementing judicial reform;
- Changing the regulatory paradigm to a "shared economic interest" model;
- Completely eliminating fuel subsidies and implementing an effective gas regulatory environment.

PSC UPDATE

CHEVRON consolidated and renamed its Indonesian business unit to Chevron IndoAsia in 2005, which includes former Caltex and Unocal operations. Both Caltex and Unocal now operate under the Chevron brand names, Chevron Pacific Indonesia (CPI) and Chevron East Kalimantan (CEK), respectively.

CPI is the single largest crude oil producer in Indonesia, accounting for almost 50 percent of the country's total production. CPI averaged 507,900 b/d and produced 34.8 BCF of gas in 2004. Most of CPI's production and operations are located in Riau province, Central Sumatra. The majority of the firm's production came from the Rokan PSC in the Duri and Minas fields. CPI also holds a 100% interest in the Kisaran block, which it acquired from the government in 2001. Outside Central Sumatra, Chevron has a 25% non-operating interest in the South Natuna Sea Block B, operated by ConocoPhillips.

In contrast with CPI, Chevron East Kalimantan (previously Unocal) leads in the exploration of Indonesia's deepwater resources with the majority of its operations located offshore. Following the merger, Chevron strengthened its position as the country's leading producer for both onshore and offshore exploration. During 2004, CEK produced 55,700 b/d of oil and condensate and a total of 124.2 BCF of gas. The acquisition added interests in 12 offshore PSCs in areas covering approximately 7 million acres and a supply contract with Bontang LNG plant.

CEK continues exploration and appraisal drillings to add to its oil and gas reserves. CEK operated Indonesia's first deep water project, the West Seno field, in the Makassar Strait PSC, offshore East Kalimantan. The field began production in 2003 and is expected to peak at 60,000 bpd and 150 mmcfd of gas when the second phase of the project is completed. The field produced 16,700 b/d of oil and 3.3 BCF of natural gas in 2004. Chevron also plans to develop the

Sadewa gas field (150-600 BCF reserves), which is expected to come online in 2010 – 2008. In the mid-term, CEK hopes to begin production at Gendalo in 2010 and Gehem in 2008.

CEK currently pipes about 150 mmcfd to the Bontang LNG plant, but, the company predicts gas production could reach 800 mmcfd or greater by 2011. A variety of sources could absorb future gas production: Bontang's planned ninth LNG production train, a proposed LNG regasification facility in Java, or a proposed East Kalimantan-Java gas pipeline (2010).

Chevron's downstream activities include sales of paraxylene, benzene and fuel catalysts to refineries in Java, and the company enjoys a sizable domestic market share of lubricants and fuel additives. Chevron is currently assessing the impact of recent deregulation for possible new opportunities in refining, distributing, and marketing its downstream products.

In the electric power business, Chevron Geothermal and Power replaced Amoseas Indonesia in 2004 as operator of the Darajat geothermal plant in West Java. In 2005 Chevron inaugurated the construction of its Darajat complex expansion, the 110 megawatt Darajat III. Darajat III is expected to start operation in the third quarter of 2009 and sell power to PLN. From the Unocal merger, Chevron acquired another geothermal facility in Gunung Salak, Central Java. In addition, the company also operates a 270 MW co-generation facility in North Duri to support its Central Sumatra activities.

EXXONMOBIL was created from the merger of Exxon and Mobil in November 1999, leading to the consolidation of Exxon, Esso, and Mobil operations in Indonesia. ExxonMobil (EM) celebrated 100 years of doing business in Indonesia in 1998, including 30 years as a production-sharing contractor, 20 years as a producer of liquefied natural gas and 10 years as a producer of liquefied petroleum gas.

One of ExxonMobil's largest endeavors during 2004 - 2009 was its effort to extend its TAC for the Cepu block in East Java. In March 2009, ExxonMobil and Pertamina signed a joint operating agreement which will pave the way to begin production in the block, possibly as early as 2008. Through purchases and acquisitions, ExxonMobil holds and operates a 100% participating interest under a production sharing arrangement awarded by Pertamina in 1990. ExxonMobil has invested over $400 million in Cepu. EM has made a significant discovery at Banyu-Urip, with estimated resources in excess of 300 million barrels of oil and significant volumes of gas. ExxonMobil proposes a $2.6 billion capital investment to fully develop the block. The company estimates peak crude oil production will be 171,000 b/d. Major gas supplies could be available for sale to meet existing shortfalls in East and Central Java. The company estimates the project would generate annual gross revenues between $700 million and $1.2 billion at peak production.

Cepu extension talks between ExxonMobil, Pertamina and the GOI lagged for the past five years. In 2005, Pertamina and ExxonMobil made progress, signing a new cooperation contract for the Cepu block, where each holds 45 percent interest in the block. In March 2009, ExxonMobil and Pertamina resolved a disagreement with EM securing the lead to develop the project and Pertamina executives playing key roles. The successful conclusion of the Cepu deal will provide substantial economic benefits to Indonesia and East and Central Java and will send a positive signal to foreign investors.

In North Sumatra, ExxonMobil's natural gas operations include the Arun, Pase, South Lhoksukon, and North Sumatra Offshore fields, which supply gas to the Arun LNG plant. Gas supply from the field is declining and not sufficient to meet export commitments and supply the local fertilizer industry in Sumatra. The government has requested that ExxonMobil divert some of its production to supply the fertilizer plants even at the cost of the GOI having to purchase LNG cargoes from the world spot market to meet its contractual export commitments.

ExxonMobil has a 50 percent participating interest in A-Block (ConocoPhillips is operator). In 2005, ExxonMobil announced plan to divest its interest in A-Block. The company also sold its 68 percent interest in the Madura Strait PSC to Husky Energy in 2004.

BP is one of the largest foreign investors in Indonesia. Through partnerships with upstream authority BP Migas, BP has invested over $5 billion in its Indonesian operations over the last 34 years. After acquiring Arco's assets in 2000, every BP business stream—exploration and production, chemicals, downstream and solar—is represented in the company's Indonesia operations.

In Java, BP realigned its strategy to concentrate on its West Java assets. BP operates the Offshore North West Java PSC (with a 46% interest), which averaged 30,000 b/d of crude oil and 225 mmbtu/d of gas during 2004. BP currently supplies 65% of the West Java gas market. In 2004 BP shed almost all of its East Java assets, including its 100 percent interests in Kangean and Muriah PSC.

BP is the major shareholder and operator of the Tangguh LNG project, which encompasses three PSCs in the Berau-Bintuni Bay region of western Papua. The Tangguh gas fields contain 14.4 trillion cubic feet (TCF) of proven and certified natural gas reserves. The planned LNG processing plant will produce 7.6 million metric tons of LNG per year from two initial processing trains starting in 2008 - 2009.

Following final Indonesian government approval in March 2005, BP appointed a consortium of Kellogg Brown Root (KBR), JGC Corporation, and PT Pertafenikki, as contractors to build the Tangguh project. The project has already obtained four market commitments for
7.65 million tons (MT) of Tangguh LNG per annum -- 2.6 MT of LNG per year to China's Fujian province for a 25 year term beginning 2010, 1.35 MT of LNG per year to South Korea's K Power and POSCO for a 20-year term beginning 2009, and 3.7 MT of LNG per year to Sempra Energy's proposed LNG receiving terminal in the West Coast for a 20-year term beginning in 2008. (Until Tangguh becomes operational LNG will likely come from the Bontang LNG facility in East Kalimantan). The GOI and BP also hope to ink new LNG supply contracts with Japan.

Through a joint venture with ENI, BP also has a 50 percent interest in VICO, Indonesia's fourth largest gas producers with gross production of 330 BCF and 28 mmbd. VICO operates the Sanga Sanga PSC in East Kalimantan, which supplies 20 percent of the gas for the Bontang LNG facility. In the downstream sector, BP distributes lubricants under the Castrol brand and produces purified terephthalic acid (PTA) in cooperation with Mitsui Chemicals and Mitsui & Co.

CONOCOPHILLIPS continues to streamline and refocus its Indonesian operations following the August 2002 merger of Conoco Inc. and Phillips Petroleum. The merger followed then- Conoco Inc.'s acquisition of Gulf Canada Resources in 2001. The company since changed its investment criteria to focus on three core areas in Indonesia: South Sumatra, South Natuna Sea and East Java. In 2003, Conoco Phillips Indonesia sold its share of the Kakap PSC (31.25 percent interest), Sebuku PSC, Makassar Strait (100 percent) and Tungkal PSC, South Sumatra (100 percent). Currently ConocoPhillips owns 13 production sharing contracts (PSCs), eight of which are operated by the company, and a 14 percent participating interest in the Transgasindo pipeline in South Sumatra.

ConocoPhillips is the largest supplier of pipeline gas in Indonesia through the South Sumatra pipeline and West Natuna pipeline. In August 2003, ConocoPhillips began supplying natural gas from its south Sumatra Corridor PSC to Singapore's PowerGas, via the Grissik-Batam-Singapore gas pipeline. The company has also supplied natural gas to Singapore's Sembawang Gas from its West Natuna gas fields since 2001 and to Petronas' Duyong Complex offshore Malaysia from South Natuna Sea Block B since August 2002. ConocoPhillips has been a major player in the pipeline gas business since 1998, when it began supplying gas from the South Sumatra Corridor Block PSC to the Chevron-operated Duri steamflood in Central Sumatra.

ConocoPhillips holds a 40 percent operating interest in the offshore Block B PSC, South Natuna Sea. The Belanak floating production, storage and offloading (FPSO) project at the Block B PSC, started oil production in December 2004. The FPSO has a capacity to process 100,000 b/d of oil and 430 million cubic feet of gas per day. Natural gas production from the field is exported via pipeline to Singapore and Malaysia.

In offshore East Java, ConocoPhillips has an operating interest in the Ketapang block. The company believes the block has significant oil potential and plans an additional 5 wells in 2009. Malaysia's Petronas has an equal, non-operating interest in the block. ConocoPhillips plans to drill to invest over $3 billion in projects in the Natuna Sea and Ketapang over the next 4 years.

ConocoPhillips is also a major player in the $900 million South Sumatra to West Java gas development project. The project includes a 660-kilometer pipeline from ConocoPhillips Suban gas field in the Corridor Block to the state-owned electricity utility PLN gas-fired power plants in West Java. The company signed a gas sales agreement in August 2004 with state gas company PGN for 2.3 TCF of gas to supply industrial customers in West Java and Jakarta over a 17 year period commencing 2010. Gas supply will come from the Suban gas field on Corridor Block PSC, South Sumatra and will be transported via the South Sumatra-West Java pipeline.

AMERADA HESS consolidated its holdings in Indonesia and sold most of its Indonesian assets during 2002 – 2003. Amerada Hess' present assets in Indonesia are a 78 percent operating interest in Pangkah PSC and a 25 percent working interest in the Jambi Merang JOB.

Amerada Hess has focused its operations in Indonesia on the development of the Ujung Pangkah gas field located in the Madura Strait, offshore East Java. The company is also constructing an offshore well head platform and an onshore gas processing facility in Gresik. Amerada Hess plans to pipe gas from the Ujung Pangkah gas field to PLN's Gresik power plant. In December 2004, the company signed a 400 BCF gas supply contract with PLN for 20 years starting at the end of 2009.

MEDCO, Indonesia's largest private oil company, began exporting crude oil in 2000. It also formally changed its name to "PT Medco Energi Internasional Tbk." at that time. Medco is 50.7 percent owned by Encore International Ltd, which is affiliated with the Panigoro family. On January 2005, Encore signed conditional sales purchase agreements to buy out 40 percent and 19.9 percent share ownerships in New Links Energy Resources from Thailand's PTTEP and Cumin Limited respectively. Encore is now the sole shareholder of New Links. In 2005, Medco launched a secondary public offering, which increased public investors' shareholding in Medco up to 42.6 percent. Medco, through its subsidiaries, owns 14 oil and gas blocks throughout Indonesia, seven of which are in production, while the rest are in the exploration phase.

Medco is the third largest crude oil producer in Indonesia. However, its crude production dropped almost 14 percent to 57,500 b/d in 2004 despite additional production from Kakap block and overseas assets. An ongoing production decline in Medco's largest fields, Kaji Semoga in Rimau PSC, South Sumatra, is the primary reason for drop off. Medco plans to utilize waterflood optimization and enhanced oil recovery (EOR) to slow down the decline rate in its Sumatra fields.

Medco's proven oil reserves now stand at 99 million barrels, while proven and probable reserves stand at 176 million barrels.

In late 2003, Medco assumed the sole risk in exploration drilling in Jeruk in the Sampang PSC. They struck oil in 2004. Other interest holders in the PSC, Singapore Petroleum Company and Cue Energy, decided to reinstate their rights to the Jeruk field at that time. Consequently, Medco will receive full reimbursement of its expenses in developing the field and additional compensation when the field comes online in 2010.

In August 2004 Medco completed its takeover of Novus Petroleum Limited, a listed Australian oil and gas company with assets in the Middle East, Australia, US and Indonesia. Through the acquisition, Medco gained interests in two Indonesian producing fields, Brantas and Kakap. Shortly there after, Medco began consolidation and shed some of Novus' assets. The company sold Novus' Pakistani, US, and Australian assets, as well as 18 percent and 6.25 percent of Brantas and Kakap PSCs in Indonesia.

The company believes its future lies in natural gas development. Medco's gas reserves stand at 221 BCF proven and 629 BCF proven and probable. Medco's gas production, more than doubled to 192 mmcfd during 2004, owing to additional production from Novus' assets.

In addition to gas blocks in south Sumatra, Medco's Exspan Tomori Sulawesi holds a 50 percent operating stake in the Senoro-Toili JOB with PT Pertamina. The block has estimated natural gas reserves of 2.5 TCF. In January 2009, Medco shipped its first oil from the Senoro's Tiaka field to Pertamina's Plaju refinery.

In July 2005 Medco entered into an Exploration Joint Venture Agreement with the US-based Anadarko Petroleum's Indonesian subsidiary. Under the agreement Anadarko will provide $80 million over three years in exchange for up to 40 percent interest in Medco's exploration assets. Medco also acquired 100 percent of the Sembakung Technical Assistance Contract (TAC), a mature producing field in Perkasa Equatorial Sembakung and signed a PSC agreement with Libya's National Oil Company for the Area 47 concession, Northwest Libya. In 2009, Medco plans $300 million in capital expenditures to continue with its acquisition strategy, of both domestic and international assets.

EMP, Energi Mega Persada, Indonesia's second largest oil and gas company, was incorporated in October 2001 and has been listed on the Jakarta Stock Exchange since June 2004. EMP is controlled by PT Kondur Indonesia and PT Brantas Indonesia, with each holding 30.1 percent shares and is affiliated withthe Bakrie Group. EMP operates three exploration blocks and has proven and probable reserves of 91 million barrels of oil and 3.3 trillion cubic feet (TCF) of gas as of 2005.

One of EMP's strategies is to strengthen its position in East Java market, mainly capitalizing on lack of gas supply in the region. EMP is a leading player in the East Java gas market after purchasing BP's 100 percent interest in the offshore Kangean PSC and Pan Asia Enterprise's 50 percent interest in the Brantas PSC, both in 2004. EMP inked gas sales agreements totaling over 970 trillion cubic feet from its Kangean block to supply PLN, PGN, petrochemicals firm Petrokimia Gresik, Pertamina, and local gas distributor Indogas. EMP is continuously seeking expansion of its portfolio via asset acquisitions. In December 2005, EMP obtained shareholder approval to acquire PT Tunas Harapan Perkasa (THP), a local oil and gas company with interests in five exploration assets mainly in located in Sumatra.

CNOOC, the China National Offshore Oil Company, is currently Indonesia's largest offshore oil producer (over 81,500 b/d) following its acquisition of RepsolYPF Indonesia in January 2002.

CNOOC's holdings now include an operating 65.34% interest in the Offshore South East Sumatra PSC, a 36.72 percent interest in the Offshore Northwest Java PSC, a 25 percent interest in the West Madura PSC offshore East Java, a 50 percent interest in the Poleng TAC in East Java, and a 39.51 percent interest in the Malacca Strait PSC. CNOOC's Indonesian operation had net proved reserves of 155 million boe, accounting for approximately 7 percent of total company reserves. In 2004, the company produced and 81.5 thousand b/d of oil and 18.8 BCF of gas.

CNOOC's Indonesia strategy is to tap into the export market as well as get more involved in the domestic natural gas industry. CNOOC entered the LNG export business when it bought a 12.5 percent stake in the $3 billion Tangguh LNG project in late 2002.

Production in CNOOC's South East Sumatra PSC continued to decline over the past 2 years by almost 30 percent compared to 2002. Main oilfields Cinta and Widuri are already 30 years old and are steadily declining. However, the company is optimistic that it will be able to maintain production level through the development of marginal fields and new gas fields in the area. In April 2005, CNOOC received increased financial incentives from the government for its 6 marginal fields. CNOOC secured a gas sales agreement with PLN in 2004 to supply 80 billion BTU to PLN's proposed Cilegon Power plant in West Java starting in 2009 and lasting 12 years. They will supply the gas mainly from the newly developed Zelda and Banuwati fields in the Southeast Sumatra PSC.

CRUDE OIL MARKETING

Indonesia, through Pertamina, BP Migas and its foreign partners, sells crude oil using the Indonesia Crude Price (ICP) formula. Indonesian crude is generally low sulfur and waxy. Indonesia's representative Minas crude (often referred to in marketing terms as Sumatra Light Crude or SLC) produced in Central Sumatra has an American Petroleum Institute (API) gravity of 34.5 degrees at 60 degrees F and a sulfur content of between 0.06 percent and 0.10 percent by weight.

Effective October 1, 1999, Pertamina changed the ICP pricing formula for official export prices of Indonesian crude. The ICP formula has three components: the Asian Petroleum Price Index (APPI), the Rim Intelligence Company price, and the Platts price. The APPI component is derived from twice weekly APPI price assessments adjusted by a basket of regionally traded crude oils (including Indonesian Sumatra Light Crude and Malaysian Tapis) using a 52-week moving average. Pertamina lowered the portion of the APPI panel quota from 33.3 percent to 20.0 percent and increased the portion of the spot assessments of Platt and RIM to 40.0 percent each. The purpose of the adjustment was to better reflect world prices through more emphasis on the spot market. The Ministry of Energy and Mineral Resources reviews the oil pricing formula semi-annually.

Asian countries are the largest markets for Indonesian crude. Japan accounted for 25 percent of Indonesian crude oil exports in 2004, followed by South Korea (20 percent), China (12 percent), Australia (9.7 percent) and the United States (5.7 percent).
Pertamina has an office in Singapore through its wholly owned Hong Kongbasedsubsidiary Pertamina Energy Trading (ex-Perta Oil). The company promotes and facilitates trade in crude oil and fuel between Singapore and Indonesia, offers logistical services to Pertamina, and represents Pertamina's interests.

IMPORTS

Indonesia remains a significant importer of crude oil. In 2005, Indonesia imported an unofficial 118 million barrels. In 2004, Indonesia imported 148.5 million barrels (an average of 406.9 thousand b/d), mainly from Saudi Arabia (25.5 %), Nigeria (18 %), Malaysia (7 percent), Vietnam

(6.4 percent) and Angola (6 %). Oil product imports rose to an unofficial 160 million barrels in 2005, up from 154 million in 2004 and 106 million barrels in 2003.

Indonesia 2004 Crude Export Destinations

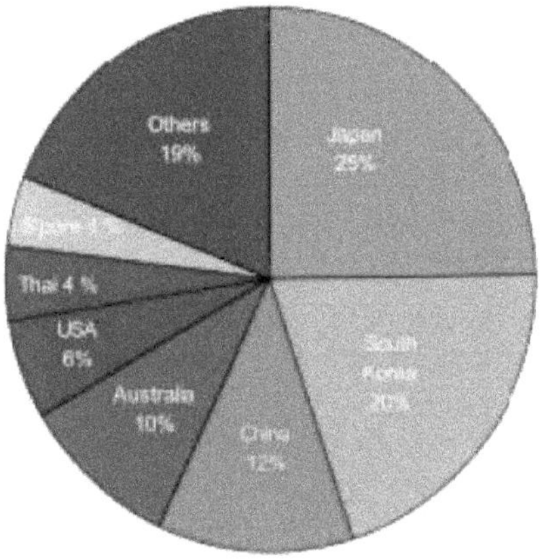

PETROLEUM PRODUCTS CONSUMPTION AND REFINING

Indonesia became a net petroleum importer on a monthly basis in July 2004. As a result, Indonesia became a net importer of fuel products for the entire year. Oil trade deficits reached 29 million barrels or almost 81,000 b/d in 2004. Full year official statistics for 2005 are likely to indicate a continued trend toward net importer status. However, the GOI move in October 2005 to remove substantial subsidies for domestic fuels, raising average fuel prices by an unweighted 126 percent, will provide a strong balance to the continued decline in domestic production and stagnant refining capacity. Fuel consumption increased 8 percent in 2004 to 64.7 million kiloliters (KL), up from 59.9 million KL in 2003 and 57.8 million KL in 2002. The GOI is projecting 41.6 million kiloliters of domestic fuel consumption in 2009, a drop of 36 percent from 2004.

Consumption in 2004 increased in each category of fuel except for kerosene and industrial diesel oil. A significant part of the increase likely resulted from the smuggling of subsidized fuel products to neighboring countries and domestic adulteration activities. In 2004, fuel product imports increased to 422,000 b/d from 292,000 in 2003.

The majority of domestic consumption is for transportation (46.7 percent), industry (24.6 percent), household use (18.2 percent) and electric power (10.5 percent). The transportation sector uses largely automotive diesel oil (ADO), while households are the largest consumers of kerosene.

Pertamina's Downstream Directorate is responsible for the distribution of fuel products to end-users from 174 storage depots throughout Indonesia. The Directorate has established eight regional representative offices to market the products. Fuel products are transported via an elaborate pipeline network and by tank trucks, rail tank wagons, tank vessels and barges. Pertamina controls the sale of gasoline and automotive diesel by direct ownership and franchise of close to 3,000 gasoline stations nationwide. Pertamina itself only owns 2% of the retail stations. The private sector also sells kerosene. The selling price of fuel oil on the domestic market, excluding industry fuels, is determined by the government. Starting in 2005, the government began to adjust prices for high grade automotive fuels and industry fuels according to market prices.

Domestic Fuel Consumption

(Million Liters)

Products	2000	2001	2002	2003	2004
Auto Diesel	21,735	23,014	24,213	25,636	26,488
Gasoline	12,422	13,057	13,732	14,112	17,027
Kerosene	12,455	12,279	11,678	12,262	11,846
Fuel Oil	6,013	6,121	6,260	6,321	5,755
IDO	1,451	1,420	1,360	1,403	1,093
Avtur	744	n/a	553	124	2,438
Avgas	5	n/a	n/a	8	3

OIL REFINING

In 2004, Indonesia's production of petroleum-based fuels and non-fuels from domestic refineries dropped to just under 1 million b/d, largely due to a decreased supply of domestic crude. Most of the petroleum products refined in Indonesia are destined for domestic consumption. Indonesia has nine oil refineries, all owned and operated by state oil and gas company Pertamina, with a combined installed capacity of 1.06 million b/d. The nine refineries are located in Sumatra, Java, East Kalimantan and Irian Jaya. They produce a mix of oil fuels (diesel, fuel oil and kerosene), liquefied natural gas, secondary fuels (such as naptha) and non-fuels (such as asphalt and lubricants).

According to government figures, on average Pertamina's refineries operated at 95% of their combined capacity of 1.056 million b/d in 2004. During a period of fuel scarcity in mid-2005, Pertamina was forced to delay maintenance of its Dumai refinery and operate its Cilacap facility above normal capacity. The lack of spare capacity also means that Indonesia must seek overseas imports when its larger refineries are closed for maintenance. In light of high global prices, Pertamina began using more domestic crude oil in its refineries in 2004 and 2005.

REFINERY PROJECTS

Pangkalan Brandan: this small, aging refinery consists of a simple (primary) distillation unit, with no secondary processing unit. Its products are premium fuels, diesel, LSWR and asphalt. Pangkalan has a processing capacity of 5,000 b/d.

Dumai: The refinery has both a primary and a secondary processing unit (Hydro Cracker), which can produce up LPG, naphtha, HVGO and green coke. Its processing capacity is 120,000 b/d.
Sungai Pakning: Built around 1957, the plant refines heavy paraffin crude oil to produce diesel and paraffin and has a capacity of 50,000 Bb/d.

Plaju: The aged refinery was built by Shell in 1930. It consists of both a primary unit and a secondary processing unit. The secondary unit, a Fuel Catalytic Cracker Unit or FCCU, can process up to 135,000 b/d and was designed to produce PTA and Polytam. In August 2003, operating problems at Plaju forced its closure for one month, delaying maintenance on the

Balongan refinery. Pertamina has proposed converting the facility into a petrochemical plant by 2008.

Oil Refinery Production (1000b/d)

Refinery	Installed Capacity	Crude Processed 2003	Crude Processed 2004
Pangkalan Brandan	5.0	2.6	2.3
Dumai	120.0	28.9	22.1
Sungai Pakning	50.0	47.0	48.6
Musi	133.7	113.3	107.4
Cilacap	348.0	351.4	332.5
Balikpapan	260.0	246.5	264.3
Balongan	125.0	114.8	111.9
Kasim	10.0	8.4	8.4
Cepu	3.8	2.3	2.2
TOTAL	**1,055.5**	**1,015.2**	**999.8**

Source: MIGAS

CILACAP

Indonesia's largest refinery, Cilacap is located in Central Java and has a 348,000 b/d capacity. Its products are premium fuel, kerosene, diesel, fuel oil, and naphtha. Its secondary processing unit is nearly the same as that of the Plaju FCCU and produces lube base products. The bulk of crude supplies (up to 75%) for the refinery are imported from Asia and the Middle East.

Pertamina has signed a long-term import contract with Saudi Aramco to supply the refinery's crude needs. Pertamina has also continued examining the cheaper option of purchasing crude from local producers. In 2005, Pertamina agreed to purchase 250,000 barrels of crude from BP's Ardjuna field, in West Java. The short term agreement was valid for 3 months starting December 2005.

BALIKPAPAN II:

The Balikpapan II refinery in East Kalimantan is more modern than Cilacap and Dumai, and consists of both a primary unit and a secondary processing (Hydro Cracker) unit. The plant has a refining capacity of 220,000 b/d. Bechtel upgraded the refinery in 1983. Due to the facility design, the plant cannot process crude from nearby domestic producers (Total, Chevron, Talisman, and VICO).

BALONGAN

Indonesia's newest state-owned refinery at Balongan in West Java has the capacity to process 125,000 b/d of domestic crude. It has two production units: the crude distillation unit (CDU) and the residue catalytic cracking unit (RCCU). The CDU processes crude oil into naphtha, kerosene,

automotive diesel and residue; the RCCU turns the residue from CDU into LPG and Premium, Super TT and Premix gasoline. The RCCU, one of the world's largest, has a processing capacity of 83,000 B/D, but has experienced problems since its commissioning in 1994. The refinery was initially designed to supply export markets, which is why it is also called the Exor (export oriented) I refinery. Balongan supplies about 70% of Jakarta's refined product demand. The plant processes Duri crude (70%), Minas crude (20%) and Jatibarang crude (10%). Pertamina closed the plant for routine maintenance during September-October 2003. However, a crude pipeline leak required Pertamina to run the refinery at 80% capacity for another month.
Balongan was upgraded in 2005 with additional capacity to produce 52,000 b/d High Octane Motor Component (HOMC) and increase LPG production by 200 tons/day. The upgrade was also part of a government effort to increase the use of unleaded fuel. Pertamina's new diesel fuel, Pertamina DEX is produced at this refinery.

KASIM

This is a small refinery located in Irian Jaya and has only a simple primary distillation unit. Its main products are premium fuel, diesel and kerosene.

New Refinery Projects?

Prior to the October 2005 fuel price hikes, the Energy Ministry estimated that Indonesia needed about $15 billion in refinery investment through 2009 to reduce the country's growing reliance on fuel imports, which accounted for 30 percent of consumption. Prior to the price hikes, domestic demand for fuel increased by 7 percent annually, but refining capacity has remained stagnant for the more than a decade.

Local firm PT Intanjaya Agromegah Abadi (backed by Saudi investors) and its joint venture partner, Texas-based Inter Global Technologies (IGT) are slated to begin construction of the country's first privately-owned refinery in early 2009. The Parepare oil refinery in South Sulawesi was initially approved nine years ago, but development stalled during the 1997-98 economic crises. IAA holds a 30% stake in PT Kilang Minyak Nusantara, owner of the proposed refinery, while IGT holds the remaining 70%. The proposed refinery will have a capacity of 300,000 barrels per-stream day (BSPD) and expects to start production in 2010.

In July 2005, Pertamina signed a memorandum of understanding (MOU) with China's Sinopec to construct a refinery in Tuban, East Java with a capacity between 150,000 to 200,000 b/d. Pertamina postponed the initial groundbreaking date in December 2005 and is reportedly considering seeking another partner to develop the project due to delays by Sinopec in moving forward with the deal.

FUEL IMPORTS

Indonesia remained a net exporter of crude oil and products in 2004, although it became a net importer on a monthly basis in July 2004. The gross output of Indonesia's nine refineries is now insufficient to meet domestic consumption. As a result Indonesia must import around 30 percent of its refined fuel products and crude oil for blending.

In 2004, fuel product imports increased
44.5 percent to 422,000 b/d from 2003's 292,000 b/d. The largest category of imported product was automotive diesel oil (52 percent) followed by High Octane Mogas Component (22 percent) and kerosene (11 percent).

Pertamina has adopted a four-pronged approach to source adequate supplies of fuel for Indonesia's domestic market:

- Production from Pertamina refineries;
- Time-limited contracts for fuel imports from the Middle East;
- Spot product purchases from Singapore; and
- Overseas crude processing deals (CPD).

Indonesia Crude Import Suppliers

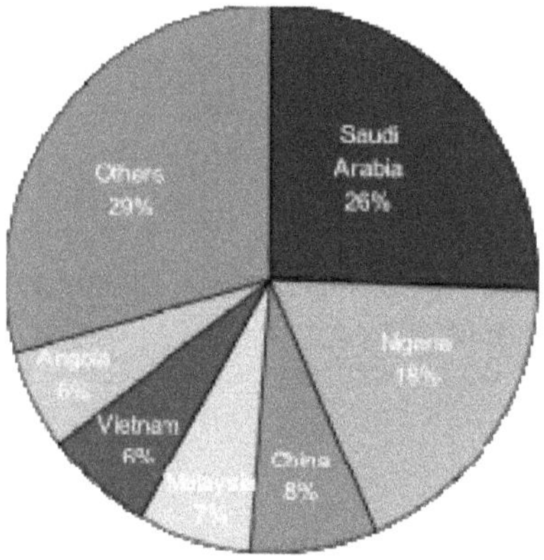

PRICING AND SUBSIDIES

The government continues to administer petroleum product prices, which remains a matter of great political sensitivity. Over the past four years, the GOI has pursued a policy to reduce fuel subsidy costs, thereby increasing fuel prices. However in the past two years, fuel subsidies have jumped back from Rp 30 trillion in 2003 to Rp 59.2 trillion in 2004. The government planned to continue significant reductions in 2005, initially budgeting only Rp 19 trillion to cover 59.6 million kiloliters (KL) of consumption. However, with the unexpected surge in global crude prices up to $70/barrel (triple the $24/barrel budget assumption), the subsidy required skyrocketed, placing a major strain on the state budget and the currency. During 2005 the government revised the fuel subsidy budget to Rp 76.5 trillion and later to Rp 89.2 trillion. This was coupled with two increases in subsidized fuel prices during. In 2009, the Government plans to allocate Rp 54.3 trillion in fuel subsidies, based on budget assumptions of a world oil price of $57/barrel and domestic fuel consumption of 41.6 million kiloliters.

Indonesia continues to phase out its fuel subsidy policy and move towards a market pricing mechanism. In 2005, the government managed to completely phased out subsidies for industrial fuel users and high-octane transportation fuels (Pertamax and Pertamax Plus). Prices for these fuels are administered monthly by Pertamina. In its Energy Blueprint, the government plans full subsidy removal for premium and diesel fuels by 2009 and kerosene by 2010. The blueprint also envisions more efficient use of fossil fuels and encourages alternative energy source development.

SUBSIDIZED FUEL

The latest fuel price increase in October 2005 raised subsidized fuel prices by an average of 105 percent. Further to Presidential Decree No. 55/2005, subsidized fuels are for the use of the following customers:

- Households (kerosene)
- Fishing boats of a maximum 30 tons in size with a maximum gasoil consumption of 25 kiloliters (KL) per month

- Transportation, including private and government vehicles, public transport and domestic route ships (premium and gasoil)
- Public services facilities, including hospitals, places of worship, education facilities, crematorium and government offices (gasoil).

Subsidized Fuel Price Changes (2004 – 2005) (in Rupiah per liter)

Fuel Type 2004		Mar-05	% Chng	Oct-05	% Chng
Premium	1,810	2,400	32.6	4,500	87.5
Gasoil	1,650	2,100	27.3	4,300	104.8
Kerosene	700	900	28.6	2,000	122.2

Source: Pertamina

The transportation and household sectors account for approximately 48 percent and 18 percent of total national fuel consumption. The price hike has been effective in suppressing domestic fuel consumption. Following the October 2005 price hike, Pertamina reported an average consumption decline of 20 percent in October and November. Premium and gasoil consumption declined by almost 36 percent and 30 percent respectively and by the end of the year, total fuel consumption fell below its national quota of 59.6 KL.

NON-SUBSIDIZED FUELS

Industry Fuels

In July 2005, Indonesia began to set its industrial fuel prices according to market forces. The market price is calculated by adding 15 % to the average monthly Mid Oil Platt Singapore (MOPS) price, plus 15% for the costs associated with administering the market mechanism and an additional 10% for the Value Added Tax (VAT) Pertamina announces price changes at the end of each month/

Industry Price Change (Rup Per Litre)

Gasoil	2,100	2,700	28.6	5,340	97.8
Kerosene	2,200	2,790	26.8	6,480	132.3
Diesel Oil 2,050		2,660	29.8	5,180	94.7
Fuel Oil	1,560	2,300	47.4	3,680	60.0

* Price as of December 2005. Prices are adjusted several times during the year. Refer to appendix 10.5 for detailed price changes during 2005. Source: Pertamina

The government defines industrial users as all of those who are not specifically identified otherwise in Presidential Decree No. 55/2005. The price disparity between subsidized and industry fuels has sparked increased smuggling activity and fuel adulteration with subsidized fuels, especially for kerosene (as of July 2005 the subsidized price was Rp 900 as opposed to Rp 4,940 for industry). The government has increased efforts to combat smuggling but reports of illicit transactions persist. Arbitrage and rent seeking remain powerful economic phenomena the world over wherever significant price disparities exist between subsidized and non-subsidized commodities.

In anticipation of downstream market liberalization and to secure its market share, Pertamina also began offering discounts to its industrial customers starting November 2005. They have offered one to four percent discounts to industrial customers willing to sign one-year contracts for a minimum of 100 KL of fuel per month.

OTHER TRANSPORTATION FUELS

Indonesia has three high grade fuels available to the transportation sector, Pertamax Plus, Pertamax and most recently Pertamina DEX. Pricing for these fuels are also adjusted according to market forces. Consumption of high-grade fuels declined considerably since Pertamina raised prices more than 50 percent in mid December 2004. Average daily consumption of these fuels fell to around 500 KL per day from 2000 KL. Consumption for these fuels accounts for less than 1 percent of national fuel consumption.

High Grade Fuel Price Changes (2004 – 2005) (in Rupiah per liter)

Fuel Type	¾	12/04	% Change	2005	% Change
Pertamax	2,450	4,000	63.3	5,400	35.0
Pertamax					
Plus	2,750	4,200	52.7	5,600	33.3
Pertamina					
DEX	n.a	n.a	n.a	5,900	n.a

* Price as of December 2005. Prices are adjusted several times during the year. Refer to appendix 10.5 for detailed price changes during 2005. Source: Pertamina

UNLEADED GASOLINE PHASE-IN

Indonesia's effort to phase out unleaded gasoline began almost a decade ago and has received significant assistance from the U.S Environment Protection Agency and USAID. The government failed to meet its original 2005 target for a complete phase-out of leaded fuel and has not yet announced a new target date as this report went to press.

Pertamina also failed to comply with the Energy Ministry's Decree No.1585/1999, which mandated that unleaded gasoline be available nationwide by January 2003. Insufficient facilities and funding constraints have limited Pertamina's ability to supply unleaded fuel nationwide. Pertamina completed the upgrade of the Balongan refinery in 2005, which produces a high-quality diesel fuel, Pertamina DEX.

Currently ULG is supplied to five areas, the greater Jakarta area (July 2001), Cirebon in West Java (October 2001), Bali (November 2002), Batam (June 2003) and Surabaya (September 2004). These areas represent more than 40 percent of the national market. The Jakarta governor announced plans in February 2009 to implement Regional Regulation No. 2/2005 on Air Pollution Control, which include provisions for an emission test for four-wheeled motor vehicles.

DOWNSTREAM MARKET LIBERALIZATION

Beginning in 1997, the GOI has moved slowly but surely to encourage greater capacity and efficiency in the downstream sector. In the early 1990's, the GOI determined that Pertamina did not have the funds to build additional refining capacity and undertook a series of measures to attract private investment in that sector. Under Presidential Decree (PD) No. 31/1997, the GOI loosened Pertamina's monopoly on refining by allowing private refineries to market their products domestically through Pertamina.

Highlights of PD 31 include:

- Private refineries may be set up by Indonesian companies in partnership with foreign firms or with Pertamina;
- Pertamina buys oil fuels and other refinery products from private companies on a long-term trade contract basis in line with Pertamina's needs and absorption capability and considering the economics of the private corporation's refinery products;
- Pertamina's offer price for fuel from those private refineries is based on the international market price;
- Oil products produced by private refineries which are not needed domestically may be sold by private companies to international markets;
- Pertamina will remain the sole distributor in the domestic market.

Oil and Gas Law 22/2001 marked another step toward liberalizing the downstream sector. The Law originally envisioned a downstream sector which:

- Eliminates Pertamina's monopoly position by November 2005;
- Ensures that investors and participants are given equal regulatory and legal treatment;
- Establishes a transparent pricing regime based on market prices;
- Rationalizes and streamlines downstream administration;
- Allows local and private investors to enter the downstream sector in four areas: processing, transportation, storage and marketing.

In 2004, the government issued implementing Regulation No. 36/2004 on the sector. The regulation stipulated that:

- The Minister of Energy and Mineral Resources is in charge of issuing licenses for businesses wishing to engage in downstream activities.
- The Ministry of Energy and Mineral Resources determines types, standard and quality of fuel oil, gas and other fuels that can be marketed domestically.
- Downstream authority BPH Migas regulates the provision, distribution, and supply of fuel products.
- BPH Migas will appoint companies with "special rights" as gas pipeline operators and determine tariffs for other pipeline users.
- BPH Migas sets prices for households and small industrial users. In addition, BPH MIGAS will supervise pricing for fuel products and gas.
- Downstream businesses can be operated by corporate entities that have obtained a business license issued by the Ministry of Energy and Mineral Resources
- Downstream activities include the processing of crude oil and gas into oil fuel and gas fuel, LPG and LNG; the transport of processed oil/gas products via pipeline and other means; the storage of such products; and the sale, purchase, export and import of such products.
- Processing of oil and gas products into lubricant and petrochemical products are categorized as downstream activities and are jointly regulated by the Ministry of Energy and Mineral Resources and Ministry of Industry

- There are separate licenses for processing, transportation, storage and trading. There are two types of fuel trading licenses: wholesale and limited trading. Wholesale licenses are for companies that intend large-scale sale/import/export of processed oil and gas products and have their own storage facilities. Limited trading licenses are for companies that do not have storage facilities.
- Wholesale license holders can distribute their commodities to end users, while limited trading license holders can only sell their commodities to users with storage facilities or receiving terminals.
- The government sets policy on the national Strategic Fuel Reserve, and can obligate downstream license holders to contribute to the reserve. The government determines the size of each company's contribution.

Foreign investors are starting to enter the downstream market. In November 2005, Shell became the first private investor to open a retail fuel station, in Jakarta's edge city Tangerang. Malaysia's Petronas followed suit and opened a retail station in Cibubur in December 2005. Shell and Petronas have announced plans to open several other outlets throughout the country.

The downstream market is now liberalized, but Pertamina will continue at least through 2009 to carry out its public service obligation (PSO) to distribute fuel to the whole nation. Presidential Decree No.71/2005 allows BPH Migas to appoint other companies to distribute fuels through an open bidding process. The tender award for subsidized fuel is based on MOPS prices plus a premium on distribution costs and a small profit margin. Any company wishing to distribute subsidized fuel must also distribute fuel to remote areas. No companies beside Pertamina expressed interest in bidding on the PSO in 2005, and it is unclear whether foreign investors are interested in this segment of the market.

Pertamina has been girding itself for increased downstream sector competition. In 2005, the company changed its corporate logo, renewed its fuel station franchising procedures, and remodeled its existing fuel stations. In conjunction with partners, Pertamina plans to add another 500 fuel stations to its existing 2,500 fuel stations jointly. Pertamina also signed a $6 billion MOU with Canada Accelon Energy to build a 28 million barrel per year synthetic diesel fuel factory in East Kalimantan. Under the MOU, Pertamina secured exclusive rights to the Euro-4 standard diesel fuel for 15 years starting 2008.

LUBE OIL

The downstream liberalization is also expected to change market trends and brings benefits to consumers in lube oils. Industry players estimate that more than 250 brands of imported and local lubricants currently exist in market. Pertamina remains the market leader with 55 percent although its share is declining from the 70 percent it enjoyed prior to liberalization. Pertamina operates 3 lube oil blending plants--in Jakarta, Cilacap and Surabaya--with a combined capacity of 573,000 liters. Other prominent players in market include Pennzoil, Evalube, BP, Shell, and Petronas. Motor vehicles manufacturers, such as Toyota, Honda and Suzuki have also entered the motor lubricant market distributing their own brands.

Three years after the start of liberalization, the industry is plagued by excess supply and production capacity. In 2005, domestic production capacity reached 1.2 million KL per year, while demand is estimated at around 700,000 KL per year. Current market competition is intense and is expected only to increase after the government decided to reduce import tariffs for mineral based lubricants from 30% to 15% starting March 2009. The Indonesian Lube Association (Aspelindo), whose members' production capacity account for half of the national production, praised the decision. As more imported products enter the market, local producers are gradually losing market share. Lubricating oil imports increased more than six times in value during the past 2 years, rising from $12.6 million in 2002 to $76.8 million in 2004. In terms of volume, import tripled from 36.3 tons in 2002 to 103.2 tons in 2004 in volume.

NATURAL GAS

Production industry and account for 90 percent of all production.
Indonesia has almost 190 trillion cubic feet (TCF) of natural gas reserves (proven and probable), the thirteenth largest in the world. In 2004, the country produced 3.03 trillion cubic feet (TCF) of gas, ranking eighth in world gas production. Gas reserves are equivalent to almost four times Indonesia's oil reserves and can supply the country for 62 years at current production rates. According to the GOI, over 71 percent of natural gas reserves are located offshore, with the largest reserves found off Natuna Island (28.8 percent), East Kalimantan (25.2 percent), South Sumatra (13 percent) and Irian Jaya (12.8 percent). However, not all of these reserves are commercially viable, due to both the quality of the gas and the distance to market.

In 2004, Indonesia supplied 19 percent of the world's LNG, down from 26 percent in 2003. LNG accounts for 43 percent of the country's total natural gas production and is exported mainly to Japan, South Korea and Taiwan. Pipeline gas exports to Singapore began in 2001, reaching 129 BCF last year. A new Sumatra-Singapore pipeline was inaugurated in late 2003. Revenues from gas exports are substantial -- $8.1 billion in 2004, about 11 percent of Indonesia's total export revenues. Domestically, gas demand comes primarily from fertilizer and petrochemical plants (34 percent) and the power industry (25 percent). Most of Indonesia's gas comes from East Kalimantan (47 TCF in reserves) and Sumatra (42 TCF in reserves), but there are large reserves in Papua (24 TCF) and other areas in the archipelago (75 TCF). Six major companies dominate the Gross Natural Gas Production

Roughly 55 percent of Indonesia's natural gas was marketed as LNG or liquefied petroleum gas (LPG) for export, 5.6 percent for electricity, 6.4 percent for fertilizer and 3.4 percent for city gas. Less than six percent was flared.

Indonesia still maintains its lead as the world's top LNG exporter; however its share in the global LNG markets is declining. Questions over supply reliability, low investment in the energy sector and uncertainty over domestic gas supply policy have contributed to Indonesia's declining market share. As a result, Oman, Qatar, Russia, and Australia are displacing Indonesian LNG on world markets. Domestically, the reduction of fuel subsidies in October 2005 eased fuel price distortions and made natural gas increasingly competitive as a fuel alternative. The GOI has indicated that gas will play a significant role in meeting the country's growing electric power demands.

As new LNG producers, Indonesia's a regional gas transmission network is developing, creating new gas markets and sources of revenue. Pipeline exports of natural gas have offset in part the greater competition in LNG markets. Pipeline gas exports increased over 131 percent between 2003 and 2004, reaching 129 BCF, accounting for 8 percent of gas export volume. Indonesia began exporting 325 mmcfd to Singapore via a subsea pipeline from West Natuna under a 22-year contract in 2001. Deliveries of natural gas to Malaysia's Duyong gas platform began in August 2002, under a 20-year contract for 250 million cubic feet per day (mmcfd). Gas sale revenues will likely total $14.2 billion over the life of both contracts. In August 2003, the South Sumatra-Singapore gas pipeline was completed; it will eventually supply 350 mmcfd over a 20-year contract.

LOWER SUBSIDIES, NEW LAWS STIMULATE DOMESTIC DEMAND

The phasing out of domestic fuel subsidies should also stimulate gas demand. The government eliminated the subsidy for industry fuels in 2005 and plans to completely phase out premium fuel and gasoil subsidies by the end of 2009. In October 2005, state gas company PGN raised industrial gas prices to $4.5 per mmbtu from $3.9 per mmbtu. In January 2009 PGN raised prices again to $5 per mmbtu. Even at this price, however, gas is still equivalent to only about 21 cents per liter of diesel oil compared to industrial diesel oil price of 56 cents/liter.

Major Producers (MMSCF)

Company	2002	2003	2004	% Change
Total	835.031	877.523	909.932	3,69
ExxonMobil	557.873	601.673	507.096	-15,72
Vico	438.982	392.625	329.511	-16,07
BP	272.113	245.296	182.209	-25,72
Pertamina	258.012	263.194	383.870	45,85
Unocal	149.317	144.844	124.199	-14,25
ConocoPhillips	233.411	297.922	319.317	7,18
Others	297.134	332.166	273.998	-17,51
Total	**3.041.873**	**3.155.243**	**3.030.132**	-3,97

Source: MIGAS

The Oil and Gas Law of 2001 introduced other changes that encourage domestic gas use. The new law permits direct "free market" negotiations of gas contracts between buyer and seller. Previously, production sharing contractors (PSCs) had to sell their gas to the state-owned petroleum company, Pertamina, which in turn sold the gas to the final buyer. Several PSCs report that the GOI's new direct negotiation mechanism is working well and that the upstream authority BP Migas has generally stayed out of the negotiations, except in cases where either the buyer or seller requested its participation.

These provisions have raised domestic demand estimates and led to a number of new gas sales agreements. In December 2004, PSCs and gas buyers signed 18 gas and LPG agreements worth $4.02 billion. During 2005, gas producers signed at least 17 agreements under the direct marketing mechanism that will supply gas to power, industry and petrochemical buyers. PGN projects conservatively that between now and 2015, Indonesia's domestic gas demand will increase by as much as 60 percent to 3.7 bcf/d.

GROWING POWER NEEDS WILL DRIVE GAS DEMAND

Power generation needs in Java and Bali will also drive growing domestic gas demand. Over the last several years, peak power demand grew by an average of six percent annually, while power capacity did not increase. Peak loads on the Java-Bali grid (which accounts for of 80 percent of Indonesia's power demand) reached a record high of 14,821 MW in April 2005. As a result, the actual reserve margin has declined from 16 percent in 2001 to a razor-thin 6 percent in 2004 in (Note: desired reserve margins are normally between 25 and 30 percent).

PLN estimates that Indonesia needs over 23,000 MW in new capacity between 2005 and 2015 to prevent a long-term power crisis and restore its power reserve margin. Much of that new capacity will be fueled by gas and coal. PLN plans to raise natural gas use by the power sector from 17

percent in 2004 to 40 percent by 2015. By volume, this means an increase networks, state gas utility PGN plans four from 483 mmcfd to 1.7 billion cubic feet new transmission projects to meet rising per day (bcfd) in 2015. Presently PLN power sector demands for gas, as follows:
plans for three new power plants to come online in 2009, including the 740 MW gas turbine combined cycle (GTCC) Cilegon.

Increasing gas consumption in the energy mix makes strong economic sense, particularly with current crude oil price levels. About 2,700 MW of PLN's GTCC plants in Java are running on fuel oil because of declining gas supply and transmission problems in East Java. Petroleum-based fuels are expensive – about 6.2 cents per kilowatt hour (kwH), or 2.5 times more costly than gas. PLN spends about $1.6 billion annually on oil-based fuels and estimates it can save up to $1 billion per year by switching to gas. This however, requires a reliable gas infrastructure and security of gas supply. The switch, when coupled with the power utility's plans to raise electricity tariffs, is an important element in restoring the financial health of Indonesia's power industry. At the same time, it also has significant implications for Indonesia's export revenues derived from natural gas.

IMPEDIMENTS TO DOMESTIC GAS GROWTH

In its Energy Blueprint, the Ministry of Energy and Mineral Resources plans to increase gas's proportion in the national energy mix to 30.6% by 2025 from the current 26.5%. However despite changes spurring gas demand, impediments limit domestic gas growth. The primary obstacles include a limited transmission and distribution system, financing limitations, and continued regulatory uncertainty. To address the inadequate state of gas transmission and distribution
In addition to these projects, the GOI is proposing to build an LNG receiving terminal in West Java, to process and distribute gas from existing LNG plants (Bontang), as well as future plants in Papua (Tangguh) and South Sulawesi (Donggi). PGN is extending its distribution network and plans to ship compressed natural gas (CNG) over short to medium distances to remote areas. In addition, PGN is also investigating the feasibility of developing an integrated mini-LNG transportation system. The project will involve a mini-LNG receiving terminal located in in Makassar, South Sulawesi, which will ship LNG from the Bontang LNG plant.

Many producers require explicit financial guarantees to sell gas domestically. The government's reluctance to provide such guarantees poses another obstacle to domestic gas growth, according to industry observers. In the power industry, a number of PSCs have requested that PLN provide standby letters of credit (SBLC) before investing in long-term gas supply agreements. According to industry analysts, PLN's credit availability with government-linked banks is limited. PLN has asked Bank Indonesia to exclude SBLCs from the legal lending limit to get around this obstacle. Some power analysts suggest that if PLN would permit higher returns on investment, companies *Petroleum Report Indonesia 2005-2009* would be willing to assume more of this risk themselves.

Projects	Length (km)	Capacity (mmscfd)	Completion
Grissik – W.Java	661	400	2007
Duri – Medan	521	250	2007
E.. Kalimantan - Central Java	1,219	1,100	2007/ 2010
E.Java-W.Java	680	350	2008/ 2010

Source: PGN

Another constraint to gas development is the absence of a competitive gas pricing system. Under the historic system, prices for gas supply contracts are negotiated on a field-by-field basis between Pertamina and individual producers after the discovery of the gas field. Prices are fixed for a designated supply for the duration of the contract. Hence, the producer's price for gas is different for each PSC. Consumer prices are set on a cost-plus basis.

Currently, the negotiated gas price for power generation is far below the global average, in the range of $2.45 to $3 per MMBTU, compared to current global natural gas prices, which currently averages at around $7 per mmbtu in early 2009. The World Bank and the Asian Development Bank (ADB) have urged Indonesia to adopt a pricing regime that creates greater incentives for companies to find and produce gas. A competitive domestic gas price would allow Indonesia to realize the full value and potential of its gas reserves. Without pricing changes, the domestic gas market provides few incentives for the exploration and development of gas fields that are too small to support LNG but more than adequate for domestic gas customers. A second major constraint is the absence of a predictable basis for forecasting the future value of gas, such as an indexed price formula. A final constraint has been the subsidy provided for alternative fuels.

REGULATIONS REQUIRE CLARIFICATION

The current regulatory environment sends mixed signals to investors which inhibits the exploration and development of potential gas reserves. Despite domestic market obligation (DMO) provisions in the 2001 Oil and Gas law promoting gas use and the issuance of downstream Regulation 36, industry players still do not see a clear set of "rule of the game." Industry players say that they want clarification of the exact DMO quantity and whether the government will honor existing PSC contracts. In addition, doubts about contract sanctity, contract extensions, security, and taxation hurt the gas investment climate.

The end result of this uncertainty, and the consequent lack of exploration, is stark: According to the American Chamber of Commerce, gas blocks signed before 1971 still account for nearly 60 percent of Indonesia's commercial reserves. Blocks signed after 1990 account for only 14 percent of commercial reserves.

EXPANDING FUTURE PRODUCTION

Indonesia is blessed with abundant reserves, although there is a geographical mismatch between location of gas reserves and energy needs. The Ministry of Energy and Mineral Resources estimates total gas demand between 2008- 2018 will reach 22,200 BSCF, while supply is estimated at 13,231 BSCF. In the long-term, Java's additional gas supply will rely on the development of gas fields outside the island and completion of pipeline projects.

In addition to geographical constraints, other barriers to developing Indonesia's gas resources include the availability of financing, long project lead-time, and the lack of incentives to explore and exploit gas reserves. Private sector participants identified the following key areas to increase development in the gas sector:

- Increase incentives to find and produce natural gas;
- Harmonize conflicting laws and eliminate the lengthy bureaucratic process for project approval;
- Clarify the gas DMO obligation;
- Promote private investment and ownership, through price stability, an equitable cost recovery mechanism;
- Address gas reliability concerns for those firms that invest in major gas facilities; and

- Government guarantees for gas payment by state owned enterprises.

A TRANS-ASEAN GAS PIPELINE?

ASEAN's Energy ministers signed a memorandum of understanding on July 5, 2002 to push ahead with a $7 billion natural gas pipeline project in a bid to alleviate concerns over supply shortages and to improve economic development. Minister of Energy and Mineral Resources Purnomo Yusgiantoro said the project's masterplan has been completed, and a council will soon be established to oversee the completion of the gas grid. Purnomo said more than 1,000 kilometers of the grid have already been constructed. ASEAN has identified the need for 4,500 kilometers of pipeline to complete the project, which might reach 6,000 kilometers, if the necessary new Indonesian domestic pipelines are included.

Purnomo said Indonesia will be a major player in the trans-ASEAN gas pipeline project because of its enormous gas reserves. ASEAN members have previously said that a regional natural gas pipeline, as well as an electricity grid, is the most efficient way for ASEAN countries to prevent a future energy crisis. Indonesia has already developed several pipelines -from West Natuna to Singapore, West Natuna to Malaysia, and from South Sumatra to Singapore. It is also studying a possible pipeline from West Natuna to Thailand.

ASEAN members will develop regulations and frameworks for the cross-border supply, transportation and distribution of natural gas throughout the region. This will be supervised by a future ASEAN Gas Consultative Council. The key reason behind the gas grid is the need to reduce oil consumption and to provide backup energy sources for ASEAN members. ASEAN members hope to complete the gas grid by 2020.

INTEGRATED TRANSMISSION SYSTEM

The South Sumatra pipeline is part of state gas company PGN's plan for an integrated gas transmission pipeline system, known as the Integrated Gas Transporation System (IGTS). The IGTS will eventually link the islands of Sumatra, Java, and Kalimantan via a 4,200-kilometer integrated gas pipeline. Reputed to be Southeast Asia's longest, the pipeline is being funded by the World Bank, ADB, other institutions, as well as PGN's own internal funding. PGN's network will flow 2.2 BCFD of natural gas after its scheduled completion in 2010.

PROJECT ONE - GRISSIK-DURI PIPELINE

Phase One became operational in 1998. The 544-kilometer Grissik/Duri gas transmission pipeline transports 310 mmscfd of natural gas from the Grissik gas plant in ConocoPhillips Indonesia's Corridor PSC in South Sumatra. The project will supply Caltex's Duri Steam Flood Project in Central Sumatra for 15 years. ConocoPhillips is the producer, Caltex is the buyer, and PGN is the pipeline network owner.

The Grissik/Duri pipeline project is the first part of an 850-kilometer gas transmission pipeline to link South Sumatra to Singapore. Phase Two, which covers a 530-kilometer leg from Grissik to Singapore by way of Batam Island was completed in August 2003. Both the Grissik/Duri pipeline and the Grissik/Singapore pipeline have been included in the TransgasIndo pipeline consortium, jointly owned and operated by PGN and a joint venture among ConocoPhillips, Petronas, Talisman, and Singapore Petroleum.

Project Two: South Sumatra–West Java Pipeline: This 1,100-kilometer pipeline project will provide gas from ConocoPhillips and Pertamina fields in Sumatra to West Java power plants and industrial users. The pipeline will be funded by a combination of JBIC loans and proceeds from a PGN bond and IPO offerings. All parties hope to complete the project and have the first gas flowing in mid 2010.

Phase I of the project involves construction of a 450 kilometers pipeline from Pagardewa, South Sumatra to Cilegon and Serpong, West Java. Phase I will provide 250 mmcfd of gas from Pertamina's Pagardewa gas field and ConocoPhillips' Grissik field to the Muara Tawar, Tanjung Priok and Muara Karang gas-fired power plants in Jakarta. Currently, Phase I completion date is scheduled for March 2010.

Phase II will connect Grissik to Pagardewa via a 270 km pipeline, a parallel line from Pagardewa to Labuhan Maringgai and a 190 km pipeline from Labuhan Maringgai to Muara Bekasi, and Rawamaju in West Java. Phase II will provide 400 mmcfd (ramping up to 600 mmcfd). PGN completed the procurement tender for the project in 2005 and aims for project completion in December 2010. This pipeline will supply natural gas from Pertamina's gas fields in Prabumulih to West Java industrial users. Pertamina and PGN have already agreed to provide 250 mmcfd to West Java once the pipeline becomes operational.

Project Three: East Kalimantan-Central Java: The most ambitious of the five projects, the 1,200-kilometer East Kalimantan-Java pipeline would transport up to 1.1 bcfd of gas through a combined offshore and onshore pipeline stretching from Kuala Badak, East Kalimantan to Semarang, Central Java. PGN would partially fund the project from a bond and IPO offering. At an estimated cost of $1.2 billion, PGN will need substantial outside financing. PGN completed the feasibility study of the project and announced the tender in December 2005. Presently, PGN plans for project construction to begin in 2010 with first gas flowing in 2010.

Project Four: East/West Java Pipeline:
This proposed project will involve construction of a 730 kilometers pipeline stretching from Gresik (East Java) to Cirebon and Muara Bekasi (West Java) along with a 300-kilometer East and Central Java distribution link. The pipeline will have the capacity to transport about 700 mmcfd of natural gas and cost an estimated $540 million. Currently PGN plans for project construction to start in 2008 with completion in 2010.

Project Five: Duri – Dumai – Medan Pipeline: An extension of the Grissik-Duri project, the 521-kilometer pipeline will transport gas from Duri, Riau to Medan, North Sumatra. The project will be the northern extension of an integrated Sumatra transmission network and supply gas to Asahan Power. PGN, Kondur Petroleum and Asahan Power signed MOU in October 2004 for the sale of 80140 mmcfd gas through the pipeline. PGN plans to finance the estimated $574 million project via internal and external finance lending. Currently, PGN plans for project completion in 2010.

LNG AND LPG

Through the end of 2004, Indonesia remained the world's leading exporter of LNG, with about 18.8 percent market share in the world and over 33 percent share in Asia and the Pacific. Currently, Indonesia has the capacity to produce a total of 31.6 million tons of LNG at the Arun plant in North Sumatra and the Badak (Bontang) plant in East Kalimantan. However, actual production in 2004 reached only 25.2 million MT, compared to a peak of 29.8 million MT in 1999. LNG is still one of the country's significant foreign exchange earners. LNG exports were valued at $7.7 billion in 2004, a 17 percent increase compared with the $6.6 billion earned in 2003. Japan remained Indonesia's top market for LNG, with 64 percent of the total, followed by South Korea (21 percent) and Taiwan (16 percent).

World LNG Trade 2004

Exporting	billion m3	percent
Indonesia	33,49	18,8
Malaysia	27,68	15,6

Algeria	25,75	14,5
Qatar	24,06	13,5
Trinidad & Tobago	13,99	7,9
Nigeria	12,59	7,1
Australia	12,17	6,8
Brunei	9,50	5,3
Oman	9,03	5,1
UAE	7,38	4,1
USA	1,68	0,9
Libya	0,63	0,4
Total	177,95	100,0

Source: BP statistical review

Indonesia signed its first long-term LNG contract in 1973, with the first shipment from Bontang in 1977 and the first shipment from Arun in 1978. Indonesia signed a number of additional LNG contracts between 1973 and 1995. Indonesia's LNG exports are under long-term contracts between Pertamina and its customers. Pertamina's role was reinforced in June 2004 when BP Migas appointed Pertamina as the sole sales agent for LNG sales to South Korea and Taiwan.

NEW LNG SALES AND CONTRACT EXTENSIONS

LNG prices are on an upward trend. Average import prices for Japan, the world's largest LNG importer, increased by 9 percent to $5.18/mmbtu in 2004 from the 2003 price of $4.77 – almost double the benchmark negotiated prices for the Guangdong and Fujian LNG terminals in China, which were agreed in 2002 for prices between $2.40-$3.00/mmbtu.

Indonesia did not gain the full benefit from rising global prices, as LNG exports have declined due to falling production and a costly domestic fertilizer policy. In 2009, the government planned to cut delivery of a total of 61 cargoes, 52 from Bontang and 9 from Arun. The downward trend in LNG exports is expected to continue at least until 2010.

Indonesia finalized two LNG contracts for its Tangguh project in 2004 to supply a total of 1.3 million MT per year to South Korea's K Power and POSCO. Future LNG contracts are likely to be affected if the government continues with its plan to implement a 25 percent domestic gas obligation. In 2005, a negotiation with a Japanese buyer for a 2010-delivery date LNG contract extension was halted pending a government decision on its gas supply policy.

Arun

The Arun LNG plant is operated by the PT Arun Natural Gas Liquefaction Company, of which 55 percent is owned by Pertamina, 30 percent by Mobil LNG Indonesia Inc. (an ExxonMobil affiliate) and 15 percent by Japan Indonesia LNG Company (JILCO). ExxonMobil/BP Migas is the sole supplier of natural gas to Arun, whose production capacity is now about 6.4 million MT per annum. Aceh gas production peaked in 1995 and gas deliveries to the six-train PT Arun LNG plant have started on a steady decline. ExxonMobil has extracted about 90 percent of the gas reserves in the field and committed reserves will run out entirely in 2018. The Arun facility produced 5.6 million MT in 2004, a decline from 6.6 million MT in 2003, and is expected to discontinue operations in 2014.

Due to the normal decline in the Arun fields there is insufficient gas to supply all domestic fertilizer plants. The government requested that ExxonMobil divert part of its gas production to fertilizer firm Pupuk Iskandar Muda (PIM). The result was a cut in Arun's delivery of export cargoes, which required the GOI to turn to the spot LNG market to meet its contractual commitment to export buyers. Arun's export commitment was 75 cargoes in 2005. The government needed to acquire between eight and ten LNG cargoes from abroad in 2005 to maintain gas supply to fertilizer plants and still comply with its LNG contractual requirements.

The Arun area fields include: the original Arun field; the South Lhoksukon A and D gas fields, located 15 kilometers from Arun; the Pase A and B gas fields, located north of Arun; and the North Sumatra Offshore (NSO) gas field. The NSO field sits 100 km offshore from the Arun LNG plant.

Bontang

The eight-train (A through H) Bontang facility in Badak, East Kalimantan is the largest LNG plant in the world and has 21.6 million MT of production capacity. The facility marked its 600th LNG shipment in November 2005.

The plant is operated by PT Badak NGL Company, which is 55-percent owned by Pertamina, 20-percent by Vico (which in turn is 50-percent owned by BP), 10percent by TotalFinaElf, and 15-percent by Japan Indonesia LNG Company (JILCO). Gas is supplied from a production sharing arrangement among Pertamina, Chevron, Vico and Total. LNG production from the Bontang facility in 2004 declined to 19.6 million MT from 20.1 million MT in 2003.

In 1995, Pertamina signed two 20-year contracts for Bontang's "H" train with the Korea Gas Company and the Chinese Petroleum Corporation (Taiwan). Indonesia also advanced plans to build a ninth LNG train (train I) at the Bontang facility. The 3 million MT per year train is scheduled for 2010 and will increase annual production by 25 million MT.

Bontang experienced a variety of challenges that constrained its ability to provide gas for both LNG production and feedstock for national fertilizer plants in East Kalimantan. The three gas suppliers (Total, Vico and Chevron) experienced problems with underproduction or inconsistent production due to maintenance, accidents or low field performance, all of which led to gas supply shortages to the plant. Despite shortfalls, the GOI diverted gas from Bontang's producers so that Pertamina could sell subsidized gas to a national fertilizer plant group and two small Japanese-owned plants. In 2005, the GOI renegotiated Bontang contracts, cutting 42 cargoes and leaving Bontang with 335 cargoes for export.

Tangguh

BP is the major shareholder and operator of the Tangguh LNG project, which encompasses three PSCs in the Berau-Bintuni Bay region of western Papua. The Tangguh gas fields contain 14.4 trillion cubic feet TCF of proven and certified natural gas reserves. The LNG processing plant will produce seven million MT of LNG per year from two initial processing trains. Following final Indonesian government approval in March 2005, BP appointed a consortium, composed of Kellogg Brown Root (KBR), JGC Corporation, and PT Pertafenikki, as contractors to build the Tangguh project. BP Indonesia holds a 37.16% stake, with the balance shared by CNOOC (16.96%), Mitsubishi (16.30%), Nippon (12.23%), KG (10.00%), and LNG Japan (7.35%).

The Indonesian government and BP have secured four market commitments for 7.65 million MT of Tangguh's LNG. In July 2004, the project won a contract to supply 550,000 MT of LNG per year to South Korean steel maker POSCO for 20 years. In August 2004, the project also signed another supply contract of 800,000 MT of LNG per year to South Korea's K Power for a 20-year term starting 2009. In addition, in 2002 the project won the contract to supply 2.6 million MT of

LNG per year to China's Fujian province for a 25-year term beginning in 2010. It also signed a HoA in 2003 with the U.S. firm Sempra Energy to supply 3.7 million MT of LNG for a 20-year term beginning in 2010. Until Tangguh becomes operational LNG will likely come from the Bontang LNG facility in East Kalimantan. Tangguh's developers are also considering a PLN-proposed LNG regasification facility in Java as another target for LNG sales.

SULAWESI -THE FOURTH LNG CENTER?

Plans to develop another LNG project and gas processing facility in Central Sulawesi still linger despite a failure to discover sufficient reserves to justify greenlighting the development. Pertamina continues with its exploration plan in an attempt to find new gas and increase reserves to at least 3.5 TCF. Pertamina is also still mulling over building a 2 million MT per year LNG plant to use gas from the Matindok block, Central Sulawesi. Matindok consists of the Donggi gas block, which is operated by Pertamina, and the Senoro-Toili gas block, which is jointly operated by Pertamina and Medco's Exspan Nusantara.

Donggi's potential initially captured the interest of foreign companies, including Chevron, Royal Dutch/Shell, Marathon Oil, Mitsui, CNOOC, PetroChina and Petronas. However a few years without significant discoveries of gas combined with a lack of clarity for LNG management and regulation resulted in several companies deciding to withdraw their expressions of interest in the project.

In 2005, Australia's LNG Limited announced a plan to build a 850,000 MT per year mini-LNG plant in Luwuk, Central Sulawesi close to the Senoro-Toili fields. Its 50 percent subsidiary, PT LNG Energi Utama, obtained foreign capital investment approval from the Investment Coordinating Board. Its joint venture partner,Maleo Energi Utama is a private Indonesian company with operations in Sulawesi area. During the year, Medco signed an exclusive agreement with LNG Limited to conduct a feasibility study for an 800 BCF, 20 year gas supply plan to the proposed LNG plant from the Senoro fields. The estimated $240 million project is planned for start up in 2010.

LIQUID PETROLEUM GAS

Total liquid petroleum gas (LPG) production declined slightly in 2004 to 1.9 million MT from 2.0 million MT in 2003. LPG production at five of Pertamina's refineries declined 1.6 percent to 896,400 MT in 2004 from 911,200 MT in 2003. LPG production dropped due to problems at the Balikpapan refinery coupled with decreased utilization of the Cilacap refinery. The Arun LNG plant has reported no LPG production from its LPG extraction plant since 2000. It produced 216,000 MT in 1999. Indonesia exported around 57 percent of its LPG production in 2004, valued at $366 million, mainly to Japan (80 percent).

PETROCHEMICALS

The Indonesian petrochemical industry is progressing slowly towards recovery after the late-1990s economic crisis. The industry has relied in the past on an abundant natural resources base of crude oil and natural gas and a large and growing market of more than 240 million people. It has been constrained by a lack of integration between the petroleum and petrochemical industries. The Asian economic crisis damaged the petrochemical industry. Many of the remaining companies have heavy debts. Furthermore, Indonesia's anemic investment climate significantly limits interest in this sector. In 2005, petrochemical producers also faced high prices for basic materials as a result of soaring global crude prices.

The sector players have called for for additional production capacity as growing demand and limited capacity have translated into increased imports of a number of key petrochemicals. They contend that the country is missing opportunities for job creation, foreign exchange revenues and a domestic buffer from international price changes. The industry got a boost as construction of the Tuban petrochemical project resumed in 2004. Once in operation, the complex will add to

Indonesia's production capacity of paraxylenes, benzene and toluene.
In 2005, PT Petrokimia Nusantara Interindo (PENI), Indonesia's largest polyethylene producer was acquired by Malaysia's Titan Chemical Corp, an integrated petrochemical producer controlled by Malaysia's state-owned asset management company Permodalan Nasional Bhd. Japan's Marubeni Corporation also divested its shareholding in Chandra Asri Petrochemical Complex (CAPC) to Commerzbank International Trust Singapore in 2005. CAPC was one of the companies restructured as a result of the financial crisis. CAPC owed $463.6 million to the Indonesian Bank Restructuring Agency (IBRA) and $731 million to private lenders, led by Marubeni Cooperation of Japan. In 2002, Marubeni agreed to convert $147 million of its loans into a 24.59 percent equity share in CAPC. CAPC produces ethylene, propylene and polyethylene.

TARIFF REDUCTION POSTPONED

The GOI had previously committed to reduce tariffs of petrochemical products to comply with the Common Effective Preferential Tariff (CEPT) and ASEAN Free Trade Agreement (AFTA) schemes. In 1998, the government lowered import tariffs on petrochemical products (ethylene, propylene, styrene, polyethylene, polypropylene, polystyrene and polyvinyl chloride) and their derivatives from 25-35 percent down to 10-20 percent, effective January 1, 1999.

Ministry of Finance Decree No. 187/2000 in May 2000 went a step further by reducing import tariffs for 708 items, including upstream and midstream petrochemical products. This decree lowered import duties on selected petrochemical products (ethylene, propylene, styrene, polyethylene, polypropylene, and their derivatives) as of June 1, 2000. In 2003 the GOI decided to postpone further reductions, however, saying that current rates already were quite low at a range between 0-10 percent.

IMPORT TARIFFS SELECTED PETROCHEMICAL PRODUCTS (PERCENT)

BENZENE & PARAXYLENE

Benzene and paraxylene are currently produced by Pertamina's Cilacap refinery with a production capacity of 123,000 tons per year and 270,000 tons per year, respectively. Production rates of the two products are insufficient to meet domestic demand, which must be met through imports. Compared to 2003, imports of Benzene and paraxylene in 2004 increased by 1.2 percent and 38 percent respectively to 301,500 tons and 778,200 tons. The country will increase its paraxlylene production by 500,000 tons once the Tuban Petrochemical's project comes online in 2009.

Products	Pre 1-Jan-99	1-Jan-99	1-Jun-00
Ethylene	25	10	0
Propylene	25	10	5
Polyethylene	35	20	5
Polypropylene	35	20	5
Polystyrene	25	20	10

35 20 10

Polyvinyl Chloride	35	20	10

PURE TEREPHTALIC ACID (PTA)

Since 1998, five PTA plants have been in operation -- Pertamina Plaju Aromatic, Bakrie Kazei PTA, Amoco Mitsui PTA Indonesia, Polysindo Eka Perkasa and Polyprima Karya Reksa, with a combined capacity of 1.98 million MT per year. PTA is produced from paraxylene and is used as raw material for polyester production in the textile industry. The growth of Indonesia's textile industry and the demand for polyester raw materials provided the stimulus for Pertamina and private investors to enter into PTA production. The bulk of production is sold to Indonesian polyester makers and for export purposes. In 2004 PTA production increased to 1.68 million tons from 1.58 million tons in 2003. In the last 5 years, PTA export has more than doubled from 244,800 tons in 2000 to 512,572 tons in 2004.

Three Japanese partners led by Mitsubishi Kasei Corp. own Bakrie Kasei, the largest PTA producer in Indonesia with a total capacity of 640,000 tons per year. (PT Bakrie Brothers sold its 20 percent share in the company to its former partners in late 2000) Bakrie Kasei's first PTA production unit commenced operation in 1994 and the second unit in 1996. Amoco-Mitsui PTA Indonesia, a joint venture of Amoco Chemical (50 percent), now incorporated into BP, Mitsui Petrochemical Industries (45 percent) and Mitsui Company (5 percent), commissioned a PTA factory in Merak, West Java, in February 1998, with an annual production capacity of 420,000 MT per year. PT Polysindo Eka Perkasa of the Texmaco Group started a PTA plant operation in April 1997 with a capacity of 340,000 MT per year. PT Polyprima Karyareksa of the Napan group commenced commercial production in 1997 with an annual capacity of 350,000 tons. Pertamina Plaju Aromatics has an annual capacity of 225,000 tons.

POLYPROPYLENE (PP)

Three plants, with a combined production capacity of 605,000 tons per year, produce polypropylene, which is a basic feedstock for plastic packaging material made from propylene. The three are Pertamina's plant in Plaju, South Sumatra (annual production capacity of 45,000 tons), Tri Polyta Indonesia's plant in Cilegon, West Java (annual capacity of 360,000 tons) and Polytama Propindo, Indramayu, West Java (annual capacity of 180,000 tons). PP's production increased 4 percent to 507,600 tons in 2004 or 84 percent of the country's total capacity.

ETHYLENE

Chandra Asri Petrochemical Center (CAPC) is the only ethylene producer in Indonesia, with an annual capacity of 550,000 tons. Actual production in 2004 of 408,000 tons (74 percent utilization) is below the country's annual demand of over 900,000 tons. As a result more than half of Ethylene demand is supplied through imports. In 2004, Ethylene import rose to 475,000 tons from 405,000 tons in 2003.

POLYETHYLENE (PE)

Indonesia has a PE production capacity of 750,000 tons from its 2 producers, PT Petrokimia Nusantara Interindo (PENI) and CAPC. Indonesia's first polyethylene plant, PT PENI in Merak, West Java, came on stream in 1993, with an annual production capacity of 250,000 MT. In August 1998, the company completed its expansion project and increased its annual capacity to 450,000 MT. In 1999, CAPC increased the country's total polyethylene production capacity to 750,000 MT.

Total imports of PE were 267,800 tons in 2004, and will likely increase as a result of insufficient production and growing demand. Although national production increased slightly to 445,000 tons, plant utilization is only 59 percent. Current demand for propylene is around 620,000 tons and demand for raw materials of plastics in Indonesia is growing around 8 percent per year.

METHANOL

The country produced almost 788,000 tons of methanols in 2004, down 2 percent from 2003's production of 792,000 tons. Prior to 1998, methanol was produced only by Pertamina's Bunyu Refinery, now operated by PT Medco Methanol Bunyu. PT Kaltim Methanol Industry in Bontang, East Kalimantan, came on stream in 1998, and brought Indonesian methanol annual production capacity to 990,000 MT. PT Kaltim Methanol has plans to be a major methanol supplier to Asia. The first shipment of methanol to Japan was in March 1998. PT Kaltim Methanol is 85 percent owned by Japan's Sojitz Corporation (formerly Nissho Iwai Corporation). The plant has an annual production capacity of 660,000 MT.

A gas supply shortage also affected the upstream chemical industry. In June 2005, Medco's methanol plant in Kalimantan temporarily ceased operation as a result of the lack of gas from Medco's Tarakan PSC and Pertamina's Bunyu gas fields.

THE PROJECTS

The long-suspended $2.3 billion Trans Pacific Petrochemical Indonesia (TPPI) project in Tuban, East Java resumed construction in June 2004 following approvals from Japanese creditors and a GOI guarantee letter for the project in 2003. The loan facility provides Pertamina with $400 million to fund the remainder of the project.

The Tuban Petrochemical Project is owned by Trans Pacific Petrochemical Indonesia (TPPI), a subsidiary of the Tirtamas Group which transferred majority ownership of the project to the state asset management company PPA (formerly IBRA) in 1998 after the conglomerate failed to repay $635 million in bank loans. At time of suspension, Tirtamas had already completed 65 percent of construction. PPA and Tirtamas set up a new company, Tuban Petro, to manage the restructuring process. Consequently through Tuban Petro, PPA and Pertamina hold 59.5 percent and 15 percent respectively in the project. Other stakeholders include Siam Cement of Thailand, Sojitz Corporation (formerly Nissho Iwai) and Itochu Corporation.

When completed, the plant will have an annual production capacity of 3.6 million tons per year. The complex will produce aromatic products consisting of paraxylene (500,000 tons), benzene (200,000 tons), and toluene (150,000 tons). It will greatly reduce imports of these products and carry a potential savings of $1 billion per year to country. In addition to the above products, the complex will also produce 1 million tons of naphtha and 1.6 million tons of kerosene and diesel. Presently the project is scheduled to come online in 2009.

FERTILIZERS

Installed production capacity at Indonesia's 12 fertilizer plants operated by six companies (five state-owned companies and one ASEAN joint venture) is 8.7 million MT of urea and 5.7 million MT of ammonia per year. Fertilizer production in 2003 and 2004 remained stagnant at 5.7 million tons (54 percent total capacity) after falling from 6 million tons in 2002.
Starting in 2004, fertilizer production was affected by the suspension of production at the two large fertilizer plants in Aceh (ASEAN Aceh Fertilizer or AAF and Pupuk Iskandar Muda or PIM I). Designated a strategic commodity, the government directs state-owned fertilizer companies to meet domestic demand first with the remainder be exported. Urea exports fell dramatically to 465,400 tons in 2004 from 946,800 tons in the previous year with main export destinations being Thailand, Australia and Malaysia.

Domestic demand for fertilizer continues to increase at average of 3.0 percent per year. With insufficient production to meet domestic demand, Indonesia imported fertilizer amounting to 2.15 million tons valued at $386 million in 2004, an increase of almost 47 percent from 2003. The largest Indonesian fertilizer import is potassium chloride, which is used as an additive to enhance the performance of other fertilizers. It is mainly used by soybeans, tobacco and tea producers. The fertilizer industry uses about 194 BSCF of natural gas per year. It purchases gas in U.S. dollars at a government subsidized price ranging from $1 to $3 per mmbtu. Despite Indonesia's abundant supply of natural gas and strong domestic and foreign demand for fertilizer, the industry is struggling for survival. Trouble in obtaining adequate gas supplies for fertilizer plants in Indonesia has became more severe in the past few years, leading ultimately to the shuttering of the production line at AAF in 2004 and its liquidation in August 2005. AAF began production in 1983 and had a capacity of 1.6 million tons per year.

Pupuk Iskandar Muda (PIM) also suspended its operation in September 2005. During 2004 PIM operated at only 28.7 percent of its total capacity and produced just 336,300 tons of fertilizers. The government plans to resume production at the plant in 2009 by diverting ExxonMobil's Arun gas to the facility. In turn, the government will replace ExxonMobil's gas deficit from Pupuk Kaltim's gas supply from East Kalimantan. Industry experts consider the GOI's plan to be detrimental to the robust development of the natural gas industry. With the halt in production from these two producers, current production comes from PT Pusri, PT Pupuk Kaltim, PT Pupuk Kujang and PT Petrokimia Gresik.

BASIC LAWS AND REGULATIONS FOR OIL AND GAS SECTOR

PETROLEUM ACT

PREAMBLE

According to international law, Timor-Leste has sovereign rights for the purpose of exploring, exploiting and managing its natural resources, including Petroleum resources. In its Territory, Timor-Leste has title to all Petroleum resources in the ground, whether on land or at sea.

The purpose of the Petroleum Act (the "Act") is to provide maximum benefit to Timor-Leste and its people from its petroleum resources by creating a regulatory regime that allows petroleum companies to develop these petroleum resources.

The Act empowers the Ministry to authorise petroleum companies to explore for and develop petroleum resources. Other petroleum regimes were considered, with a view to creating a regime that is internationally competitive, and will promote investment in the development of the petroleum sector.

The petroleum resources that belong to Timor-Leste are a strategic component of the economy, have great potential value, and are expected to generate significant revenues for Timor-Leste. Besides aiming to generate maximum revenues to Timor-Leste from these resources, the Act also aims to contribute to Timor-Leste's broader development goals. Revenues from, and development of, petroleum will allow Timor-Leste to address more fully its development needs and priorities, further strengthen its human resources, consolidate the gains achieved so far, accelerate and sustain economic growth, reduce poverty and improve the welfare of the people of Timor-Leste.

The Act aims to ensure stability and transparency in the regulation of petroleum development. In this regard, it is complemented by existing and future transparency requirements in Timor-Leste, including in relation to the publication and saving of petroleum revenues.

Pursuant to Section 95.1 and Article 139 of the Constitution of Timor-Leste, the National Parliament enacts the following that shall have the force of law:

CHAPTER I – GENERAL PROVISIONS

Article 1 Citation

This Act may be cited as the "Petroleum Act".

ARTICLE 2 DEFINITIONS

In this Act: "Access Authorisation" means an authorisation granted pursuant to Article 11; "Act" means this *Petroleum Act*, as amended or modified from time to time, and regulations made and directions given under it; “Affiliate” means, in respect of an Authorised Person (or, if more than one Person, in respect of

each such Person), a Person that Controls, is Controlled by, or is under common Control with, the Authorised Person or any such Person, as the case may be; “Authorisation” means an Access Authorisation, a Petroleum Contract, a Prospecting

Authorisation or a Seepage Use Authorisation or any agreement made in respect of such an Authorisation or Contract; “Authorised Area” means the area from time to time the subject of an Authorisation; “Authorised Person” means:

(a) in respect of a Petroleum Contract, a Contractor; and

(b) in respect of any other Authorisation, the Person to whom the Authorisation has been granted; “Calendar Year” means a period of twelve months commencing on January 1 and ending on the following December 31, according to the Gregorian calendar;

“Code” means the *Petroleum Mining Code* adopted pursuant to Article 7, paragraph (a) of the Treaty, as amended, varied, modified or replaced from time to time, and regulations made and directions given under it;

“Contract Area” means the Authorised Area under a Petroleum Contract; “Contractor” means a Person with whom the Ministry has made a Petroleum Contract; “Control” means, in relation to a Person, the power of another Person to secure:

(i) by means of the holding of shares or the possession of voting power, in or in relation to the first Person or any other Person; or

(ii) by virtue of any power conferred by the articles of association of, or any other document regulating, the first Person or any other Person, that the affairs of the first Person are conducted in accordance with the wishes or directions of that other Person;

“Crude Oil” means crude mineral oil and all liquid hydrocarbons in their natural state or obtained from Natural Gas by condensation or extraction; “Decommission” means, in respect of the Authorised Area or a part of it, as the case may be, to abandon, decommission, transfer, remove and/or dispose of structures, facilities, installations, equipment and other property, and other works, used in Petroleum Operations in the Authorised Area, to clean up the Authorised Area and make it good and safe, and to protect the environment;

“Good Oil Field Practice” has the meaning in Section 23.1; “Government” means the Government of the Democratic Republic of Timor-Leste; “Inspector” has the meaning in Section 26.1; “Ministry” means the ministry or other agency, from time to time, responsible for the administration of this Act; “Natural Gas” means all gaseous hydrocarbons and inerts, including wet mineral gas, dry mineral gas, casing head gas and residue gas remaining after the extraction of liquid hydrocarbons from wet gas, but not Crude Oil; “Operator” means an Authorised Person or other Person named in an Authorisation or unitisation agreement to organise and supervise Petroleum Operations; “Parliament” means the National Parliament of Timor-Leste; “Person” includes a corporation or other legal entity; “Petroleum” means:

(i) any naturally occurring hydrocarbon, whether in a gaseous, liquid or solid state;

(ii) any mixture of naturally occurring hydrocarbons, whether in a gaseous, liquid or solid state; or

(iii) any Petroleum (as defined above) that has been returned to a reservoir;

"Petroleum Contract" means a contract, licence, permit or other authorisation made or given pursuant to Article 10; "Petroleum Operations" means activities for the purposes of:

(i) prospecting for Petroleum;

(ii) exploration for, development, exploitation, sale or export of Petroleum; or

(iii) construction, installation or operation of any structures, facilities or installations for the development, exploitation and export of Petroleum, or decommissioning or removal of any such structure, facility or installation;

"Prospecting Authorisation" means an authorisation granted pursuant to Article 9; "Public Officer" means a civil servant or equivalent individual, members of Parliament or of Government, Judges or Public Prosecutors;

"Reservoir" means a porous and permeable underground formation containing an individual and separate natural accumulation of producible hydrocarbons (oil and/or gas) that is confined by impermeable rock and/or water barriers and is characterized by a single natural pressure system;

"Seep" means, in respect of Petroleum, Petroleum which is seeping to the surface, naturally, through natural conduits;

"Seepage Use Authorisation" means an authorisation granted pursuant to Article 12;

"State-Owned Contractor" means the Contractor incorporated under the laws of Timor-Leste which is controlled, directly or indirectly, by Timor-Leste;

"Territory of Timor-Leste" consists of the territory of Timor-Leste, including its territorial sea, together with its exclusive economic zone and continental shelf where, by international law, Timor-Leste has sovereign rights for the purposes of exploring for and exploiting its natural resources;

"Timor-Leste" means the Democratic Republic of Timor-Leste;

"Treaty" means the Timor Sea Treaty between the Government of Timor-Leste and the Government of Australia signed on 20th May 2002;

"Well" means a perforation in the earth's surface dug or bored for the purpose of producing Petroleum; and

"Wellhead" means the point where Petroleum exits the confines of the Well and associated systems.

ARTICLE 3 TERRITORIAL SCOPE OF ACT

This Act applies to the Territory of Timor-Leste.

Except as otherwise provided, this Act does not apply to any area that is subject to a provisional arrangement within the meaning of Section 83(3) of the United Nations Convention on the Law of the Sea, done at Montego Bay December 10, 1982.

ARTICLE 4 MATERIAL SCOPE OF ACT

This Act applies to Petroleum Operations.

The existence of an Authorisation in force in a given area does not prevent authorisation of the exploration and exploitation of mineral substances other than Petroleum, provided that such other activity does not hinder the proper performance of the Petroleum Operations.

Article 5 Title to Petroleum

Title to, and control over, Petroleum in the Territory of Timor-Leste are vested in Timor-Leste.

A Person may acquire title to Petroleum only after it has been lawfully recovered.

Article 6 Exercise by the Ministry of its Powers and Functions

1. The Ministry shall exercise its powers and discharge its functions under this Act, including under Authorisations made hereunder, in such a manner as:

(a) to ensure sound resource management;

(b) to ensure that Petroleum is developed in a way that minimises damage to the natural environment, is economically sustainable, promotes further investment and contributes to the long-term development of Timor-Leste;

(c) is reasonable; and

(d) is consistent with Good Oil Field Practice.

2. Before exercising any such power or discharging any such function, the Ministry may give opportunity to Persons likely to be affected to make representations to it, and shall give consideration to the relevant representations received by it

Article 7 Restrictions to Rights of Public Officers

1. A Public Officer shall not acquire, attempt to acquire or hold:

(a) an Authorisation or an interest, whether direct or indirect, in an Authorisation; or

(b) a share in a corporation (or an Affiliate of it) that holds an Authorisation.

Any instrument that grants or purports to grant, to a Public Officer, an interest, whether direct or indirect, in an Authorisation shall, to the extent of the grant, be void.

The acquisition or holding of an Authorisation, interest or share by the minor children or spouse of a Public Officer shall be deemed to be an acquisition or holding by the Public Officer.

Article 8 Graticulation

For the purposes of this Act, the Territory of Timor-Leste, or parts thereof, shall be divided into blocks according to a grid system.

CHAPTER II – AUTHORISATION OF PETROLEUM OPERATIONS

Article 9 Prospecting Authorisations

The Ministry may grant a Prospecting Authorisation, in respect of a specified area, to a Person or a group of Persons.

(a) A Prospecting Authorisation grants a right to perform geological, geophysical, geochemical and geotechnical surveys in the Authorised Area.

The Prospecting Authorisation shall require the Authorised Person to report on the progress and results of such prospecting, and to maintain confidentiality with respect thereto.

Nothing in a Prospecting Authorisation authorises the holder to drill a Well or to have any preference or right to make a Petroleum Contract.

Prior to granting a Prospecting Authorisation in respect of an area that is the subject of an existing Authorisation, the Ministry shall give written notice to the holder of the existing Authorisation.

(a) The holder of a Prospecting Authorisation may surrender it at any time by written notice to the Ministry, provided that the Authorised Person has fulfilled all its obligations thereunder.

(b) If the holder has not complied with a condition to which the Prospecting Authorisation is subject, the Ministry may terminate it by written notice to the holder.

Article 10 Petroleum Contracts

The Ministry may conclude a Petroleum Contract, in respect of a specified area, with a Person or a group of Persons provided that if a group, such group has entered into a joint operating agreement approved by the Ministry under Section 18.1.

In order to be eligible to enter into a Petroleum Contract, a Person must:

have, or have access to, the financial capability, and the technical knowledge and technical ability, to carry out the Petroleum Operations in the Contract Area;

not have a record of non-compliance with principles of good corporate citizenship; and be a limited liability corporation or entity with limited liability.

(a) Without prejudice to Articles 11 and 12, a Petroleum Contract grants to the Contractor the exclusive right to conduct Petroleum Operations in the Contract Area.

(b) The Petroleum Contract may be limited to Crude Oil, Natural Gas or other constituents of Petroleum.

(a) A Contractor shall give written notice to the Ministry within twenty four (24) hours whenever any Petroleum is discovered in its Authorised Area.

(b) The Contractor shall provide such information relating to the discovery requested by the Ministry.

A Petroleum Contract shall oblige the Contractor to carry on Petroleum Operations only in accordance with work programmes, plans and budgets approved by the Ministry.

Article 11 Access Authorisations

1. (a) The Ministry may grant an Access Authorisation, in respect of a specified area, to a Person or a group of Persons.

(b) The Ministry may not grant an Access Authorisation in respect of an area that is the subject of a Petroleum Contract, a Prospecting Authorisation or a Seepage Use Authorisation until it has taken into account any submissions made by the holders of such Authorisations in such a way that there is no undue interference with the rights of that other Authorised Person.

2. (a) An Access Authorisation, while it remains in force, authorises the holder to do one or more of the following:

(i) construct, install and operate structures, facilities and installations; and

(ii) carry out other works; as specified in the Authorisation in the Authorised Area.

(b) Nothing in an Access Authorisation authorises the holder to drill a Well.

3. (a) An Access Authorlsatlon:

(i) may be surrendered by the holder by written notice to the Ministry, provided that the Authorised Person has fulfilled all its obligations thereunder; and

(ii) may be terminated by the Ministry at any time by written notice to the holder, if the holder has not complied with a condition to which the Authorisation is subject.

(b) The Ministry shall provide written notice of the surrender or termination to any Authorised Person in whose Authorised Area operations were authorised to be carried on by the Access Authorisation concerned.

4. The Ministry may give a direction to the holders of Access Authorisations and to other Authorised Persons regarding the coordination of their respective Petroleum Operations.

Article 12 Seepage Use Authorisations

a) The Ministry may grant a Seepage Use Authorisation in respect of a specified area.

b) The Ministry may grant a Seepage Use Authorisation to a Person who is acting for this purpose on behalf of a class of Persons specified in the Authorisation.

(a) A Seepage Use Authorisation grants an exclusive right to exploit a Seep in a specified area.

A Seepage Use Authorisation shall require the Authorised Person to report on the progress and results of such exploitation.

A Seepage Use Authorisation shall specify the maximum depth to which the Authorised Person may drill a Well.

(a) Notwithstanding paragraph 10.3(a), a Seepage Use Authorisation may be granted in respect of an area that is already the subject of an Authorisation other than a Seepage Use Authorisation, and the Seepage Use Authorisation prevails if there is conflict.

Prior to granting a Seepage Use Authorisation in respect of an area that is the subject of an existing Authorisation, the Ministry shall give written notice to the holder of the existing Authorisation.

Any Authorisation granted subsequent to the Seepage Use Authorisation shall be subject to the rights of holders of Seepage Use Authorisations.

(a) A Seepage Use Authorisation:

(i) may be surrendered by the holder by written notice to the Ministry, provided that the Authorised Person has fulfilled all its obligations thereunder; and

(ii) may be terminated by the Ministry at any time by written notice to the holder, if the holder has not complied with a condition to which the Seepage Use Authorisation is subject.

(b) The Ministry shall provide written notice of the surrender or termination to any Authorised Person in whose Authorised Area operations were authorised to be carried on by the Seepage Use Authorisation concerned.

(iii) training of, and giving preference in employment in the Petroleum Operations to, nationals of Timor-Leste; and (iv) the acquisition of goods and services from Persons based in Timor-Leste.

(b) An Authorisation awarded to an applicant obliges it to comply with its proposals as mentioned in paragraph 13.3(a).

Article 13 Invitation to Apply

1. (a) The Ministry shall invite, by public notice, applications for Authorisations.

(b) Notwithstanding paragraph 13.1(a), the Ministry may elect to award Authorisations through direct negotiation without issuing such invitations:

(i) in the case of Access Authorisations; or

(ii) in the case of all other Authorisations, where it is in the public interest to do so.

(c) If the Ministry grants an Authorisation without inviting applications, it shall

provide reasons for its so doing.

(d) The application shall be submitted in one of the official languages of Timor-Leste or, in the event that they are written in any other language, be accompanied by an official translation into one of the official languages of Timor-Leste, and shall be submitted in a closed envelope.

2. (a) An invitation shall specify the area concerned, the proposed activities, the criteria upon which applications will be assessed, the applicable fees (if any) to be paid with the application, and the time by which, and the manner in which, applications may be made.

(b) Unless the invitation otherwise states, the Ministry may choose not to award an Authorisation to any of the applicants.

3. (a) An application for an Authorisation shall include proposals for:

(i) securing the health, safety and welfare of persons involved in or affected by the Petroleum Operations;

(ii) protecting the environment, preventing, minimising and remedying pollution, and other environmental harm from the Petroleum Operations;

4. The Ministry shall not grant an Authorisation in respect of an area until it has given due consideration to all applications made in response to, and in compliance with, an invitation.

Article 14 Succession of Petroleum Operations Under the Treaty

Once the Treaty is no longer in force, the Ministry shall grant an Authorisation or conclude a Petroleum Contract with those Persons who were engaged in Petroleum Operations under the terms of the Treaty under conditions equivalent to those that were in place under the Treaty, with the addition of incorporation of the terms included in Article 22.

Article 15 Petroleum Operations Generally

Every Petroleum Contract, Access Authorisation and Seepage Use Authorisation shall require that third party access be granted on reasonable terms and conditions.

(a) If there is more than one Authorised Person in respect of a particular Authorisation, the obligations and liabilities of the Authorised Person under an Authorisation are the obligations and liabilities of them all, jointly and severally.

(b) With respect to a Petroleum Contract, the State-Owned Contractor may be exempted by the Ministry of the requirement set out in paragraph 15.2(a).

An Authorisation is void *ab initio*, if obtained in violation of the laws of Timor-Leste, including laws concerning corruption.

Article 16 Restitution and Reparation

1. Without prejudice to any criminal liability of that Person, a Person who engages in Petroleum Operations other than pursuant to an Authorisation shall:

(a) make restitution to Timor-Leste of an amount equal to the market value of Petroleum developed, exploited or exported, together with late payment interest thereon at a rate not to exceed the legal rate of interest to be determined by the Ministry;

(b) either forfeit all infrastructure and equipment used in engaging in those Petroleum Operations, or remove such infrastructure and equipment or be liable for the payment of the costs of such removal; and

(c) clean-up pollution resulting from those Petroleum Operations, or reimburse the costs of clean-up to Timor-Leste.

The liabilities under Section 16.1 shall apply cumulatively, or not, as is determined to be appropriate by the Ministry, with a view to place Timor-Leste in the position in which it would have been were it not for the Petroleum Operations engaged in other than pursuant to an Authorisation.

The liabilities under Section 16.1 of Persons who, together, are engaged in, or have engaged in, Petroleum Operations are the liabilities of them all, jointly and severally.

Article 17 Restrictions on Exercise of Rights

1. (a) An Authorised Person shall not exercise any of the rights granted under an Authorisation or under this Act:

(i) on any public immovable property without the consent of the responsible authority;

(ii) on any private immovable property of the State without the consent of the responsible authority; or

(iii) on any private immovable property without payment of fair and reasonable compensation to the owner.

(b) The owner of any immovable property in an Authorised Area retains rights to the use of its land except in so far as the use interferes with Petroleum Operations.

(c) An Authorisation may limit or otherwise control the use by an Authorised Person of public infrastructure, and the consumption of other natural resources, including trees, sand, gravel, rock and water.

(d) An Authorisation does not constitute a waiver of the obligation to seek the written consent of responsible authorities.

An Authorised Person shall not exercise any of the rights under an Authorisation or under this Act in a way that interferes with fishing, navigation or any other lawful offshore operation without the written consent of the responsible authority.

(a) The Authorised Person is liable to pay fair and reasonable compensation if, in the course of Petroleum Operations, it:

disturbs the rights of the owner of any immovable property, or causes any damage thereon; or

demonstrably interferes with fishing, navigation or any other lawful offshore activities.

(b) Where the value of any rights have been enhanced by the Petroleum Operations, compensation payable in respect of such rights shall not exceed any amount which would be payable if the value had not been so enhanced.

What constitutes fair and reasonable compensation under this Article 17 shall be decided by the Ministry, after having considered representations by interested parties.

Article 18 Approvals by Ministry

A joint operating agreement, a lifting arrangement and any agreement related to the Petroleum Operations, as well as any changes to such agreements, shall be subject to prior approval by the Ministry.

(a) All changes in Control of an Authorised Person shall be subject to prior approval by the Ministry.

Where a change in Control occurs without the prior approval of the Ministry, the Ministry may terminate the applicable Authorisation.

Paragraph 18.2(a) does not apply if the change in Control is the direct result of an acquisition of shares or other securities listed on a recognised stock exchange.

For the purposes of paragraph 18.2(a), change in Control includes a Person ceasing to be in Control (whether or not another Person becomes in Control), and a Person obtaining Control (whether or not another Person was in Control).

Except with the prior written consent of the Ministry, or as explicitly provided in the terms of the Authorisation, no assignment, transfer, conveyance, novation, merger, encumbrance or other similar dealing in respect of an Authorisation shall be of any force or effect.

Article 19 Unitisation Contract

1. (a) Where a Reservoir is partly within a Contract Area, and partly in another Contract Area:

(i) the Ministry may require by written notice the Contractors to enter into a unitisation agreement with each other for the purpose of securing the more effective and optimised production of Petroleum from the Reservoir; and

(ii) if no agreement has been reached within a period of eighteen (18) months from receipt of written notice as required in sub-paragraph 19.1(a)(i), the Ministry shall decide on the unitisation agreement.

(b) Where a Reservoir is partly within a Contract Area and partly in an area that is not the subject of a Petroleum Contract:

(i) the Ministry may require by written notice the Contractor to enter into a unitisation agreement with the Ministry for the purpose of securing the more effective and optimised production of Petroleum from the Reservoir; and

(ii) if no agreement has been reached within a period of eighteen (18) months from receipt of written notice as required in sub-paragraph 19.1(b)(i), the Ministry shall decide on the unitisation agreement, unless otherwise provided in the Petroleum Contract.

Without limiting the matters to be dealt with, the unitisation agreement shall define the amount of Petroleum in each area covered by the unitisation agreement, and shall appoint the Operator responsible for production of the Petroleum covered by the unitisation agreement.

The Ministry may approve the development or exploitation of the Reservoir only after it has approved or decided the unitisation agreement.

Any changes to the unitisation agreement shall be subject to prior approval by the Ministry.

Article 20 Resolution of Disputes

1. (a) The Ministry may inquire into and decide all disputes involving Persons engaged in Petroleum Operations, either:

(i) among themselves, where agreements between them do not specify a dispute resolution mechanism; or

(ii) in relation to third parties (other than the Government) not so engaged, as long as these third parties accept the jurisdiction of the Ministry for the resolution of the dispute.

(b) The Ministry may refuse to decide any dispute referred to it and, if it does so, it shall notify the parties to the dispute in writing.

(c) The Ministry may, taking into account all relevant circumstances, give any direction which may be necessary for the purpose of giving effect to its decision in proceedings pursuant to this Article 20, including ordering the payment, by any party to a dispute, to any other party to the dispute of such compensation as may be fair and reasonable.

2. (a) If a dispute arises relating to the interpretation and/or application of the terms of an Authorisation between an Authorised Person and the Ministry, the parties shall attempt to resolve that dispute by means of negotiation.

(b) If the dispute cannot be resolved by negotiation, either party may submit the dispute to arbitration or to the competent judicial authority.

Article 21 Exemption from or Variation of Conditions

The Ministry may exempt an Authorised Person from complying with the conditions of its Authorisation, and may also agree to vary or suspend those conditions, either with or without conditions and either temporarily or permanently

CHAPTER III – STATE PARTICIPATION

Article 22 State Participation in Petroleum Operations

The decision by Timor-Leste to participate in Petroleum Operations shall be made by the Council of Ministers, which can delegate such competence to the Prime Minister.

This Act shall apply to the State-Owned Contractor in the same terms as is applicable to any other Contractor, with the required adaptations

Each Authorisation shall stipulate the right of Timor-Leste to participate in Petroleum Operations, up to a maximum equity of 20%.

The participation of Timor-Leste may occur during any phase of Petroleum Operations in accordance with the terms and conditions to be established by contract.

CHAPTER IV – CONDUCT OF PETROLEUM ACTIVITIES

Article 23 Work Practices

1. Petroleum Operations shall be conducted in accordance with Good Oil Field Practice, that is, in accordance with such practices and procedures employed in the petroleum industry worldwide by prudent and diligent operators under conditions and circumstances similar to those experienced in connection with the relevant aspect or aspects of the Petroleum Operations, principally aimed at guaranteeing:

(i) conservation of Petroleum resources, which implies the utilization of adequate methods and processes to maximize the recovery of hydrocarbons in a technically and economically sustainable manner, with a corresponding control of reserves decline, and to minimize losses at the surface;

(ii) operational safety, which entails the use of methods and processes that promote occupational security and the prevention of accidents;

(iii) environmental protection, that calls for the adoption of methods and processes which minimize the impact of Petroleum Operations on the environment;

2. Production of Petroleum shall take place:

(a) in such a manner that as much as possible of the Petroleum in place in each individual Petroleum deposit, or in several deposits in combination, will be produced;

(b) in accordance with Good Oil Field Practice and sound economic principles; and

(c) in such a manner that waste of Petroleum or reservoir energy is avoided.

3. Contractors shall carry out continuous evaluation of production strategy and technical solutions, shall take the necessary measures in order to achieve this, and shall inform the Ministry of any relevant changes, in accordance with Good Oil Field Practice.

Article 24 Decommissioning

1. An Authorised Person shall Decommission on the earlier of:

(a) termination of the Authorisation; and

(b) when no longer required for Petroleum Operations; and, in either case:

(c) except with the consent in writing of the Ministry and in accordance with the conditions of the consent; or

(d) unless the Authorisation otherwise provides.

CHAPTER V – INFORMATION AND INVESTIGATION

Article 25 Data and Information

Timor-Leste shall have title to all data and information, whether raw, derived, processed, interpreted or analysed, obtained pursuant to any Authorisation.

Data and information acquired during the course of Petroleum Operations may be freely exported by Authorised Persons provided that the Ministry may require that an original, or in the case of a core, rock, fluid or other physical sample, a usable portion of the original, of all data and information, both physical and electronic, be kept in Timor-Leste.

Article 26 Audit and Inspection

1. (a) The Ministry may appoint a person to be an inspector for the purposes of this Act (an "Inspector").

(b) The Inspector will have the powers and rights provided to it in the regulations.

2. On request, an Authorised Person shall make its books and accounts available to the Ministry for auditing.

Article 27 Termination of Authorisations

1. (a) Termination of an Authorisation for any reason is without prejudice to rights and obligations expressed in this Act or the Authorisation to survive termination, or to rights and obligations accrued thereunder prior to termination, and all provisions of an Authorisation reasonably necessary for the full enjoyment and enforcement of those rights and obligations survive termination for the period so necessary.

(b) The Ministry shall have the power to terminate an Authorisation as set out in the Authorisation.

2. (a) If there is more than one Authorised Person in respect of a particular Authorisation and circumstances arise in which the Ministry may terminate an Authorisation, the Ministry may elect to terminate an Authorisation only in respect of those Authorised Persons whose acts or omissions (or in relation to whom acts, omissions or events have occurred which) have led to such circumstances, and shall so notify the remaining Authorised Persons.

(b) Should the Ministry terminate an authorisation under paragraph 27.2(a), it shall give the remaining Authorised Persons right of preference in the acquisition of the terminated share, in proportion to their respective shares. Any share not acquired by the remaining Authorised Persons shall revert to Timor-Leste.

Article 28 Indemnification of the Government and Ministry

1. An Authorised Person shall:

(a) defend, indemnify and hold harmless the Government and Ministry from all claims by third parties resulting, directly or indirectly, from Petroleum Operations, and pay all compensations relating to any civil liability claims, pretensions or demands; and

(b) unless the Ministry is satisfied, after consultation with the Authorised Person, that the potential liability under Article 28, paragraph (a) can be covered by other means, maintain insurance in respect thereof on a strict liability basis for such amount as the Ministry requires from time to time.

CHAPTER VI – PUBLIC INFORMATION

Article 29 Publication by Ministry

1. The Ministry shall publish, in the *Jornal da República*:

(a) notice of the grant of Authorisations, and a summary of the terms of such Authorisations;

(b) invitations for applications for Authorisations under Section 13.1(a); and

(c) notice of the termination of Authorisations.

2. The Ministry shall publish invitations for applications for Authorisations under Section

13.1 (a) in the media, in such manner as is required by regulation.

Article 30 Public Information

1. (a) The Ministry shall make available to the public:

(i) copies of all Authorisations and amendments thereto, whether or not terminated;

(ii) details of exemptions from, or variations or suspensions of, the conditions of an Authorization under Article 21; and

(iii) copies of all unitisation agreements.

(b) The Ministry shall make available to the public, within a reasonable period of time of a request having been made therefor, summary details of:

(i) the Authorisations (and amendments thereto, whether or not terminated) and unitisation agreements contemplated in paragraph 30.1(a);

(ii) an approved Development Plan;

(iii) all assignments and other dealings consented to in respect of Authorisations, subject to commercial confidence as to the commercial terms; and (iv) all Authorisations (and amendments thereto, whether or not terminated) and unitisation agreements in compliance with the Code.

(c) The Ministry shall make available to the public, within a reasonable period of time of a request having been made therefor, the summary details pertaining to Petroleum Operations in the area covered by the Treaty, provided in compliance with the Code.

2. Within ten (10) business days of a request having been made, the Ministry shall publish brief reasons for:

(a) granting an Authorisation subsequent to an invitation, as contemplated at paragraph 13.1(a);

(b) granting an Authorisation without inviting applications, as contemplated at paragraph 13.1(b);

(c) approving a Development Plan under a Petroleum Contract;

(d) granting an exemption from, or agreeing to a variation or suspension of, the conditions of an Authorization under Article 21; and

(e) making any decision or granting any approval that, under an Authorisation, requires publication.

3. (a) Companies shall report on their compliance with requirements under the Act and Authorisations in such manner and detail as required by their Authorisation and as provided by regulation.

(b) The Ministry shall make available such reports to the public.

The Ministry shall make available to the public such reports by Authorised Persons on payments relating to Petroleum Operations made to the Government of Timor-Leste as are required by law.

The information contemplated in this Article 30 shall be available to any Person on payment of the fee therefor, to be provided by regulation.

The information contemplated in paragraphs 30.1(b) and 30.1(c) shall be available in at least one official language of Timor-Leste.

CHAPTER VII – REGULATIONS AND DIRECTIONS

Article 31 Regulations

1. The Government may make regulations under this Act relating to the following:

(a) graticulation of the Territory of Timor-Leste;

(b) the exploration for and the production of Petroleum;

(c) the use and disclosure of data, information, records and reports;

(d) the measurement and sale or disposal of Petroleum;

(e) health and safety;

(f) protection and restoration of the environment;

(g) resource management;

(h) structures, facilities and installations;

(i) the clean-up or other remedying of the effects of the escape of Petroleum;

(j) abandonment and decommissioning;

(k) the control of movement into, within and out of Timor-Leste of persons, vessels, aircraft, vehicles and any other man-made platforms and structures;

(l) work programmes and budgets;

(m) the control of tariffs charged for third party access;

(n) the auditing of an Authorised Person and of its accounts and records;

(o) reporting by Authorised Persons on compliance with obligations set out in the Act and Authorisations, including in relation to:

(i) the training and employment of Timor-Leste nationals,

(ii) procurement of Timor-Leste goods and services,

(iii) occupational health and safety, and (iv) environmental protection.

(p) fees to be paid, including by applicants for Authorisations, Authorised Persons, and Persons wishing to inspect the public register; and

(q) any other matters relating to this Act.

2. The Ministry shall publish regulations in the *Jornal da República*.

Article 32 Directions

In addition to its power to give directions under paragraph 11.4(a) and paragraph 20.1(c), the Ministry may give a direction to an Authorised Person:

(a) relating to any matter set out in Section 31.1; or

(b) otherwise requiring compliance with this Act or its Authorisation.

CHAPTER VIII – PENALTY PROVISIONS

Article 33 Territorial and Material Scope of this Chapter

Articles 34, 35, 37, 39, 40, 41 and 43 are, with the required adaptations, applicable to the areas that are subject to the Treaty.

The provisions of this Chapter are without prejudice to criminal and civil liability under the general law.

Article 34 Unauthorised Activities

Whoever engages in Petroleum Operations other than pursuant to an Authorisation shall be punished by imprisonment from three (3) months up to five (5) years or fine of no less than one hundred (100) days.

If the damaged caused to the State is of an amount of fifty thousand United States Dollars (USD $50,000.00) or greater, the penalty shall be imprisonment from one (1) up to eight

(8) years or fine of no less than one hundred and fifty (150) days.

Article 35 Danger to People, Property and Environment

1. Whoever, by conduct that contravenes the provisions of this Act or the Code, endangers the life or physical integrity of a person, endangers property of high value, or gravely endangers the environment, shall be punished by:

(a) Imprisonment from one (1) up to eight (8) years or fine of no less than two hundred (200) days, if the conduct and the creation of the danger are malicious;

(b) Imprisonment up to five (5) years or fine of no less than one hundred (100) days, if the conduct is malicious and the creation of the danger is negligent.

Article 36 Hindering the Exercise of Powers by the Inspector

Whoever, directly or indirectly, in any measure or by any means, hinders, or leads someone else to hinder, the exercise of powers and rights by the Inspector, shall be punished by imprisonment from three (3) months up to four (4) years or fine of no less than one hundred (100) days.

An attempt is punishable.

Article 37 Misleading Information

1. Whoever,

(a) in, or in connection with, any application under this Act or the Code, knowingly or recklessly gives information that is materially false or misleading; or

(b) in any report, return or affidavit submitted under any provision of this Act or the Code or an Authorisation thereunder, knowingly or recklessly includes or permits to be included, any information which is materially false or misleading;

shall be punished by imprisonment up to three (3) years or fine of no less than seventy five (75) days.

2. An attempt is punishable.

Article 38 Non-compliance with Regulations or Directions

Where a Person fails or neglects to comply with a regulation to which Article 31 refers, and/or with a direction to which Article 32 refers, the Ministry may cause to be done all or any of the things required by the regulation or direction to be done at the cost and expense of that Person.

Costs and expenses incurred by the Ministry under the previous paragraph, together with interest thereon at a rate to be determined by the Ministry, shall be a debt due to the Government.

Article 39 Accessory Penalties

1. In relation to the crimes provided for in the Act, the following accessory penalties may be applied:

(a) Temporary deprivation of the right to participate in public tenders concerning Petroleum Operations, in particular those regarding Authorisations and the procurement of goods and services;

(b) Embargo of any construction works, in such cases as they may result in irreversible damage to relevant public interests;

(c) Disability, up to a maximum of two (2) years, of the exercise of activities, if the Person has, within the period of one (1) year starting from the date of the first contravention, contravened this Act, or regulations or directions issued thereunder;

(d) Termination of Authorisations;

(e) Good conduct bond;

(f) Disability of rights to subsidies awarded by public entities or services;

(g) Publication of the sentence; and/or

(h) Other writs of prevention which are adequate taking into account the circumstances of the case in question.

Article 40 Liability of Legal Persons, Corporations and Other Legal Entities

Legal persons, corporations or any other legal entities, including those without juridical personality, are liable for contraventions provided for in this Chapter when committed by its organs or representatives in its name and in the collective interest.

The liability is excluded where the agent has acted against express orders or instructions properly issued.

The liability of the entities mentioned in Section 40.1 does not exclude the individual liability of the respective agents.

The entities mentioned in Section 40.1 are jointly and severally liable, as provided for in civil law, for the payment of any fines or compensations, or for the fulfillment of any obligations, derived from the facts or with incidence on matters covered by the scope of this Act.

Article 41 Fines to Legal Persons, Corporations and Other Legal Entities

In the case of legal persons, corporations or any other legal entities, including those without juridical personality, the daily rate for fines corresponds to an amount between five United States Dollars (USD $5.00) and ten thousand United States Dollars (USD $10,000.00), as determined by the court, taking into account the economic and financial situation and burdens of the legal person, corporation or other legal entity.

If the fine is applied to an entity without juridical personality, its payment will be guaranteed by the entity's assets and, in the event of non-existence of such assets or under-capitalisation, jointly and severally, the assets of each of the associates.

Article 42 Inspection

It is the competence of the Ministry and the Inspector, as well as any other organs of the Public Administration to whom such competence is delegated, in accordance with law and regulations, to ensure the inspection of compliance with the provisions of this Act, without prejudice of competences which the law confers upon other public entities.

Article 43 Extrajudicial Writ of Execution

For purposes of coercive collection under general law, a certification issued by the Ministry in relation to a debt constituted, or amount due, as a result of the application of the provisions of this Act, which is not paid within a reasonable period to be determined by the Ministry, and which shall be notified in writing to the debtor, constitutes an extrajudicial writ of execution.

Article 44 Subsidiary Legislation

General criminal law, as well as relevant administrative and civil legislation, are applicable in a subsidiary manner, with the required adaptations, to give effect to the provisions of this Chapter.

CHAPTER IX – OTHER AND FINAL PROVISIONS

Article 45 Transitional Provision

Article 16 applies, with the required adaptations, to all Petroleum Operations engaged in other than pursuant to an Authorisation from 28 November 1975.

At its discretion, the Ministry may issue regulations setting out the administrative procedure to be followed, as well as obligations to be undertaken, by Persons who have engaged in or are engaging in Petroleum Operations other than pursuant to an Authorisation as of the date of entry into force of this Act in order for past and/or ongoing such Petroleum Operations to be deemed, for purposes of this Act, to be engaged in pursuant to an Authorisation.

Article 46 Non-Transfer

An Authorisation granted to an individual cannot be transferred by inheritance, without prejudice to the ability of the value of that Authorisation to be transferred by inheritance.

Article 47 Entry into Force

This Act shall enter into force on the day after its publication in the *Jornal da República*.

Approved on 29th July 2005

LAW NO. 22/2001 ON PETROLEUM AND NATURAL GAS

BY GRACE OF THE GOD ALMIGHTY THE PRESIDENT OF THE REPUBLIC OF INDONESIA

Considering :

a. that the national development must be directed to creation of people's welfare by reforming all aspects of national and state life on the basis of the state ideology Pancasila and the Constitution of 1945;

b. that since petroleum and natural gas are non-renewable strategic natural-resources controlled by the state and vital commodities controlling life of public at large and play important role in the national economy, the exploitation of petroleum and natural gas must be capable of contributing maximally to the people's prosperity and welfare;

c. that petroleum and natural gas related business activities play important role in proving real added value for the national economic growth which is increasing and sustainable;

d. that Law No. 44 Prp./1960 on petroleum and natural gas mining, Law No. 15/1962 on the stipulation of Government Regulation in lieu of Law No. 2/1962 on the obligation of oil companies to meet the domestic need and Law No. 8/1971 on state-owned oil and gas mining companies are no longer suitable to developments of petroleum and natural gas mining businesses;

e. that by continuously observing national and international developments, it is necessary to amend legislation on petroleum and natural gas mining so as to be capable of creating independent, reliable, transparent, competitive, efficient and environmental friendly petroleum and natural gas business activities as well as boosting the growth of national potential and role;

f. that base on the considerations as meant in letters a, b, c, d and e as well as to provide legal basis for steps of renewal and arrangement of petroleum and natural gas exploitation, it is necessary to promulgate a law on petroleum and natural gas;

In view of :

Article 5 paragraph (1), Article 20 paragraphs (1), (2), (4) and (5), Article 33 paragraphs (2) and (3) of the Constitution of 1945 as already amended by the Second Amendment to the Constitution of 1945;

Stipulation of the People's Consultative Assembly of the Republic of Indonesia No. XV/MPR/1998 on the realization of regional autonomy; regulation, sharing and exploitation of national resources on the basis of the principle of justice; as well as financial equilibrium between the central government and regional governments in the framework of the Unitary State of the Republic of Indonesia.

With the collective approval of THE HOUSE OF REPRESENTATIVES OF THE REPUBLIC OF INDONESIA

DECIDES :

To stipulate : LAW ON PETROLEUM AND NATURAL GAS.

CHAPTER I GENERAL PROVISION

Article 1

Petroleum shall be a result of the natural process in the form hydrocarbon in a pressure condition and at atmosphere temperature which constitutes liquid or solid material, including asphalt, mineral candle or ozokerit and bitumen obtained from a mining process, excluding coal and sediments of other hydrocarbon in the form of solid material obtained from activities not connected with petroleum and natural gas-related business activities.

Natural gas is shall a produce of the natural process in form of hydrocarbon in a pressure condition and at an atmosphere temperature that in the form of gas, which is obtained from a petroleum and natural gas mining process.

Petroleum and natural gas shall be natural oil and gas.

Fuel oil shall be fuel derived and/or processed from petroleum.

Mining concession shall be the authority delegated by the state to the government to manage exploration and exploitation activities.

General survey shall field activities covering the collection, analysis and presentation of data connected with information on geological condition to predict the location and potential of petroleum and natural gas resources outside the working area.

Upstream business activities shall be business activities focused or based on exploration and exploitation business activities.

Exploration shall be activities aimed at obtaining information on geological condition to find and obtain the estimated reserves of petroleum and natural gas in the working area stipulated.

Exploitation shall be a series of activities aimed at producing petroleum and natural gas from the working area stipulated, consisting of drilling and completion of wells, the building of transport, storage and processing facilities to separate and purify petroleum and natural gas in the field as well as other activities supporting the exploitation.

Downstream business activities shall be business activities focused or based on processing, transport, storage and/or commercial business activities.

Processing shall be activities to purify, obtain parts, increase the quality and added value of petroleum and/or natural gas, excluding on-sight processing.

Transport shall be activities to move petroleum, natural gas and/or their processed products from the working area or storage and processing places, including the transport of natural gas through transmission and distribution pipeline.

Storage shall be activities to receive, collect, store and release petroleum and/or natural gas.

Commerce shall be activities to purchase, sell, export and import petroleum, natural gas and/or their processed products, including commerce of natural gas through pipeline.

The Indonesian mining jurisdiction shall be all Indonesian mainland, waters and continental shelf territories.

Working area shall be a certain region within the Indonesian mining jurisdiction used for the exploration and exploitation.

Business entities shall be companies in the form of statutory body which undertake businesses permanently, continuously and are established in accordance with laws in force as well as operate and are domiciled in the territory of the Unitary State of the Republic of Indonesia.

Permanent establishments shall be business entities established and being in the form of statutory body outside the territory of the Unitary State of the Republic of Indonesia that undertake activities in the territory of the Unitary State of the Republic of Indonesia and are obliged to comply with legislation in force in the territory of the Unitary State of the Republic of Indonesia.

Joint cooperation contract shall be a production sharing contract or other models of joint cooperation contract in exploration and exploitation activities, which is better in favor of the state and whose output is maximally used for improving people's welfare.

Business license shall be a license granted to a business entity to process, transport, store and/or trade for obtaining a benefit and/or profit.

The central government hereinafter called the government shall be the element of the Unitary State of the Republic of Indonesia consisting of the President and ministers.

The regional government shall be the head of the region along with other elements of autonomous region as the regional executive board.

Executing agency shall be an agency established to control upstream business activities in the petroleum and natural gas sector.

Regulatory board shall be a board established to regulate and supervise the supply and distribution of fuel oil and natural gas as well as the transport of natural gas through pipeline in the downstream business activities.

Minister shall be the minister in charge of petroleum and natural gas business activities.

CHAPTER II PRINCIPLE AND OBJECTIVE ARTICLE 2

The implementation of petroleum and natural gas-related business activities stipulated in this law shall be based on the principles of populist economy, integration, benefit, balance, equitable distribution, collective prosperity and public welfare, security, safety and legal certainty as well as the environmentally friendly principle.

Article 3

The implementation of petroleum and natural gas-related business activities shall aim at :

a. guaranteeing the effective implementation and control over business activities of effective, efficient, highly

   competitive and sustainable exploration and exploitation of state-owned petroleum and natural gas which

   are strategic and not renewable through an open and transparent mechanism;

b. assuring the effective implementation and control over the accountable processing, transport, storage and

   commercial businesses executed through a mechanism of reasonable, fair and transparent business

   competition;

c. guaranteeing the efficient and effective supply of petroleum and natural gas as both a source of energy and

   material for the domestic need;

d. supporting and promoting the national capacity so as to be more capable of competing nationally, regionally

   and internationally;

e. increasing state income to contribute maximally to the national economy and developing as well as

   strengthening the position of Indonesian industry and trade;

f. creating job opportunities, enhancing the public welfare and prosperity fairly and equitably as well as

   continuously maintaining the conservation of the environment.

CHAPTER III CONTROL AND CONCESSION

Article 4

(1) Petroleum and natural gas as non-renewable strategic natural-resources contained in the Indonesian mining jurisdiction shall constitute national assets controlled by the state.

(2) The control by the state as meant in paragraph (1) shall be executed by the government as the holder of mining concession.

(3) The government as the holder of mining concession shall establish the executing agency as meant in Article 1 point 23.

Article 5

Petroleum and natural gas-related business activities shall consist of :

1. Upstream business activities composed of :

a. exploration;

b. exploitation.

2. Downstream business activities comprising :

a. processing;

b. transport;

c. storage;

d. commerce.

Article 6

(1) The upstream business activities as meant in Article 5 point 1 shall be executed and controlled through the joint cooperation contracts as meant in Article 1 point 19.

(2) The joint cooperation contracts as meant in paragraph (1) shall at least contain the following requirements :

a. the ownership of natural resources is still on the hand of the government up to the delivery point;

b. the control over the operational management lies on the executing agency;

c. capital and risks are wholly borne by business entities or permanent establishments.

Article 7

(1) The downstream business activities as meant in Article 5 point 2 shall be executed by the business licenses as meant in Article 1 point 20.

(2) The downstream business activities as meant in Article 5 point 2 shall be realized through a mechanism of reasonable, fair and transparent business competition.

Article 8

(1) The government shall prioritize to the exploitation of natural gas for the domestic need and have the task of preparing strategic petroleum reserves to support the supply of fuel oil in the country, which is further stipulated by a government regulation.

(2) The government shall guarantee the availability and smooth distribution of fuel oil being a vital commodity and controlling the life of public at large throughout the territory of the Unitary State of the Republic of Indonesia.

(1) The implementation of transport business activities of natural gas through pipeline connected with public interests shall be regulated so that its utilization is open for all users.

(2) The government in this case a regulating agency shall be responsible for the regulation and supervision over the business activities as meant in paragraphs (2) and (3).

Article 9

(1) The upstream and downstream business activities as meant in Article 5 point 1 and 2 shall be executed by :

a. state-owned enterprises;

b. regional administration-owned companies;

c. cooperatives, small-scale businesses;

d. private business entities.

(2) Permanent establishments shall only be allowed to undertake upstream business activities.

Article 10

(1) Business entities or permanent establishments undertaking upstream business activities shall be prohibited from executing downstream business activities.

(2) Business entities undertaking downstream business activities shall be disallowed to execute upstream business activities.

CHAPTER IV UPSTREAM BUSINESS ACTIVITIES ARTICLE 11

(1) The upstream business activities as meant in Article 5 point 1 shall be executed by business entities or permanent establishments on the basis of joint cooperation contracts with the executing agency.

(2) Every joint cooperation contract already signed shall contain at least the following principal provisions :

a. state revenue;

b. working area and reversion;

c. obligation to disburse funds;

d. transfer of ownership of production results of petroleum and natural gas;

e. period and conditions of the extension of contract;

f. settlement of any dispute;

g. obligation to supply petroleum and/or natural gas to meet the domestic need;

h. expiration of contract;

i. post-mining operation obligations;

j. working safety and security;

k. environmental management;

l. transfer of right and obligation;

m. necessary reporting;

n. plan for the development of field;

o. prioritization of the use of domestic goods and services;

p. development of surrounding communities and guarantee for rights of communal society;

q. prioritization of recruitment of Indonesian workers.

Article 12

(1) The working area to be offered to business entities or permanent establishments shall be stipulated by the minister after consulting with the regional government.

(2) The offering of the working area as meant in paragraph (1) shall be done by the minister.

(3) The minister shall stipulate business entities and permanent establishments authorized to undertake exploration and exploitation business activities in the working area as meant in paragraph (2).

Article 13

(1) Every business entity or permanent establishment shall be given only one working area.

(2) In the case of a business entity or permanent establishment managing more than one working areas, separate statutory body shall be established in every working area.

Article 14

(1) The validity period of the joint cooperation contracts as meant in Article 11 paragraph (1) shall be 30 (thirty) years at the maximum.

(2) Business entities or permanent establishments can apply for the extension of the validity period of the joint cooperation contracts as meant in paragraph (1) to another term of 20 (twenty) years at the maximum.

Article 15

(1) The validity period of the joint cooperation contracts as meant in Article 14 paragraph (1) shall consist of the period of exploration and period of exploitation.

(2) The period of exploration as meant in paragraph (1) shall be 6 (six) years and extendible to only another term of 4 (four) years at the maximum.

Article 16

Business entities or permanent establishments shall be obliged to revert gradually part or all of their working areas to the minister.

Article 17

Business entities or permanent establishments already securing the first approval of development of field in a working area but not realizing their activities for the maximum period of 5 (five) years as from the date of expiration of the exploration period shall be obliged to return their working areas wholly to the minister.

Article 18

Guidances, procedures and requirements for the joint cooperation contracts, stipulation and offering of working areas, alteration and extension of joint cooperation contracts as well as the reversion of the working areas as meant in Articles 11, 12, 13, 14, 15, 16 and 17 shall be further stipulated in a government regulation.

Article 19

(1) General survey executed by or under a license of the government shall be done to support the preparation for the working area as meant in Article 12 paragraph (1).

(2) Procedures and requirements for the implementation of the general survey as meant in paragraph (1) shall be further stipulated by a government regulation.

Article 20

(1) Data obtained from the general survey and/or exploration and exploitation shall be the state property controlled by the government.

(2) Data obtained by business entities or permanent establishments in their working areas can be used by the relevant business entities or permanent establishments for the validity period of the joint cooperation contracts.

(3) In the case of the joint cooperation contracts expiring, business entities or permanent establishments shall be obliged to give up the whole data obtained during the period of the joint cooperation contracts to the minister through the executing agency.

(4) The secrecy of the data obtained by business entities or permanent establishments in their working areas shall be effective for a specified period.

(5) The government shall regulate, manage and utilize the data as meant in paragraphs (1) and (2) to plan the preparation for the opening of working areas.

(6) The implementation of the provisions on ownership, period of the use, secrecy, management and utilization of the data as meant in paragraphs (1), (2), (3), (4) and (5) shall be further stipulated by a government regulation.

Article 21

(1) The plan for the first time development of field to be used for production activities in a working area shall secure the approval of the minister on the basis of considerations of the executing agency after consulting with the relevant provincial government.

(2) In developing and producing petroleum and natural gas fields, business entities or permanent establishments shall be obliged to optimize and utilize them or on accordance with good technical norms.

(3) Provisions on the development of field, production of petroleum and natural gas reserves and provisions on the technical norms as meant in paragraphs (1) and (2) shall be further stipulated by a government regulation.

(1) Business entities or permanent establishments shall give up maximally 25% (twenty five percent) of their portion resulting from the production of petroleum and natural gas to meet the domestic need.

(2) The implementation of the provisions as meant in paragraph (1) shall be further stipulated by a government regulation.

CHAPTER V DOWNSTREAM BUSINESS ACTIVITIES ARTICLE 23

(1) The downstream business activities as meant in Article 5 paragraph (2) can be executed by business activities after securing business licenses from the government.

(2) The business licenses needed for the implementation of the petroleum and/or natural gas-related business activities as meant in paragraph (1) shall be distinguished by :

a. processing business license;

b. transport business license;

c. storage business license;

d. commercial business license.

(3) Every business entity can be given more than one business licenses as long as the licensing does not contravene provisions of laws in force.

Article 24

(1) The business licenses as meant in Article 23 shall at least contain :

a. name of operator;

b. kind of business granted;

c. obligations in the implementation of the operation;

d. technical requirements.

(2) Every business license already granted as meant in paragraph (1) only can be used in accordance with its designation.

Article 25

(1) The government can issue a written warning, suspend activities, freeze activities or revoke the business licenses as meant in Article 23 on the basis of :

a. violation against any of the requirements mentioned in business licenses;

b. repetition of violation against requirements for business licenses;

c. failure to meet the requirements stipulated on the basis of this law.

(2) Before revoking the business licenses as meant in paragraph (1), the government shall firstly open opportunity for business entities to abolish the violation already committed of fulfill the stipulated requirements in a specified period.

Article 22 Article 26

Activities of field processing, transport and sales of production as the continuation of exploration and exploitation executed by business entities or permanent establishment shall not need the separate business licenses as meant in Article 23.

Article 27

(1) The minister shall stipulate the national master plan for transmission and distribution of natural gas.

(2) Only certain transport segments can be granted to business entities holding business licenses to transport natural gas through pipeline.

(3) Only certain commercial regions can be granted to business entities holding business licenses to transport natural gas through pipeline.

Article 28

(1) Fuel oil and certain processed products marketed in the country to meet the public need shall comply with the standards and quality stipulated by the government.

(2) Prices of fuel oil and natural gas shall be entrusted to the mechanism of fair and reasonable business competition.

(3) The implementation of the pricing policy as meant in paragraph (2) shall not reduce the social responsibility of the government for certain groups of communities.

Article 29

(1) In regions facing scarcity of fuel oil and remote areas, the transport and storage facilities, including their supporting facilities can be utilized in cooperation with other parties.

(2) The utilization of the facilities as meant in paragraph (1) shall be regulated by the executing agency by continuously observing technical and economic aspects.

Article 30

Provisions on the processing, transport, storage and commercial businesses as meant in Article 23, 24, 25, 26, 27, 28 and 29 shall be further stipulated by a government regulation.

CHAPTER VI STATE REVENUE ARTICLE 31

(1) Business entities or permanent establishments undertaking the upstream business activities as meant in Article 11 paragraph (1) shall pay state revenue in the form of taxes and non-tax state receipts.

(2) The state revenue in the form of taxes as meant in paragraph (1) shall consist of :

a. taxes;

b. import duty, and other levies on the import and excise;

c. regional taxes and levies.

(3) The non-tax state receipts as meant in paragraph (1) shall consist of :

a. state portion;

b. state levies in the form of permanent contribution and exploration and exploitation contributions;

c. bonuses.

(4) Joint cooperation contracts shall mention that the obligation to pay the taxes as meant in paragraph (2) is executed in accordance with :

a. provisions of taxation laws effective upon the signing of the joint cooperation contracts;

b. provisions of taxation laws in force.

(5) Provisions on the stipulation of amounts of the state portion, state levies and bonuses as meant in paragraph

(3) as well as procedures for remitting them shall be further stipulated by a government regulation.

(6) The non-tax state receipts as meant in paragraph (3) shall be the revenue of the central government and regional governments, which is shared in accordance with provisions of laws in force.

Article 32

Business entities undertaking the downstream business activities as meant in Article 22 shall pay taxes, import duty and other levies on the import, excise, regional taxes and regional levies as well as other liabilities in accordance with laws in force.

CHAPTER VII RELATIONS BETWEEN PETROLEUM AND NATURAL GAS-RELATED BUSINESS ACTIVITIES AND LAND TITLE ARTICLE 33

(1) The petroleum and natural gas-related business activities as meant in Article 5 shall be executed in the Indonesian mining jurisdiction.

(2) Rights to working areas shall not cover rights to land being earth surface

(3) Petroleum and natural gas-related business activities cannot be executed in :

a. cemeteries, places considered sacred, public places, public facilities and infrastructures, nature preserve, cultural preserve as well as land belonging to communal society;

b. state defense fields and buildings as well as surrounding land;

c. historic building and state symbols;

d. buildings, residences or factories along surrounding yard land, except under a license from government institutions, approval of communities and individuals with regard to the said matter.

(4) Business entities or permanent establishments planning to undertake their activities can remove the buildings, public places, public facilities and infrastructures as meant in paragraph (3) letters a and b after securing prior licenses from the authorized government institutions.

Article 34

(1) In the case of business entities or permanent establishments planning to use land attached to a right or state land in their working areas, the relevant business entities or permanent establishments shall firstly make a kind of settlement with the right holder or users of the state land in accordance with the right holder or users of the state land in accordance with laws in force.

(2) The settlement as meant in paragraph (1) shall be done under a way of deliberation to reach a consensus by means of transactions, granting a reasonable compensation, recognition or other forms of compensation to the right holder or users of the state land.

Article 35

Holders of land title shall be obliged to allow business entities or permanent establishments to carry out exploration and exploitation on the relevant land if :

a. before activities start, business entities or permanent establishments firstly show joint cooperation contracts or their legitimate copies as well as notify the objective and place of activities to be executed;

b. business entities or permanent establishments firstly make the settlement or a guarantee for the settlement approved by the right holder or users of the state land as meant in Article 34.

Article 36

(1) Business entities or permanent establishments being already given working areas shall be granted a right to use land plots used directly for petroleum and natural gas-related business activities and their safety areas in accordance with the provisions of laws in force and be obliged to maintain and keep the land plots.

(2) In the case of the granted working areas as meant in paragraph (1) covering a wide area on the state land, land plot not used for petroleum and natural gas-related business activities can be given to other parties by the minister in charge of the agrarian affairs or land affairs by prioritizing local communities after securing recommendation from the minister.

Article 37

Provisions or procedures for the settlement of the use of land title or state land as meant in Article 35 shall be further regulated by a government regulation.

CHAPTER VIII FOSTERING AND SUPERVISION PART ONE FOSTERING ARTICLE 38

The government shall foster petroleum and natural gas-related business activities.

Article 39

(1) The fostering as meant in Article 38 shall cover :

a. the implementation of government affairs in the field of petroleum and natural gas-related business activities;

b. the stipulation of policies on petroleum and natural gas-related business activities on the basis of reserves and potentials of petroleum and natural gas which are owned, production capacity, domestic need for fuel oil and natural gas, technology mastery, environmental aspect and conservation of the environment, national capacity and development policies.

(2) The fostering as meant in paragraph (1) shall be applied carefully, transparently and fairly to the implementation of petroleum and natural gas-related business activities.

Article 40

(1) Business entities or permanent establishments shall guarantee the effective standard and quality in accordance with provisions of laws in force as well as apply good technical norms.

(2) Business entities or permanent establishments shall guarantee working safety and security as well as the environmental management and abide by provisions of laws in force in the petroleum and natural gas-related business activities.

(3) The environmental management as meant in paragraph (2) shall be in the form of obligations to prevent and overcome pollution as well as to restore the environmental damages, including obligation of post-mining operation.

(4) Business entities or permanent establishments undertaking the petroleum and natural gas-related business activities as meant in Article 5 shall prioritize to the use of local manpower, goods and services as well as domestic design and engineering capacities transparently and competitively.

(5) Business entities or permanent establishments undertaking the petroleum and natural gas-related business activities as meant in Article 5 shall be responsible for the development of the environmental and local communities.

(6) Provisions on working safety and security as well as the environmental management as meant in paragraphs

(1) and (2) shall be further stipulated by a government regulation.

PART TWO SUPERVISION

Article 41

(1) Responsibility for activities of supervision over jobs and the implementation of petroleum and natural gas-related business activities with regard to the compliance to provisions of laws in force shall be at the ministry whose tasks and authority cover petroleum and natural gas-related business activities and other ministries concerned.

(2) The supervision over the implementation of upstream business activities based on joint cooperation contracts shall be executed by the executing agency.

(3) The supervision over the implementation of downstream business activities based on business licenses shall be executed by the executing agency.

Article 42 The supervisions as meant in Article 41 paragraph (1) shall include :

a. conservation of resources and petroleum and natural gas reserves;
b. management of data on petroleum and natural gas;
c. application of good technical norms;
d. kind and quality of processed products of petroleum and natural gas;
e. allocation and distribution of fuel oil and raw materials;
f. working safety and security;
g. environmental management;
h. utilization of domestic goods, services and design and engineering capacities;
i. development of Indonesian manpower;
j. development of the environmental and local communities;
k. mastery, development and application of petroleum and natural gas technology;
l. other activities in the field of petroleum and natural gas related business activities as long as they are
connected with public interests.

Article 43

Provisions on the fostering and supervision as meant in Articles 38, 39, 41 and 42 shall be further stipulated by a government regulation.

CHAPTER IX EXECUTING AGENCY AND REGULATING AGENCY ARTICLE 44

(1) The supervision over the implementation of joint operation contracts of the upstream business activities as meant in Article 5 point 1 shall be executed by the executing agency as meant in Article 4 paragraph (3).

(2) The executing agency as meant in paragraph (1) shall have the function of supervising the upstream business activities so that the exploitation of petroleum and natural gas resources belonging to the state can give a maximal benefit and revenue to the state for increasing the public welfare maximally.

(3) The executing agency as meant in paragraph (1) shall have the following tasks :

a. giving considerations to the minister with regard to the minister's policies on the preparation and offering of working areas as well as joint cooperation contracts;

b. signing joint cooperation contracts;

c. assessing and conveying plans for the development of fields for the first time to be used for production activities in a working area to the minister for securing approval;

d. approving plans for the development of fields other than those mentioned in letter c;

e. approving working plans and budgets;

f. monitoring and reporting the implementation of joint cooperation contracts to the minister;

g. appointing sellers of petroleum and/or natural gas being the state portion which can produce a maximum profit to the state.

Article 45

(1) The executing agency as meant in Article 4 paragraph (3) shall constitute a state-owned statutory body.

(2) The executing agency shall consists of managerial elements, experts, technical personnel and administrative personnel.

(3) The head of the executing agency shall be appointed and relieved by the President after consulting with the House of Representatives of the Republic of Indonesia and be responsible to the President in executing his/her tasks.

Article 46

(1) The regulating agency as meant in Article 8 paragraph (4) shall supervise the supply and distribution of fuel oil and transport of natural gas through pipeline.

(2) The regulating agency as meant in paragraph (1) shall function to regulate so that the supply and distribution of fuel oil and natural gas stipulated by the government can be guaranteed throughout the territory of the Unitary State of the Republic of Indonesia as well as the domestic use of natural gas increases.

(3) The regulating agency as meant in paragraph (1) shall have the tasks of regulating and stipulating the following matters :

a. supply and distribution of fuel oil;

b. national fuel oil reserves;

c. utilization of fuel oil transport and storage facilities;

d. tariff of transport of natural gas through pipeline;

e. selling price of natural gas to households and small-scale customers;

f. operation of natural gas transmission and distribution.

(4) The tasks of the executing agency as meant in paragraph (1) shall also cover the supervision over the fields as meant in paragraph (3).

Article 47

(1) The structure of the regulating agency as meant in Article 8 paragraph (4) shall consist of a committee and a division.

(2) The committee as meant in paragraph (1) shall comprise one chairman concurrently member and 8 (eight) members, originating from professionals.

(3) The chairman and members of the committee of the regulating agency as meant in paragraph (1) shall be appointed and relieved by the President after securing the approval of the House of Representative of the Republic of Indonesia.

(4) The regulating agency as meant in Article 8 paragraph (4) shall be responsible to the President.

(5) The establishment of the regulating agency as meant in Article 8 paragraph (4) shall be stipulated by a presidential decree.

Article 48

(1) The budget of operational costs of the executing agency as meant in Article 45 shall be based on the fee of the government in accordance with laws in force.

(2) The budget of operational costs of the regulating agency as meant in Article 46 shall be based on the State Budget of Revenue and Expenditure and contributions from business entities which are regulated in accordance with laws in force.

Article 49

Provisions on organizational structures, status, function, tasks, personnel, authority and responsibility as well as working mechanism of the executing agency and the regulating agency as meant in Article 41, 42, 43, 44, 45, 46, 47 and 48 shall be further stipulated by a government regulation.

CHAPTER X INVESTIGATION

Article 50

(1) In addition to investigators of the Police of the Republic of Indonesia, certain civil servant officials within the ministry in charge of petroleum and natural gas-related business activities shall be authorized specially to act as the investigators as meant in Law No. 8/1981 on the criminal code to investigate crimes in petroleum and natural gas-related business activities.

(2) Civil servant investigators shall be authorized to :

a. examine the truth of reports and information on crimes in petroleum and natural gas-related business activities;

b. investigate persons or statutory bodies allegedly committed crimes in petroleum and natural gas-related business activities;

c. summon persons for testifying and investigating as witnesses or suspects in petroleum and natural gas-related business activities;

d. raid place and/or facilities allegedly used for committing crimes in petroleum and natural gas-related business activities;

e. inspect facilities and infrastructures of petroleum and natural gas-related business activities and stop the use of equipment allegedly used for committing crimes;

f. sealing and/or confiscating equipment of petroleum and natural gas-related business activities used for committing crimes as evidences;

g. invite necessary experts in connection with the investigation of crimes in petroleum and natural gas-related business activities;

h. stop investigating crimes in petroleum and natural gas-related business activities.

(3) The civil servant investigators shall notify the commencement if investigation into crimes to police officials of the Republic of Indonesia in accordance with the provisions of laws in force.

(4) The investigators as meant in paragraph (1) shall be obliged to stop the investigation in the case of the events as meant in paragraph (2) letter a having no sufficient evidence and/or the events being not a crime.

(5) The exercise of the authority as meant in paragraph (2) shall be done in accordance with provisions of laws in force.

CHAPTER XI CRIMINAL PROVISION ARTICLE 51

(1) Everyone who undertakes the general survey as meant in Article 19 paragraph (1) without right shall be subjected to one-year imprisonment or a fine of Rp. 10,000,000,000.00 (ten billion rupiahs) at the maximum.

(2) Everyone who sends or gives up or transfers the data as meant in Article 20 without right in whatever from shall be subjected to one-year imprisonment or a fine of Rp. 10,000,000,000.00 (ten billion rupiahs) at the maximum.

Article 52

Everyone who undertake exploration and/or exploitation without the joint cooperation contracts as meant in Article 11 paragraph (1) shall be subjected to 6 (six)-year imprisonment or a fine of Rp. 60,000,000,000.00 (sixty billion rupiahs) at the maximum.

Article 53

Everyone who undertakes :

a. the processing as meant in Article 23 without a processing business license shall be subjected to 5 (five)-year imprisonment or a fine of Rp. 50,000,000,000.00 (fifty billion rupiahs) at the maximum.

b. the transport as meant in Article 23 without a transport business license shall be subjected to 4 (four)-year imprisonment or a fine of Rp. 40,000,000,000.00 (forty billion rupiahs) at the maximum.

c. the storage as meant in Article 23 without a storage business license shall be subjected to 3 (three)-year imprisonment or a fine of Rp. 30,000,000,000.00 (thirty billion rupiahs) at the maximum.

d. the commerce as meant in Article 23 without a commerce business license shall be subjected to 3 (three)year imprisonment or a fine of Rp. 30,000,000,000.00 (thirty billion rupiahs) at the maximum.

Article 54

Everyone who imitates or falsify fuel oil and natural gas and the processed products as meant in Article 28 paragraph (1) shall be subjected to 6 (six)-year imprisonment or a fine of Rp. 60,000,000,000.00 (sixty billion rupiahs) at the maximum.

Article 55

Everyone who abuses the transport and/or commerce of fuel oil subsidized by the government shall be subjected to 6 (six)-year imprisonment or a fine of Rp. 60,000,000,000.00 (sixty billion rupiahs) at the maximum.

Article 56

(1) In the case of the crimes as meant in this chapter being committed for and on behalf of business entities or permanent establishments, charges and sentence shall be imposed on the business entities or permanent establishments and/or their executives.

(2) In the case of the crimes being committed by business entities or permanent establishments, sentence imposed on the said business entities or permanent establishments shall be a fine as high as the maximum fine of the crimes plus one thirds of the fine.

Article 57

(1) The crimes as meant in Article 51 shall be violations.

(2) The crimes as meant in Articles 52, 53, 54 and 55 shall be crimes.

Article 58

In addition to the criminal provisions as meant in this Chapter, the additional sentence shall be the revocation of right or seizure of goods used for and obtained from crimes in petroleum and natural gas-related business activities.

CHAPTER XI TRANSITIONAL PROVISION Article 59

With the enforcement of this law :

a. the executing agency shall be established not later than one year;

b. the regulating agency shall be established not later than one year

Article 60

With the enforcement of this law :

a. the status of Pertamina shall be changed into a state limited liability company (Persero) by a government regulation not later than 2 (two) years;

b. as long as the state limited liability company as meant in paragraph (1) is not established yet, Pertamina which was established on the basis of Law No. 8/1971 (Statute Book of 1971 No. 76, Supplement to Statute

Book No. 2971) shall be obliged to undertake petroleum and natural gas-related business activities as well as regulate and manage assets, personnel and other important matters needed;

c. upon the establishment of the new state limited liability company, the obligation of Pertamina as meant in letter b shall be transferred to the relevant company.

Article 61

With the enforcement of this law :

a. Pertamina shall continue executing the task and function of supervision over the operation of exploration and exploitation contractors, including production sharing contractors up to the establishment of the executing agency;

b. upon the establishment of Persero as the substitute to Pertamina, the state-owned enterprise shall be obliged to make a production sharing contract with the executing agency to continue exploration and exploitation in ex-mining concession areas of Pertamina and be considered already securing the business licenses as meant in Article 24, needed for the implementation of processing, transport, storage and commercial businesses.

Article 62

Upon the enforcement of this law, Pertamina shall continue executing the task of supplying and serving fuel oil for the domestic need for a period of no later than 4 (four) years.

Article 63

With the enforcement of this law :

a. following the establishment of the executing agency, all rights, obligations and consequences resulting from the production sharing contracts between Pertamina and other parties shall transfer to the executing agency.

b. following the establishment of the executing agency, other contracts connected with the contracts as meant in latter a between Pertamina and other parties shall shift to the executing agency.

c. all contracts as meant in letters a and b shall be declared to remain effective up to the expiration of the relevant contracts;

d. rights, obligations and consequences resulting from the contracts, agreements or commitments other than those mentioned in letters a and b shall continue to be exercised by Pertamina up to the establishment of Persero set up for the purpose and shift to Persero afterwards;

e. the implementation of dealings or negotiations between Pertamina and other parties in the framework of joint cooperation in exploration and exploitation shall shift to the minister.

Article 64

With the enforcement of this law :

a. state-owned enterprises other than Pertamina, which undertake petroleum and natural gas-related businesses shall be considered already securing the business licenses as meant in Article 23;

b. the development which is being executed by the state-owned enterprises as meant in latter a upon the enforcement of this law shall continue to be executed by the state-owned enterprises;

c. not later than one year, the state-owned enterprises as meant in letter a shall be obliged to establish business entities set up for undertaking their business activities in accordance with the provisions of laws in force;

d. contracts or agreements between the state-owned enterprises as meant in letter a and other parties shall continue to remain effective up to the expiration of the period of the relevant contracts or agreements.

CHAPTER XIII MISCELLANEOUS ARTICLE 65

This law shall apply to petroleum and natural gas-related business activities other than those mentioned in Article 1 points 1 and 2, as long as they are not yet or are not regulated by other laws.

CHAPTER XIV CONCLUSION ARTICLE 66

(1) With the enforcement of this law, the following laws :

a. Law No. 44 Prp/1960 on petroleum and natural gas mining (Statute Book of 1960 No. 133, Supplement to Statute Book No. 2070);

b. Law No. 15/1962 on the stipulation of government regulation in lieu of a law No. 2/1962 concerning the obligation of oil companies to meet the domestic need (Statute Book of 1962 No. 80, Supplement to Statute Book No. 2505);

c. Law No. 8/1971 on state-owned oil and gas mining company (Statute Book of 1971 No. 76, Supplement to Statute Book No. 2971) as well as the whole amendments, amended the latest by Law No. 10/1974 (Statute Book of 1974 No. 3045);

(2) All technical directives for Law No. 44 Prp/1960 on petroleum and natural gas mining (Statute Book of 1960 No. 133, Supplement to Statute Book No. 2070) and Law No. 8/1971 on state-owned oil and gas mining company (Statute Book of 1971 No. 76, Supplement to Statute Book No. 2971) shall remain effective as long as they do not contravene or are not yet replaced by new regulations on the basis of this law.

Article 67

This law shall come into force as from the date of promulgation.

For public cognizance, this law shall be promulgated by placing it in Statute Book of the Republic of Indonesia.

Ratified in Jakarta On November 23, 2001

THE PRESIDENT OF THE REPUBLIC OF INDONESIA sgd. MEGAWATI SOEKARNOPUTRI

Promulgated in Jakarta On November 23, 2001

THE SECRETARY OF STATE sgd. BAMBANG KESOWO

ELUCIDATION ON LAW NO. 22/2001 CONCERNING PETROLEUM AND NATURAL GAS

GENERAL

Article 33 paragraphs (2) and (3) of the Constitution of 1945 affirms that the state controls production branches important for the state and dominating the life of public at large. The state also controls the earth and water as well as natural resources contained inside the earth and water and uses them maximally for increasing the people's prosperity and welfare. In view of the fact that petroleum and natural gas are non-renewable strategic natural resources controlled by the state and vital commodities playing important role in the provision of raw materials for industries, fulfillment of the domestic need for energy as well as a important source of foreign exchange earnings, they must be managed optimally so that they can be used maximally for the people's prosperity and welfare.

In the framework of complying with the provisions of the Constitution of 1945, and following the enforcement of law No 44/Prp/1960 on petroleum and natural gas mining and law No 8 /1971 on state-owned oil and natural gas mining company over four decades, various obstacles are found in the implementation of the laws because their materials substances are no longer suitable to the current and future developments.

In order to face the global need and challenges in the future, petroleum and natural gas-related business activities are demanded to be more capable of supporting the sustainability of the national development in the framework of improving the people's prosperity and welfare.

Based on the above mentioned matters, it is necessary to formulate a law on petroleum and natural gas to provided the legal foundation for steps of renewal and rearrangement of petroleum and natural gas-related business activities.

The formulation of law aims at :

exploiting and controlling petroleum and natural gas as natural and development resources which are strategic and vital;

supporting and driving up national capacity so as to be more competitive;

in creasing the state revenue and contributing maximally to the national economy, developing and strengthening Indonesia's industries and trade;

creating job opportunities, improving the environment and increasing the people's prosperity and welfare.

This law makes out a principal substance of the provision that petroleum and natural gas as strategic natural resources contained in the Indonesian mining jurisdiction constitute national assets controlled by the state and the control is executed by the government as the holder of mining concession in the upstream business activities, while the downstream business activities are executed after securing business licenses from the government.

In order to ensure the more efficient execution of the function of the government as the regulator, fostering agency and supervisor, the executing agency is established in the upstream business activities, while in the downstream business activities, the regulatory board is set up.

ARTICLE BY ARTICLE

Article 1 up to Article 3 Sufficiently clear Article 4

Paragraph (1) Base on the gist of Article 33 paragraph (3) of the Constitution of 1945, petroleum and natural gas as strategic natural resources deposited in the earth of the Indonesian mining jurisdiction constitute national assets controlled by the state. The above mentioned control by the state is meant to ensure that the state assets can be utilized maximally for the welfare of the whole Indonesian people. Therefore, individuals, communities and business people having a right to a land plot on the surface have not right to control or own petroleum and natural gas contained inside the land.

Paragraph (2) and (3) Sufficiently clear

Article 5 Point 1 Sufficiently clear

Point 2 Referred to in this provision as commerce includes natural gas commerce through both transmission and distribution pipelines.

Article 6

Paragraph (1) Besides fulfilling the laws in force, business entities or permanent establishments also must abide by certain obligation in executing their business activities.

Paragraph (2) The model of the joint cooperation contracts in this provision is production sharing contracts and other exploration and exploitation contracts more beneficial to the state. Hereinafter referred to as :

The delivery point is the selling point of petroleum and natural gas.

The control over the operational management is the approval of working plans and budget, field development plans as well as supervision over the realization of the said plans.

The capital and risks wholly borne by business entities or permanent establishment is that in the joint cooperation contracts, the government through the executing agency on the basis of this law is not allowed to invest in bear financial risks of joint cooperation contracts.

Article 7 Paragraph (1) Sufficiently clear

Paragraph (2) The realization through a mechanism of reasonable, fair and transparent business competition does not mean that the social responsibility of the government is ignored.

Article 8

Paragraph (1) The government regulation as the implementation of this provision contains, among others, principal substances : priority of natural gas exploitation, quantity, kind and locations of strategic petroleum reserves.

Paragraph (2) The government is obliged to ensure the sufficient supply of fuel oil throughout the country, including remote areas, the availability of a national stock at a sufficient quantity for as certain period.

Paragraph (3) Since the petroleum pipeline networks constitute naturally monopolistic facilities, their utilization needs to be regulated and supervised in the framework of guaranteeing the equal treatment of services for all users. Referred to public interest in this provision is interests of producers, consumers and other communities connected with the transport of natural gas.

Paragraph (4) Sufficiently clear

Article 9

Paragraph (1) This provision is meant to open widest opportunities for large, medium and small-scale business entities to undertake the upstream business activities with the operational scale on the financial and technical capacity of the relevant business entities.

Paragraph (2) Most of the highly-risky upstream business-activities (2) are executed by international companies having a broad range of international networks . In order to create an investment climate conducive to investments, including foreign investment, the opportunities to not establish business entities is provided.

Article 10 Paragraph (1)

Since the upstream business activities are activities of exploration of non-renewable natural resources being the state assets, the state must obtain the maximal benefit for the people's prosperity in the said activities.

The downstream business activities constitute activities of the business characteristics in general, in which the production costs and possible risks cannot be charged (consolidated) to the costs of upstream business activities. The prohibition of consolidation of the cost of upstream and downstream business activities also aims at ensuring the clear sharing of revenue between the central government and regional government as meant in Article 31 paragraph (6)

In the case of business entities undertaking upstream and downstream activities at the same time, they must establish separate statutory bodies, among others, by holding company. Paragraph (2) Sufficiently clear

Article 11

Paragraph (1) The government mentions obligations in joint cooperation contracts so that the government can control the joint cooperation contracts through requirements for the said contracts and the legislation in force as meant in Article 6 paragraph (1)

Paragraph (2) The copy of every joint cooperation contract already approved collectively and signed by the two parties must be sent to the commission of the house of Representatives of the Republic of Indonesia in charge of petroleum and natural gas affairs.

Paragraph (3) This provision is meant to provide legal certainty for parties committed themselves to joint cooperation contracts.

Article 12

Paragraph (1) Consultation with the regional government is done to give explanations and obtain information on plans for the offering of certain regions deemed potential to contain petroleum and natural gas resources to become working areas. The consultation with the regional government is done with the governor leading the administration of the regional government in accordance with provisions of the regional administration laws.

Paragraph (2) In its implementation, the minister coordinates with the executing agency. Paragraph (3) In its implementation, the minister coordinates with the executing agency

Article 13 Paragraph (1) Sufficiently clear

Paragraph (2) This provision is meant to avoid the consolidation of encumbrance and/or return of costs of exploration and exploitation of a working area by other working area. This provision also aims at preventing the unclear sharing of revenue between the central government and the respective regional governments connected with the said working areas.

Article 14 Sufficiently clear

Article 15 Paragraph (1) Sufficiently clear

Paragraph (2) If business entities or permanent establishments found no petroleum and/or natural gas reserves which can be produced during the exploration period, they must return their working areas wholly.

Article 16 This provision is meant to ensure that part and/or the whole of working areas not used can be offered to other parties as new working areas. Therefore, the government can obtain optimal results from the utilization of potentials of natural resources in a working area.

Article 17 Sufficiently clear

Article 18 The government regulation as technical directives for this provision contains, among others, principal substances : provisions and requirements for joint cooperation contracts, requirements and procedures for stipulation and offering of working areas, extension of joint cooperations contracts and stipulation and intake of working areas.

Article 19 Paragraph (1) Sufficiently clear

Paragraph (2) The government regulation on the general survey contains, among others, principal substances : the execution of general survey, kinds of activities, timetable of implementation, procedures for implementation and processing of data resulting from the survey.

Article 20 Paragraph (1) up to paragraph (3) Sufficiently clear Paragraph (4)

Data or information on the underground condition resulting from investments made by business entities or permanent establishments cannot be opened directly for the public to protect their investment interests. Data can be declared opened after a certain period and interesting parties can used the said data. The period of secrecy of data is dependent on kinds and classifications of data.

Paragraph (5) Sufficiently clear

Paragraph (6) The government regulation as technical directives for this provision contains, among others, principal substances : authority and responsibility of the government, kinds of data, classifications and periods of secrecy, administration and maintenance of data as well as periods of utilization and re-delivery of the data.

Article 21

Paragraph (1) The approval of the minister in this provision is needed because the development of the first field in a working area determines whether the operation of the working area is returned or continued by the executing agency or permanent establishments The approval of plans for the development of the subsequence fields in the working area will be granted by the executing agency . The consultation with regional governments as meant in this provisions is needed for ensuring that the proposed plans for development of fields can be coordinated with regional governments of provinces especially for regional lay-out plans and plans for regional revenue from petroleum and natural gas in the regions in accordance with laws in force

Paragraph (2) This provision is meant to ensure that business entities or permanent establishments in exploiting petroleum and natural resources observe optimalization and conservation of petroleum and natural gas resources and implement them in accordance of good technical norms.

Paragraph (3) The government regulation as technical directives for this provision contains, among others, principal substances : Kinds and plans for developments of fields, technical norms, reporting obligations as well as procedures for the approval of plans for developments of fields.

Article 22

Paragraph (1) This provision is meant to provide a guarantee for the availability of supply of petroleum and natural gas resulting from the Indonesia mining jurisdiction to meet the domestic need for fuel. The delivery as high as 25% (twenty five percent) at the maximum of their portion resulting from the production of petroleum and/or natural gas in this provision is meant to ensure that if a working area produces petroleum and natural gas, business entity or permanent establishment is obliged to give up maximally 25% (twenty five percent) of its portion from the petroleum production and maximally 25% (twenty five percent) of its portion from the natural gas production.

Paragraph (2) The government regulation as meant in this provision contains, among others, principal substances : condition of the domestic need, mechanism of implementation and provision of price as well policies on the granting of incentives connected with the exercise of obligation of the delivery of petroleum and/or natural gas being portion of business entities or permanents establishments from their production.

Article 23 Paragraph (1) Business licenses are licenses granted by the go vernment to business entities in accordance with their respective scopes of authority to undertake processing, transport storage and/ or commercial business activities after fulfilling the necessary requirements. In the case of matters being connected with regional interests, the government issues business licenses after the said business entities secure recommendations from the regional governments.

Paragraph (2) This provision is meant to ensure the more effective supervision and control over business entities operating in processing, transport, storage and / or commercial fields. The government is obliged to approve or reject applications for business licenses submitted by business entities in a certain period in accordance with laws in force.

Paragraph (3) Sufficiently clear

Article 24 Sufficiently clear

Article 25 Paragraph (1) Sufficiently clear

Paragraph (2) Based on considerations, among others that the downstream business activities deal with commodities controlling the life of public at large and huge investment, the central government and regional government according to their respective scopes of authority can open opportunity for business entities to eliminate the violations committed before their business licenses are revoked . In addition to the violations, business licenses also can be revoked based on requests of holders of the business licenses.

Article 26. In view of the fact that in activities of fields processing, transport and sales of petroleum and natural gas in the framework of the continuation of exploration and exploitation , facilities which are built are not destined to obtain benefits and /or profits from the activities, business licenses are not needed. This provisions is not effective if facilities owned by business entities or permanent establishments are used collectively with other parties by collecting a cost or rental fee so as to obtain benefits and / or profits, so that the business entities or permanent establishment must secure business licenses.

Article 27

Paragraph (1) The master plan stipulated by the government will be used as an investment reference to the development and building of natural gas transmission and distribution network by the interesting business entities.

Paragraph (2) This provision is meant to encourage fair business competition and enhance efficiency in the use of infrastructure as well as the quality of service.

The segments of transport businesses are distributed by considering technical, economic, security and safety aspects. Paragraph (3)

This provision is meant to encourage fair business competition and enhance efficiency in the use of infrastructures as well as the quality of service.

Article 28 Paragraph (1) This provision is meant to protect interests of consumers, health of communities and the environment. Paragraph (2)

Sufficiently clear

Paragraph (3) The government can grant special aid as the substitute to subsidy to certain consumers for certain kinds of fuel oil. The government stipulates the natural gas pricing policy for the need of households and small-scale consumers as well as other certain users.

Article 29

Paragraph (1) This provision is meant to open opportunity for other parties to use collectives facilities belonging to a business entity on the basis of a joint agreement in the framework of ensuring the optimal use of the facilities and the efficient operation to reduce distribution costs, particularly in the case of the shortage of supply of fuel oil in a region and relatively isolated area.

Paragraph (2) Sufficiently clear

Article 30 The government regulation as technical directives for this provision contains, among other, principal substances : kinds of business activities, procedures for submission of applications and implementation of business licenses, standards and quality, obligations of business entities, classifications of violations, procedures for warning, cancellation, freezing and revocation of business licenses and the authority of regional governments connected with business licensing.

Article 31

Paragraph (1) Since the provision as meant in this article is based on the understanding that upstream business activities in the form of exploration and exploitation are activities of intake of non-renewable natural resources being the state assets, business entities or permanent establishments are obliged to give up non tax state revenue consisting of the portion of the state, state levies and bonuses, besides paying taxes, import duty and other liabilities.

Paragraph (2) Letters a and b Sufficiently clear

Letter c Besides paying regional taxes, business entities or permanent establishments are also obliged to pay regional levies.

Paragraph (3)

Letter a The state portion of production given up by business entities or permanent establishments to the state as the owner of petroleum and natural gas resources.

Letter b This provision is based on the understanding that business entities or permanent establishments are obliged to pay a regular contribution in accordance with the size of working areas as a compensation for the opportunity to undertake exploration and exploitation activities. The exploration and exploitation contributions are imposed on business entities or permanent establishments as a compensation for the intake of non renewable petroleum and natural gas resources. State levies being a revenue of the central government constitute non-tax state revenue (PNBP) in accordance with the provisions of law in force.

Letter c Referred to in this provision as bonuses are data, signature and production bonuses based on the accomplishment of a certain cumulative production level.

Paragraph 4 The provision article is meant to enable business entities or permanent establishment to alternatives for taxation regulations which will be enforced to joint cooperation contracts. The opening of the opportunity constitutes freedom of business entities of permanent establishments to choose taxation provisions in accordance the feasibility of their business because exploration and exploitation are long – term businesses, need huge capital and are highly risky.

Paragraph (5) The government regulation as technical directives for this provision contains, among other, principal substances : regulation of amount of the state portion based on net production percentage, and state levies consisting of regular contribution per unit of working area, exploration and exploitation levies per production volume, bonuses and regulation of certain requirements for joint cooperation contracts.

Paragraph (6) Referred to in this provision as "which is shared in accordance with provisions of law in force" is in accordance with provisions on the financial equilibrium between the central government and regional administration.

Article 32 Given the downstream business activities in the form of the processing, transport, storage and commerce are not business activities directly connected with the intake of non-renewable natural resources, the obligations to pay taxes, import duty and other liabilities to the state as like industrial and/or trading business activities in general apply.

Article 33 Paragraph (1) and (2) Sufficiently clear

Paragraph (3) Principally, all petroleum and natural gas related business activities executed in a location need a license from the government institution. Yet, in certain places before securing license from the government institution, the businesses must secure prior approval from communities and/ or individuals

Letter a Referred to as public places, public facilities and infrastructures are facilities provided by the government for interests for the public at large and having social functions, such as road, market, cemetery, park and worship places.

Letter b up to letter d Sufficiently clear

Paragraph (4) Since public places, facilities and infrastructures, defense fields and buildings constitute facilities built by the government for the public or defense interests, licenses from the government institutions concerned are needed, by observing suggestions of communities.

Article 34 Paragraph (1) Sufficiently clear

Paragraph (2) Referred to in this provision as recognition is the recognition to communal rights of traditional communities in a region so that their settlement can be done through deliberation and consensus on the basis of the relevant communal law.

Article 35 Sufficiently clear

Article 36

Paragraph (1) In view of the fact that a right to working area does not cover a right to land surface, business entities or permanent establishments do not automatically have a right to use land plots in the working area. In the case of business entities directly using the land plots, the right to use the land must be exercised in accordance with provisions of law in force.

Paragraph (2) Sufficiently clear

Article 37 The government regulations as technical directives for this provision contains, among other, principal substances : procedures for the settlement or negotiation rights and obligations of the respective parties, guidances on the amount of compensations and technical; provisions on the settlement pattern of land use.

Article 38 The fostering executed by the government in petroleum and natural gas- related business activities is based on the state control over natural resources and production fields controlling the life of public at large.

Article 39 Paragraph (1) Letter a

The implementation of government affairs in the field of petroleum and natural gas-related business activities include, among others, the dissemination of information, education, training, technological research and development, enhancement of added value of products, application of standardization, accreditation, fostering of supporting industrial/business activities, fostering of small/medium-scale businesses, the utilization of domestic goods and services, maintenance of working security and health, environmental conservation, creation of a conducive business climate as well as maintenance of security and orderliness.

Letter b Sufficiently clear Paragraph (2) Sufficiently clear

Article 40 Paragraph (1) up to paragraph (3) Sufficiently clear

Paragraph (4) This provision is meant to support and drive up the national capacity so as to be more capable of competing.

Paragraph (5) Referred to in this provision as being responsible for the development of the environment and local communities is the involvement of business entities or permanent establishment in the development and utilization of potentials and capacities of local communities, among others by means of employing workers in certain quantity and quality as well as improving the resettlement of communities to create the harmony between business entities or permanent establishments and surrounding communities.

Paragraph (6) The government regulations as technical directives for this provision contains, among others, principal substances covering the following obligations of business entities or permanent establishments :

a. in the field of working safety and security, which covers safety and health of workers, conditions and requirements for working places and environment and standards of installation and equipment;

b. in the field of the environmental management which covers prevention and overcoming of environmental pollution and restoration of environmental damages during and after joint cooperation contracts.

Article 41 Sufficiently clear

Article 42 Letter a up to letter g Sufficiently clear

Letter h In its implementation, the utilization continues to observe economic values in the respective projects or activities.

Letter i In the use of foreign manpower, procedures in force and requirements in accordance with the need must be observed.

Letter j up to letter m Sufficiently clear

Article 43 The government regulation as technical directives for this provision contains, among others, the principal substances as mentioned in elucidation on article 39 paragraph (1) letter a

Article 44 Sufficiently clear

Article 45

Paragraph (1) The state-owned statutory body as meant in this provision has the status of a civil law subject and constitutes a non profit institution and is managed professionally.

Paragraph (2) Referred to in this provision as the managerial elements are the head and vice head as well as deputies . technical personnel are functional personnel having expertise in their fields.

Paragraph (3) The consultation aims at testing the capability and feasibility of prospective head of the executing agency by the House of Representatives of the Republic of Indonesia in this case the commission in charge of petroleum and natural gas affairs.

Article 46

Paragraph (1) This provision is meant to protect interests of consumers in the continuous supply and distribution of fuel oil throughout Indonesia. The supervision over the transport of natural gas through pipeline is done to optimize and prevent monopoly in the utilization of transmission, distribution and storage pipe facilities by certain business entities.

Paragraph (2) The government is responsible for the sustainability of stocks and service as well as avoiding the scarcity of fuel oil throughout Indonesia.

Paragraph (3) Referred to in this provision as the utilization of fuel oil transport and storage facilities is prioritized to certain regions or remote areas whose market mechanism cannot run so that the existing transport and storage facilities need to be regulated to be usable for achieving an optimal result and a lowest price.

Household is every consumer utilizing natural gas for the household purpose. The operation of gas transmission and distribution is regulated by the regulatory board connected with business aspects of the said natural gas distribution and distribution activities.

Paragraph (4)

Sufficiently clear Article 47 Paragraph (1)

Sufficiently clear

Paragraph (2) Referred to in this provision as professionals are parties having necessary expertise, experience and knowledge in the oil , environmental, law, economies and social fields as well as having high integrity in executing their tasks and obligations.

Paragraph (3) The regulatory board is independent and since its tasks and functions deal with interests of the public at large, the appointment and relief of its personnel need to secure the approval of the House of Representatives of the Republic of Indonesia.

Paragraph (4) In view of the fact that the tasks and functions of the regulatory board is directly connected with commodities badly needed by the public at large so as to be very influential to the national economy and able to cause a board impact of vulnerability in the society as well as having inter-sectoral regulation, the regulatory board is responsible to the President.

Paragraph (5) Sufficiently clear

Article 48

Paragraph (1) Every state revenue resulting from business entities or permanent establishments which undertake upstream business activities is directly remitted to the state cash. In controlling joint cooperation contracts with business entities or permanent establishments, the regulatory board earns a fee as the managerial wage received from the government for activities which are executed.

Paragraph (2)

The operational cost of the regulatory board originating from the State Budget of revenue and Expenditure (APBN) is meant as the authorized capital of the regularity board. Subsequently, the operational cost of the regulatory board are obtained from contributions of business entities that the board regulates.

Article 49 up to article 54 Sufficiently clear

Article 55 Referred to in this provision as the abuse is activities intended to obtain benefits of individuals or business entities by means harmful to interests of the public at large and the state, such as illegal mixing of fuel, deviation from the allocation of fuel oil. Transport and sales of fuel oil to other countries.

Article 56 up to article 59 Sufficiently clear

Article 60

Letter a The status of limited liability company as meant in this provision is the status of company mentioned in law on state-owned enterprises.

Letter b and c

Sufficiently clear

Article 61 Letter a Sufficiently clear

Letter b The joint cooperation contracts as meant in this provision contain payment liabilities to the state whose amount is in accordance with provisions in force in Pertamina's mining concession areas so far by including CHAPTER V.

Article 62 Sufficiently clear

Article 63 In order to implement this provision, joint cooperation contracts connected with parties making contracts are changed/amended without altering conditions and requirements for the contracts.

Letter b and c Sufficiently clear

Letter d Referred to in this provision as contracts, agreements or commitments include selling contracts of liquefied natural gas.

Letter e Sufficiently clear

Article 64

Letter a State–owned enterprises other than Pertamina, which undertake petroleum and natural gas-related businesses include PT Perusahaan Gas Negara (Persero) established on the basis of Government Regulation No 37/1994.

Letter b and c Sufficiently clear

Article 65

Referred to in this provision as petroleum or natural gas is oil and gas resulting from artificial process (instead or results of natural process)

Article 66 and 67 Sufficiently clear

PETROLEUM MINING CODE FOR THE JOINT PETROLEUM DEVELOPMENT AREA

[Insert Date]

JPDA PETROLEUM MINING CODE PREAMBLE

In accordance with Article 7(a) of the Timor Sea Treaty, and subject to the terms of that Treaty, the following Petroleum Mining Code is adopted to govern the exploration, development and exploitation of Petroleum within the JPDA, as well as the export of Petroleum from the JPDA.

PART I PRELIMINARY

SECTION 1 INTERPRETATION

1.1 DEFINITIONS

In this Code:

"Access Authorisation" means an authorisation granted pursuant to Section 9.1;

"Affiliate" means, in respect of an Authorised Person, (or, if more than one person, in respect of each such person), a person that Controls, is Controlled by, or is under common Control with, the Authorised Person or any such person, as the case may be;

"Authorisation" means an Access Authorisation, a Production Sharing Contract or a Prospecting Authorisation, or an agreement (if any) made in respect of such an Authorisation or Production Sharing Contract;

"Authorised Activities" means the activities authorised by an Authorisation; "Authorised Area" means the area from time to time the subject of an Authorisation; "Authorised Person" means:

(a) in respect of a Production Sharing Contract, the Contractor; and

(b) in respect of any other Authorisation, the person to whom the Authorisation has been granted;

"Block" has the meaning in sub-Section 2.2;

"Calendar Year" means a period of twelve months commencing on January 1 and ending on the following December 31, according to the Gregorian calendar;

"Code" means this Petroleum Mining Code, as amended, modified or replaced from time to time, and regulations made and directions given under it;

"Commencement Date" means the date upon which the Joint Commission adopts this Code;

"Contract Area" means the Authorised Area from time to time the subject of a Production Sharing Contract; "Contractor" means a person with whom the Designated Authority has made a Production Sharing Contract;

"Control" means, in relation to a person, the power of another person to secure:

(a) by means of the holding of shares or the possession of voting power, in or in relation to the first person or any other person; or

(b) by virtue of any power conferred by the articles of association of, or any other document regulating, the first person or any other person, that the affairs of the first person are conducted in accordance with the wishes or directions of that other person;

"Crude Oil" means crude mineral oil and all liquid hydrocarbons in their natural state or obtained from Wet Gas by condensation or extraction;

"Designated Authority" means the Timor Sea Designated Authority for the JPDA established pursuant to Article 6 of the Treaty;

"Field Export Point" means:

(a) in circumstances where petroleum has gone through field level separation, is made ready for sale, further processing, or transportation and exported from the Contract Area by tanker - the point of tanker loading;

(b) in circumstances where petroleum has gone through field level separation, is made ready for sale, further processing, or transportation and exported from the Contract Area by pipeline - the inlet flange of the export pipeline;

(c) in circumstances where petroleum is processed beyond field level separation within the Contract Area - no later than the point at which the petroleum is input to such further processing; or

(d) such other point within the JPDA as approved in a development plan in accordance with an Authorisation;

"Good Oil Field Practice" means such practices and procedures employed in the petroleum industry worldwide by prudent and diligent operators under conditions and circumstances similar to those experienced in connection with the relevant aspect or aspects of the Petroleum Operations, having regard to relevant factors including:

(a) conservation of petroleum and gas resources, which includes the utilization of methods and processes to maximise the recovery of hydrocarbons in a technically and economically efficient manner, and to minimize losses at the surface;

(b) operational safety, which entails the use of methods and processes aimed at preventing major accident events and occupational health and safety incidents, and

(c) environmental protection, that calls for the adoption of methods and processes which minimize the impact of the Operations on the environment;

"Infrastructure Provider" has the meaning in sub-paragraph 9.1(a)(iii);

"Insolvency Event" means:

(a) the Authorised Person is insolvent, is adjudged bankrupt or makes any assignment for the benefit of its creditors, or is adjudged to be unable to pay its debts as the same fall due;

(b) an application (other than a vexatious or frivolous application) to, or order is made by, a court having jurisdiction or, an effective resolution is made for the dissolution, liquidation or winding up of the Authorised Person and in the case of an application to a court, the application is not withdrawn or dismissed within thirty (30) days;

(c) a receiver is appointed or an encumbrancer or security holder takes possession of a majority of the assets or undertaking of the Authorised Person;

(d) the Authorised Person ceases or threatens to cease to carry on its business or execution is forced against all or a majority of the Authorised Person's property and is not discharged or set aside within fourteen (14) days;

(e) an administrator is appointed or a resolution that an administrator be appointed to the Authorised Person is passed or any formal steps are taken to appoint an administrator to the Authorised Person; or

(f) the Authorised Person, without the consent of the Designated Authority, enters into, or resolves to enter into, an arrangement, compromise, or composition with any of, or any class of its creditors or members or process is filed in a court seeking approval of such arrangement, compromise or composition where the proposed arrangement, compromise or composition could, in the opinion of the Designated Authority, materially affect the ability of the Authorised Person to discharge its obligations under its Authorisation.

"Inspector" has the meaning in sub-Section 15.2;

"Interim Petroleum Mining Code" means the interim code governing the exploration, development and exploitation of petroleum within the JPDA, and adopted by the Joint Commission on 2 April 2003 pursuant to Article 7(b) of the Treaty;

"Joint Commission" means the Joint Commission for the JPDA established pursuant to Article 6 of the Treaty;

"Joint Operating Agreement" means any agreement or contract, among all of the Contractors with respect to their respective rights and obligations under a Production Sharing Contract;

"JPDA" means the Joint Petroleum Development Area established pursuant to Article 3 of the Treaty;

"Natural Gas" means all gaseous hydrocarbons and inerts, including wet mineral gas, dry mineral gas, casing head gas and residue gas remaining after the extraction of liquid hydrocarbons from Wet Gas;

"Operator" means the person appointed from time to time to organise and supervise Authorised Activities;

"Petroleum" means:

(a) any naturally occurring hydrocarbon, whether in a gaseous, liquid, or solid state;

(b) any naturally occurring mixture of hydrocarbons, whether in a gaseous, liquid or solid state; or

(c) any naturally occurring mixture of one or more hydrocarbons, whether in a gaseous, liquid or solid state, as well as other substances produced in association with such hydrocarbons;

and includes any petroleum as defined by paragraphs (a), (b) or (c) that has been returned to a Reservoir;

"Petroleum Operations" means any activity authorised by the Designated Authority, and includes:

(a) the exploration for, development and exploitation of Petroleum in the Contract Area, and the export of that Petroleum from the Contract Area;

(b) the construction, installation and operation of structures, facilities, installations, equipment and other property, and the carrying out of other works, necessary for the purposes mentioned in paragraph (a) above;

(c) Decommissioning, including removal of items referred to in paragraph (b) above;

(d) the marketing of that Petroleum; and

(e) planning and preparation for the activities mentioned in paragraphs (a), (b),

(c) and (d) above;

"Pipeline" means a pipe or system of pipes, and associated equipment, for exporting Petroleum from the JPDA, but not a field gathering or flow line;

"Production Sharing Contract" means a contract between the Designated Authority and a limited liability corporation or entity with limited liability under which production from a specified area of the JPDA is shared between the parties to the contract;

"Prospecting Authorisation" means an authorisation granted pursuant to Section 8;

"Reservoir" means a porous and permeable underground formation containing an individual and separate natural accumulation of producible hydrocarbons (oil and/or gas) that is confined by impermeable rock and/or water barriers and is characterized by a single natural pressure system;

"Sub-Block" has the meaning in sub-Section 2.2;

"Treaty" means the Timor Sea Treaty between the Government of Timor-Leste and the Government of Australia signed on 20t May 2002; and

"Wet Gas" means a mixture of hydrocarbons, inerts and impurities that is recoverable from a Reservoir and is gaseous at the conditions which its volume is measured or estimated.

1.2 HEADINGS

As used herein, headings are for convenience and do not form a part of, and shall not affect the interpretation of, this Code.

1.3 FURTHER INTERPRETATION

In this Code, unless the contrary intention appears:

(a) the words "including" and "in particular" shall be construed as being by way of illustration or emphasis only, and shall not be construed as, nor shall they take effect as, limiting the generality of any preceding words;

(b) a reference to a Section, sub-Section, paragraph and sub-paragraph, is to a Section, sub-Section, paragraph and sub-paragraph of this Code;

(c) a reference to an agreement or instrument is to the same as amended, varied, novated, modified or replaced from time to time;

(d) an agreement includes an arrangement, whether or not having the force of law;

(e) a reference to the consent or approval of the Designated Authority means the consent or approval, in writing, of the Designated Authority and in accordance with the conditions of that consent or approval;

(f) "person" includes a corporation or other legal entity;

(g) the singular includes the plural, and vice versa;

(h) any gender includes the other; and

(i) where a word or expression is defined, cognate words and expressions shall be construed accordingly.

1.4 Exercise by the Designated Authority of its Powers and Functions

(a) The Designated Authority shall exercise its powers and discharge its functions under the Treaty, the Code and Authorisations in accordance with Good Oil Field Practice with a view to contributing to further investment in the JPDA and to the long-term development of Timor-Leste and Australia.

(b) Unless otherwise provided in this Code, before exercising any such power or discharging any such function, the Designated Authority shall, subject to paragraph 1.4(c):

(i) give opportunity to Authorised Persons, and others reasonably likely to be affected by the exercise of the power or by the discharge of the function to make representations to it; and

(ii) give consideration to representations received by it.

(c) The Designated Authority may exercise a power or discharge a function referred to in paragraph 1.4(a) without complying with the requirements of paragraph 1.4(c) where the Designated Authority considers that there are compelling reasons for doing so. Where the Designated Authority does exercise a power or discharge a function under this paragraph, it shall notify the Joint Commission within fourteen

(14) days of doing so.

(d) The forgoing provisions of this sub-Section 1.4 are without prejudice to the power of the Joint Commission, in Annex D of the Treaty, to give directions to the Designated Authority on the discharge of its powers and functions.

SECTION 2 GRATICULATION OF THE JOINT PETROLEUM DEVELOPMENT AREA

2.1 SECTIONS AND SUB-SECTIONS

For the purposes of this Code:

(a) the surface of the Earth shall be divided:

(iii) by the meridian of Greenwich and by meridians that are at a distance from that meridian of five (5) minutes, or a multiple of five (5) minutes, of longitude; and

(iv) the equator and by parallels of latitude that are at a distance from the equator of five (5) minutes, or a multiple of five (5) minutes, of latitude;

into sections, each of which is bounded:

(v) by portions of two (2) of those meridians that are at a distance from each other of five (5) minutes of longitude; and

(vi) by portions of two (2) of those parallels of latitude that are at a distance from each other of five (5) minutes of latitude; and

(b) the surface of the Earth shall further be divided:

(i) by the meridian of Greenwich and by meridians that are at a distance from that meridian of one (1) minute, or a multiple of one (1) minute, of longitude; and

(ii) the equator and by parallels of latitude that are at a distance from the equator of one (1) minute, or a multiple of one (1) minute, of latitude;

into sub-sections, each of which is bounded:

(iii) by portions of two (2) of those meridians that are at a distance from each other of one (1) minute of longitude; and

[Insert Date]

(iv) by portions of two (2) of those parallels of latitude that are at a distance from each other of one (1) minute of latitude. Page 10

2.2 BLOCKS AND SUB-BLOCKS

A section that is wholly or partly within the JPDA is a Block. A sub-section that is wholly or partly within the JPDA is a Sub-Block. The Designated Authority shall allocate an identifying number to each Block and Sub-Block. Where a Sub-Block is divided by depth, the Designated Authority shall allocate an identifying letter to each part.

Section 3 Geodetic Datum

3.1 DETERMINING A POSITION OF A POINT IN THE JPDA

Whenever it is necessary to determine the position of a point in the JPDA, that position shall be determined by reference to a spheroid having its centre at the centre of the Earth and a major (equatorial) radius of 6378160 metres and a flattening of 100/29825 and by reference to the position of the Johnson Geodetic Station in the Northern Territory of Australia. The Johnson Geodetic Station shall be taken to be situated at 133 degrees, 12 minutes and 30.0771 seconds of East Longitude and at 25 degrees, 56 minutes and 54.5515 seconds of South Latitude and to have a ground level of 571.2 metres above the spheroid referred to above.

3.2 Using the World Geodetic System 84

For reasons of practicality, positions in the JPDA may be expressed by reference to the spheroid World Geodetic System 84 (WGS 84), which has its centre at the centre of the Earth and a major (equatorial) radius of 6378137 metres and a flattening of 100/29825.7223563. To transform geographic coordinates from the reference system mentioned in the previous paragraph to WGS 84, the Designated Authority shall resort to

internationally recognised datum transformation parameters.

PART II AUTHORISATION OF ACTIVITIES

SECTION 4 GENERAL PROVISIONS

4.1 Prohibited without Authorisation

(a) Except pursuant to an Authorisation, a person shall not explore for, develop or exploit Petroleum within the JPDA, nor export Petroleum from the JPDA.

(b) Paragraph 4.1(a) includes the construction, installation and operation of any structure, facility, installation, equipment or other property, and the carrying out of any other works, in the JPDA.

4.2 Acquisition of Title to Petroleum

A person shall not acquire title to Petroleum before it has been recovered from a Reservoir and delivered at the Field Export Point.

4.3 Joint and Several Liability

If there is more than one Authorised Person in respect of a particular Authorisation, the obligations and liabilities of the Authorised Person under an Authorisation are the obligations and liabilities of them all, jointly and severally.

4.4 Joint Operating and Other Agreements

(a) Except with the consent in writing of the Designated Authority and unless in accordance with the conditions of the consent, where any agreement (whether an agreement commonly referred to as a Joint Operating Agreement, or otherwise) is made by and between any two or more persons with respect to any share of:

(i) the rights, interests, benefits, obligations and liabilities of the Authorised Person under the Authorisation; or

(ii) any Petroleum, or any proceeds of sale of any Petroleum, which, at the time the agreement is made, has not been, but might be, produced from the Authorised Area, the Designated Authority may terminate the Authorisation.

(b) Paragraph 4.4(a) does not apply to an agreement for the sale or exchange of Crude Oil where the sale or exchange occurs after title thereto has passed to the Authorised Person.

(c) A consent by the Designated Authority under this sub-Section 4.4 is without prejudice to sub-Section 4.3.

4.5 Approval of Operator

(a) The appointment of an Operator shall be subject to the prior approval of the Designated Authority where:

(i) there is more than one Authorised Person in respect of a particular Authorisation and the person appointed as Operator is one of those Authorised Persons, and

(ii) the person appointed as Operator is not an Authorised Person.

(b) Any change in Operator shall be subject to the prior approval of the Designated Authority.

(c) Where the Designated Authority determines that an Operator is no longer competent to be an Operator, the Designated Authority, with the approval of the Joint Commission, may, by written notice to the Operator and to the Authorised Person, revoke its approval.

[Insert Date] Page 12

4.6 Change in Control

(a) All changes in Control of an Authorised Person shall be subject to the prior approval of the Designated Authority.

(b) Where a change in Control occurs without the prior approval of the Designated Authority, the Designated Authority may terminate the applicable Authorisation.

(c) Paragraph 4.6(a) does not apply if the change in Control is the direct result of an acquisition of shares or other securities listed on a recognised stock exchange.

(d) For the purposes of this sub-Section 4.6, "change in Control" includes a person ceasing to be in Control (whether or not another person becomes in Control), and a person obtaining Control (whether or not another person was in Control).

4.7 Restrictions on Assignment

(a) Except with the consent in writing of the Designated Authority, and unless in accordance with the conditions of the consent, where an assignment or other dealing occurs in respect of an Authorisation by an Authorised Person the Designated Authority may terminate the Authorisation.

(b) Paragraph 4.7(a) includes any assignment, transfer, conveyance, novation, merger, encumbering or other dealing in any manner whatsoever or howsoever (whether legally, beneficially or otherwise, and whether conditionally or not) by an Authorised Person with:

(i) an Authorisation, or all or any part of its rights, interests, benefits, obligations and liabilities under it;

(ii) Petroleum which has not then been, but might be, recovered in the Contract Area, or any proceeds of sale of such Petroleum; and

(iii) anything whereby the Authorisation, that Petroleum or any of those rights, interests and benefits would, but for this sub-Section 4.7, be held for the benefit of, or be exercisable by or for the benefit of, any other person.

(c) Sub-paragraph 4.7(b)(ii) does not apply to an agreement for the sale or exchange of Crude Oil where the sale or exchange occurs after title thereto has passed to the Authorised Person.

(d) The Designated Authority may not consent to a dealing which would result in a person other than a limited liability corporation, or an entity with limited liability, specifically established for the sole purposes of the Production Sharing Contract, becoming a Contractor, and any consent otherwise is of no force or effect.

(e) For the purposes of paragraph 4.7(b), encumbrance includes any mortgage, charge, pledge, hypothecation, lien, assignment by way of security, title retention, option, right to acquire, right of pre-emption, right of set off, counterclaim, trust arrangement, overriding royalty, net profits interest, or any other security, preferential right, equity or restriction, any agreement to give or to create any of the forgoing and any transaction which, in legal terms, is not a secured borrowing but which has an economic or financial effect similar to that of a secured borrowing.

4.8 Indemnification of Designated Authority and Joint Commission

An Authorised Person shall:

(a) at all times defend, keep effectually indemnified and hold harmless the Designated Authority and the members of the Joint Commission against all actions, suits, proceedings, costs, charges, claims and demands whatsoever (including for economic loss) which may be made or brought against the Designated Authority and/or the members of the Joint Commission wheresoever by any third party in relation to or in connection with its Authorisation or resulting, directly or indirectly, from Authorised Activities under its Authorisation or any other matter or thing done or purported to be done in pursuance of that Authorisation or in the conduct of those Authorised Activities, notwithstanding that the Designated Authority and/or the members of the Joint Commission may have approved in any manner or form whatsoever thereof or that such may have been permitted or required by the terms of the Treaty, the Code (including any regulation made or direction given thereunder) or that Authorisation, or that the Designated Authority and/or the members of the Joint Commission could have exercised, but did not exercise, any power, function, right or authority to prohibit the same;

(b) unless the Designated Authority is satisfied from time to time, after consultation with the Authorised Person, that the potential liability under paragraph 4.8(a)can be covered by other means, including self-insurance, maintain insurance in respect thereof for such amount and on such terms as the Designated Authority requires from time to time; and

(c) take out and maintain insurance in respect of such other matters as the Designated Authority requires (including in respect of pollution), for such amounts as the Designated Authority requires from time to time and otherwise as required by Good Oil Field Practice, unless the Designated Authority is satisfied from time to time, after consultation with the Authorised Person, that the potential liability can be covered by other means, including self-insurance.

SECTION 5 APPLICATIONS

5.1 INVITATION

(a) The Designated Authority shall, by notice in official Timor-Leste and Australian Government gazettes, and in such other manner, if any, as it decides, from time to time invite applications to enter into an Authorisation.

(b) Notwithstanding paragraph 5.1 (a), the Designated Authority may, with the approval of the Joint Commission, elect to award Authorisations without issuing such invitations:

(i) in the case of Access Authorisations; or

(ii) in the case of all other Authorisations, where it is in the public interest to do so.

(c) if the Designated Authority grants an Authorisation without inviting applications, it shall publish a brief explanation of its reasons in a convenient manner.

5.2 CONTENT OF INVITATION

An invitation mentioned in sub-Section 5.1 shall specify:

(a) the area concerned, and the activities the Designated Authority proposes to authorise in respect of it;

(b) the criteria upon which applications will be assessed;

(c) the time by which (not to be less than four (4) weeks), and the manner in which, applications may be made;

(d) the fees, if any, which are to accompany the application; and

(e) such other matters as the Designated Authority considers material or convenient to specify.

Unless the invitation specifically so states, the Designated Authority is not obliged to grant an Authorisation to any applicant.

5.3 APPLICANT'S PROPOSALS IN RESPECT OF HEALTH, SAFETY AND THE ENVIRONMENT

(a) An application for an Authorisation shall include proposals:

(i) for securing the health, safety and welfare of persons in or about the Authorised Activities; and

(ii) for protecting the natural and marine environment, and for preventing, minimising and remedying pollution and other environmental harm from the Authorised Activities.

(b) An Authorisation awarded to an applicant obliges it to comply with its proposals as mentioned in paragraph 5.3(a), but without prejudice to its obligation to comply with more stringent requirements (if any) in the Treaty, the Code, the Authorisation or Good Oil Field Practice.

5.4 Applicant's Proposals in respect of Training and Employment, and Local Goods and Services

An application for an Authorisation shall include proposals for:

(a) training, and, with due regard to occupational health and safety requirements, giving preference in employment in the Authorised Activities to nationals and permanent residents of Timor-Leste; and

(b) the acquisition of goods and services from persons based in Timor-Leste.

5.5 Designated Authority to Consider Applications

The Designated Authority may not grant an Authorisation in respect of an area to the extent to which applications in respect of that area have been invited, until all applications submitted in compliance with the terms of such invitation have finally been considered.

5.6 False or Misleading Information in an Application

The knowing or reckless giving of information that is false or misleading in a material respect in, or in connection with, any application under the Code, shall be grounds on which the Designated Authority may terminate any Authorisation granted as a result of that application.

SECTION 6 MAKING OF PRODUCTION SHARING CONTRACTS

6.1 Power of Designated Authority

The Designated Authority may, with the approval of the Joint Commission:

(a) subject to sub-Sections 6.2 and 5.5; and

(b) in respect of all or any part of the JPDA (subject to any other Production Sharing Contract authorising activities in that area);

make a Production Sharing Contract with any person.

6.2 Restrictions on Choice of a Contractor

(a) The Designated Authority may only make a Production Sharing Contract with a person, or group of persons, which:

(i) it is satisfied has, or has access to, the financial capability, and the technical knowledge and ability, to carry on the Petroleum Operations in a manner wholly consistent with the Treaty, the Code and the Production Sharing Contract; and

(ii) does not have a record of non-compliance with principles of good corporate citizenship; and

(iii) if a group, has made an agreement of a kind which, if the Production Sharing Contract were made with it, would be an agreement of the kind mentioned in sub-Section 4.4, and the Designated Authority has given its consent to the agreement and the group has agreed to act (and has acted and is acting) in accordance with the conditions (if any) of the consent.

(b) A Production Sharing Contract may only be made with a person which is a limited liability corporation or entity with limited liability, or with persons who are limited liability corporations or entities with limited liability, specifically established for the sole purpose of the Production Sharing Contract. A Production Sharing Contract made other than with such a person or persons, as the case may be, is of no force or effect.

(c) If a Contractor engages in a business other than the Authorised Activity, the Designated Authority may terminate the Production Sharing Contract.

SECTION 7 RIGHTS AND OBLIGATIONS CONFERRED BY PRODUCTION SHARING CONTRACT

7.1 Principal Rights and Exclusivity

(a) Subject to this Code, a Production Sharing Contract authorises the Contractor exclusively to explore for, develop and exploit Petroleum in the Contract Area, and to export that Petroleum from the JPDA.

(b) Paragraph 7.1(a) includes:

(i) the construction, installation and operation of structures, facilities, installations, equipment and other property, and the carrying out of other works, necessary for the purposes mentioned in it, in the Contract Area; and

(ii) the marketing of that Petroleum.

(c) Without limiting the generality of the forgoing provisions of this sub-Section 7.1, the Petroleum Operations may be limited to Crude Oil, Natural Gas or other constituents of Petroleum, and the Contract Area may be delineated vertically as well as horizontally.

7.2 Mandatory Provisions

A Production Sharing Contract obliges the Contractor to comply with its obligations under the Treaty and the Code. Subject thereto, the Production Sharing Contract shall:

(a) oblige the Contractor to fund the Petroleum Operations;

(b) oblige the Contractor to carry on the Petroleum Operations in accordance with programmes and budgets approved by the Designated Authority;

(c) oblige the Contractor periodically to submit to the Designated Authority, in respect of the Petroleum Operations, data, information, reports, assessments and plans;

(d) provide for the Contractor to share Petroleum from the Contract Area with the Designated Authority;

(e) permit the Contractor to lift, dispose of and export from the Contract Area, its share of Petroleum from the Contract Area, and (without prejudice to its obligations under the Treaty, the Code and the Contract) to retain the proceeds from the sale thereof;

(f) subject to sub-Section 4.2, specify the point or points at which title to the Contractor's share of Petroleum from the Contract Area will pass to it;

(g) oblige the Contractor, at the request of the Designated Authority, to lift, dispose of and export from the Contract Area, all or a portion of the Designated Authority's share of Petroleum on terms no less favourable to the Designated Authority than those which the Contractor receives for its own share, and to account to the Designated Authority for the value thereof;

(h) require the Contractor to provide for third party access to structures, facilities, installations, equipment and other property, and other works, constructed, installed or operated in the course of the Petroleum Operations on reasonable terms and conditions; and

(i) provide for disputes between the Designated Authority and the Contractor to be resolved by an independent tribunal.

7.3 Other Provisions

A Production Sharing Contract may:

(a) oblige the Contractor to carry out specified minimum levels of work and expenditure;

(b) provide for the periodic relinquishment of parts of the Contract Area;

(c) provide for the Contractor to maintain insurances in addition to those mentioned in sub-Section 4.8;

(d) provide for the consequences of a failure of the Contractor to fulfil its obligations under the Production Sharing Contract;

(e) oblige the Contractor to provide security for the funding and performance of its obligations under the Production Sharing Contract, including in respect of decommissioning;

(f) specify the actions, in addition to those mentioned in sub-Section 7.4, to be taken by the Designated Authority and the Contractor, on the discovery of Petroleum;

(g) oblige the Contractor to transfer title, to the Designated Authority, to structures, facilities, installations, equipment and other property, and to other works, constructed, installed or operated in the course of Petroleum Operations;

(h) provide that the Contract is a commercial agreement and that both the Designated Authority and the Contractor waive any claim to sovereign immunity which they may have, both as to process and execution; and

(i) provide for such other matters as may be convenient.

7.4 Discovery of Petroleum

A Contractor shall notify the Designated Authority in writing within twenty four (24) hours whenever any Petroleum is discovered in its Authorised Area, and shall provide such information in regard thereto as the Designated Authority may request, including details in writing of the chemical composition and physical properties of the Petroleum, and the nature of the sub-soil in which the Petroleum occurs.

SECTION 8 PROSPECTING AUTHORISATION

8.1 Grant

(a) The Designated Authority may grant a Prospecting Authorisation to any person, subject to such conditions as the Designated Authority specifies in the Authorisation.

(b) Notwithstanding paragraph 8.1(a), a Prospecting Authorisation does not enable the holder of the Prospecting Authorisation to enter any part of the JPDA that is the subject of a Production Sharing Contract, without the written agreement of the Contractor, and such agreement shall not be unreasonably withheld.

(c) A Prospecting Authorisation, while it remains in force, authorises the holder to acquire data and other information for the purposes of exploration, in the area specified in the Prospecting Authorisation.

(d) Nothing in a Prospecting Authorisation authorises the holder to drill a well or to have any preference or right to make a Production Sharing Contract.

8.2 Notice to Other Persons

Where:

(a) a person holds a Prospecting Authorisation in respect of an area; and

(b) a Prospecting Authorisation is granted to another person in respect of that area;

the Designated Authority shall, by written notice served on each of those persons, inform them of:

(c) the Authorised Activities of the other; and

(d) the conditions to which the Prospecting Authorisation granted to the other is subject.

8.3 Surrender and Cancellation

A Prospecting Authorisation:

(a) may be surrendered by the holder at any time by instrument in writing served on the Designated Authority, provided that the Authorised Person has fulfilled all its obligations thereunder; and

(b) may, if the holder has not complied with a condition to which the Prospecting Authorisation is subject, be cancelled by the Designated Authority by instrument in writing served on the holder.

SECTION 9 ACCESS AUTHORISATION

9.1 GRANT

(a) The Designated Authority may grant:

(i) a person wishing to undertake a survey to facilitate the, development or exploitation of Petroleum within the JPDA, or the export of Petroleum from the JPDA (in respect of all or a part of the JPDA);

(ii) with the approval of the Joint Commission in the case of a Contractor wishing to drill a well into a Reservoir that is within the Contract Area under its Production Sharing Contract, a Contractor (in respect of a part of the JPDA which is not within its Contract Area);

(iii) with the approval of the Joint Commission if in regard to a Pipeline, a person (an "Infrastructure Provider"), not being a Contractor, wishing to construct, install or operate, in the JPDA, structures, facilities, installations, equipment or other property, or carry out other works, development or exploitation of Petroleum within the JPDA, or the export of Petroleum from the JPDA (in respect of a part of the JPDA); or (iv) an Access Authorisation, subject to such conditions as the Designated Authority thinks fit and specifies in the Access Authorisation;

(b) An Access Authorisation authorises the holder:

(i) if a Contractor, to carry on, in the area specified in the Access Authorisation, and in relation to the Petroleum Operations authorised by its Production Sharing Contract, the operations so specified (including the construction, installation and operation of structures, facilities, installation, equipment and other property, and the carrying out of other works);

(ii) if a person undertaking a survey, to carry on, in the area specified in the Access Authorisation, and in relation to the matters mentioned in subparagraph 9.1(a)(i), the operations so specified; and

(iii) if an Infrastructure Provider, to carry on, in the area specified in the Access Authorisation, and in relation to the matters mentioned in sub-paragraph 9.1(a)(iii), the operations so specified.

(c) Except in relation to a Contractor wishing to drill a well into a Reservoir that is within its Contract Area, nothing in an Access Authorisation authorises the holder to drill a well.

9.2 NOTICE TO OTHER PERSONS

The Designated Authority may not grant an Access Authorisation with any person in respect of an area that is the subject of a Production Sharing Contract with, or a Prospecting Authorisation held by, another person, or vary an Access Authorisation in force in respect of such an area, unless:

(a) it has, by instrument in writing served on that other person, given not less than one

(1) month's notice of its intention to grant, or vary, as the case may be, the Access Authorisation;

(b) it has served a copy of the instrument:

(i) on such other persons as it thinks fit; and

(ii) in a case where it intends to vary an Access Authorisation, on the holder of the Access Authorisation;

(c) it has, in the instrument:

(i) given particulars of the Access Authorisation proposed to be granted, or of the variation proposed to be made, as the case may be; and

(ii) specified a date on or before which a person on whom the instrument, or a copy of the instrument, is served may, by instrument in writing served on the Designated Authority, submit any matters that it wishes the Designated Authority to consider; and

(d) it has taken into account any matters so submitted to it on or before the specified date by such a person in such a way that there is no undue interference with the rights and obligations of that other person, and the terms are not inconsistent with general commercial practice in similar circumstances.

9.3 Surrender and Cancellation

(a) An Access Authorisation:

(i) may be surrendered by the holder at any time by instrument in writing served on the Designated Authority, provided that the Authorised Person has fulfilled all its obligations thereunder; and

(ii) may, if the holder has not complied with a condition to which the Access Authorisation is subject, be cancelled by the Designated Authority by instrument in writing served on the holder.

(b) The Designated Authority shall serve a copy of the instrument concerned on any Contractor or holder of a Prospecting Authorisation in whose Authorised Area operations were authorised to be carried on by the Access Authorisation concerned.

9.4 Reports to Other Persons

An Access Authorisation in respect of an area that is the subject of a Production Sharing Contract shall,

(a) to the extent that the Designated Authority is satisfied that it is right and proper to do so having regard to the operations authorised by the Access Authorisation and to the rights, interests, benefits, obligations and liabilities of the Contractor under the Production Sharing Contract, and

(b) having taking into account any matters submitted to it by the Contractor and those other persons mentioned in sub-Section 9.2, require that the holder of the Access Authorisation furnish to the Contractor, at such times and in such manner as are specified in the Access Authorisation, such data, information and reports as are so specified.

9.5 Third Party Access

(a) The conditions to which an Access Authorisation granted to a Contractor or to an Infrastructure Provider are subject shall include conditions as to third party access to the structures, facilities, installations, equipment and other property, and other works concerned.

(b) Third-party access shall be on commercial terms and in accordance with Good Oil Field Practice.

9.6 Directions

The Designated Authority may give directions to the holders of Access Authorisations and to other Authorised Persons, regarding the coordination of their respective operations.

SECTION 10 UNITISATION

10.1 Power of Designated Authority to Require Unitisation

(a) Where a Reservoir is partly within a Contract Area and partly within another Contract Area, but wholly within the JPDA, the Designated Authority may require by written notice the Contractors to enter into a unitisation agreement for the purpose of securing the more effective recovery of Petroleum from the Reservoir.

(b) If no agreement has been reached within a period of eighteen (18) months from receipt of written notice as required in paragraph 10.1(a), the Designated Authority shall, with the approval of the Joint Commission, determine the terms of the unitisation agreement.

(c) Where a Reservoir is partly within a Contract Area and partly within an area not the subject of a Production Sharing Contract, but wholly within the JPDA, the Designated Authority, with the approval of the Joint Commission, may require by written notice the Contractor to enter into a unitisation agreement with the Designated Authority for the purpose of securing the more effective recovery of Petroleum from the Reservoir. The unitisation agreement is subject to the approval of the Joint Commission.

(d) If no agreement has been reached within a period of eighteen (18) months from receipt of written notice as required in paragraph 10.1(c), an independent expert approved by the Contractor and the Designated Authority shall determine the terms of the unitisation agreement. In the absence of agreement on the choice of the independent expert within thirty (30) days, an expert shall be appointed by the Joint Commission at the request of either party.

10.2 Timing

Approvals for the development or exploitation of the Reservoir shall not be granted by the Designated Authority before the terms of the unitisation agreement are agreed or determined.

10.3 Changes to Unitisation

Any changes to the unitisation agreement shall be subject to the prior approval of the Designated Authority with the approval of the Joint Commission.

SECTION 11 ADDITIONAL POWERS

11.1 Agreements with Other Persons

The Designated Authority may make an agreement with a person with respect to any matter incidental to or connected with an Authorisation, including assurances to providers of finance to the Contractor regarding the exercise of the Designated Authority's power and functions in regard to assignments, termination and rates of production of Petroleum, as requested and agreed to by the Contractor.

11.2 Exemptions by the Designated Authority

Subject to sub-Section 11.3, the Designated Authority may, at the request of an Authorised Person, exempt that Authorised Person from complying with the conditions of its Authorisation, and may also agree to vary or suspend those conditions, either with or without conditions and either temporarily or permanently, except insofar as this would be inconsistent with the Treaty and this Code.

11.3 Approval of Joint Commission

The Designated Authority may not, without the approval of the Joint Commission, exempt an Authorised Person from complying with, or vary or suspend:

(a) any condition of a Production Sharing Contract; or

(b) any condition of an Authorisation in respect of a Pipeline.

PART III CONDUCT OF AUTHORISED ACTIVITIES

SECTION 12 WORK PRACTICES

12.1 Proper and Workmanlike Manner

An Authorised Person shall carry out Authorised Activities in a proper, efficient and workmanlike manner, and in accordance with the Treaty and the Code, its Authorisation and Good Oil Field Practice.

12.2 Particular Obligations

In particular, an Authorised Person shall carry out Authorised Activities in such a manner as is required by sub-Section 12.1 to:

(a) protect the environment in and about the Authorised Area, ensure that Authorised Activities result in minimum ecological damage or destruction, and clean up pollution;

(b) ensure the health, safety and welfare of persons in or about the Authorised Activities;

(c) maintain in safe and good condition and repair, the Authorised Area and all structures, facilities, installations, equipment and other property, and other works, used or to be used, in Authorised Activities;

(d) manage the resources in a way that promotes further investment and contributes to the long term development of Timor-Leste and Australia;

(e) on the earlier of:

(i) termination of the Authorisation; and

(ii) when no longer required for Authorised Activities; and, in either case:

(iii) except with the consent in writing of the Designated Authority and in accordance with the conditions of the consent; or

(iv) unless the Authorisation otherwise provides,

abandon, decommission, transfer, remove and/or dispose of all structures, facilities, installations, equipment and other property, clean up the Authorised Area and make it good and safe, and protect the environment, to the satisfaction of the Designated Authority.

PART IV INFORMATION AND INVESTIGATION

SECTION 13 DATA AND INFORMATION

13.1 Ownership of Data

(a) The Designated Authority shall have title to all technical data and information acquired in the course of, or as a result of, Authorised Activities.

(b) Paragraph 13.1(a) includes all raw data and information (including cores, cuttings, samples, and all other geological, geophysical, geochemical, drilling, well, production and engineering data and information) that the Authorised Person collects and compiles through Petroleum Operations. It does not include data obtained from special studies carried out by or for the Authorised Person that uses special proprietary software or procedures. It also does not include interpretations that have particular commercial or regional significance to a Contractor (over and above that which is necessary for the commercial evaluation and development of a Contract Area) and in respect of which the eligible recoverable cost attributable to the Contract Area is a small proportion of the total cost of the interpretations.

13.2 Records and Reporting to the Designated Authority

An Authorised Person shall, unless otherwise required by law:

(a) keep such financial, commercial, legal, operational, technical and other data, information and records relating to Authorised Activities (including the sale or other disposition of Petroleum, and the data and information mentioned in sub-Section 13.1) in such manner and at such place;

(b) make available to the Designated Authority such data, information and records in such manner and at such time and at such place; and

(c) provide the Designated Authority with such reports in respect thereof and otherwise in respect of Authorised Activities, as the Designated Authority specifies.

SECTION 14 RELEASE OF INFORMATION AND DATA

14.1 Use of Data and Information

(a) The Designated Authority may make such use as it wishes of the data and information mentioned in Section 13, and nothing in sub-Sections 14.2 or 14.3 prevents the Designated Authority using data and information for the purposes of general statistical and other general reporting (publicly or otherwise) on its activities.

(b) Except with the consent in writing of the Designated Authority and in accordance with the conditions (if any) of the consent, the Authorised Person may only use the data and information mentioned in sub-Section 13.1 for its Authorised Activities or for an application for an Authorisation or for reporting information to its Affiliates provided that the Authorised Person first procures that any such Affiliates agree to be bound by this paragraph 14.1(b).

14.2 Confidentiality of Data and Information

(a) Except as otherwise provided in the Authorisation or with the consent of the Authorised Person, the Designated Authority shall not publicly disclose or, other than for the purpose of the administration of the Treaty or the Code, or as otherwise required by the Treaty or the Code, make available to any person, any data or information mentioned in sub-Section 13.1 until the earlier of:

(i) five (5) years after the data or information was acquired by the Authorised Person; and

(ii) the Authorisation under which the data or information was acquired ceasing to apply;

(b) Except with the consent of the Designated Authority, and in accordance with the conditions (if any) of the consent, an Authorised Person shall not disclose the data or information mentioned in sub-Section 13.1 other than:

(i) to its employees, agents, contractors and Affiliates to the extent necessary for the proper and efficient carrying on of its Authorised Activities;

(ii) as required by law;

(iii) for the purpose of the resolution of disputes under its Authorisation; or (iv) as required by a recognised stock exchange.

(c) The Authorised Person shall procure that a person mentioned in sub-paragraph 14.2(b)(i) maintains the data and information disclosed to it confidential in the terms of this sub-Section 14.2.

14.3 Trade Secrets

(a) Except as otherwise provided in the Authorisation or with the consent of the Authorised Person, and notwithstanding sub-Sections 14.1 and 14.2, the Designated Authority shall not publicly disclose or, other than for the purpose of the administration of the Treaty or the Code, or as otherwise required by the Treaty or the Code, make available to any person, any data or information submitted to it by an Authorised Person which:

(i) is a trade secret of, or other data and information the disclosure of which would, or could reasonably be expected to, adversely affect, the Authorised Person in respect of its lawful business, commercial or financial affairs; and

(ii) was clearly marked as such when it was submitted to the Designated Authority.

(b) Without prejudice to sub-paragraph 14.3(a)(i):

(i) the Designated Authority may, at any time and from time to time, serve notice on an Authorised Person requiring it to show cause, within the time specified for the purpose in the notice, why information which it has marked pursuant to sub-paragraph 14.3(a)(ii) above should still be considered a trade secret or other information as mentioned in that sub-paragraph 14.3(a)(ii); and

(ii) if the Authorised Person does not show cause within that time, the data and information shall no longer be a trade secret or other such information for the purposes of this sub-Section 14.3.

14.4 Speculative Seismic Surveys

The Designated Authority may, in an agreement of a type as is mentioned in sub-Section 11.1, agree longer periods of confidentiality with a person wishing to engage in a speculative seismic survey where it is the intention of that person to sell the data and information acquired on a non-exclusive basis.

14.5 Public Announcement

Except with the consent of the Designated Authority and in accordance with the conditions (if any) of the consent, subject to law and/or the rules of an established stock exchange, an Authorised Person shall not make any public statement about its Authorisation or the results of its Authorised Activities. In no event shall such a public statement state or imply that the Designated Authority approves or agrees with its contents.

SECTION 15 INSPECTIONS

15.1 Power of Appointment

(a) The Designated Authority may, by instrument in writing, appoint a person to be an inspector for the purposes of the Code.

(b) An inspector must possess qualifications and experience that are appropriate to the areas of duty of that Inspector.

(c) An inspector is required to be bound by strict confidentiality provisions and must have no conflicts of interest in respect of duties undertaken.

15.2 Powers of Inspector

A person so appointed may, at all reasonable times and on production of the appropriate credentials:

(a) enter any area, structure, vehicle, vessel, aircraft or building in the JPDA that, in their opinion, has been, is being or is to be used for or in connection with the Authorised Activities or the furnishing of information mentioned in sub-Section 17.1 or in which, in their opinion, there may be documents or records relating to such activities;

(b) inspect and test any machinery or equipment that has been, is being, or is to be, used in Petroleum Operations in the JPDA;

(c) within the JPDA, take or remove, for the purpose of analysis or testing, or for use in evidence, samples of Petroleum, water or other substances;

(d) inspect, take extracts from and make copies of, any document, book or other record relating to, or which in his opinion might relate to, such activities or matters; and

(e) make inquiries concerning compliance with the provisions of the Code and Authorisation, and any direction issued, restrictions imposed or orders made under the Code.

15.3 Powers of the Designated Authority

The Designated Authority may;

(a) with respect to the health, safety and welfare of persons in or about such activities in the JPDA, issue directions to, and impose restrictions on, the Authorised Person or any person so engaged;

(b) order, by instrument in writing:

(i) the cessation of operations on or in, and the withdrawal of any person from, any area, structure, facility, installation or other works in the JPDA that is being used in connection with such activities; or

(ii) the discontinuance of the use of any machinery or equipment in the JPDA;

which it considers unsafe, unless and until such action as is necessary for safety and specified in the instrument is taken and completed.

15.4 Provision of Facilities

An Authorised Person and any person who is the occupier or person in charge of any structure, facility, installation, works or place, or the person in charge of any vehicle, vessel, aircraft, machinery or equipment referred to in sub-Section 15.2 shall provide an inspector with all reasonable facilities and assistance (including, if an Authorised Person and the inspector requires access to its offshore facilities, the provision of necessary means of transport) that the inspector requests for the effective exercise of his powers.

15.5 Complaints

(a) A person aggrieved by an action of an inspector under Section 15 may complain in writing to the Designated Authority, which shall as soon as practicable consider the complaint.

(b) The Designated Authority may take such reasonable action as is necessary in response to the complaint.

15.6 Inspector may be Accompanied

An inspector may be accompanied by any person who has written authorisation from the Designated Authority and who the Designated Authority believes has special or expert knowledge of any matter being investigated, tested or examined.

15.7 Inspector not to be Hindered

An Authorised Person shall not:

(a) hinder an inspector in the exercise of their powers under this Code;

(b) make a statement or produce a document that is false or misleading in a material aspect to an inspector engaged in carrying out his duties and functions; or

(c) withhold any information from an inspector without lawful excuse.

SECTION 16 AUDITING

16.1 Audit

An Authorised Person's books and accounts shall be audited at such times and in such manner as may be provided in this Code and its Authorisation.

16.2 Independent Audit

Notwithstanding sub-Section 16.1, at the written request of the Designated Authority, an Authorised Person shall arrange for, and pay for, an independent audit of its activities under its Authorisation. There shall be a period of at least twelve (12) months between independent audits except in the case of manifest error or fraud.

SECTION 17 INVESTIGATIONS

17.1 Power of Designated Authority

Where the Designated Authority has reason to believe that an Authorised Person in the JPDA, Australia or Timor-Leste is capable of giving information or producing or making available documents or records relating to Authorised Activities which have been, or are being, carried on, it may, by instrument in writing served on that Authorised Person, give to that person a direction:

(a) to furnish to it in writing, within the period and in the manner specified in the instrument, any such information;

(b) requiring a senior representative of the Authorised Person, with decision making authority in relation to the issue under investigation, to meet with it, or with any person specified in the instrument, at such time and place as is so specified and there to answer questions and discuss issues relating to those matters; or

(c) to make available to it or a person specified in the instrument, at such time and place as is so specified, such documents or records.

17.2 Self-Incrimination no Excuse

An Authorised Person shall not be excused from furnishing information on the grounds that the information might tend to incriminate that person unless the information is likely to be admissible in evidence against that person in criminal proceedings in Australia.

17.3 Right to copy

Where documents or records are made available pursuant to a requirement under this

Section 17, the Designated Authority or the inspector may make copies of, or take extracts from, them.

17.4 Misleading Information

An Authorised Person who, in purported compliance with a direction under sub-Section

17.1, provides or permits to be provided any information which is false or misleading in a material respect shall have failed to comply with that direction.

PART V SAFETY ZONES

SECTION 18 SAFETY ZONES

To promote the safety of navigation and Authorised Activities, the Designated Authority may, consistent with international law, declare safety zones around structures, installations equipment and other property, and other works, in the JPDA. The Designated Authority may also require the installation, maintenance and provision of such navigation, fog and illumination lighting, acoustic and other devices and equipment as it considers necessary for the safety of Authorised Activities.

PART VI PUBLIC INFORMATION

SECTION 19 PUBLICATION OF DETAILS OF AUTHORISATIONS

The Designated Authority shall publish, in official Australian and Timor-Leste Government gazettes, summary details of Authorisations made or terminated in part or in whole.

SECTION 20 PUBLIC INFORMATION

20.1 Authorisations and Other Documents

(a) The Designated Authority shall make available to the public copies of all Authorisations and amendments thereto, whether or not terminated within thirty (30) days of their conclusion.

(b) The Designated Authority shall make available to the public, within a reasonable period of time of a request having been made therefor, summary details of:

(i) an approved Development Plan;

(ii) the original Authorised Area and all changes thereto;

(iii) the original Authorised Person (and, if a group, the undivided participating interest of each member of the group) and the identity of the Operator, and all changes thereto;

(iv) subject to commercial confidence as to the commercial terms, all assignments and other dealings consented to in respect thereof, and

(v) all unitisation agreements and determinations.

20.2 Decision-Making

Within ten (10) business days of a request having been made, the Designated Authority shall publish brief reasons for:

(a) granting an Authorisation subsequent to an invitation, as contemplated at paragraph 5.1(a);

(b) granting an Authorisation without inviting applications, as contemplated at paragraph 5.1(b);

(c) approving a Development Plan;

(d) granting an exemption from, or agreeing to a variation or suspension of, the conditions of an Authorisation under sub-Section 11.2; and

(e) making any decision or granting any approval that, under an Authorisation, requires publication.

20.3 Compliance Reports

(a) Authorised Persons shall report on their compliance with requirements under the Code and Authorisations in such manner and detail as required by their Authorisation and as provided by regulation.

(b) The Designated Authority shall make available such reports to the public.

20.4 Publication of Payments

The Designated Authority shall, in such a manner and detail as prescribed, publish payments made to the Designated Authority under an Authorisation.

20.5 Public Access

The information contemplated in this Section 20 shall be available to any person at all convenient times and the Designated Authority may require payment of a fee therefor.

PART VIII TERMINATION

SECTION 21 TERMINATION OF AUTHORISATIONS

21.1 GROUNDS FOR TERMINATION

(a) Where an Authorised Person:

(i) has not complied with a condition or term to which an Authorisation is subject;

(ii) has not complied with this Code;

(iii) has knowingly provided false information to the Designated Authority in connection with an Authorisation;

(iv) has not paid any amount payable by it under this Code or under an Authorisation within a period of three (3) months after the day on which the amount became payable; or

(v) is subject to or commits an Insolvency Event, the Designated Authority may, with the approval of the Joint Commission, on that ground, by instrument in writing served on the Authorised Person terminate the Authorisation.

(b) The Designated Authority shall not terminate the Authorisation due to one or more of the relevant grounds identified in sub-paragraphs 21.1(a)(i) –(iv) unless there has been a material breach by the Authorised Person of one of those grounds.

(c) Where this Code or an Authorisation expressly grants the Designated Authority a right to terminate an Authorisation, that right shall be exercised in compliance with the requirements of this Section 21.

21.2 DESIGNATED AUTHORITY TO GIVE NOTICE

Except in relation to an Insolvency Event, in which case the Designated Authority may terminate an Authorisation forthwith, the Designated Authority shall not terminate an Authorisation unless:

(a) it has, by instrument in writing served on the Authorised Person, given not less than thirty (30) days notice of its intention to so cancel the Authorisation;

(b) it has, in the instrument, specified a date on or before which the Authorised Person may submit in writing to the Designated Authority any matters that it wishes to be considered; and

(c) it has taken into account any information provided under paragraph 21.2(b) and any action taken by the Authorised Person or other parties to remove that ground or to prevent the recurrence of similar grounds.

21.3 GENERALLY

Termination of an Authorisation for any reason (including the passage of time) is without prejudice to rights and obligations expressed in the Code or the Authorisation to survive termination, or to rights and obligations accrued thereunder prior to termination, and all provisions of an Authorisation reasonably necessary for the full enjoyment and enforcement of those rights and obligations survive termination for the period necessary.

21.4 PARTIAL TERMINATION

If the Authorised Person is more than one Authorised Person in respect of a particular Authorisation and circumstances arise in which the Designated Authority may terminate an Authorisation, the Designated Authority may:

(a) elect to terminate an Authorisation only in respect of those Authorised Persons whose acts or omissions (or in relation to whom acts, omissions or events have occurred which) have led to such circumstances, and shall so notify the remaining Authorised Persons; or

(b) allow other Authorised Persons to remedy the breach of the defaulter to the satisfaction of the Designated Authority.

PART IX MISCELLANEOUS

SECTION 22 REGULATIONS

22.1 PROVISIONS IN REGULATIONS

(a) The Designated Authority, with the approval of the Joint Commission, may make regulations prescribing all matters that by the Code are required or permitted to be prescribed or are necessary or convenient to be prescribed for carrying out or giving effect to the Code.

(b) Without limiting the generality of paragraph 22.1(a), the regulations may make provision for all or any of the following matters:

(i) the exploration for Petroleum and the carrying on of operations, and the execution of works, for that purpose;

(ii) the production of Petroleum (including the rate at which it is recovered) and the carrying on of operations, and the execution of works, for that purpose;

(iii) the measurement and sale or disposal of the Designated Authority's and a Contractor's Petroleum, and the carrying on of operations for that purpose;

(iv) the conservation, and prevention of the waste, of natural resources, whether Petroleum or otherwise;

(v) the construction, erection, maintenance, operation, use, inspection, certification and re-certification of structures, facilities, installations, other works, equipment and other property;

(vi) the control of the flow or discharge, and the prevention of the escape, of Petroleum, water or drilling fluid, or a mixture of water and drilling fluid with Petroleum or any other matter;

(vii) the clean-up or other remedying of the effects of the escape of Petroleum;

(viii) the prevention of damage to Petroleum-bearing strata;

(ix) the prevention of waste or escape of Petroleum;

(x) the abandonment, decommissioning, removal and disposal of structures, facilities, installations, equipment and other property, and of other works, used or held for use in Authorised

Activities and the cleaning up of Authorised Areas, including steps required to prevent hazard to human life, property and the environment;

(xi) the carrying on of Authorised Activities in a safe and environmentally sound manner;

(xii) the preparation of assessments of the impact of Authorised Activities on the environment;

(xiii) the authorisation by the Designated Authority of entry into the JPDA by the employees of Authorised Persons and the employees of their sub-contractors;

(xiv) the control of movement into, within and out of the JPDA of vessels, aircraft, structures, facilities, installations, equipment and other property used or held for use in Authorised Activities;

(xv) the actions, in addition to those mentioned in sub-Section 7.4, to be taken by the Designated Authority and the Contractor on the discovery of Petroleum;

(xvi) the content and information to be provided in respect of programmes and budgets requiring the prior approval of the Designated Authority;

(xvii) the control of tariffs charged for the use of structures, facilities, installations and other works, and the conditions of such use;

(xviii) the auditing of an Authorised Person and of its accounts and records;

(xix) reporting by Authorised Persons on compliance with proposals set out in this Code and Authorisations, including in relation to

(aa) the training and employment of Timor-Leste nationals, (bb) procurement of Timor-Leste goods and services,

(cc) occupational health and safety, and
(dd) environmental protection.

(xx) fees, to be paid to the Designated Authority, in order to cover the costs of its activities (any changes in fees shall not be made to apply retrospectively). These include fees to be paid by:

(aa) applicants for Authorisations;

(bb) Authorised Persons; and

(cc) persons wishing to inspect the register mentioned in sub-Section 20.1;

(xxi) the publication of payments made by an Authorised Person to the Designated Authority under an Authorisation; and

(xxii) any other matters relating to the Code.

(c) The power under this Section 22 to make regulations may be exercised:

(i) either in relation to all cases to which the power extends, or in relation to all of those cases subject to specified exceptions, or in relation to any specified cases or classes of cases; and

(ii) so as to make, as respects the cases in relation to which it is exercised:

(aa) the same provision for all those cases, a different provision for different cases or classes of cases, or different provisions as respects the same case or classes of case for different purposes of the Code; or

(bb) any such provision either unconditionally or subject to any specified condition.

(d) The Designated Authority may, by instrument in writing served on a person or a class of person, make a regulation on a matter consistent with the forgoing provisions of this sub-Section 22.1 to apply to that person or class of persons.

22.2 Failure to Comply

(a) Where a person fails or neglects to comply with a regulation, the Designated Authority may cause to be done all or any of the things required by the regulation to be done.

(b) Costs and expenses incurred by the Designated Authority under paragraph 22.2(a) shall be a debt due to the Designated Authority by the person to whom the regulation was given and may be recovered in a court of competent jurisdiction.

SECTION 23 DIRECTIONS

23.1 Issue Directions

(a) The Designated Authority may, by instrument in writing served on an Authorised Person, give to that person a direction as to any matter with respect to which regulations may be made under Section 22, or as otherwise provided in the Code.

(b) Directions given by the Designated Authority under sub-Section 23.1 are subject to any regulations made under Section 22.

23.2 Failure to Comply

(a) Where a person fails or neglects to comply with a direction given to it under sub-Section 23. 1, the Designated Authority may cause to be done all or any of the things required by the direction to be done.

(b) Costs and expenses incurred by the Designated Authority under sub-Section 23.1 in relation to a direction shall be a debt due to the Designated Authority by the person to whom the direction was given and may be recovered in a court of competent jurisdiction.

SECTION 24 REMOVAL OF PROPERTY

(a) Without prejudice to the generality of sub-Section 23.2, where an Authorised Person fails or neglects to comply with a direction to remove and dispose of property from an Authorised Area, the Designated Authority may remove all or any of the property, and dispose of all or any of it in any manner it thinks fit (including by sale, whether at public auction or otherwise).

(b) The Designated Authority may deduct from the proceeds of any sale of any such property all or any part of any costs and expenses incurred by it under sub-Sections

22.2 and 23.2 in relation to that property and any other amounts owed to the Designated Authority by the Authorised Person pursuant to the Treaty, the Code or an Authorisation.

SECTION 25 ARBITRATION

25.1 Settlement of Disputes

(a) Any dispute between Timor-Leste and Australia concerning the interpretation or application of the Code shall, as far as practicable, be settled by consultation or negotiation.

(b) Any dispute which is not settled in the manner set out in paragraph 25.1(a) shall, at the request or Timor-Leste or Australia, be submitted to an arbitral panel in accordance with the procedure set out in Annex B to the Treaty.

SECTION 26 TRANSITIONAL PROVISION

26.1 Interim Petroleum Mining Code

(a) This Code shall commence on, and the Interim Petroleum Mining Code shall be repealed from, the Commencement Date.

(b) Notwithstanding paragraph 26.1(a), the Interim Petroleum Mining Code, as in force immediately before the Commencement Date, continues to apply in relation to production sharing contracts numbered 03-12, 03-13, 03-19 and 03-20.

MINERALS EXPLORATION - IMPORTANT INFORMATION

Indonesia's mineral resources were dominated by crude petroleum and natural gas but included significant reserves of coal, tin, nickel, copper, gold, and bauxite. Much industrial development was based on increased domestic processing of oil and natural gas. Most mineral production was exported after some degree of domestic processing to industrial nations, primarily Japan. In some cases, Indonesia's own mineral intensive industries, such as steel and aluminum, relied on imports of raw materials. Krakatau Steel imported about 2 million tons of high-grade iron ore in 1989, and P.T. Indonesia Asahan Aluminum imported 360,000 tons of alumina from Australia. On balance, however, Indonesia was a net exporter of minerals in large part because of petroleum exports. In 1989 the total value of mineral exports was US$10 billion, almost 90 percent of which was oil or liquefied natural gas; mineral imports were only US$1.4 billion

PETROLEUM, LIQUEFIED NATURAL GAS, AND COAL

PETROLEUM

Indonesia's oil production was formally governed by a quota allocation from OPEC. At the March 1991 OPEC ministerial meeting, Indonesia's quota was set at 1.445 million barrels per day, below the country's estimated production capacity of 1.7 million barrels per day. Indonesia's quota represented about 6 percent of total OPEC production. About 70 percent of Indonesia's annual oil production was exported on average during the late 1980s, but domestic consumption was increasing steadily and reached half of annual oil production by 1990.

Indonesia's oil industry is one of the oldest in the world. Oil in commercial quantities was discovered in northern Sumatra in 1883, leading to the establishment of the Koninklijke Nederlandsche Maatschappij tot Exploitatie van Petroleum-bronnen in NederlandschIndië (Royal Dutch Company for Exploration of Petroleum sources in the Netherlands Indies) in 1890, which was merged in 1907 with the Shell Transport and Trading Company, a British concern that had been drilling in Kalimantan since 1891, to form Royal Dutch Shell. Royal Dutch Shell dominated colonial oil exploration for more than thirty years. By 1911 Royal Dutch Shell operated concessions in Sumatra, Java, and Kalimantan (then called Borneo), and Indonesian oil was almost 4 percent of total world production. Indonesia's most important oil fields, the Duri and Minas fields in the central Sumatran basin, were discovered just prior to World War II by Caltex, a joint venture between the American companies Chevron and Texaco, although production did not begin until the 1950s. By 1963 the Duri and Minas oil fields, located in Riau Province near the town of Dumai, accounted for 50 percent of oil production.

The postindependence government increased its control over the oil sector during the 1950s and 1960s by increasing operations of several government-owned oil companies and by stiffening the terms of contracts with foreign oil firms. In 1968 the government companies--Indonesian Oil Mining company (Pertamin), National Oil Mining Company (Permina), and the National Oil and Gas Company (Permigan)--were consolidated into a single operation, the National Oil and Natural Gas Mining Company (Pertamina). At this time, a new form of contract--the production-sharing contract--was introduced. A production-sharing contract split total oil production between the contractor and the government, represented by Pertamina, and allowed the government to assume ownership of structures and equipment used for exploration and production within Indonesia. Indonesia's contract terms were considered among the toughest in the world, with the government in most cases receiving 85 percent of oil produced once the foreign company recovered costs.

Annual oil production in Indonesia peaked in 1977 at over 600 million barrels. The official price of Minas crude was then about US$14 per barrel, a substantial rise from the 1973 price of about

US$4 per barrel as a result of OPEC's successful market manipulations. Prices continued to soar in 1981, reaching US$35 per barrel, and oil exports peaked at US$15 billion, or about 70 percent of total export earnings. In 1982, however, production declined, reaching a low of 460 million barrels and the oil market began to weaken that same year, when Indonesia's Minas crude was priced at US$29. The market collapsed in 1986, bringing the Minas price to below US$10 per barrel. Recovery of oil prices began slowly, and by 1989 Minas was priced at about US$18 per barrel. Total production in 1989 was almost 500 million barrels, and oil exports were valued at US$6 billion.

Indonesia had proven oil reserves in 1990 equal to 5.14 billion barrels, with probable reserves of an additional 5.79 billion barrels. Throughout the archipelago there were sixty known basins with oil potential; only thirty-six basins had been explored and only fourteen were producing. The majority of unexplored areas were more than 200 meters beneath the surface of the sea. Indonesia's oil reserves were usually found in medium- and small-sized fields, so that continued exploration was vital to maintain production and known reserves.

In 1989 and 1990, the government loosened some provisions for new contracts to stimulate exploration, particularly in frontier areas. Improved oil market conditions in the late 1980s also contributed to a surge in production-sharing contracts. Fifty-seven of the 100 contracts active in 1992 were signed from 1987 to 1991. The newer contracts committed US$2.8 billion in exploration during the 1990s. Production from existing oil fields was still dominated by Caltex's operations in Sumatra, which accounted for 47 percent of Indonesian oil production in 1990. Twenty foreign oil companies, primarily United States-based, were active producers in 1990.

Pertamina operated eight petroleum refineries with a total capacity to produce 400,000 barrels per day of a variety of distilled products for domestic use and export. The Indonesian government subsidized the domestic prices of distillates, and in spite of several price increases during the 1980s, prices in Indonesia were well below international market prices by 1990. For example, kerosene, used primarily for cooking, was priced at Rp190 per liter following a 15 percent price hike in May 1990; the price of kerosene in Singapore was then equivalent to Rp643 per liter and in the Philippines, Rp512 per liter. The total cost of fuel subsidies amounted to Rp2.6 trillion (US$1.3 billion) in FY 1990. Pertamina forecast an increase in domestic demand for distilled products of 7 percent per year, and hoped to meet this demand and, simultaneously, to expand exports. Four new refineries with a total capacity of 500,000 barrels per day intended entirely for export were in various stages of planning in 1990.

LIQUEFIED NATURAL GAS

Indonesia was the world's largest producer and exporter of liquefied natural gas. Two major facilities, P.T. Arun at Lhokseumawe, Special Region of Aceh, and P.T. Badak, in Bontang, Kalimantan Timur Province, condensed natural gas through refrigeration to one-six hundredth of its volume for shipment in tankers. Both facilities were built in the late 1970s under supply contracts to Japan, although excess production was shipped to other destinations. After several expansions, the total capacity had reached 22.6 million tons per year by 1990. Exports of liquefied natural gas in 1990 were 20.6 million tons, valued at US$3.7 billion.

Although most of Indonesia's natural gas was supplied to liquefying plants for export in the early 1990s, about 20 percent was used for domestic consumption, primarily in fertilizer plants, where it was processed into ammonia and urea. Natural gas reserves were estimated in 1990 at 67.5 trillion standard cubic feet of proven reserves and 12 trillion standard cubic feet of probable reserves. Growing domestic and export demand encouraged plans for the development of the Natuna gas field, the nation's largest field, located in the South China Sea northeast of the

Natuna Islands. The high carbon dioxide content of this field had previously deterred investment, but Esso Indonesia indicated willingness to invest US$12 billion to $US15 billion to treat and market the gas. Pertamina authorized further negotiations with Esso after reviewing the proposal in 1991.

COAL

Coal production declined in the 1970s because of increasing use of subsidized petroleum fuels. However, in the late 1970s Suharto announced a new effort to increase domestic coal use, especially in cement and electric power plants. Total coal production rose steadily in the 1980s to reach 11 million tons in 1990. Most coal reserves were located in southern Sumatra and eastern and southern Kalimantan. Total measured reserves were 4.2 billion tons, with an additional 12.9 billion tons classified as inferred reserves and 15 billion tons of hypothetical reserves. A government mining company, P.T. Tambang Batubara Bukit, produced the majority of coal in 1991, but ten coal cooperation contracts signed between 1981 and 1987 with foreign investors were expected to produce a total of 20 to 25 million tons per year by 1994.

OTHER MINERALS

TIN

Indonesia was one of the world's four major tin producers, behind Brazil but close in ore production to Malaysia and China in the late 1980s. Tin ore production was centered on Bangka Island, part of Sumatera Selatan Province. New exploration was planned in 1989 on Sumatra and offshore Bangka Island. Indonesia is a member of the Association of Tin Producing Countries and was required in FY 1989 to restrict tin exports to no more than 31,500 tons as part of the association's Supply Rationalization Scheme. The government enterprise P.T. Timah controlled the majority of tin mining and, together with an Australian mining firm, operated a tin smelter in Muntok, located in northwestern Bangka Island. In 1989 the smelter, which had a capacity of 32,500 tons per year, produced 29,900 tons of refined tin from local ore. In the late 1980s, Indonesia exported 80 percent of its tin production. Some tin ore was shipped to Malaysia for processing, although tin metal was shipped primarily to Singapore. Most of the growing domestic tin consumption was used in tin plating and for solder. Official proven reserves of tin were 740 million tons.

NICKEL

Indonesia was among the world's top five producers of nickel ore in 1989, although Canada and the then-Soviet Union produced much greater quantities. The major nickel mining operations were run by P.T. Aneka Tambang (also known by the abbreviated P.T. Antam), the Indonesian government mining firm, and by P.T. Inco, an international firm owned primarily by the Canadian firm Inco Limited, with a minority share owned by Sumitomo Metal Mining Company of Japan. At its integrated nickel complex at the Soroako Concession in Sumatera Selatan Province, P.T. Inco processed ore into nickel matte, which was then exported to Japan. Plans were underway in 1989 to expand the capacity of the complex from 35,000 tons to 47,630 tons capacity. P.T. Inco also planned to issue from US$300 million to US$400 million in stock shares on the Jakarta Stock Exchange in 1990 to meet the 20 percent domestic equity ownership requirement mandated in its 1967 contract with the Indonesian government. P.T. Aneka Tambang had mine operations in the Pomalaa area of Sulawesi Selatan Province and on Gebe Island, Maluku Province. A joint venture between P.T. Aneka Tambang and Australian Queensland Nickel planned to open a new nickel mine on Gag Island, Irian Jaya Province, in 1991. P.T. Aneka Tambang also operated a ferronickel processing plant in Sumatera Selatan Province with a capacity of 4,800 tons per year of contained nickel. Total nickel ore reserves in Indonesia represented 12 percent of world reserves, or 367 million tons with a nickel content between 1.5 to 2 percent.

COPPER

Copper mining in the late 1980s was dominated by the FreeportMcMoRan Copper and Gold Company, a United States firm, which, through its joint venture subsidiary Freeport Indonesia, had operated the Ertsberg Mountain mine in the Jayawijaya Mountains of Irian Jaya Province since the early 1970s. The mined ore was milled and then sent 115 kilometers by pipeline to Freeport's Amamapare port. The mine produced 32 million tons before becoming depleted. To expand its operations, in 1989 Freeport Indonesia was granted an exploration license by the Indonesian government that added 2.5 million hectares to its original 10,000-hectare concession. A major new discovery on Grasberg Mountain, three kilometers north of the Ertsberg Mountain site, was expected to come under production in 1990 and to produce around 270,000 tons annually by the end of 1992. It was projected to become the world's largest open-cast mine, and at one of the lowest costs in the world. Total proven and probable reserves of copper, centered in the Ertsberg and Grasberg areas of Irian Jaya, were 15 billion tons. In a related joint venture, Freeport Indonesia, Nippon Mining (Japan), Metallgesselschaft (Germany), and a private Indonesian investor had plans to start construction of a 150,000-ton annual production capacity, US$600 million copper smelter in Gresik, Jawa Timur Province. Given its 10 percent ownership of Freeport Indonesia, the Indonesia government had high profits at stake.

GOLD

Most gold production officially reported in government statistics was a byproduct of Freeport Indonesia's copper mining. In 1989 total official gold production was about 6,000 kilograms, of which about 4,000 kilograms was extracted by Freeport Indonesia with a 15,000 kilogram production expected by the end of 1992. However, a large number of small-scale mining operations in Kalimantan may have produced as much as 18,000 kilograms of gold in 1989. Many of these small mines were operated illegally on foreign concessions. In 1989 there were approximately eighty foreign contractors with concessions for gold exploration, primarily in Kalimantan, but only a small number had producing mines.

BAUXITE

Bauxite was being mined in the early 1990s by P.T. Aneka Tambang on Bintan Island and three neighboring islands, and most bauxite was exported to Japan. Total bauxite reserves of 396 million tons were found in the Bintan Island area and in Kalimantan Barat Province. Reserves of commercially exportable bauxite were much more limited, although on-site processing into alumina had the potential to be commercially feasible with below export grade reserves. Bauxite, the demand for which had increased during Repelita V after having slowed down during Repelita IV, is a primary input in the production of aluminum. It must first be refined into alumina. Plans were underway in 1991 for an alumina refinery, and the Department of Mining and Energy had been seeking an interested foreign partner to develop a US$600 million facility on Bintan Island since the late 1980s. Alumina input for P.T. Indonesia Asahan Aluminum was imported from Australia.

LARGEST OIL AND GAS COMPANIES OPERATING IN INDONESIA

Company Members are companies who hold a percentage working interest in petroleum and/or geothermal rights within Indonesia and whose interest in such rights has been recognized by the Government of the Republic of Indonesia. "Company" in this context shall include the Research and Development Center for Oil and Gas Technology - "LEMIGAS" and any other organization which may, from time to time, be deemed by the Board of Directors to be so included for the purpose of Company membership of this Association.

No.	Company	Representative	Phone

1.	ANADARKO INDONESIA COMPANY	Gary Ford	(62-21) 3006-1600
2.	BONTANG EXPLORATION COMPANY PTE. LTD.	J.R. Henriksen	(62-21) 5140-0193
3.	BP INDONESIA	John Minge	(62-21) 7883-8800
4.	BUMI PARAHYANGAN RANHILL ENERGIA CITARUM	Abdul Wahab	(62-21) 527-7002
5.	CHEVRON INDOASIA COMPANY	Steve W. Green	(62-21) 573-1020
6.	CITIC SERAM ENERGY LTD.	Tang Zhongfu	(62-21) 766-2840
7.	CNOOC SES Ltd.	Fang Zhi	(62-21) 515-1001
8.	CONOCOPHILLIPS INDONESIA LTD.	Trond-Erik Johansen	(62-21) 574-2120
9.	ENERGI PASIR HITAM INDONESIA, PT	Sammy Hamzah	(62-21) 524-6001
10.	ENERGY EQUITY EPIC (SENGKANG) PTY. LTD.	Paul Edwards	(62-21) 522-2806
11.	ENI INDONESIA LTD.	Roberto Lorato	(62-21) 3000-3200
12.	EXXONMOBIL OIL INDONESIA INC.	Terry S. McPhail	(62-21) 574-0707
13.	FREEPORT INDONESIA, PT	Armando Mahler	(62-21) 259-1818
14.	GENTING OIL NATUNA PTE. LTD.	Stephen Jacobs	(62-21) 527-3828
15.	HESS (INDONESIA-PANGKAH) LTD.	Tracy Mosness	(62-21) 572-5744
16.	HUSKY OIL (MADURA) LTD.	Kevin Moore	(62-21) 7179-4777
17.	INDELBERG INDONESIA, PT	Radhi Budiman	(62-21) 520-7828
18.	INPEX CORPORATION (INPEX)	Hirohisa Ota	(62-21) 570-0557
19.	IRIAN PETROLEUM LTD.	Li Lanzhong	(62-21) 5290-7026
20.	JAPEX BUTON LTD.	Shigeru Mitsuya	(62-21) 390-1507
21.	KALREZ PETROLEUM (SERAM) LTD.		(62-21) 8379-3125
22.	KANGEAN ENERGY INDONESIA LIMITED	Keisuke Inoue	(62-21) 2550-4880
23.	KODECO ENERGY CO. LTD.	James Albert Hendricks	(62-21) 515-9047
24.	KONDUR PETROLEUM S.A.	Amir Balfas	(62-21) 5290-6100

25.	LAPINDO BRANTAS, INC.	Dharma Irawan Jenie	(62-21) 5290-6336
26.	LEKOM MARAS PENGABUAN INC.	Bur Maras	(62-21) 7884-6221
27.	LUNDIN OIL & GAS B.V.	Andrew Harber	(62-21) 526-2611
28.	MARATHON INT'L PETROLEUM IND. LTD.	Woody Pace	(62-21) 2757-9000
29.	MEDCO ENERGI INTERNASIONAL TBK	Rashid I. Mangunkusumo	(62-21) 250-5112
30.	MITRA ENERGY (INDONESIA SIBARU) LTD.	Chandra Daud Tiranda	(62-21) 515-2245
31.	OPIC	Yii-Wen Lin	(62-21) 720-5625
32.	PACIFIC OIL & GAS INDONESIA, PT	A.R. Natanegara	(62-21) 314-9189
33.	PEARLOIL (TUNGKAL) LIMITED	John N. Grant	(62-21) 5790-3903
34.	PERTAMINA Directorate of Upstream	Sukusen Soemarinda	(62-21) 350-8048
35.	PETROCHINA INT'L COMPANIES IN INDONESIA	Wei Zhigang	(62-21) 5794-5300
36.	PETROLIAM NASIONAL BERHAD/PETRONAS	Ismail Abdul Rahman	(62-21) 526-6782
37.	PETROSELAT LTD.	Charlie Wu	(62-21) 386-2550
38.	PPPTMGB "LEMIGAS"	Hadi Purnomo	(62-21) 739-4422
39.	PREMIER OIL NATUNA BV	Peter Mills	(62-21) 515-1800
40.	PROVIDENT INDONESIA ENERGY LLC	Bambang Haryanto	(62-21) 5289-2248
41.	SANTOS (SAMPANG) PTY. LTD.	Eko Lumadyo	(62-21) 270-0410
42.	SHELL COMPANIES IN INDONESIA	Darwin Silalahi	(62-21) 7883-8838
43.	STAR ENERGY (KAKAP) LTD.	Bret Mattes	(62-21) 5290-6070
44.	STATOIL	Tor Fjaeran	(62-21) 515-7777
45.	TALISMAN (ASIA) LTD.	Ron Aston	(62-21) 521-0650
46.	TOTAL E&P INDONESIE	Philippe Armand	(62-21) 523-1999
47.	VICO INDONESIA	Chris Phillips	(62-21) 520-0250

COMPANIES AND ORGANIZATIONS RELATED TO OIL AND GAS INDUSTRY

No.	Company	Representative	Telephone
1.	ABHITECH MATRA INDAH, PT	Arief Karnadi	(62-21) 640-0805, 640-0904
2.	ACCENTURE, PT	Neneng Goenadi	(62-21) 574-6575
3.	AMEC BERCA INDONESIA, PT	Ben Dowson	(62-21) 315-9040
4.	APEXINDO PRATAMA DUTA Tbk., P.T.	Hertriono Kartowisastro	(62-21) 780-4766, 780-0840
5.	ARMINDO PRIMA, PT	Winniarlita Irmawati, MM	(62-21) 4584-1330
6.	BADAK NGL	Yoga P. Suprapto	(62-21) 3193-0243, 3193-6317
7.	BAKER ATLAS INDONESIA, PT	Ivo Nuic	(62-21) 780-0737
8.	BAKER HUGHES INTEQ	John Grindrod	(62-21) 780-0737
9.	BECHTEL INDONESIA, PT	Herado Panjaitan	(62-21) 5291-6000
10.	BGP INDONESIA, PT	Zhang Haitao	(62-21) 522-9948
11.	BJ SERVICES INDONESIA	Scoot Stainback	(62-21) 780-6393, 780-6343
12.	BMT ASIA PACIFIC INDONESIA, PT	Johnny Tjea	(62-21) 782-7639
13.	BORMINDO NUSANTARA, PT	Iskandar Muda Kamil	(62-21)
14.	CENTURY DINAMIK DRILLING	Linus Setiadi	(62-21) 520-1518
15.	CITRA TUBINDO, PT	Frankie Setiadi	(62-21) 525-0609, 571-2603
16.	CITRABUANA INDOLOKA, PT	Taufik Hidayat	(62-21) 780-3370
17.	COMPACTO SOLUSINDO, PT	R. Bagdja Hardjakaprabon	(62-21) 740-8476
18.	COOPER CAMERON	Dave Oakden	(62-21) 780-8044
19.	CORELAB INDONESIA, PT	Bob East	(62-21) 780-1533
20.	DAYA TURANGGA, PT	R.J. Lumenta	(62-21) 7590-0233
21.	DELOITTE PETROLEUM SERVICES	Simon Crellin	+ (65) 6224-8288
22.	DIMAS UTAMA, PT	Indra Wardhana	(62-21) 830-0390, 830-0392
23.	ERNST & YOUNG	General Manager	(62-21) 5289-5685
24.	EXLOG SARANA INDONESIA, PT	Wimborn M. Hutapea	(62-21) 794-3155, 7919-3904/05
25.	FLUOR DANIEL INDONESIA, PT	Gempar Sumitro	(62-21) 570-2880
26.	FMC SANTANA PETROLEUM EQUIPMENT IND.	Onky Pudjarminta	(62-21) 440-4151, 440-0307
27.	GAFFNEY, CLINE & ASSOCIATES	David S. Ahye	(65) 6225 6951

28. GEOPROLOG INTIWIJAYA, PT Diah Sulasmo (62-21) 789-2077

29. GEOSERVICES, PT H.L. Ong (62-21) 830-5555, 831-8989

30. GERARD DANIELS Chris Chapman 0407-335900

31. GRANT GEOPHYSICAL INDONESIA, PT Craig Walker (62-21) 720-7509/7515

32. HALLIBURTON INDONESIA, PT Mark Phillips (62-21) 780-110

33. HANOVER INDONESIA, PT Robert Harvie (62-21) 7279-2839; 739-3268

34. HITEK NUSANTARA
35. OFFSHORE DRILLING Kaustubh (62-21) 522-7250

35. HORIZON GEOCONSULTING, PT Andy Livsey (62-21) 7918-1559

36. IMECO INTER SARANA, PT Sarwi H. Notoatmodjo (62-21) 780-8068

36. INSTITUTE TECHNOLOGY BANDUNG Geophysics Dept - Dr. Wawan Gunawan; Petroleum Engineering Dept. - Dr. Ir. Sutopo; Geophisics & Meteorology Dept. - Dr. hendra Grandis; Geology Dept. - Dr. Ir. Dardji Noeradi (62-22) 250-9168

37. INSTITUTE TECHNOLOGY MEDAN Ir. Azhari Fithrah Nst, MT (62-61) 736-3771

38. INSTITUTE TECHNOLOGY SEPULUH NOPEMBER Seno Pudji Sardjono (62-31) 594-3351, 599-2933

40. INTERTEK UTAMA SERVICES, PT John Fowler (62-21) 780-8011

41. ITOCHU CORPORATION Horiguchi Jun (62-21) 3193-1647, 3193-6502

42. JGC CORPORATION Takeshi Goto (62-21) 572-3320

43. KALIRAYA SARI, PT Ir. Vincent Darja (62-21) 536-3118

44. LANDMARK CONCURRENT SOLUSI IND. Jonathan Zwaan (62-21) 3003-9000

45. LERINDRO INTERNATIONAL Andrew H. Suryadi (62-21) 781-7056

46. McDERMOTT INDONESIA Asan Sofian (62-21) 520-8611

47. M-I INDONESIA, PT David Paterson (62-21) 780-6578

48. MITSUBISHI CORPORATION Yutaka Takei (62-21) 515-1519

49. MURPHY OIL CORPORATION Hans F. Schwing (62-21) 576-2003

50. MUTIARA BIRU PERKASA, PT Malcolm Andrew Robbins 5794-1429

51. OSCO UTAMA, PT Antonius Nurimba (62-21) 692-8772, 690-9522

52. PAMERINDO BUANA ABADI, PT Ian Douglas Roberts (62-21) 316-2001

53. PELITA AIR SERVICE, PT	Hariadi Soepangkat	(62-21) 231-2030
54. PETRATAMA NUSAPERTIWI (PETRANUSA), PT	Ir. Mohamad Noer	(62-21) 797-3106 (62-21) 7919-7673
55. PETROSEA Tbk, PT	John Sheridan	(62-21) 718-3255
56. PGS NUSANTARA, PT	Simon Irwin	(62-21) 769-8038
57. PricewaterhouseCoopers	William Deertz	(62-21) 521-2901
58. PURNA BINA INDONESIA, PT	Herado Panjaitan	(62-21) 5291-6000
59. PUSDIKLAT "MIGAS" CEPU	Dr. Ir. Zuhdan Fathoni	(62-296) 421-888
60. RESOURCES JAYA TEKNIK MGMNT IND., PT	Rohmad Hadiwijoyo	(62-21) 739-4588, 739-6871
61. RIAU ISLAMIC UNIVERSITY	Iskandar Zulkarnain	(62-761) 674-717
62. SAIPEM INDONESIA, PT	Michel Laine	(62-21) 3002-2100
63. SANTA FE SUPRACO INDONESIA	Jeff Durham	(62-21) 721-1700
64. SCHLUMBERGER GEOPHYSICS NUSANTARA, PT	Iwan Chandra	(62-21) 522-7050 ext 249
65. SCOMI OILTOOLS, PT	Setyadi Pudjantoro	798-9140
65. SEAMLESS PIPE INDONESIA JAYA, PT	Raul Garcia	(62-21) 525-7863
67. SIDDHARTA & SIDDHARTA, DRS.	Agung Nugroho Soedibyo	(62-21) 574-2333, 574-2888
68. STTNAS YOGYAKARTA	Ir. Iman W. Sumarinda MSc	(62-274) 485-390, 486-986
69. SUCOFINDO, PT	Iqbal Akbar	(62-21) 798-3666
70. SUDJACA PALEMBANG, PT	Hendra Sudjaka	(62-21) 632-7326
71. SUMBER DAYA KELOLA, PT	Arief Soesilo	(62-21) 721-1046
72. SUPRACO INDONESIA, PT	Ir. Sofwan Farisyi, MM	(62-21) 719-1070
73. SYNERGY DOWNSTREAM SOLUTIONS PTE. LTD.	Jeff Wilson	(62-21) 527-2222
74. TIDEWATER OPERATORS INDONESIA, PT	Dirk J. Jol	(62-21) 798-1682
75. TRANS NUSANTARA MULTI CONS., PT	Anton Tjahjono	(62-21) 390-9211, 390-0310
76. TRIPATRA ENGINEERING, PT	Pandri Prabono	(62-21) 750-0701
76. TUGU PRATAMA INDONESIA, PT	Mohammad Jusuf Adi	(62-21) 520-8814, 829-1717

78. UNIVERSITY OF BRAWIJAYA Adi Susilo (62-341) 575-833

79. UNIVERSITY OF GADJAH MADA Geology Dept. - Dr. Ir. Heru Hendrayana; Physics Dept. - Drs. Sismanto MSi (62-274) 513-668, 901-380

80. UNIVERSITY OF HASANUDDIN Geology Dept. - Ir. Hamid Umar; Geophysics Dept. - M. Altin Massinai (62-411) 580-202

81. UNIVERSITY OF INDONESIA Gas & Petrochemical Dept. - Mahmud Sudibandriyo, PhD; Physics Dept. - DR. Abd. Haris (62-21) 786-3516

82. UNIVERSITY OF LAMPUNG Ordas Dewanto, M.Si. (62-721) 701-609 ext 719

83. UNIVERSITY OF LONDON Simon Suggate 44 1784 443592

84. UNIVERSITY OF PADJADJARAN Dr. Ir. Ildrem Syafri, DEA (62-22) 779-6515, 421-8040

85. UNIVERSITY OF PAKUAN Ir. Agus Karmadi (62-251) 311-007

86. UNIVERSITY OF PROKLAMASI 45 Sari Wulandari (62-274) 485-517 ext 26

87. UNIVERSITY OF SRIWIJAYA Dr. Ir. H. Marwan Asof DIE, DEA (62-711) 580-137

88. UNIVERSITY OF TRISAKTI Geology Dept. - Ir. Agus Guntoro; Petroleum Engineering Dept. - Djoko Sulistiyanto (62-21) 566-3232 ext 506

89. UPN "VETERAN" Geology Dept. - Ir. Achmad Subandrio MT; Applied Geophysics Dept. - Ir. Agus Santoso, MSi; Petroleum Engineering Dept. - Ir. Joko Pamungkas (62-274) 486-403

90. VELISIA LARASATI Law Offices Velisia P.D. Sitanggang (62-21) 252-6558

91. VERITAS DGC MEGA PRATAMA, PT Tjandra Siswojo (62-21) 252-2240

92. WELLTEKINDO NUSANTARA, PT Ermin S. Nasution (62-21) 5793-8938/39/40

93 WOOD MACKENZIE LIMITED Vijay Krishnan +65 65180820

INVESTING IN INDONESIA: IMPORTANT INFORMATION

INVESTMENT CLIMATE

OPENNESS TO FOREIGN INVESTMENT

Since the middle of 1997, Indonesia has faced its most severe economic crisis in three decades. The economic downturn has coincided with a prolonged political crisis, which culminated in severe rioting in the capital and other cities, and the resignation of President Soeharto, Indonesia's leader for more than 30 years.

The Indonesian government turned to the International Monetary fund in October 1997 for assistance in surmounting its economic difficulties which included a substantial depreciation of the Indonesian Rupiah, rising inflation, and a collapsing banking system. The program has had several major revisions and includes major structural reforms, which should ultimately result in an improved investment climate.

The Indonesian government continues its policy of actively encouraging foreign investment and issued several new regulations in 1998 to ease the entry of foreign firms and capital into Indonesia. The Foreign Capital Investment Law of 1967, however, continues to provide the basic framework for foreign investment.

The Capital Investment Coordinating Board (BKPM) plays a key role in promoting foreign investment and approving project applications. The relevant technical government departments handle investments in the oil and gas, mining, banking and insurance industries. All other foreign investment must be approved by BKPM, which also approves domestic investments when the owners seek investment incentives. BKPM aims to function as a one-stop investor service; however, investors are routinely required to work closely with relevant technical government departments and regional and local authorities. A recent package of reforms unveiled in June 1998 freed investors from some of the cumbersome documentary requirements resulting from the need to work with local governments. Other reforms have been announced but not finalized which would free small investments from the Jakarta-based approval process by granting greater autonomy to the regional foreign investment boards.

Private entities may establish, acquire, and dispose of interests in business enterprises. Current regulations permit foreign firms to acquire domestic firms in sectors open for foreign investment without referring the purchase to BKPM. In practice, however, foreign firms are required to petition BKPM for approval. When reviewing applications from foreign firms seeking to acquire locally established firms, BKPM frequently requires the buyer to reserve a small stake for a local buyer or the original owner and, in cases where the local firm is being "rescued" by a foreign buyer, to inject capital, not just provide management expertise, technology or assume outstanding loans. The approval process to take over a "sick" firm may take as long as two months. In all cases, the purchase of domestic firms is limited to sectors open to foreign investment.

Indonesia encourages the participation of small and medium sized indigenous firms in certain sectors of the economy. Foreign investors in these sectors are required to partner with small businesses or cooperatives before investment applications are approved. A "negative" list published by the Ministry of Investment outlines sectors closed to foreign investment as well as those which require the participation of small and medium sized partners. The most recent revision of the negative list for investment was released in July 1998. Copies of the negative list are available from U.S. Commercial Center, Jakarta (See Chapter XI for Contact Information).

In June 1998, the government of Indonesia eliminated many restrictions on foreign investment retail operations. Foreign firms are now allowed to operate retail outlets in most major urban areas although restrictions remain in the provinces. In addition, many foreign firms use franchising, licensing, and technical service agreements to distribute their goods.

In June 1998, Indonesia also lifted many restrictions on foreign participation in domestic distribution services. Under the present regulations, foreign companies manufacturing in Indonesia may distribute their locally produced goods at the wholesale level and may apply for permits to import and distribute other products as well. Companies engaging in wholesale distribution may not conduct retail operations directly, but must form a separate retail company. The number of expatriate employees, which may be granted visas to work in any single wholesale and retail business, is limited.

In June 1994 and May 1995 several previously restricted sectors were opened, some conditionally, to foreign investment, including harbors, electricity generation, telecommunications, shipping airlines, railways, and water supply. Foreign investment opportunities in many services remain restricted, however. The government is continuing to develop policies on the private provision of infrastructure through build-own-operate and build operate-transfer schemes, particularly for electric power, telecommunications, and roads.

Oil and gas: The state owns all oil and mineral rights; foreign firms participate in their extraction through exploration and production sharing contracts. The Department of Mines and Energy has the primary responsibility for oil and energy; it oversees the state oil company, Pertamina, and its production-sharing contractors. Contractors are required to finance all exploration, production, and development costs in their contract areas; they are entitled to recover operating, exploration, and development costs out of the oil and gas produced. The government is considering changes to the basic petroleum law to allow private sector participation in downstream marketing of petroleum products.

Mining: Foreign investors operate under contracts of work for general mining and production sharing contracts for coal. The contractor conducts all stages of the operation and assumes all financial and operational risks. Changes in mining law now under consideration may allow coal producers to operate under contracts of work. After the Busang affair, touted in 1996 as the world's richest gold strike but determined to contain no significant gold in May 1997, some anticipated that the government may tighten regulations regarding foreign prospecting and mining operations. This has not occurred.

Banking, Securities and Insurance: A 1988 deregulation package opened the banking, securities and insurance industries to foreign investment; all entrants had to be in the form of joint ventures, and foreign insurance and securities firms were subject to discriminatory capital requirements. In 1997, the government lifted restrictions on foreign ownership of non-bank firms listed on Indonesian stock exchanges. It intends to submit amendments to the banking law to Parliament in 1998 to ease restrictions on foreign investment in the banking sector. The Department of Finance licenses new securities and insurance ventures; Bank Indonesia, the central bank, licenses banks and regulates banking activity.

New programs to enhance the efficiency of state-owned enterprise and to expose them to greater competition have been announced as part of the Indonesia's ongoing IMF program. Specifically, the government has committed to divest majority ownership in at least 7 major parastatals, including parts of the state-owned steel, telecommunications, mining, plantation, and cement firms. International investment houses have been appointed to assist the government in evaluating and packaging these firms and foreign investors are actively being sought.

CONVERSION AND TRANSFER POLICIES

The Indonesian rupiah has depreciated in excess of 70 percent since July 1997 and remains volatile. The Indonesian rupiah is freely convertible and is traded on in an interbank market in Jakarta. Indonesia maintains no capital controls and foreign exchange may flow freely in and out of the country. No prior permits are necessary to transfer foreign exchange. Foreign investors have the right to repatriate capital and profits at the prevailing rate of exchange. The government does not place restrictions on outward direct investment. In comparison with recent years, however, the foreign exchange market is extremely thin. Prior to the onset of the economic crisis, more than USD 5 billion of rupiah routinely changed hands each day. At the present time, exchange flows rarely amount to more than a few hundred million per day.

In July 1997, the Indonesian rupiah began to weaken and Indonesia was forced to widen its trading band to 12 from 8 percent. As other regional currencies slumped and the rupiah faced even greater depreciation pressures, the government chose in August 1997 to abandon its managed float entirely to allow the rupiah to float freely. Since the last quarter of 1997, the rupiah has been extremely volatile and depreciated very sharply against the dollar.

The rapid depreciation comes against a backdrop of exchange rate predictability against the dollar. Since 1986, the rupiah's depreciation against the dollar had ranged between 2.3 percent and 5.9 percent. Depreciation against currencies of other trading partners has been larger, reflecting the changing value of the dollar. In 1991, the government instituted a system of ceilings for foreign commercial borrowing by public sector entities, commercial banks and private sector projects that have a connection with the government.

EXPROPRIATION AND COMPENSATION

Article 21 of the 1967 Foreign Capital Investment Law stipulates that the government shall not initiate nationalization of foreign investments except by law and when such action is necessary in the interest of the state. According to BKPM, no foreign investment has been expropriated since the passage of the 1967 law. There is concern at the present time that the government may nationalize projects or abrogate contracts awarded to firms connected to the family of former President Soeharto. Government officials have stated that foreign firms will not be expropriated as it dismantles the business empires of former first family members.

DISPUTE SETTLEMENT

The Indonesian government has agreed to submit any investment disputes to the International Center for the Settlement of Investment Disputes (ICSID) in Washington, D.C. An investment arbitration board, BANI, is available when both parties to a dispute agree to submit to its arbitration. A long-pending investment dispute involving a U.S. investor was resolved through the ICSID in 1993.

Indonesia is also party to the 1958 New York Convention on Recognition and Enforcement of Foreign Arbitral Awards. The record of enforcement of foreign arbitral awards is, however, negative. In one recent case, Indonesian courts refused to recognize the applicability of third country negotiation clauses in a joint venture contract. Although the suit continues, the

Indonesian court's refusal to recognize international arbitration resulted in the foreign investor's abandoning its assets in Indonesia.

The court system has not provided effective recourse for solving commercial disputes. The judiciary has not been independent and there is no law requiring Indonesian courts to enforce money judgements of non-Indonesian courts.

The GOI has recognized that the legal system must be modernized. The tax code was reformed in 1983 and amended in 1991 and 1995. New laws on banking, insurance, and pensions were passed in 1992, which codify deregulation measures previously contained in ministerial decrees. Comprehensive company and capital markets laws were enacted in 1996. Work has begun on a new commercial code. One of the government's priorities is the continuing rationalization and modernization of laws and regulations.

As part of Indonesia's program with the IMF, a new bankruptcy law has been promulgated to assist foreign creditors in collecting outstanding obligations. This law is scheduled to come into effect August 20, 1998.

PERFORMANCE REQUIREMENTS AND INCENTIVES

Various fiscal incentives are available to both foreign and domestic investors. A company producing for the domestic market may apply for import duty exemptions on all required machinery and equipment as well as on raw and supporting materials needed during the first two years of commercial production.

A company producing 65 percent for export has additional incentives. It may apply for restitution of import duties paid on inputs, which are subsequently re-exported in finished form. In June 1998, the Ministry of Investments announced that it was revising the criteria for the provision of tax holidays to make them transparent and more easily applied. Several drafts have been proposed but no official version has been issued. Various criteria include investments in the less-developed eastern provinces, employment-generating industries, export-oriented industries, and risky high-tech investments.

Special investment incentives in the form of income tax, value-added tax, and luxury tax facilities are made available on a case-by-case basis by BKPM.

Indonesia has a relatively open foreign investment regime and looks to foreign investment to help the country out of the current economic crisis. The government expects foreign investors to contribute to the training and development of Indonesian nationals, allowing the transfer of skills and technology required for their effective participation in the management of foreign companies. As a general rule, a company can hire foreigners only for positions, which the government has deemed open to non-Indonesians. Employers must have manpower training programs aimed at replacing foreign workers with Indonesians.

Indonesia does not have rules requiring that investors purchase from local sources or export a certain percentage of output. Rules that encouraged investors to locate in industrial estates were diluted in June 1998. Foreign firms are not required to disclose proprietary information to the government as a requirement to invest.

PRIVATE OWNERSHIP

Indonesia recognizes the right to private ownership and establishment and has relied heavily on the private sector as the principal engine of its economic growth. Parastatals have traditionally played an important role as well. Their role shrunk in recent years as private sector activity grew and privileges awarded to state-owned enterprises decreased.

PROTECTION OF PROPERTY RIGHTS

Indonesia has suspended many private infrastructure projects, especially in the field of private power generation, for economic and political reasons. The Embassy has vigorously emphasized to the Indonesian government the importance of honoring internationally binding contracts and that all project reviews should be conducted in a rule-based, consistent, objective, and transparent manner. Many government officials recognize the importance of honoring contracts, but a risk remains that the Indonesian government may unilaterally abrogate projects and contracts. Mortgages and secured interests in chattels and real property are recognized but a recording system is not in place. Enforcement of secured interests is problematic. The court system does not provide effective recourse for settling property disputes.

Although it remains on the Special 301 priority watch list, Indonesia has made considerable progress in improving regulatory protection for intellectual property rights. Enforcement is an ongoing problem. Indonesia is a member of the World Intellectual Property Organization and a party to the Paris Convention for the Protection of Intellectual Property. In March 1997, the Parliament passed amendments to Indonesia's patent, copyright and trademark laws designed to bring them into compliance with the TRIPS agreement of the Uruguay Round. In 1997, Indonesia also reacceded to the Berne Convention and signed the Trademark Law Treaty. Other international agreements to which Indonesia is party include the Nice Agreement for the International Classification of Unclassified Goods and Services, the Strasbourg Agreement Concerning the International Patent Classification, and the Budapest Treaty on the International Recognition of the Deposit of Microorganisms.

Patents: Indonesia's first patent law entered into effect on August 1, 1991. The law and its implementing regulations outline patent application procedures, application fees, registration of patent consultants, and patent announcements. Products and production processes are in principle patentable subject to certain requirements for a period of 14 years commencing from filing of the patent application.

The duration of a patent may be extended for another two years. In addition to this relatively short term of patent protection, other drawbacks in the law include compulsory licensing provisions, and a provision allowing importation of 50 specific pharmaceutical products by non-patent holders.

Trademarks: The current trademark law took effect on April 1, 1993. This act states that trademark rights are determined on a first-to-file basis rather than on a first use basis. After registration, the mark must actually be used in commerce. The law offers protection for service marks and collective marks and sets forth a procedure for opposition prior to examination by the trademark office. It also provides well-known mark protection, although, to the detriment of several foreign marks, procedures for registering trademarks as well known have not been fully developed. Cancellation actions must be lodged within five years of the trademark registration date.

Copyright: Parliament passed amendments to the 1982 copyright law in 1987 and March 1997. The amended law affords protection to foreign works, expands the scope of coverage and raises the terms of protection to international standards. The United States and Indonesia concluded a bilateral copyright agreement extending reciprocal protection in 1989. In May 1997, Indonesia reacceded to the Berne Convention on copyright protection.

New technologies: Indonesian law does not include specific protection for biotechnology. Legislation covering integrated circuits is being drafted for presentation to Parliament. The U.S.-Indonesia Science and Technology Agreement ensures protection for intellectual property derived from cooperative activities under the agreement's umbrella.

TRANSPARENCY OF THE REGULATORY SYSTEM

Indonesia has a tangled regulatory and legal environment where most firms, both foreign and domestic, attempt to avoid the justice system. Laws and regulations are often vague and require substantial interpretation by implementing offices, leading to business uncertainty. Deregulation has been somewhat successful in removing barriers, creating more transparent trade and investment regimes, and has alleviated, but not eliminated, red tape. Transparency problems and red tape are routinely cited by U.S. businesses as factors hindering their operations in Indonesia.

EFFICIENT CAPITAL MARKETS AND PORTFOLIO INVESTMENT

Indonesia's banking sector was in dire condition as of June 1998, when a major effort to restructure the sector was taking shape. The economic crisis that swept Southeast Asia starting in July 1997 had nearly paralyzed Indonesia's financial sector. Most bank loans were not being serviced; banks were in turn unable to service their debts; and the collapse in bank credibility had all but shut off the flow of interbank credit.

After a decade of banking sector liberalization, the Government of Indonesia found itself forced to play an increasing role in banking as the economic crisis deepened. Bank Indonesia first provided a substantial amount of liquidity credits to banks -- in effect becoming the part owner of many troubled banks -- after several potentially disastrous runs on banks. As the extent of banking sector weakness became clear, the Government established the Indonesian Bank Restructuring Agency, charged with supervising and eventually recapitalizing ailing banks. The Government also issued a sweeping guarantee on bank deposits and other liabilities.

Because of the overall weakness of the commercial and banking sector, very little credit is available on the local market. BKPM has also announced that it is contemplating rules barring foreign investors from borrowing locally. Individual banks determine deposit and lending rates. Accounting standards and practices are not consistent with international norms. All the major international accounting firms operate in Indonesia under arrangements with domestic accounting firms.

Indonesia's capital market expanded rapidly over the last decade, led by growth of the equity market. Trading on the Jakarta Stock Exchange - the dominant securities market in the country - increased from only 27,000 shares per day in 1988 to 254 million shares per day in mid-1998. Like the banking sector, however, the stock market was hard hit by the economic crisis that struck Indonesia beginning in mid-1997. Market capitalization declined by 30 percent in Rupiah terms from May 1997 to May 1998, and by an even more dramatic 83 percent in U.S. dollar terms (see table 2). Indonesians described this collapse with the proverb, "already brought down, then hit by the falling ladder."

The lack of a well-developed bond market remained a limiting factor for Indonesia's financial sector, and arguably contributed to the financial and economic crisis. Lacking a deep domestic market for bond financing, and facing relatively high domestic interest rates for bank loans, many rapidly expanding Indonesian companies borrowed abroad during the early 1990s, running up private offshore debts of about US$ 80 billion by 1997. These loans were largely unhedged, because companies counted on the Rupiah's continuing depreciation at a slow and predictable rate against the U.S. dollar. The loans were also largely short-term, but it was common practice for lenders to roll over the principal on a yearly basis.

When the exchange rate crisis hit in mid-1997, companies suddenly faced loan payments that were very large in Rupiah terms. In addition, lenders balked at providing new loans and became increasingly reluctant to roll over short-term loans. The supply of foreign capital that Indonesia had come to rely on abruptly dried up. The flow of capital reversed course as foreigners and Indonesians alike began taking their wealth out of the country. As of mid-1998, a priority issue for the Indonesian Government and business sector was to restore confidence so that capital inflow would resume. A longer-term issue was development of a more vibrant and self-reliant domestic capital market.

Foreign firms generally enjoy good access to the Indonesian securities market. Financial reforms introduced in 1987 allowed foreign firms to form joint ventures with Indonesian partners in the securities market as underwriters, broker-dealers, and investment managers. The 49-percent restriction on foreign purchases of all listed firms, with the exception of banks, was lifted in 1997. Discriminatory capital requirements on foreign securities firms are expected to be removed in 1998. Portfolio investment is regulated by BAPEPAM, the Indonesian equivalent of the Securities and Exchange Commission.

There are no formal restrictions regarding mergers and acquisitions. However, Indonesian companies are closely held and, prior to the economic crisis, their owners rarely put up more than 20 percent of their stock for public offering. The Indonesian Parliament has enacted a comprehensive capital markets law with the aim of increasing transparency, certainty, and accountability.

Powerful business conglomerates own Indonesia's largest private companies. The companies within each conglomerate share directors and major shareholders. Articles of association and incorporation do not limit or prohibit foreign investment or participation.

POLITICAL VIOLENCE

In May 1998, major rioting in Jakarta and other cities and towns led the U.S. Department of State to recommend that all American citizens depart Indonesia and, with the exception of essential staff, all U.S. government employees and their dependents were ordered to leave. Many other countries, including Canada, Australia, Singapore, and Japan, issued similar warnings. By mid-June the Department of State authorized the return of all U.S. government employees and dependents, but continued to warn American citizens to exercise caution.

Because of the continuing potential for civil unrest, Indonesia has recently been added to the War Risk Rating List for insurance underwriters. Nascent insurrections exist in several parts of the country including East Timor, Irian Jaya and Aceh.

CORRUPTION

In recent years, considerable attention has focused on the costs of corruption and influence peddling to local and foreign businesses, and the economy as a whole. Local and foreign companies have long reported that corruption is commonplace, and surveys of business executives working in Asia have ranked Indonesia among countries where corrupt practices are most pervasive and act as a disincentive to direct foreign investment. Demands for "facilitation fees" to obtain required permits or licenses, government award of contracts and concessions based on personal relations, and a legal system that is often perceived as arbitrary are frequently cited problems. Foreign companies have had little success in filing formal complaints, either through legal or administrative channels that lead to corrective action. Foreign companies frequently report difficulties in obtaining and renewing necessary immigration permits for expatriate staff based in Indonesia.

Efforts to combat corruption have not been effective although a 1996 report from the National Planning and Development Board recognized the judicial system's shortcomings. Since the resignation of President Soeharto in May 1998, however, the identification and elimination of corruption, collusion and nepotism has become a national obsession. Untangling the webs the former first-family and crony-controlled businesses and contracts has been problematic for the Indonesian authorities and there is considerable maneuvering on this front.

BILATERAL INVESTMENT AGREEMENTS

Indonesia has signed investment protection agreements with many countries, including the United States, Belgium, Denmark, France, Germany, the Republic of Korea, the Netherlands, Norway, Switzerland, and the United Kingdom. It has also signed treaties for the avoidance of double taxation with several countries, including the United States. On February 1, 1997, a new U. S. - Indonesia tax treaty went into effect that reduced withholding rates to 10 percent, on par with rates accorded by Indonesia to Japan and major European countries.

OPIC AND OTHER INVESTMENT INSURANCE PROGRAMS

Since 1967, all three types of Overseas Private Investment Corporation (OPIC) insurance -- inconvertibility, expropriation, and war, revolution and insurrection -- have been available to U.S. investors in Indonesia. OPIC coverage was extended to bid bonds on service contracts in 1987. OPIC also offers project financing to U.S. firms. At this time, OPIC is not processing any applications for insurance in Indonesia, but this policy may change because of improved labor rights since June 1998.

LABOR

The labor force is estimated at about 90 million, of which about 75 percent are between the ages of 15 and 34. The labor force has grown by an average of 2.5 percent over the past 30 years, though this rate is decreasing with the drop in fertility rates, increasing urbanization and lengthening school attendance. Women make up approximately 40 percent of the work force. Before the economic crisis began in 1997, the Indonesian government estimated "open" unemployment (defined as a person who is working less than one hour a week) to be roughly 5 percent. Now the government estimates that 15 million persons, 17 percent of the labor force and 50 percent of the industrial work force, is unemployed. Unions and non-governmental observers estimate that more than half of the population is under-employed.

Before the economic crisis, the education level of Indonesia's labor force had risen to the point that some 26 percent of non-agricultural workers have graduated from high school, and about five percent had educational achievement at a university level. Only 25 percent of the non-agricultural workers had not completed primary school, although this figure reached almost 50 percent within the agricultural work force. However, high price inflation and large-scale layoffs have squeezed family incomes and caused at least 20 percent of all students to drop out of school during the last year, according to Indonesian government estimates.

The United States has traditionally been a top choice for Indonesians who wish to study abroad. In 1996, there were an estimated 12,000 Indonesians studying in the United States, most in the fields of business and engineering. The sharp drop in the rupiah's value in relation to the dollar, however, has significantly reduced the number of Indonesians who can afford foreign study.

Job creation and the alleviation of underemployment are targets of economic policy making, especially in light of the massive layoffs caused by the economic crisis. The unemployment rate for higher education graduates was much higher than the overall unemployment rate even before the crisis. At the same time, Indonesia is experiencing shortages of managerial and professional personnel. Education and human resource development remain high priorities for the government.

The government sets minimum wages by region. The minimum wage in Jakarta and West Java was set at Rp. 198,500 (approx. $17.00 at Rp. 14,100 per dollar) per month as of August 1, 1998. Regulatory requirements, such as that for 30 days full pay per month, increase the take home amount. Labor strikes have been common in recent years. Strikes usually relate to failure of employers to pay the minimum wage, denial of benefits, lack of an effective union, and termination of employees. The Indonesian government promulgated a new regulation in May 1998 which make it easier for labor organizations to register as trade unions, and several new unions have formed to join the Federation of All-Indonesian Trade Unions (FSPSI), which was the sole government-recognized union prior to 1998.

Indonesia's industrial relations system is based on the national ideology of Pancasila. In its industrial relations application, Pancasila emphasizes the traditional Indonesian values of harmony and consultation leading to consensus. In reality, such consensus is hard to reach and enforcement of labor regulations is a major problem. However, a foreign joint venture can expect more rigorous enforcement of labor regulations as well as other laws than a local firm.

FOREIGN TRADE ZONES/FREE PORTS

Investments in the manufacturing sector which are located in designated bonded zones pay no duty on imported inputs until the portion of production destined for the domestic market is "exported" to Indonesia, in which case duty is owed on that portion. This benefit is available to domestic and foreign firms alike.

FOREIGN DIRECT INVESTMENT STATISTICS

Foreign investment interest in Indonesia has fallen substantially since the onset of the economic crisis in mid-1997. From 1967 through 1996, BKPM approved foreign investment applications worth more than $173 billion; over half were approved after 1993. Foreign investment approvals reached almost $24 billion in 1994, $40 billion in 1995, and $30 billion in 1996. In 1996, foreign investors were most attracted to the chemical industry, including two oil refineries that accounted for 25 percent of approved investment. BKPM also approved significant foreign investment for infrastructure (electric/gas/water) and housing projects, with 13 and 9 percent respectively. Metal goods and the pulp/paper industry each attracted some 10 percent of approved foreign projects in 1996. Foreign investment in oil, gas, mining, banking and insurance all fall outside BKPM's purview; there are several billion dollars more annual foreign investment in these sectors.

Japan is the biggest cumulative foreign investor in Indonesia, excluding the oil/gas sector. Between 1967 and 1996, BKPM- approved Japanese investment applications reached some $35 billion, 20 percent of the total. Indonesia's second largest company, Indonesia Petroleum, is a Japanese joint venture, as is the largest automobile manufacturer, P.T. Astra. Japanese partners also figure heavily in the pulp, paper and petrochemicals industries. Japan was Indonesia's largest foreign investor in 1996, with approvals worth some $7.7 billion.

The United States ranks fifth in cumulative BKPM-approved investment from 1967-1996, with a total of $12.5 billion. However, the BKPM statistics do not include investment in the oil and gas sector, where the United States is by far the largest player. U.S. companies, including Caltex, Maxus, Arco, Mobil, Union Texas, and Unocal pump the lion's share of Indonesia's crude petroleum and natural gas. U.S. oil services companies have significant investments in Indonesia to serve the oil fields, including fabrication yards for offshore oil platform development.

P.T. Freeport Indonesia, an affiliate of the U.S. mining firm Freeport McMoRan, is the largest direct U.S. investment. Freeport Indonesia is implementing a $500 million mine and mill expansion and recently signed a new 30-year contract of work for its copper and gold concession in Irian Jaya.

Major U.S. companies produce consumer and other products and provide services for the domestic market. General Motors is building a $110 million vehicle assembly plant and the General Electric Capital Corporation has established a multi-million dollar automobile financing joint venture. In 1996, General Electric opened the first locomotive factory in Southeast Asia and created the second largest lighting company in Indonesia.

Mission Energy has taken the lead in a consortium to build a multi-billion dollar coal-fired power plant in East Java. Investors have been increasingly interested in producing in Indonesia for export, with Batam Island a newly favored investment site. Four U.S. banks have branches in Indonesia and there are nine U.S. bank representative offices.

Indonesia's other major foreign investors include the United Kingdom, Hong Kong, Singapore, the Netherlands, Taiwan, and South Korea.

SELECTED INVESTMENT OPPORTUNITIES

Indonesia's impressive growth rate over the past quarter century has created a diverse, modern economy with opportunities for trade and foreign investment in a variety of manufacturing and service sectors.

Both domestic and foreign investment are rising rapidly, proof of a high level of confidence in the economic and investment climate of Southeast Asia's emerging giant.

The following is a description of five sectors of the Indonesian economy that have a particularly promising outlook for future growth.

THE ELECTRONICS INDUSTRY

The electronics industry has experienced rapid and sustained growth in Indonesia in recent years. The value of Indonesian electronic exports rose from $1.2 billion in 1993 to more than $2.0 billion in 1994, an increase of 61.7 percent. In 1995, exports exceeded $2.5 billion.

Indonesia's electronics industry is still relatively small compared to neighboring Malaysia and Singapore. Indonesia has only recently promoted development in this industry. But analysts predict that Indonesia's electronics sector will outpace both countries in the near future; today it already has both comparative and competitive advantages over its Southeast Asian neighbors.

Indonesia has a large pool of both skilled and semi-skilled labor, including electronic engineers. (Labor costs in both Malaysia and Singapore have risen rapidly in recent years, at a higher rate than improvements in productivity.) Moreover, Indonesia has a large domestic consumer market for electronics. With a population of 200 million persons and a per capita income exceeding $1,000, Indonesia is experiencing very heavy demand for consumer electronics, including audio, video, television, computer and home theater products.

Production in Indonesia comprises a wide range of electronics products, including molds and dies for metal and plastic components, electronic components, semi conductors, televisions, a variety of audio and video products, computers and telecommunications products.

PAPER AND PULP

The paper and pulp industry is one of the foundations of Indonesia's economy for the foreseeable future. By the year 2000, Indonesia's paper and pulp industry is expected to rival Brazil's as the world's largest. Paper production could reach the 10 million tons per year level. Indonesia's pulp production does not yet meet the country's annual needs, resulting in imports of used paper.

Indonesia represents both a large domestic and export market for paper and pulp products. With Indonesia's large and increasingly literate population, promising growth is expected in newsprint writing, and printing papers. And with Indonesia's economic growth expected to continue at more than 7 percent for the remainder of the decade, high growth is also projected for industrial papers, wrapping papers and cement bags.

Its paper industry is already growing at a rate of 20 percent per year. Indonesia's paper and pulp exports are expected to rise from an estimated $1 billion in 1995/1996 to more than $1.5 billion in 1996/1997, an increase of 36 percent.

PETROCHEMICALS

Even though Indonesia is a nation of abundant natural resources, its petrochemical industry has only recently been developed. Indonesia still imports more than $2 billion in petrochemical products each year.

Indonesia recently inaugurated the $1.8 billion petrochemical megaproject of PT Chandra Asri Petrochemical Center in Cilegon, West Java, the country's first olefin center. It has an installed capacity of 510 thousand tons of ethylene, 300 thousand tons of polyethylene and 245 thousand tons of propylene. The increased production will still not generate enough to meet the increasing demands of Indonesia's rapidly growing industrial and consumer society. It is estimated that four additional olefin centers are needed to anticipate the rising need for plastics.

Investment opportunities in the petrochemical industry are very diverse. At present, Indonesia has only upstream petrochemical industries limited to propylene, ethylene, and methanol. The industry has been accorded priority development by the Indonesian government.

AGRIBUSINESS

Indonesia's agrarian land mass, tropical climate and large domestic population provides a potential for it to emerge as a world market leader in several agribusiness commodities.

Indonesia's horticultural potential is especially promising. The country already produces a variety of high-quality fruits and vegetables, many of which are difficult to produce elsewhere. Two horticultural seed centers - the Mekarsari Fruit Park and the Nusantara Flower Park - have recently been opened. Palm oil is another leading investment prospect. Production of Crude Palm Oil (CPO) exports exceeded $1 billion in 1995-1996. Analysts predict Indonesia will surpass neighboring Malaysia as the world's largest producer of CPO within the next 15 years.

Indonesia is a maritime nation with abundant ocean wealth. To date, however, its fisheries have not yet developed into a major export industry. Of Indonesia's total potential of an estimated 5.3 million tons of fisheries, only about 2.7 million tons were utilized in 1993. Leading fisheries exports include shrimp (at 61 percent of total) and tuna (14 percent). At present, Indonesia is the world's second largest producer of shrimp, after Thailand. In addition, the availability of quality meats in Indonesia is lower than present domestic demand, resulting in Indonesia having to import more than 10 thousand tons of meat annually.

Agribusiness areas include fish, fruit and vegetable production. Domestic demand for food and beverage products, as well as production for export to neighboring markets, creates outstanding business opportunities for multinational companies. Indonesia needs to import agribusiness technology to increase its agricultural productivity and international competitiveness in this growing and promising manufacturing sector.

TOURISM

Indonesia has unlimited potential for tourism development. In 1996, tourist visitors exceeded 4 million persons and contributed $6.4 billion to the country's Gross Domestic Product. The government projects tourist arrivals will grow to 9 million persons by the year 2000. Indonesia has all the elements necessary for a successful and diverse tourism industry: thousands of unspoiled tropical islands with unmatched scenic beauty, a variety of cultures and peoples, a central location among other tourism destinations in Southeast Asia, and a tradition of warmth and hospitality toward visitors.

The Asia-Pacific region is experiencing a rapid growth in tourism, fueled in large part by rapidly rising inter-regional travel. Analysts predict that growth in Indonesia's tourism industry will be one of the strongest in the region over the next decade. Internationally travelers are already familiar with tourism development on Bali, home to some of the world's most exclusive hotels and resorts, and a truly unique culture and environment. But today, Indonesia is beginning to develop facilities in other areas of the vast archipelago, including Lombok (the island paradise east of Bali), Bintan (near Singapore), North Sulawesi (a major diving destination), northern Sumatra, and near the antiquities of Central Java, including Bourbador. And with more than a quarter of Indonesia's land mass covered with vast tropical forests - home to thousand of species of flora and fauna - Indonesia has a potential to become one of the world's major destination for ecotourists.

Indonesia already boasts 29 five-star hotels and resorts, many managed by well-known management companies with networks throughout the world. The Indonesian government is also making significant investments in tourism-related infrastructures, including improvement in airport facilities, roads and highways, passenger railways (on Java) and tourist attractions.

SELECTED LAWS AND REGULATIONS ON INVESTMENTS

SELECTED BUSINESS REGULATIONS

- Decree of the Minister of Industry and Trade No. 726/MPP/Kep/12/2004 on STIPULATION OF THE AMOUNTS OF REFERENCE PRICES FOR THE CALCULATION OF RESOURCES ROYALTY PROVISION (PSDH), dated December 31, 2004

- Decree of the Minister of Industry and Trade No. 550/MPP/Kep/10/2004 on IMPORTER IDENTITY NUMBER (API), dated October 5, 2004 (Attachment)

- Decree of the Minister of Industry and Trade No. 366/MPP/Kep/8/2004 on AMENDMENT TO ARTICLE 1 1 OF THE DECREE OF THE MINISTER OF INDUSTRY AND TRADE NO. 374/MPP/KEP/8/2004 CONCERNING EXPORT PROVISIONS ON QUOTAS OF TEXTILE AND CLOTHING , dated August 5, 2004

- Decree of the Minister of Industry and Trade No. 365/MPP/Kep/8/2004 on THE APPOINTMENT OF THE EXECUTING AGENCY FOR MONITORING INTERNATIONAL TRADE AND INDUSTRIAN DEVELOPMENT, dated August 5, 2004

- Decree of the Minister of Industry and Trade No. 364/MPP/Kep/8/2004 on THE IMPORT TRADE SYSTEM OF SUGAR, dated August 5, 2004

- Circular of the Director General of Taxation No.SE-29/PJ.44/2004 on THE VALIDITY PERIOD OF FISCAL CLEARANCE (SKF), dated July 8, 2004

- Decree of the Minister of Finance No. 349/KMK.01/2004 on AMENDMENT TO THE DECREE OF THE MINISTER OF FINANCE NO.291/KMK.051/1997 ON BONDED WAREHOUSES AS ALREADY AMENDED THE LATEST BY THE DECREE OF THE MINISTER OF FINANCE NO. 292/KMK.01/1998 , dated June 24, 2004

- Decree of the Minister of Finance No. 348/KMK.01/2004 on VARIANTS AND TYPES OF MOTOR VEHICLES SUBJECTED TO SALES TAX ON LUXURY GOODS , dated June 24, 2004

- Decree of the Minister of Finance No. 347/KMK.01/2004 on THE EXEMPTION FROM IMPORT DUTY ON THE IMPORT OF GOODS AND/OR MATERIALS FROM BONDED WAREHOUSES TO BE PROCESSED, ASSEMBLED OR INSTALLED IN OTHER GOODS FOR MANUFACTURING MOTOR VEHICLES DESTINED FOR EXPORT , dated June 24, 2004

- Decree of the Minister of Finance No. 346/KMK.01/2004 on THE EXEMPTION FROM IMPORT DUTY ON GOODS AND MATERIALS FOR THE PRODUCTION OF COMPONENTS, ACCESSORIES AMD COACHWORK OF SPECIAL MOTOR VEHICLES , dated June 24, 2004

- Decree of the Minister of Finance No. 345/KMK.01/2004 on THE EXEMPTION FROM IMPORT DUTY ON BASIC MATERIALS FOR AUTOMOTIVE COMPONENT PRODUCTION, dated June 24, 2004
- Decree of the Minister of Finance No. 344/KMK.01/2004 on AMANDEMENT TO DECREE OF THE MINISTER OF FINANCE NO. 444/KMK.05/1996 ON STIPULATION OF CLASSIFICATION SYSTEMS OF GOODS AND TARIFFS OF IMPORT DUTY ON IMPORTED GOODS, dated June 24, 2004 (Attachment)
- Decree of the Minister of Finance No. 189/KMK.017/2004 on THE STIPULATION OF TARIFS OF EXPORT TAX ON OIL PALM, PALM OIL, COCONUT OIL AND THEIR DERIVATIVE PRODUCTS , dated June 3, 2004
- Decree of the Minister of Industry and Trade No.146/MPP/Kep/4/2004 on AMENDMENT TO THE ATTACHMENT TO THE DECREE OF THE MINISTER OF INDUSTRY AND TRADE NO.558/MPP/KEP/12/1998 ON GENERAL PROVISIONS IN THE EXPORT SECTOR, dated April 22, 2004
- Decision of the Director General of International Trade No. 19/DJ-PLN/KP/III/2004 on THE DETERMINATION OF GROWTH QUOTAS (KPt) FOR THE EXPORT OF TEXTILE AND CLOTHING TO THE UNITED STATES, EUROPEAN UNION, NORWAY, CANADA AND TURKEY FOR 2004, dated March 19, 2004
- Decision of the Director General of International Trade No. 18/DJ-PLN/III/2004 on TECHNICAL DIRECTIVES FOR THE DETERMINATION OF GROWTH QUOTAS (KPt) OF TEXTILES AND CLOTHING (tpt) FOR APPROVED EXPORTERS OF TEXTILE AND CLOTHING OF SMALL-SCALE BUSINESSES AND COOPERATIVES (ETTPT-PKK) IN THE QUOTA YEAR OF 2004 AND PROCEDURES FOR PARTNERSHIP IN THE EXPORT QUOTAS OF TPT BY ETTPT-PKK, dated March 19, 2004
- Law of the Republic of Indonesia No. 8/2004 on CONSUMERS' PROTECTION, dated April 20, 2004 (Elucidation)
- Law of the Republic of Indonesia No. 5/2004 on PROHIBITION AGAINST MONOPOLISTIC PRACTICES AND UNFAIR BUSINESS COMPETITION, dates March 5, 2004
- Decree of the Minister of Industry and Trade No. 29/MPP/Kep/1/2004 on PROVISIONS ON THE EXPORT OF COFFEE, dated January 29, 2004
- Decree of the Minister of Industry and Trade No. 84/MPP/Kep/3/2004 dated March 17, 2004 on Textile and Clothing Growth Quotas of The Quota Year of 2004 For Export Destinations : United States, European Union, Norway, Canada, Turkey, And Partnership in The Export of Textile And Clothing
- Decree of the Minister of Industry and Trade No. 384/MPP/Kep/8/2004 dated August

	18,2004 on The Second Amendment to The Decree of The Minister of Industry and Trade No. 108/Mpp/Kep/5/1996 on Standardization, Certification, Accrediation Of And Supervision Over The Quality of Products Within The Ministry of Industry And Trade
▪	Decision of the Director General of Metal, Machine, Electronic and Multifarious Industries No. 007/SK/DJ-ILMEA/VI/2004 dated June 24, 2004 on Procedural Requirements for The Registration of Types and Variants of Motor Vehicles
▪	Decree of the Minister of Industry and Trade No. 274/MPP/Kep/6/2004 dated June 21, 2004 on Prohibition of and Supervision Over The Distribution and Production of Dioxin Contaminated Products
▪	Decree of the Minister of Industry and Trade No. 231/MPP/Kep/6/2004 dated June 3, 2004 on Revocation of The Decree of The Minister of Industry and Trade No. 108/Kp/1/1984 on The Appointment of PT Berdikari as The Sole Distributor of Aluminium Ingots Produced by PT Inalum
▪	Decree of the Minister of Industry and Trade No. 230/MPP/Kep/6/2004 dated June 4, 2004 on Revocation of The Decree of The Minister of Industry and Trade No. 505/Mpp/Kep/10/1998 on The Trade In and Distribution of Cooking Oil and Granulated Sugar
▪	Decree of the Minister of Finance No. 349/KMK.01/2004 dated June 24, 2004 on Amendment To The Decree of The Minister of Finance No. 291/Kmk.05/1997 on Bonded Warehouses As Already Amended The Latest by The Decree of The Minister of Finance NO. 292/KMK.01/1998
▪	Decree of the Minister of Finance No. 348/KMK.04/2004 dated June 24, 2004 on Variants and Types of Motor Vehicles Subjected To Sales Tax on Luxury Goods
▪	Decree of the Minister of Finance No. 347/KMK.01/2004 dated June 24, 2004 on The Exemption from Import Duty on The Import of Goods and/or Materials From Bonded Warehouses to be Processed, Assembled or Installed in Other Goods for Manufacturing Motor Vehicles Destined for Export
▪	Decree of the Minister of Industry and Trade No. 327/MPP/Kep/7/2004 dated July 14, 2004 on The Amendment to The Decree of The Minister of Industry and Trade No. 12/Mpp/Kep/I/1998 on The Implementation of Corporate Registry

▪	Decree of the Minister of Finance No. 502/KMK.01/1998 on THE CHANGE IN IMPORT DUTY RATES ON CERTAIN PRODUCTS, dated December 14, 1998
▪	Decree of the Minister of Industry and Trade No. 525/MPP/Kep/XI/1998 on GOVERNMENT REGULATIONS THE ORGANIZATION OF REGISTRATION OF CORPORATE ANNUAL FINANCIAL STATEMENTS, dated November 13, 1998

- Decree of the Minister of Industry and Trade No. 442/MPP/Kep/9/1998 on AMENDMENT TO THE ATTACHMENT TO THE DECREE OF THE MINISTER OF INDUSTRY AND TRADE NO. 182/MPP/Kep/9/1998 ON GENERAL PROVISIONS IN THE EXPORT SECTOR, dated September 25, 1998

- Decree of the Minister of Industry and Trade No. 441/MPP/Kep/9/1998 on PROVISIONS ON THE EXPORT OF TIMBER, dated September 25, 1998

- Decree of the Minister of Industry and Trade No. 440/MPP/Kep/9/1998 on PROVISIONS ON THE EXPORT OF ROUND RATTANS, dated September 25, 1998

- Decree of the Minister of Industry and Trade No. 438/MPP/Kep/9/1998 on AMENDEMENT TO DECREE OF THE MINISTER OF INDUSTRY AND TRADE No. 350/MPP/KEP/7/1998 ON THE RESTRICTION OF EXPORT OF CERTAIN GOODS SECURING SUBSIDY FROM THE GOVERNMENT, dated september 22, 1998

- Decree of the Minister of Industry and Trade No. 350/MPP/Kep/7/1998 on THE RESTRICTION OF EXPORT OF CERTAIN GOODS SECURING SUBSIDY FROM THE GOVERNMENT, dated July 27, 1998

- Decree of the Minister of Industry and Trade No. 349/MPP/Kep/7/1998 on THE EX-FACTORY TRANSACTION PRICE OF GRANULATED SUGAR PURCHASED BY BULOG FROM PT PERKEBUNAN NUSANTARA/PT RAJAWALI NUSANTARA INDONESIA AND FARMERS AS WELL AS OTHER PRODUCERS, dated July 24, 1998

- Decree of the Minister of Industry and Trade No. 348/MPP/kep/7/1998 on THE TRADING AND DISTRIBUTION OF COOKING OIL AND GRANULATED SUGAR, dated July 24, 1998

- Joint Decree of the Minister of Industry and Trade, the Minister of Agriculture and the Minister of Cooperatives and Small-scale Business Development No. 24/MPP/Kep/1/1998, No. 30/Kpts/TN.320/1/1998 and No. 01/SKB/M/1/1998 on REVOCATION OF THE JOINT DECREE OF THE MINISTER OF TRADE AND COOPERATIVES, THE MINISTER OF INDUSTRY AND THE MINISTER OF AGRICULTURE NO. 236/Kpb/VII/82, NO. 341/M/SK/7/1982 AND NO. 21/Kpts/UM/7/1982 ON BUSINESS DEVELOPMENT FOR THE PROMOTION OF DOMESTIC MILK PRODUCTION, MANUFACTURING AND NIARKETING, dated January 22, 1998

- Decree of the Minister of Industry and Trade of the Republic of Indonesia No. 307/MPP/Kep/6/1998 on 2004 CALIBRATION MARKS, dated June 24, 1998

- Decree of the Minister of Industry and Trade No. 187/MPP/Kep/4/1998 on STIPULATION ON THE EXPORT OF RATTAN, dated April 20, 1998

- Decree of the Minister of Industry and Trade No. 186/MPP/Kep/4/1998 on STIPULATION

ON THE EXPORT OF SAWN TIMBER AND PROCESSED TIMBER, dated April 20, 1998
▪ Decree of the Minister of Industry and Trade No. 185/MPP/kep/4/1998 on STIPULATION ON THE EXPORT OF LOGS, dated April 20, 1998
▪ Decree of the Minister of Industry and Trade No. 184/MPP/Kep/4/1998 on REVOCATION OF THE DECREE OF THE MINISTER OF INDUSTRY AND TRADE NO. 34/MPP/Kep/1/1998 ON THE EXPORT OF RATTAN MATS, dated April 20, 1998
▪ Decree of the Minister of Industry and Trade No. 183/MPP/Kep/4/1998 on REVOCATION OF THE DECREE OF THE MINISTER OF INDUSTRY AND TRADE NO. 32/MPP/Kep/1/1998 ON THE EXPORT OF SAWN TIMBER AND WOOD PRODUCTS, dated April 20, 1998
▪ Decree of the Minister of Industry and Trade No. 182/MPP/Kep/4/1998 on GENERAL PROVISIONS IN THE EXPORT SECTOR, dated April 20, 1998
▪ Decree of the Minister of Industry and Trade No. 181/MPP/Kep/4/1998 on REVOCATION OF THE DECREE OF THE MINISTER OF INDUSTRY AND TRADE NO. 102/MPP/Kep/2/1998 ON THE DOMESTIC SUPPLY OF CRUDE PALM OIL (CPO), REFINED BLEACHED DEODORIZED PALM OIL (RBD PO), CRUDE OLEIN (CRD OLEIN) AND REFINED BLEACHED DEODORIZED OLEIN (RBD OLEIN), dated April 17, 1998
▪ Decree of the Minister of Industry and Trade No. 105/MPP/Kep/2/1998 on THE REORDERING AND FOSTERING OF THE DEVELOPMENT OF WAREHOUSES, dated February 27, 1998
▪ Decree of the Minister of Industry and Trade No. 97/MPP/Kep/2/1998 on AMANDEMENT TO THE DECREE OF THE MINISTER OF INDUSTRY AND TRADE NO. 228/MPP/Kep/7/1997 ON GENERAL PROVISION IN THE EXPORT SECTOR, dated February 26, 1998
▪ Government Regulation No. 24/1998 on CORPORATE ANNUAL FINANCIAL INFORMATION, dated February 14, 1988
▪ Decree of the Minister of Finance No. 30/KMK.01/2004 on THE STIPULATION OF THE EXPORT TAX ON OIL PALM, PALM OIL, COCONUT OIL AND THEIR DERIVATIVE PRODUCTS, dated January 29, 1998
▪ Presidential Decree No. 27/1998 on THE ESTABLISHMENT OF THE INDONESIAN BANK RESTRUCTURING AGENCY, dated January 26, 1998
▪ Presidential Decree No. 26 of 1998 on GUARANTY FOR COMMERCIAL BANK REPAYMENT OBLIGATION, dated January 26, 1998

- Decree of the Minister of Industry and Trade No. 34/MPP/Kep/1/1998 on PROVISION ON THE EXPORTS OF RATTAN MATS, dated January 21, 1998
- Decree of the Minister of Industry and Trade No. 33/MPP/Kep/1/1998 on REVOCATION OF THE DECREE OF THE MINISTER OF TRADE NO. 410/KP/XII/88 CONCERNING THE EXPORT TRADE CONTROL OVER RATTAN MATS, dated January 21, 1998
- Decree of the Minister of Industry and Trade No. 32/MPP/Kep/1/1998 on PROVISION ON THE EXPORT OF SAWN TIMBER AND PROCESSED TIMBER, dated January 21, 1998
- Decree of the Minister of Industry and Trade No. 30/MPP/KEP/1/1998 on REVOCATION OF THE DECREE OF THE MINISTER OF TRADE NO. 119/KP/V/87 ON THE EXPORT TRADE CONTROL OVER SAWN TIMBER AND PROCESSED TIMBER, dated January 21, 1998
- Decree of the Minister of Industry and Trade No. 29/MPP/KEP/I/1998 on REVOCATION OF THE DECREE OF MINISTER OF TRADE NO. 128/KP/IV/86 ON PLYWOOD EXPORT QUOTAS, dated January 21, 1998
- Decree of the Minister of Industry and Trade No. 28/MPP/Kep/I/1998 on PROVISIONS ON PLYWOOD EXPORTS, dated January 21, 1998
- Decree of the Minister of Industry and Trade No. 27/MPP/Kep/1/1998 on REVOCATION OF THE DECREE OF THE MINISTER OF TRADE NO. 1198/KP/X/84 CONCERNING THE CONFIRMATION OF THE ESTABLISHMENT OF JOINT MARKETING AGENCY GROUPS AND THE EXPORT TRADE CONTROL OVER PLYWOOD, dated January 21, 1998
- Decree of the Minister of Industry and Trade No. 26/MPP/Kep/1/1998 on REVOCATION OF THE DECREE OF THE MINISTER OF TRADE AND COOPERATIVES NO. 152/KP/V/82 ON THE PLYWOOD EXPORT TRADE SYSTEM, dated January 21, 1998
- Decree of the Minister of Industry and Trade No. 25/MPP/Kep/1/1998 on AMENDMENT TO THE DECREE OF THE MINISTER OF INDUSTRY AND TRADE NO. 230/MPP/Kep/1/1997 ON GOODS SUBJECT TO THE IMPORT TRADE SYSTEM AS ALREADY AMENDED BY THE DECREE OF THE MINISTER OF INDUSTRY AND TRADE No. 406/MPP/Kep/I/1997, dated January 21, 1998
- Presidential Decree No. 24 of 1998 on THE ISSUING OF BANK INDONESIA'S GUARANTY, AND THE ISSUING OF BANK GUARANTY FOR RECEIVING FOREIGN LOAN BY STATE-OWNED BANKS AND REGIONAL DEVELOPMENT BANKS HAVING A LICENSE IN FOREIGN EXCHANGE OPERATION, dated January 23, 1998
- Presidential Decree No. 23/1998 on THE GRANTING OF AUTHORITY TO BANK INDONESIA IN THE FIELD OF MONETARY CONTROL, dated January 21, 1998

- Decree of the Minister of Industry and Trade No. 23/MPP/Kep/1/1998 on TRADE BUSINESS INSTITUTIONS, dated January 21, 1998
- Decree of the Minister of Industry and Trade No. 22/MPP/Kep/1/1998 on THE GUIDELINE FOR CLOVE TRADING, dated January 21, 1998
- Decree of the Minister of Industry and Trade No. 21/MPP/Kep/1/1998 on REVOCATION OF THE DECREE OF THE MINISTER OF INDUSTRY AND TRADE NO. 407/MPP/Kep/11/1997 ON THE DOMESTIC PROCUREMENT AND DISTRIBUTION OF WHEATFLOUR, dated January 21, 1998
- Decree of the Minister of Industry and Trade No. 20/MPP/Kep/1/1998 on REVOCATION OF THE DECREE OF THE MINISTER OF INDUSTRY AND TRADE NO. 142/MPP/Kep/6/1996 ON THE PRODUCTION OF NATIONAL CARS, dated January 21, 1998
- Presidential Decree No. 20/1998 on THE REVOCATION OF PRESIDENTIAL DECREE NO. 42/1992 ON THE PRODUCTION OF NATIONAL CAR, dated January 21, 1998
- Presidential Decree No. 19/1998 on AMENDMENT TO PRESIDENTIAL DECREE NO. 50/1995 ON THE LOGISTIC BOARD AS ALREADY AMENDED BY PRESIDENTIAL DECREE NO. 45/1997, dated January 21, 1998
- Decree of the Minister of Industry and Trade No. 19/MPP/Kep/1/1998 on REVOCATION OF THE DECREE OF THE MINISTER OF INDUSTRY AND TRADE NO. 31/MPP/SK/2/1996 ON NATIONAL MOTOR VEHICLES, dated January 21, 1998
- Presidential Decree No. 18/1998 on THE EXPERT TEAM FOR THE COUNCIL FOR ECONOMIC AND MONETARY RESILIENCE, dated January 21, 1998
- Decree of the Minister of Finance No. 17/KMK.0111998 on THE REDUCTION OF IMPORT DUTY RATES ON SELECTED IMPORT PRODUCTS, dated January 21, 1998
- Government Regulation No. 16/1998 on AMENDMENT TO GOVERNMENT REGULATION NO.2/1996 ON THE ACTIVITIES OF COMPANIES SET UP UNDER FOREIGN CAPITAL INVESTMENTS IN THE EXPORT AND IMPORT SECTORS, AS ALREADY AMENDED BY GOVERNMENT REGULATION NO. 42/1997, dated Januari 21, 1998
- Decree of the Minister of Finance No. 16/KMK.01/1998 on THE REDUCTION OF IMPORT DUTY RATES ON SELECTED AGRICULTURAL PRODUCTS, dated Januari 21, 1998
- Government Regulation No. 15/1998 on AMENDMENT TO GOVERNMENT

	ACTIVITIES IN THE TRADE SECTOR AS ALREADY AMENDED THE LATEST BY GOVERNMENT REGULATION NO. 41/1997, dated January 21, 1998
▪	Decree of the Minister of Finance No. 15/KMK.017/1998 on AMENDMENT TO THE DECREE OF THE MINISTER OF FINANCE NO. 220/KMK.017/1993 ON COMMERCIAL BANKS, dated January 21, 1998
▪	Government Regulation No. 14/1998 on AMENDMENT TO GOVERNMENT REGULATION NO.50/1994 ON THE IMPLEMENTATION OF LAW NO.8/1983 ON VALUE ADDED TAX OF GOODS AND SERVICES AND SALES TAX ON LUXURY GOODS AS ALREADY AMENDED BY LAW NO. 11/1994, AS ALREADY AMENDED THE LATEST BY GOVERNMENT REGULATION NO. 36/1996, dated January 21, 1998
▪	Presidential Instruction No. 6/1998 on FOREIGN CAPITAL INVESTMENTS IN THE FIELD OF OILPALM ESTATES, dated January 21, 1998
▪	Presidential Instruction No. 5/1998 on DISCONTINUATION OF IMPLEMENTATION OF PRESIDENTIAL INSTRUCTION NO. 5/1997 ON THE SMALLHOLDER SUGARCANE DEVELOPMENT PROGRAM, dated January 21, 1998
▪	Presidential Instruction No. 4/1998 on COORDINATION OF NATIONAL MILK DEVELOPMENT AND PROMOTION, dated January 21, 1998
▪	Presidential Instruction No. 3/1998 on THE TERMINATION OF FINANCIAL AID TO PT INDUSTRI PESAWAT TERBANG NUSANTARA (IPTN), dated January 21, 1998
▪	Presidential Instruction No. 2/1998 on TRADE BETWEEN FIRST LEVEL REGIONS AND BETWEEN SECOND LEVEL REGIONS/ISLANDS, dated January 21, 1998
▪	Presidential Instruction No.1/1998 on THE PROHIBITION TO IMPOSE LEVIES ON EXPORT GOODS, dated January 21, 1998
▪	Government Regulation No. 13/1998 on PUBLIC CORPORATIONS (PERUM), dated January 17, 1998
▪	Government Regulation No. 12/1998 on THE LIMITED LIABILITY COMPANY (PERSERO), dated January 17, 1998
	Presidential Decree No. 7/1998 on COOPERATION BETWEEN THE GOVERNMENT AND PRIVATE COMPANIES IN THE DEVELOPMENT AND OR MANAGEMENT OF INFRASTRUCTURES, dated January 12, 1998

LAW ON FOREIGN INVESTMENT

CONSIDERING:

a. that, throughout the territory of this country, as blessing of God, potential economic resources are found abundantly which have not yet been transformed into real economic strength because of among other things, a lack of capital, experience and technology.

b. that Pancasila is the spiritual basis for the development of the Indonesian economic system and should always be reflected in economic policy.

c. that economic development requires transformation of potential economic resources into real economic strength through investment, utilization of technology, expansion of knowledge, improvement of skills, and increases in organizational and managerial ability.

d. that efforts to overcome economic decline and further develop our economic potential should be based on the capabilities and capacities of the Indonesian people themselves.

e. that nevertheless this principle of relying on our own capability and capacity should not lead to reluctance to make use of foreign capital, technology and skill, so long as these are truly devoted to serving the economic interests of the people without causing dependence on foreign countries.

f. that foreign capital should be utilized to maximum advantage in order to accelerate the economic development of Indonesia, as well as utilized in other fields and sectors, where Indonesian capital for the time being is not yet being employed.

g. that it is imperative to device clear regulations in order to fill the need for capital for national development, as well as to avoid uncertainty on the part of foreign investors.

IN OBSERVANCE OF:

1. Article 5 section (1), article 20 section (1), article 27 section (2) and article 33 of the Constitution.

2. Decree of the Provisional People's Consultative Assembly of the Republic of Indonesia No. XXIII/MPRS/1966, concerning the reform of the basic policies on the Economy, Finance and Development.

3. Note 1 of the MPRS of 1966 concerning Foreign Policy based on Pancasila.

4. Law No. 5 of 1960 concerning the Basic of Agrarian Regulation.

5. Law No. 37 Prp. of 1960 on Mining, and Law No. 44 Prp. of 1960 on Oil and Natural Gas.

6. Law No. 32 of 1964 concerning Regulations on Foreign Exchange Transactions.

With the approval of the Gotong Royong People's Representative Council, has decided:

To enact:

THE LAW CONCERNING FOREIGN INVESTMENT

Article 1

Investment in this Law denotes only direct investment of foreign capital made in accordance with or based upon the provision of this Law for the purpose of carrying on the enterprise in Indonesia, with the understanding that the owner of the capital directly bears the risk of the investment.

Article 2

Foreign investment in this Law means:

a. foreign exchange that does not form a part of the foreign exchange resources of Indonesia, and which with the approval of the Government is utilized to finance an enterprise in Indonesia.

b. equipment for an enterprise, including rights to technological development and materials imported into Indonesia, provided the said equipment is not financed from Indonesian foreign exchange resources.

c. that part of the profits which in accordance with this Law is permitted to be transferred, but instead is utilized to finance an enterprise in Indonesia.

CHAPTER II LEGAL FORM, DOMICILE AND AREA OF AN ENTERPRISE

Article 3

(1) An enterprise as instead by Article 2, which is operated wholly or for the greater part in Indonesia as a separate business unit, must be a legal entity organized under Indonesian Law and have its domicile in Indonesia.

(2) The Government shall determinated whether an enterprise is operated entirely or for the greater part in Indonesia as a separate business unit.

Article 4

The Government shall determine the operating area for foreign capital enterprise in Indonesia, in accordance with national and regional economic developments, the type of enterprise, the amount of capital to be invested and the desires of the capital owner.

CHAPTER III FIELDS OF ACTIVITY FOR FOREIGN INVESTMENT

Article 5

(1) The government shall determine the fields of activity open to foreign investment, according to an order of priority, and shall decide upon the conditions to be met by the investor of foreign capital in each such field.

(2) The order of priority shall be determined whenever the Government prepares medium and long-terms development plans, taking into consideration developments in the economy and technology.

Article 6

(1) Fields of activity, which are closed to foreign investment exercising full control, are those of importance to the country and in which the lives of a great deal of people are involved, such as the following.

a. harbors;

b. production, transmission and distribution of electric power for the public;

c. shipping;

d. telecommunications;

e. aviation;

f. drinking water;

g. public railways;

h. development of atomic energy;

i. mass media.

(2) Industries performing a vital function in national defense, among others, the productions of arms, ammunition, explosive, and war equipment, are absolutely prohibited to foreign investment.

Article 7

In addition to those mentioned in Article 6 Section (1), the Government may determine certain fields of activity in which foreign capital may no longer be invested.

Article 8

(1) Foreign investment in the field of mining shall be carried out in cooperation with the Government on the basis of a Working Contract *(Kontrak Karya)* or other from in accordance with prevailing regulations.

(2) The system of cooperation on the basis of working contract or other form can be implemented in other field of activity which will be determined by the Government.

CHAPTER IV MANPOWER

Article 9

The owner of foreign capital has full authority to appoint the management of the enterprise in which his capital is invested.

Article 10

Foreign capital enterprise are required to meet their needs for manpower with Indonesian nationals, expert in cases mentioned in Article 11.

Article 11

Foreign capital enterprises are allowed to bring and employ foreign managerial and expert personnel in position, which cannot yet be filled by Indonesian nationals.

Article 12

Foreign capital enterprises are required to conduct and/or provide regular and systematic training and educational facilities in Indonesia and/or abroad for Indonesian nationals with the aim of gradually replacing foreign employees by Indonesian nationals.

Article 13

The Government shall supervise the execution of the provisions of Article 9, 10, 11 and 12.

CHAPTER V USE OF LAND

Article 14

To meet the requirements of foreign capital enterprise, land may be provided, with the right of construction, the right of exploitation and the right of use in accordance with prevailing regulations.

CHAPTER VI CONCESSION ON TAXES AND OTHER LEVIES

Article 15

Foreign capital enterprises are granted the following concessions on taxes and other levies:
a. Exemption from:
1. Company tax on profits during a specified period not exceeding five years from the moment the enterprise commences production.

2. Dividen tax on that part of accrued profits paid to shareholders, as long as these profits are earned during a period not exceeding five years from the moment the enterprise commences production.

3. Company tax on profits referred to in Article 19 subsection (a) which are reinvested in the enterprise in Indonesia, for a specified period not exceeding five years from the time of reinvestment.

4. Import duties at the time of entry into Indonesia of fixed assets such as machinery, tools or instruments needed for the operation of said enterprise.

5. Capitals stamp duties on the issuance of capital originating from foreign investment.

b. Relief:
1. In the levy of company tax through a proportional rate of not more than 50% for a period not exceeding five years after expiration of the exemption period as intended by section (a) sub 1 above.

2. by off-setting loses suffered during the period of exemption intended by section (a) sub 1, against profits subject to tax following the period mentioned above.

3. by allowing accelerated depreciation of fixed assets.

Article 16

(1) The concessions on taxes and other levies mentioned in Article 15 shall be granted after consideration of the priority on fields of activity as intended by Article 5.

(2) Besides the concessions on taxes and other levies referred to in section (1) of this article, additional privileges may be granted by Government Regulations to any foreign capital enterprise, which is extremely important for economic development.

Article 17

Execution of provision of Article 15 and 16 shall be stipulated by the Government.

CHAPTER VII DURATION OF FOREIGN INVESTMENT, RIGHT OF TRANSFER AND REPATRIATION

Article 18

Every permit for investment of foreign capital shall specify the duration of its validity, which shall not exceed 30 (thirty) years.

Article 19

(1) Foreign capital enterprise shall be granted the right of transfer in the original currency of the invested capital at the prevailing exchange rate, for:

a. profits accruing to capital subtraction of taxes and other financial obligations in Indonesia;

b. costs related to the employment of foreign personnel working in Indonesia;

c. other cost which shall be subsequently determined;

d. depreciation of fixed assets;

e. compensation in case of nationalization.

(2) Transfer procedure shall be subsequently determined by the Government.

Article 20

Transfer constituting capital repatriation can not be permitted as long as the concessions concerning taxes and other levies as mentioned in Article 15 remain in effect. The implementation of this article shall be further regulated by the Government.

CHAPTER VIII NATIONALIZATION AND COMPENSATION

Article 21

The Government shall not undertake a total nationalization/revocation of ownership right of foreign capital enterprises nor take steps to restrict the rights of control and/or management of the enterprises concerned, except when it shall be declared by law that the interest of the State requires such a step.

Article 22

(1) In case of the measures referred to in Article 21, the Government has the obligation to provide compensation, the amount, type and method of payment of which shall have been agreed upon by parties, in accordance with valid principles of international law.

(2) If no agreement can be reached between the two parties with regard to the amount, type and method of payment for compensation, arbitration shall take place which shall be binding on both parties.

(3) The arbitration board shall consist of three persons: One appointed by the Government, one by the owner of the capital, and a third person as chairman selected jointly by the Government and the owner of the capital.

CHAPTER IX COOPERATION BETWEEN FOREIGN AND NATIONAL CAPITAL

Article 23

(1) In the fields of activity open to foreign capital, cooperation may be effected between foreign and national capital, with due consideration to the provision of Article 3.

(2) The Government shall further determine the fields of activity, forms and methods of cooperation between foreign and national capital, utilizing foreign capital and expertise in the fields of export and the production of goods and services.

Article 24

Profits obtained by foreign enterprises resulting from cooperation between foreign capital and national capital as mentioned in Article 23, after subtraction of taxes and other obligations payable in Indonesia, are permitted to be transferred in the original currency of the foreign capital invested.

Article 25

The provisions of this law regarding tax concession and guarantees regarding nationalization and compensation are also valid for foreign capital mentioned in Article 23.

CHAPTER X OTHER RESPONSIBILITIES OF THE FOREIGN INVESTOR

Article 26

Foreign capital enterprises are obligated to manage and control their enterprises in accordance with the principles of good business administration without harming the interest of the State.

Article 27

(1) Enterprises mentioned in Article 3 of which the capital is entirely foreign, are obligated to provide opportunities for participation by national capital, following specified period and in proportions to be determined by the Government.

(2) When participation as intended by section (1) of this article is effected by selling pre-existent shares, the proceeds of such can be transferred in the original currency of the foreign capital concerned.

CHAPTER XI OTHER PROVISIONS

Article 28

(1) Provisions of this Law shall be implemented by coordinating among the Government agencies concerned in order to ensure harmonization of Government policies regarding foreign capital.

(2) Procedures for such coordination shall be subsequently determined by the government.

Article 29

Provisions of this Law shall apply to investment of foreign capital effected after this Law comes into force, either in new enterprises of in already existing enterprises for expansion and/or modernization.

CHAPTER XII TRANSITIONAL PROVISION

Article 30

Matters not yet regulated in this Law shall be subsequently stipulated by the Government.

CHAPTER XIII FINAL PROVISION

Article 31

This Law shall take effect on the day of its enactment. In order that every person may be informed, promulgation of this Law is ordered through publication in the State Gazette of the Republic of Indonesia.

A PRESIDENTIAL DECREE CONCERNING THE SECTORS/TYPE OF BUSINESSES RESERVED FOR SMALL-SCALE ENTERPRISES AND SECTORS/TYPES OF BUSINESSES OPEN TO MEDIUM-SCALE OR LARGE-SCALE ENTERPRISES UNDER A PARTNERSHIP REQUIREMENT

Article 1

Referred to in this presidential decree as:

a.
a small-scale enterprise shall be small-scale people's economic activities fulfilling the criteria as meant in Law No. 9/1995 on small-scale enterprises;
b.

the sectors/types of businesses reserved for small-scale enterprises shall be the sectors/types of businesses which in terms of majority shall constitute the activities of small-scale enterprises and must be protected to prevent them from being subjected to unfair business competition;

c.

partnership shall be the cooperation between small-scale enterprises and medium-scale and large-scale enterprises coupled with foresting and development of small-scale enterprises by medium-scale or large-scale enterprises with the observance of the principles of mutual need, mutual reinforcement and mutual benefits;

Article 2

(1)

The sectors/types of businesses reserved for small-scale enterprises shall be as set forth in Attachment I, which shall constitute an inseparable part of this presidential decree.

(2)

The sectors/types of businesses open to medium-scale and large-scale businesses under a partnership requirement shall be as set forth in Attachement II, which shall constitute an inseparable part of this presidential decree.

(3)

The sectors/types of businesses as meant in sub-article (2) shall, by way of obligation, be counducted together with small-scale enterprises in various froms of partnership through the patterns of share participation, germ, plasm, sub-contracting, franchising, general trading, agency and other forms, to be realized on the basis of a written agreement.

(4)

The sectors/types of businesses as meant in sub-article (2) may also be conducted by medium-scale or large-scale enterprises established in framework of foreign investments with the exception of the sectors/types of businesses closed for foreign investments.

(5)

The stipulation of the sectors/types of businesses which are open under the partnership requirement shall be expanded gradually in a decree of the state minister of investment/head of the Investment Coordinating Agency, after coordination with technically relevant ministries and the Ministry of Cooperatives. Small-and-Medium-Scale Enterprises, with account being taken of the priorities in the national-scale fostering of small-scale enterprises.

Article 3

(1)

In the realization of partnership as meant in Article 2 sub-articles (3) and (4), medium-scale or large-scale enterprises shall be obligated to foster small-scale enterprises so that business opportunities and managerial capability in one or more aspects in the sectors of production and processing, marketing, human resources, technology, supplies of raw materials, business management and financing may be promoted.

(2)

Partnership realized through capital participation by small-scale enterprises shall be conducted in at least of 20% of the entire equity capital of the company which has just been set up and this percentage shall be raised gradually.

(3)

Fulfillment of equity by small-scale enterprises as meant in sub-article (2) may be conducted through the payment of dividends of the shares purchased by the small-scale enterprises in the said partnership.

Article 4

Licenses in the sectors/types of businesses as set forth in Attachment I and II of this presidential decree implemented in the framework of domestic and foreign investments shall be granted by the state minister of investment/head of the investment coordinating agency pursuant to the prevailing provisions.
(2)
Licenses in the sectors/types of businesses as set forth in Attachement I and II of this presidential decree implemented not in the framework of domestic and foreign investment shall be granted by the technically relevant minister in charge of the respective business sectors pursuant to the prevailing laws.
(3)
The minister in charge of fostering small-scale enterprises and the minister in charge of investment affairs shall be responsible for coordination in the enforcement of this presidential decree.

Article 5

(1)
A technically relevant minister shall stipulate sectoral technical policies, undertake fostering and development of small-scale enterprises in an integrated manner in the sectors of production and processing, marketing, human resources, capital and technology in conformity with the sectors/types in businesses as set forth in Attachment I and II of this presidential decree.
(2)
Operational implementation of fostering and development of small-scale enterprises shall be undertaken by relevant region government agencies, the business community and non-governmental organizations.
(3)
Monitoring and control of the enforcement of this presidential decree shall be undertaken by the technically relevant minister in charge of the respective business sectors pursuant to the prevailing laws.

Article 6

Financing sources for small-scale enterprises in the framework of the development of the sectors/types of businesses as set forth in Attachement I and II of this presidential decree may use financial sources originating from banks and other financing institutions specifically stipulated by the government.
(2)
Financing sources for small-scale enterprises as meant in sub-article (1) shall adopt a pettern of loans for small-scale enterprises extended by banks or other financial intsitutions available for financing in terms of working capital and or investments.

Article 7

Further provisions required for the implementation of this presidential decree shall be regulate jointly or separately by technically relevant ministries, in conformity with their respective areas and duties.

Article 8

This presidential decree shall take effect as from the date of promulgation. For public cognizance this presidential decree be promulgated by publishing it in the Statute Book of the Republic of Indonesia.

Presidential Decree
No. 96/1998
Concerning

LIST OF SECTORS CLOSED FOR INVESTMENT

Considering: that in the framework of anticipating global economic development and increasing flows of investment, it is necessary to review the List of Sectors Closed for Investment.

In view of:

1. Article 4 Section (1) of the Constitution of 1945;
2. Law No. 1/1967 on Foreign Investment (State Gazette No. 1/1967, Supplement to State Gazette No. 2818), as already amended by Law No. 11/1970 (State Gazette No. 46/1970, Supplement to State Gazette No. 2943);
3. Law No. 6/1968 on Domestic Investment (State Gazette No. 33/1968, Supplement to State Gazette No. 2853), as already amended by Law No. 12/1970 (State Gazette No. 47/1970, Supplement to State Gazette No. 2944);
4. Government Regulation No. 20/1994 on share ownership in companies set up in the framework of foreign investment (State Gazette No. 28/1994, Supplement to State Gazette No. 3552);
5. Presidential Decree No. 26/1980 on the Establishment of Regional Investment Coordinating Board;
6. Presidential Decree No. 25/1991 on the position, tasks, functions and organizational structure of the Investment Coordinating Board;
7. Presidential Decree No. 97/1993 on Investment Procedure;

D E C I D E S

By revoking the Presidential Decree No. 31/1995 on the list of sectors closed for investment;

To stipulate : THE PRESIDENTIAL DECREE ON THE LIST OF SECTORS CLOSED FOR INVESTMENT.

Article 1

1) The list of sectors absolutely closed for investment and sectors closed for investment in which part of the shares are owned by foreign citizens and/or foreign legal entities, is attached in the Presidential Decree.

2) The list of sectors closed for investment as meant in section (1) shall take effect in entire territory of the Republic of Indonesia.

Article 2

Business sectors listed in the attachment to this Presidential Decree, are available for indirect investment through purchasing of shares of existing companies on the Domestic Stock Exchange.

Article 3

Except otherwise stipulated by Law, the business sectors not mentioned in the attachment to this Presidential Decree shall be open for investment.

Article 4

The list of sectors for investment as mentioned in Article 1 Section (1) shall be valid for 3 (three) years and subject to annual review if it is necessary, in accordance with the requirements of developments.

Article 5

This Presidential Decree shall come into force as from the date of stipulation.

For public awareness, this Presidential Decree shall be announced by publishing it in the State Gazette of the Republic of Indonesia.

REFORMATION POLICY ON INVESTMENT

Jakarta, 29 May 1998

Office of the Ministry of Investment/

Investment Coordinating Board (BKPM) of the Republic of Indonesia

In the efforts to recover the investors' confidence due to sharp depreciation of Indonesia's rupiah, the Government of the Republic of Indonesia introduces a new package policy on private investment, which is now recognized as New Reformation Policies, as follows:

1. The delegation of authority from the President of the Republic of Indonesia to the Minister of Investment/Chairman of the Investment Coordinating Board (BKPM) to issue foreign investment approval up to US$100,0 million. Previously, foreign investment approval in Indonesia, at any amount, was issued by the President of the Republic of Indonesia, Foreign investment approval of more than US$100,0 million would still be issued by the President.
2. The delegation of authority from the Minister of Investment to the Provincial Governor/Chairman of the Regional Investment Coordinating Board (BKPMD) to issue the domestic investment approvals. If the mechanism will run very smoothly at the regional level, the value of investment of Rp.10,0 billion will be increased.
3. Reinstating of "one roof services" in the office of Ministry of Investment/Investment Coordinating Board (BKPM). In the last few years, the evaluation and approval of Master List for project expansion and restructurization was issued by the office of Director General of Customs. With the new reformation policy, investors should not go to various government institutions in order to get such approval or licensing either at the preparation or implementation stage. It will be issued by the office of the Ministry of Investment/Investment Coordinating Board (BKPM). For further clarification, under"one roof services", does not mean that the Director General of Customs will delegate the authority to the Ministry of Investment/Investment Coordinating Board (BKPM) for the above Master List's evaluation and approval. However, the Customs Office may assign their officials to the office of Ministry of Investment/Investment Coordinating Board (BKPM) and provide such services to the investors. The time frame of such services would be under the coordination of the Minister of Investment/Chairman of BKPM.

4. Reinstating of the "one roof services" at the Second Level Region/Regency to issue local permits such as building, nuisance and location permits. The service is provided under the coordination of Bupati (Head of Second Level Region Government) where each of Technical Department/Institution is stationed in the building. In this regard, there would be no delegation of authority between the government office at the second level region in order to avoid confusion.
5. The deletion of the Principle Approval which is normally issued by the Governor of Provinces before the investor could begin implementation or construction of the project. The reason for the deletion is that, each investor has received an official goverment approval from the office of Ministry of Investment/Investment Coordinating Board (BKPM).
6. The deletion of all kind of recommendation letters from the Technical Department/Directorate General Offices to the Investment Coordinating Board before the project application can be processed. With the new reformation policy, the Investment Coordinating Board will use the "Negative List" as guidance, and any further technical guidance of Technical Department/Directorate Generals will be put at the "Negative List Directory".
7. The transferring of Environmental Impact Analysis's appraisal (AMDAL) from AMDAL Commission in Jakarta (Central Government) to the Regional AMDAL Commission. The transferring of appraisal authority to the region will cut a substantial amount of time for the investors, therefore reduce cost.
8. In order to make tax incentives policy, based on the Government Regulation No.45/1996, clear and transparent to the public, the domestic and foreign investors, the criterias for such tax incentives will be established under a Presidential Decree. The criterias will include investment priority sectors, strategic role in economic development, market orientation (e.q. high export content), location, applied technology, investment risks, etc.
9. On the choice of project location, foreign investors may now choose whether to locate their project in industrial estate or in industrial zone. The previous policy required the foreign investors to locate only the industrial estate, and the foreign investors had no other choices although the price of land per meter square was relatively high. In order to locate the project in industrial zone, the foreign investor must use the regional spatial planning as guidance, therefore to avoid the use of residential, agricultural or productive land.
10. In order to widen opportunities to foreign investors and improve competitiveness among ASEAN countries, Indonesia has opened retail and wholesaler trading and palm oil sectors to foreign investment. On top of this new policy, import-export trading has also been opened earlier for foreign investment. In the meantime, foreign investment in retail and wholesaler trading should be conducted in the form of joint ventures with the Indonesian nationals/Indonesian companies.
11. The investment licensing/approval services in the Office of Investment Coordinating Board are also being streamlined. The time frame to issue a foreign investment approvals has been reduced from 42 days to only 10 working days. The other implementation permits (such as Master List's approval, expatriate approvals) will be finalized between 4 to 10 working days. With this new and streamlined services, investors would not spend too much time on getting the necessary permits.

GOVERNMENT REGULATION ON INVESTMENT

THE PRESIDENT OF THE REPUBLIC OF INDONESIA

CONSIDERING:

a. that, in the context of accelerating the growth and expansion of the national economic, and development activities in general, it is deemed necessary to develop the business climate which will enhance stability and sustainability of foreign investment;

b. that, to this end, it is deemed necessary to revise the provisions of share ownership in companies established in the context of foreign investment as contained in Government Regulations No. 50 of 1993;

IN VIEW OF:

1. Paragraph (2) of Article 5 of the 1945 Constitution.

2. Law No. 1 of 1967 on Foreign Investment (State Gazette No. 1 of 1967, Addendum to State Gazette No. 2818) as amended by virtue of Law No. 11 of 1970 (State Gazette No. 46 of 1970, Addendum to State Gazette No. 2943);

DECIDES:

To stipulate: **GOVERNMENT REGULATION OF THE REPUBLIC OF INDONESIA ON INVESTMENT**

Article 1

An approval on foreign investments is granted to a Foreign Direct Investment (FDI) company, which is established in the form of Limited Liability Company subject to the Indonesian Law and Domiciled in Indonesia.

Article 2

(1) The FDI may be established in the form of:

a. Joint venture between foreign capital and domestic capital owned by Indonesian citizens, and/or Indonesian legal entities; or

b. Straight investment, in the sense of that the entire capital is owned by foreign citizens and/or foreign legal entities.

(2) The amount of investment shall be determined by investor in accordance with the economic feasibility of the business activity.

Article 3

(1) Business license is granted to the FDI company for a period of thirty (30) years since the commencement of commercial operation.

(2) The business license may be renewed by the Minister for Investment/Chairman of the Investment Coordinating Board if the company continue to carry out its business for the benefit of the national economy and development.

(3) The minister for Investment/Chairman of the Investment Coordinating Board shall stipulate further provision of the renewal of business license, after consultation with the related Minister.

Article 4

(1) The business activity of the FDI Company may be located throughout the territory of the Republic of Indonesia.

(2) In the regions that have had the Bonded Zone and Industrial Estate, the business activity shall preferably be located in the above mentioned areas.

Article 5

(1) A joint venture company as referred to in Article 2 paragraph (1) point a, may carry out business activities categorized as important to the State and serving the public, such as ports, generation and transmission as well as distribution of electricity for public use, telecommunications, shipping lines, airlines, potable water, public railways, atomic energy reactors and mass media.

(2) A straight investment company as referred to in Article 2 paragraph (1) point b, is not permitted to carry out the business activities in the business sectors as referred to in paragraph (1) above.

Article 6

(1) The Indonesian partners' shares in the joint venture company shall be at least five percent (5%) of the total paid-up capital of the company upon its establishment.

(2) The company's shares in excess of 5% as mentioned in paragraph (1) can be sold to Indonesian citizens or Indonesian legal entities owned entirely by Indonesian citizens by way of direct ownership as agreed by the parties and/or through the domestic stock exchange.

Article 7

(1) The straight investment company shall sell a parts of its shares to Indonesian citizen and/or Indonesian legal entities within a maximum of fifteen years after the commencement of commercial operation, by way of direct ownership and/or through the domestic stock exchange.

(2) The transfer of the above mentioned company's share shall not alter the status of the company.

Article 8

(1) In addition to increase its own equity, the FDI company which has been commercially operating may also:

a. establish a new company; and/or

b. buy shares of existing domestic company except for existing FDI company, whether or not they are already commercially operating, through the domestic stock exchange.

(2) The shares as referred to in paragraph (1) point b, may also be bought by the joint venture company through direct ownership on the basis of an agreement between the parties.

3. The purchase of existing domestic company's shares as referred to in paragraph (1) and (2) can only be carried out if the fields business concerned are open to foreign direct investment at the time of the purchase.
4. The purchase of the existing domestic company's shares as referred to in paragraph (1) point b, shall not alter status of the company.

Article 9

(1) The foreign enterprises may buy the shares of the existing domestic company including the existing FDI company, irrespective as to whether they are in commercial operation.

(2) The purchase of the shares as referred to in paragraph (1) except for existing FDI company can only be carried out if the fields of business concerned are open to foreign direct investment at the time of the purchase.

(3) The purchase of the existing domestic company's shares as referred to in paragraph (1) shall be completed through direct ownership and/or through domestic stock exchange.

(4) The direct ownership by the foreign enterprises as referred to in paragraph (3) can only be carried out in the effort to rescue and restore the company concerned.

(5) The purchase of existing domestic company's shares as referred to in paragraph (1) and (2) shall not alter the status of the company.

Article 10

The further provisions required for the implementation of this Government Regulation shall be stipulated by the Minister for Investment/Chairman of the investment Coordinating Board, after hearing the opinion of the relevant Minister(s).

Article 11

Through the enactment of this Government Regulation, Government Regulation No. 50 of 1993 on the Share Ownership Requirements in Foreign Investment Company shall be declared and void.

Article 12

The company established under foreign investment law, which has been established and/or has been commercially operating before the enactment of this Government Regulation, shall comply with the provisions of this Government Regulation on the basis of the agreement of their shareholders.

Article 13

This Government Regulation shall come into effect as of the date of promulgation. For public cognizance, this Government Regulation shall be promulgated by publishing it in the State Gazette of the Republic of Indonesia.

TRAVEL TO INDONESIA

TRAVEL WARNING (Issued on February 27, 2001): The Department of State urges American citizens to defer nonessential travel to Indonesia and all travel to Aceh, Maluku, Papua, West Timor, Central Kalimantan (Borneo) and Central Sulawesi. Those who must travel to Indonesia, or who are resident there, should exercise extreme caution. Indonesia is experiencing a major political transition, and unrest and violence can erupt with little forewarning anywhere in the country. Bombings of religious, political and business targets have occurred throughout the country. In addition, events in the Middle East have sparked anti-American protests in the past.

Due to the continuing threat of serious violence, all travel should be avoided to the regions of Aceh, Maluku, West Timor, Central Kalimantan and Central Sulawesi. Further, all travel by U.S. and other foreign government officials to Aceh, Papua and the Moluccas (provinces of North Maluku and Maluku) has been restricted by the Indonesian government because of security concerns. Private Americans should adhere to these same restrictions.

A massive bombing campaign struck churches throughout Indonesia on Christmas Eve, leaving at least 16 dead and over one hundred injured. Bombings occurred in the cities of Medan, Pekanbaru, Batam, Bandung, Sukabumi, Bekasi, Jakarta, Mojokerto, Surabaya and Mataram. Bombings have also occurred over the past several months at Indonesian government buildings, foreign diplomatic facilities and business and financial centers, including the Jakarta Stock Exchange. More explosive devices have been discovered in Jakarta since Christmas, and there are indications that the bombings may continue.

On occasion, the U.S. mission in Indonesia may have to suspend services to the public or close because of security concerns. In those situations, the U.S. Embassy will continue to be available by telephone to offer emergency services to American citizens. Some foreign travelers in troubled areas of Indonesia have been subject to arbitrary arrest, detention and deportation and, on at least one occasion, false accusations of espionage. In November, 2000, in the central Java city of Solo, groups opposed to U.S. policy undertook or threatened "sweeps," trying to identify American citizens and order them to depart the country. There also have been a number of acts of intimidation and violence directed at American companies and U.S. diplomatic facilities. Indonesian security officials have sometimes been unwilling or unable to respond.

The Abu Sayyaf terrorist group has been active throughout the islands in the extreme southwest Philippines, near Indonesia, and continues to hold hostage an American citizen kidnapped in the Philippines. American citizens traveling to the border regions in Northern Kalimantan and North Sulawesi, in particular the smaller islands closer to the Philippines, are urged to review their security procedures.

American citizens resident or traveling in Indonesia are advised to exercise caution at all times, be alert to suspicious or unclaimed packages, vary times and routes and other aspects of personal daily routine and keep a low profile.

COUNTRY DESCRIPTION: Indonesia is an independent republic consisting of more than 13,500 islands spread over 3,000 miles. Indonesia's economy is developing, and tourist services are plentiful in the major tourist areas. East Timor voted for independence from Indonesia on August 30, 2004 and is currently under the authority of the United Nations Transitional Administration in East Timor (UNTAET). Please refer to the separate Consular Information Sheet available on East Timor.

ENTRY REQUIREMENTS: A passport valid for six months beyond the intended date of departure from Indonesia is required. A visa is not required for tourist stays up to two months. As of November 2000 the Government of Indonesia has been discussing implementing visa requirements for foreign travelers. Travelers should reconfirm entry requirements before traveling. For additional information about entry requirements for Indonesia, travelers may contact the Embassy of the Republic of Indonesia, 2020 Massachusetts Avenue, N.W., Washington, D.C. 20046, telephone (202) 775-5200, Internet address http://www.kbri.org.

DUAL NATIONALITY: Indonesian law does not recognize dual nationality. Because of this, U.S. citizens who are also documented as Indonesian nationals may experience difficulties with immigration formalities in Indonesia. It may also hamper efforts to provide consular protection when abroad. In addition to being subject to all Indonesian laws affecting U.S. citizens, dual nationals may also be subject to other laws that impose special obligations on Indonesian citizens. For further information, please see the Consular Affairs home page on the Internet at http://travel.state.gov for our Dual Nationality flyer.

SAFETY AND SECURITY: Indonesia is experiencing a major political transition, and unrest and violence can erupt with little forewarning anywhere in the country. Due to the continuing threat of serious violence, American citizens should avoid all travel to the regions of Aceh, Irian Jaya (also known as West Papua), the Moluccas, Central Sulawesi and West Timor. All travel by U.S. and other foreign government officials to Aceh, Irian Jaya and the Moluccas (provinces of North Maluku and Maluku) has been restricted by the Indonesian government because of security concerns. Private Americans should adhere to these same restrictions. Travelers should consult the most recent Public Announcement or Travel Warning for Indonesia for updated information on travel within the country. Public Announcements and Travel Warnings can be found on the Bureau of Consular Affairs' home page at http://travel.state.gov/. American citizens in all parts of Indonesia should exercise prudence, remain vigilant and avoid demonstrations and other situations that could turn violent.

Serious sectarian violence has occurred in the Moluccas, Central Sulawesi and the island of Lombok. Violence broke out on the island of Ambon in January 2004, spreading throughout the Moluccas and eventually leading the Government of Indonesia to declare a "Civil State of Emergency" on June 26, 2000. Violence in Central Sulawesi culminated in the death of some 200 people in May 2000. On January 17, 2000, anti-Christian violence broke out on the resort island of Lombok, leading to looting and the burning of a number of churches.

The cities of Jakarta, Medan, Bandung and Surabaya, among others, have been struck by a number of bombings in recent months. The most recent bombing campaign struck churches across Indonesia on Christmas Eve 2000, leaving at least 16 dead and one hundred injured. The Jakarta Stock Exchange, foreign diplomatic facilities and Indonesian government buildings have also been targeted. There are indications that this wave of bombings may continue.

In November 2000, in the central Java city of Solo, groups opposed to U.S. policy undertook "sweeps," trying to identify American citizens and order them to depart the country. There also have been a number of acts of intimidation and violence directed at American companies and U.S. diplomatic facilities. Security officials have sometimes been unwilling or unable to intervene in instances of unrest. Also, Indonesian authorities arbitrarily detained an American tourist in Irian Jaya without formal charges for two weeks and then deported him after a high ranking Indonesian government official publicly accused him of espionage.

The Abu Sayyaf terrorist group has been active throughout the islands in the extreme southwest Philippines, near Indonesia, and continues to hold an American citizen kidnapped in the Philippines. American citizens traveling to the border regions in Northern Kalimantan and North

Sulawesi, in particular the smaller islands closer to the Philippines, are urged to review their security procedures.

On September 6, 2000, a militia mob in West Timor attacked United Nations offices, killing three UN international staff members. The militias have specifically targeted foreigners. American citizens are strongly advised to avoid all travel to West Timor.

The tourist destination of Bali has been largely free of the disturbances seen in other parts of Indonesia. All tourist facilities are operating normally, and to date foreigners have not been the specific target of any group.

Travelers and residents should ensure that their passports and important personal papers are ready for a quick departure from the country should it become necessary for any reason. Americans traveling in Indonesia should remember that much of the country, including many tourist destinations, can be isolated and difficult to reach by available transportation or communication links.

CRIME: Indonesia has a high crime rate. Credit card fraud is a growing problem. Minor crimes, such as pickpocketing and thefts, occur in popular tourist sites throughout the country. Incidents of robbery are on the increase. One common criminal technique is to puncture automobile tires so that the occupants can be robbed while changing the tire. Thefts and robberies from cars stopped at traffic lights have been reported on occasion. American citizens are advised to keep car doors locked and windows rolled up. Americans in Jakarta are also advised to engage a taxi either from a major hotel queue or by calling a taxi company, rather than hailing one on the street. Poachers and illegal loggers operating in Indonesian parks and nature preserves have threatened researchers, tourists and others in order to discourage foreign presence in those areas.

Claiming to act in the name of religious or moral standards, certain extremist groups have begun attacking nightspots and places of entertainment. Most attacks have been aimed at property destruction rather than injury to individuals. However, in November 2000 similar groups attacked an international HIV/AIDS conference, injuring 25, including two foreigners. These groups have on occasion carried out or threatened hunts for Americans and members of certain religious groups to demand they leave the country.

A number of racially motivated incidents of harassment have recently been reported. Persons of African descent, including American citizens, may be subject to arbitrary stops and questioning by both private and public security officials. There are several credible reports that such incidents have led to harassment and physical abuse. To minimize the risk of an incident with local law enforcement authorities, Americans should carry photocopies of their passports at all times. If stopped and detained, Americans should attempt to comply with all instructions from law enforcement officers, but also make it clear that they are American citizens and that they wish to contact the U.S. Embassy. Any incidents should be reported to the U.S. Embassy immediately.

Maritime piracy is a persistent and growing problem in Indonesian waters, targeting both pleasure and commercial vessels. Pleasure yachters are advised to review the current security situation with their local agent when planning itineraries and to exercise particular care when sailing in the Strait of Malacca between Riau Province and Singapore and in the waters north of Sulawesi and Kalimantan.

The loss or theft abroad of a U.S. passport should be reported immediately to the local police and the nearest U.S. embassy or consulate. U.S. citizens may refer to the Department of State's pamphlet, *A Safe Trip Abroad*, for ways to promote a more trouble-free journey. The pamphlet is available by mail from the Superintendent of Documents, U.S. Government Printing Office, Washington, D.C. 20402, via the Internet at http://www.access.gpo.gov/su_docs, or via the Bureau of Consular Affairs home page at http://travel.state.gov/.

MEDICAL FACILITIES: The general level of sanitation and health care in Indonesia is far below U.S. standards. Some level of routine medical care is available in all major cities, although most expatriates choose to leave the country for serious medical procedures. Serious medical problems requiring hospitalization and/or medical evacuation to Singapore or Australia, the closest locations with acceptable medical care, or the United States, can cost thousands of dollars. Doctors and hospitals often expect immediate cash payment for health services.

MEDICAL INSURANCE: U.S. medical insurance is not always valid outside the United States. U.S. Medicare and Medicaid programs do not provide payment for medical services outside the United States. Doctors and hospitals often expect immediate cash payment for health services. Uninsured travelers who require medical care overseas may face extreme difficulties.

Please check with your own insurance company to confirm whether your policy applies overseas, including provision for medical evacuation, and for adequacy of coverage. Serious medical problems requiring hospitalization and/or medical evacuation to the United States can cost tens of thousands of dollars. Please ascertain whether payment will be made to the overseas hospital or doctor or if you will be reimbursed later for expenses that you incur. Some insurance policies also include coverage for psychiatric treatment and for disposition of remains in the event of death.

Useful information on medical emergencies abroad, including overseas insurance programs, is provided in the Department of State's Bureau of Consular Affairs brochure, Medical Information for Americans Traveling Abroad, available via the Bureau of Consular Affairs home page or autofax: (202) 647-3000.

OTHER HEALTH INFORMATION: Information on vaccinations and other health precautions may be obtained from the Centers for Disease Control and Prevention's hotline for international travelers at 1-877-FYI-TRIP (1-877-394-8747); fax 1-888-CDC-FAXX (1-888-232-3299), or via CDC's Internet site at http://www.cdc.gov/.

TRAFFIC SAFETY AND ROAD CONDITIONS: While in a foreign country, U.S. citizens may encounter road conditions that differ significantly from those in the United States. The information below concerning Indonesia is provided for general reference only, and it may not be totally accurate in a particular location or circumstance.

Safety of Public Transportation: Poor
Urban Road Conditions/Maintenance: Good to Fair
Rural Road Conditions/Maintenance: Fair to Poor
Availability of Roadside Assistance: Poor

In general, traffic in Indonesia is congested and undisciplined. The number and variety of vehicles on the road far exceed the capacity of existing roadways to handle the traffic. Road conditions vary from good (in the case of toll roads and major city roads) to dangerously poor.

There is generally a very low level of road safety awareness in Indonesia, although this situation is improving. Buses and trucks are often dangerously overloaded and tend to travel at high speeds. Most roads outside major urban areas have a single lane of traffic in each direction, making passing dangerous. Most Indonesian drivers do not maintain safe following distance in a manner familiar to U.S. drivers and tend to pass or maneuver with considerably less margin for error than in the United States. Although traffic in Indonesia moves on the left side of the road, drivers tend to pass on both sides and may use the shoulder for this purpose. It is common for drivers to create extra lanes regardless of the lane markings painted on the roads. Throughout the country, motor vehicles share the roads with other forms of transportation such as bicycle pedicabs, horse and ox carts, and pushcarts.

Although Indonesia has a seat belt law requiring the use of seat belts in front seats, most Indonesian automobiles do not have seat belts in the rear passenger seats. The use of infant and child car seats is not common, and it can be very difficult to rent a car seat for temporary use. Helmets are required on motorcycles, but this law is inconsistently enforced. Passengers rarely wear helmets. Accidents on rented motorcycles constitute the largest cause of death and serious accident among foreign visitors to Bali.

The use of professional drivers is common among the expatriate and upper class Indonesian communities. All car rental firms are able to provide drivers for a nominal additional fee.

Driving at night can be extremely dangerous outside of major urban areas. It is common to encounter drivers who refuse to use their lights, and most rural roads are unlit. Residents in rural areas may also sometimes congregate on road surfaces after dark, and at least one American citizen was recently involved in a fatal accident when his car hit a group lying on an unlit stretch of road.

In the event of an accident, Indonesia law requires that both drivers await the arrival of a police officer to report the accident. Although Indonesian law requires third party insurance, most Indonesian drivers are uninsured, and even when a vehicle is insured it is common for insurance companies to refuse to pay damages. If a pedestrian is injured, the driver of the vehicle is normally expected to assist in transporting the injured party to the hospital. (Indonesian ambulance services are unreliable.) In cases of traffic accidents resulting in death, it is not uncommon for bystanders to attack the driver perceived to be responsible. This is more common in rural areas and in accidents involving Indonesian drivers, but expatriate drivers have occasionally been attacked by crowds at the scene of an accident. When an accident occurs outside of a major city, it may be advisable to drive to the nearest police station before stopping.

For additional general information about road safety, including links to foreign government sites, please see the Department of State, Bureau of Consular Affairs home page at http://travel.state.gov/road_safety.html. For specific information concerning Indonesian driving permits, vehicle inspection, road tax and mandatory insurance, please contact the Indonesian national tourist organization via the Internet at http://www.indonesia-tourism.com. Please see also road safety information from the U.S. Embassy home page at http://www.usembassyjakarta.org.

AVIATION OVERSIGHT: In 1997, the U.S. Federal Aviation Administration (FAA) has assessed the government of Indonesia's civil aviation authority as Category 1 - in compliance with international aviation safety standards for oversight of Indonesia's air carrier operations.

For further information, travelers may contact the Department of Transportation within the U.S. at telephone 1-800-322-7873, or visit the FAA's Internet web site at http://www.faa.gov/avr/iasa. The U.S. Department of Defense (DOD) separately assesses some foreign air carriers for suitability as official providers of air services. For information regarding the DOD policy on specific carriers, travelers may contact the DOD at telephone (618) 229-4801.

CUSTOMS REGULATIONS: Indonesia's customs authorities may enforce strict regulations concerning temporary importation into or export from Indonesia of personal and commercial use items such as prescription medicines and Chinese-language material or videotapes. It is advisable to contact the Embassy of Indonesia in Washington, D.C. at telephone (202) 775-5200, or one of Indonesia's consulates in the United States, for specific information regarding customs requirements. Enforcement of customs regulations is not always consistent or transparent.

CRIMINAL PENALTIES: While in a foreign country, a U.S. citizen is subject to that country's laws and regulations, which sometimes differ significantly from those in the United States and do not afford the same protections available to the individual under U.S. law. Penalties for breaking the law can be more severe than in the United States for similar offenses. Persons violating the laws of Indonesia, even unknowingly, may be expelled, arrested, or imprisoned. Penalties for possession, use, or trafficking in illegal drugs in Indonesia are strict, and convicted offenders can expect severe jail sentences and fines. The death sentence can be handed down in cases of drug trafficking, and one U.S. citizen was recently given a life sentence for trafficking.

CONSULAR ACCESS: U.S. citizens are encouraged to carry a copy of their U.S. passports with them at all times, so that, if questioned by local officials, proof of identity and U.S. citizenship are readily available. When U.S. citizens are arrested or detained, formal notification of the arrest is normally provided to the U.S. Embassy in Jakarta in writing, a process that can take several weeks. If detained, U.S. citizens are encouraged to attempt to telephone the nearest U.S. consular office. **SPECIAL CIRCUMSTANCES:** U.S. citizens involved in commercial or property matters should be aware that the business environment is complex. In many cases, trade complaints are difficult to resolve.

DISASTER PREPAREDNESS: Indonesia is located in an area of high seismic activity. Although the probability of a major earthquake occurring during an individual trip is remote, earthquakes can and will continue to happen. General information about natural disaster preparedness is available via the Internet from the U.S. Federal Emergency Management Agency (FEMA) at http://www.fema.gov/.

CHILDREN'S ISSUES: For information on international adoption of children or international parental child abduction, please refer to our Internet site at http://travel.state.gov/children's_issues.html or telephone (202) 736-7000.

REGISTRATION AND EMBASSY LOCATION: Americans living in or visiting Indonesia are encouraged to register at the U.S. Embassy or Consulate where they may obtain updated information on travel and security within the country. The U.S. Embassy is located in Jakarta at Medan Merdeka Selatan 5; telephone:(62)(21)3435-9000; fax (62)(21)3435-9922. The Embassy's web site is located at http://www.usembassyjakarta.org. The consular section can be reached by e-mail at jakconsul@state.gov. The U.S. Consulate General is in Surabaya at Jalan Raya Dr., Sutomo 33; telephone: (62)(31) 567-2287/8; fax (62)(31)567-4492;e-mail consularsuraba@state.gov.

There is a Consular Agency in Bali at Jalan Hayam Wuruk 188, Denpasar, Bali; telephone: (62)(361)233-605; fax (62)(31) 222-426; e-mail amcobali@indo.net.id.

The U.S. Consulate in Medan closed in May 1996. American citizens needing assistance in Sumatra should contact the U.S. Embassy in Jakarta.

SUPPLEMENTS

US AND COUNTRY CONTACTS

1. CHAMBERS OF COMMERCE

Based in New York City, the membership of the American-Indonesian Chamber of Commerce is comprised of over 150 companies and individuals doing business in Indonesia. It has an active program of monthly luncheons, featuring speakers knowledgeable about Indonesia and briefing programs for newly appointed American and Indonesian Government officials. The Chamber also publishes "OUTLOOK/ INDONESIA," a quarterly publication containing interpretations of new Indonesian policies, sectoral reviews, summaries of recent Chamber activities, and an Executive Director's column. In addition, the American-Indonesian Chamber of Commerce provides business translations, either from English to Indonesian or Indonesian to English. Their contact information is as follows:

The American-Indonesian Chamber of Commerce
317 Madison Avenue, Suite 520New York, NY 10017
Tel.: (212) 687-4505
Fax : (212)687-5844
Email: aiccny@bigplanet.com
Internet: http://www.aicc.globalnetlink.com
Contact: Wayne Forrest, Executive Director

The American Chamber of Commerce in Indonesia, known as AMCHAM, is affiliated with the Asia-Pacific Council of American Chambers of Commerce (APCAC). Its 600 members include leading U.S. firms with offices in Indonesia, associates, individuals, and special members. The chamber prepares a number of useful guides to doing business in Indonesia and a membership directory. AMCHAM assists U.S. firms in assessing business opportunities by staging briefing breakfasts at the requestor's expense. Their contact information is as follows:

American Chamber of Commerce (AMCHAM)
World Trade Center, 11th Floor,
Jl. Jendral Sudirman Kav. 29 - 31
Jakarta 12920, Indonesia
Tel: (62-21) 526-2860
Fax: (62-21) 526 2861
Email: amcham_indonesia@ibm.net
Internet: http//www.amcham.or.id
Contact: James W. Castle, President

2. RELATED BUSINESS COUNCILS AND ASSOCIATIONS IN THE U.S.A.:

California-Asia Business Council
1946 Embarcadero, Suite 200
Oakland, CA 94606
Tel.: (510) 536-1967
Fax : (510) 261-9598
E-mail: shanahan@calasia.org
Internet: www.CalAsia.org
Contact: Mr. Shanahan Lim, Program Manager, Ms. Jeremy W. Potash, Executive Director

Indonesian American Business Association
P.O. Box 420398 Houston, TX 77242-0398
10900 Richmond Avenue, Houston, TX 77242
Tel.: (713) 789-0702
Fax : (713) 789-0559
E-mail: iaba@onramp.net
Internet: www.iaba-usa.org
Contact: Engeline Tan, Executive Director

Pacific Basin Economic Council
PBEC International Secretariats
900 Fort St., suite 1080
Honolulu, Hawaii, USA 96813
Tel.: (808) 521-9044
Fax : (808) 521-8530
E-mail: info@pbec.org
Internet: www.pbec.org
Contact: Robert G. Lees, Secretary General

U.S.-ASEAN Business Council
Support Services/MIS
1400 L Street NW #375
Washington, DC 20005
Tel.: (202) 289-1911
Fax : (202) 289-0519
E-mail: mail@usasean.org
Internet: www.us-asean.org
Contact: Jackie Darden

3. INDONESIAN TRADE ASSOCIATIONS

The major trade association in Indonesia is the Indonesian Chamber of Commerce and Industry (KADIN). Members include representatives from private industry, cooperatives, public corporations, utilities, as well as state-owned enterprises. In addition, there are numerous other specialized and professional organizations that represent the interests of various other sectors and trades in the economy. Contact information for KADIN is as follows:

Indonesian Chamber of Commerce & Industry (KADIN)
Menara Kadin, 29th Floor
Jl. H.R. Rasuna Said X-5 Kav. 2-3
Jakarta 12940
Tel.: (62-21) 916-5535, 916-5538, 527-4485
Fax : (62-21) 527-4486
Associations of importers and exporters, most of whom are organized on a commodity basis, include the Importers Association of Indonesia (GINSI) and the Indonesian Association of Exporters (GPEI). Both organizations have head offices in Jakarta. Contact information is as follows:

Importers Association of Indonesia (GINSI)
Gedung Bank Niaga, 1st Floor
Jl. Raya Pasar Minggu #45
Jakarta Selatan
Tel.: (62-21) 7919-8986, 7919-8987, 7919-8988

Fax : (62-21) 790-0808
Contact: Mr. H. Amirudin Saud, Chairman

Indonesian Exporters Association (GPEI)
21 Jl. Wolter Monginsidi No. 88A
Jakarta 12170
Tel.: 725-2612, 725-2613
Fax : 725-2615
Contact: Dipl. Ing. H. Benny Soetrisno

The Indonesian Government established the National Agency for Export Development within the Ministry of Trade to promote the export of less renowned products. These products include handicrafts (ie, jewelry, batik, handwoven fabric, and wood carvings), agricultural and cottage industry products, and new manufactured products. The agency will also assist foreign buyers and importers in establishing contacts with Indonesian companies. Contact information is as follows:

National Agency for Export Development
Jl. Gajah Mada No. 8
Jakarta 10130
Tel.: (62-21) 634-1082
Fax : (62-21) 633-8360

4. TRADE AND PROJECT FINANCING

U.S. Trade and Development Agency
American Business Center
25th Flr., Ayala Life-FGU Center
6811 Ayala Ave., Makati City
Philippines
Tel: (632) 887-1196/-1192
Fax: (632) 887-1225 fax
E-mail: tdasia@skyinet.net

Commercial Liaison to the Asian Development Bank
U.S. and Foreign Commercial Service
2nd Floor, GSO Building Seafront Compound
Roxas Boulevard, Pasar City
Manila, Philippines
Tel.: (632) 804-0460
Fax : (632) 804-0357
E-mail: Stewart.Ballard@mail.doc.gov
Internet: http://www.ita.doc.gov/mdbo
Contact: Stewart Ballard, Senior Commercial Officer

U.S. Trade and Development Agency
1621 North Kent Street, Suite 300
Arlington, VA 22209-2131
Tel: (703) 875-4357
Fax: (703) 875-4009
Internet: www.tda.gov

TDA Regional Office – Manila
John Herrman, Deputy Regional Manager
2/F, RSC Bldg. Seafront Compound
Roxas Blvd.
Manila, Philippines
Tel: (632) 804-0381 or –0363
Fax: (632) 804-0367
E-mail: tdasia@skyinet.net

Overseas Private Investment Corporation (OPIC)
1100 New York Avenue, N.W.
Washington, D.C. 20527
Tel.: (202) 336-8799
Fax : (202) 408-9859
Internet: http://www.opic.gov

Export-Import Bank of the United States (EX-IM Bank)
811 Vermont Ave., NW
Washington, D.C. 20571
Tel.: (800) 565-EXIM(3946), (202) 565-3946
Fax : (202)565-3380
Asia hotline : (800) 565-3946 ext.3905
Internet: http://www.exim.gov

Islamic Development Bank
P.O. Box 5925
Jeddah, 21432
Kingdom of Saudi Arabia
Tel.: (966-2) 636-1400 (10 lines)
Fax : (966-2) 636-6871
Tlx: 601 137 ISDB SJ
E-mail idb.comm@mail.oicisnet.org or idb.archives@mail.oicisnet.org
Internet: http://www.isdb.org

The World Bank
Office of the U.S. Executive Director
Commercial Service Liaison Staff
Jill Wilkins or Kimberly Versak
1818 H Street, NW
Washington, DC 20433
Tel.: (202) 477-1234
Fax : (202) 522-3405
Internet: http://www-esd.worldbank.org/
E-mail: kversak@worldbank.org or jwilkins@worldbank.org

In Indonesia:
Mark Baird, Indonesia Country Manager
Jakarta Stock Exchange Building
Tower 2, 12th Floor
Jl. Jendral Sudirman, Kav. 52-53
Jakarta 12190 Indonesia
Tel.: (62-21) 529-93000
Fax : (62-21) 529-93111

5. INDONESIAN GOVERNMENT CONTACTS

The following is a listing of President Abdurraham Wahid's cabinet as of March 2000. Because of the uncertainties surrounding the Indonesian government at the time, business persons who wish to get in touch with these cabinet members can contact the U.S. Commercial Service in Jakarta for up-to-date contact information or to forward correspondence.

6. Coordinating Ministers:

Political and Security: Lt. Gen (Ret.) Suryadi Sudirja
Economic, Finance, and Industry: Drs. Kwik Kian Gie
People's Welfare and Poverty Alleviation: Basri Hasanuddin, MA

Ministry:
Agriculture: Dr. Ir. Muhammad Prakosa, Ph.D
Defense/Armed Forces Commander: Prof. DR Juwono Sudarsono
Education: DR Yahya A. Muhaimin
Finance: DR. Bambang Sudibyo, MBA
Foreign Affairs: DR Alwi Shihab
Forestry and Plantation: DR Nurmahmudi Ismail
Health: Dr. Achmad Suyudi, MHA
Home Affairs: Lt. Gen. (Ret.) Suryadi Sudirja
Industry and Trade: Lt. Gen. Luhut B. Panjaitan
Law and Legislation: DR Yusril Ihza Mahendra, SH, MSC
Manpower: DR Bomer Rasaribu, SH
Maritime Exploration: Ir. Sarwono Kusumaatmadja
Mining and Energy: Lt. Gen. (Ret.) Susilo Bambang Yudhoyono
Religious Affairs: Drs. K.H. Muhammad Tolchah Hasan
Residential and Area Development: Ir. Erna Witoelar, M. Si
Transportation and Communications: Lt. Gen. Agum Gumelar

State Ministers:
State Secretary: Dr. Ali Rahman, M. Sc.
Cooperatives, Small and Medium Enterprises: Drs. Zarkasih Noer
Environment: DR Soni Keraf
Human Rights: Dr. Hasballah M. Saad
Investment/Head of BKPM: H.M. Rozy Munir, S.E., MSC
Public Affairs: DR Anak Agung Gde Agung
Public Works: Dr. Ir. Rozik Boedioro Soetjipto
Reform of State Apparatus: Rear Adm. Freddy Numberi
Regional Autonomy: DR Ryaas Rasyid
Research and Technology: Dr. A.S. Hikam
Tourism, Art and Culture: Drs. Hidayat Djaelani
Transmigration and Population: Ir. Al-Hilal Hamdi
Women's Affairs: Dra. Khofifah Indar Parawansa (Ms)
Youth and Sports: Drs. Mahadi Simambela

Officials of Ministerial Rank:
Attorney General: Marzuki Darusman, SH
Governor of the Bank of Indonesia: DR. Syahril Sabrin
Indonesian Armed Forces (TNI) Commander-in-Chief: Admiral Widodo A.S.

*In Indonesia DR refers to a male with a Doctorate degree; Dr. refers to a male with a medical degree; Drs. refers to a male with a bachelor degree; Dra. refers to a female with a bachelor degree; SH. refers to a male or female with a law degree; MSC is a male or female with a Master of Science

6. U.S. GOVERNMENT CONTACTS

U.S. Embassy, Jakarta

Mailing Address from U.S.: International Mail:
American Embassy - Jakarta American Embassy-Jakarta
Box 1 Unit 8129 Jl. Medan Merdeka Selatan #5
FPO, AP 96520 Jakarta 10110, Indonesia

U.S. Ambassador Robert S. Gelbard Deputy Chief of Mission Stephen Mull
1st Aide to Ambassador Janice G. Smith Sec. to DCM Brenda Dudley

Internet: http://www.usembassyjakarta.org

U.S. Commercial Center
Alice Davenport, Counselor for Commercial Affairs
Judy R. Reinke, Commercial Attaché
Michael Carroll, Commercial Officer
Wisma Metropolitan II, 3rd Floor
Jl. Jendral Sudirman Kav. 29-31
Jakarta 12910, Indonesia
(From the U.S., use Embassy's FPO mailing address – see above)
Tel.: (62-21) 526-2850
Fax : (62-21) 526-2855
Email : jakarta.office.box@mail.doc.gov
Internet : http://www.jakarta.uscc.org

U.S. Asian Environmental Partnership
Gerald Sanders, Technical Representative
Wisma Metropolitan II, 3rd Floor
Jl. Jendral Sudirman Kav. 29-31
Jakarta 12910, Indonesia
Tel.: (62-21) 526-2844, 526-2848
Fax : (62-21) 526-2846, 526-2849
Email: usaepdir@rad.net.id
Internet : http://www.usaep.org

U.S. Asian Environmental Partnership
Office of Environmental Infrastructure
Tel.: (62-21) 344-2211 Ext. 2480
Fax : (62-21) 380-6694

U.S. Agricultural Trade Office (ATO)
Dennis Voboril, Agricultural Attaché
Wisma Metropolitan II, 3rd Floor
Jl. Jendral Sudirman Kav. 29-31
Jakarta 12910, Indonesia

Tel.: (62-21) 526-2850
Fax : (62-21) 571-1251

The following U.S. Embassy Offices are located at:
Jl. Medan Merdeka Selatan #5
Jakarta 10110, Indonesia

Foreign Agricultural Service
Kent D. Sission, Counselor for Agricultural Affairs
Deanna M. Johnson, Agricultural Attaché
Tel.: (62-21) 344-2211 (ext. 2161)
Fax : (62-21) 380-1363

Economic Section
Judith Fergin, Economic Counselor
Michael Uyehara, Resources Officer
Robin McClellan, Science and Technology Officer
David DiGiovanna, Trade Officer
William Heidt, Finance Officer
Vicky Alvarado, Economic Officer
Tel.: (62-21) 344-2211 (ext. 2073)
Fax : (62-21) 386-2259

Public Affairs Section
Greta Morris, Public Affairs Counselor
Karl Fritz, Press Attaché
Tel.: (62-21) 344-2211 (ext. 2500)
Fax : (62-21) 381-0243
E-mail: gmorris@pd.state.gov/kfritz@pd.state.gov

Informational Resource Center (IRC)
Melling Simanjuntak, Library Director
Tel.: (62-21) 350-8467
Fax : (62-21) 350-8466
E-mail: irc@usembassyjakarta.org

Agency for International Development (U.S. AID)
Terry Myers, Director
Paul Deuster, Chief, Private Sector Development Office
Tel.: (62-21) 344-2211 (ext. 2308)
Fax : (62-21) 380-6694

Defense Attaché Office (DAO)
Col. Joseph H. Daves, Defense Attaché
Tel.: (62-21) 344-2211 (ext. 2191)
Fax : (62-21) 386-2259

Office of the Military Attaché for Defense Programs
Col. James Tompkins, Military Attaché
Tel.: (62-21) 344-2211 (ext. 2601)
Fax : (62-21) 386-2259

U.S. Consulate General – Surabaya
Robert Pollard, Consul General
Joaquin F. Monserrate, Pol/Econ/Commercial Officer
Lina Jusuf, Commercial Specialist
American Consulate General-
Jl. Raya Dr. Sutomo #33
Surabaya, Indonesia 60264
Tel.: (62-31) 567-6880, 568-2287, 568-2288
Fax : (62-31) 567-4492 Telex : 34331
E-mail: amconsby@rad.net.id

U.S. Consulate Medan (to be opened sometime in the year 2000)
Ronald Deutch
Jl. Walikota No. 13
Medan, Sumatra Utara
Tel.: (62-61) 415-2200, 453-1251
Fax: (62-61) 451-8711

U.S. Consular Agent Bali
Andrew Toth, Executive Office
Jl. Hayam Wuruk 188, Denpasar, Bali, Indonesia 80235
Tel.: (62-361) 233-605, 222-424
Fax : (62-361) 222-426
E-mail : tabuh@denpasar.wasantara.net.id

7. U.S. GOVERNMENT – WASHINGTON D.C.

Trade Information Center
U.S. Department of Commerce
Ronald Reagan Building, Mezzanine Level
Washington, D.C. 20230
Tel.: 1-800-USA-TRAD(E)8723 or (202) 482-0543
Fax : (202) 482-4473
Internet: http://www.ita.doc.gov/tic or http://tradeinfo.doc.gov//
Flashfax: 1-800-872-8723 (Use flashfax for rapid access to the most frequently requested information on doing business throughout Asia.)

Elena Mikalis / Farah Press
Desk Officers for Indonesia (Policy Issues)
U.S. Department of Commerce
Room 2324
14th and Constitution Ave., N.W.
Washington, D.C. 20230
Tel.: (202) 482-3894
Fax : (202) 482-3316
E-mail: Elena_Mikalis@ita.doc.gov, Farah_Press@ita.doc.gov
Internet: http:\\www.ita.doc.gov

U.S. Department of State Office of Business Affairs
Commercial Coordinators
22201 C St., N.W., Room 2318
Washington D.C., 20520
Tel.: (202) 647-1625

Fax : (202) 647-3951
E-mail: cbaweb@state.gov
Internet: www.state.gov/www/about_state/business/index.html

U.S. Department of Agriculture, Foreign Agricultural Service, Trade Assistance and Promotion Office
1400 Independence Ave., S.W., Room 6958-8
Washington D.C. 20250
Tel.: (202) 720-7349
Contact: Scott Cook, Contracting & Acquisition Management Division

United States-Asia Environmental Partnership (US-AEP)
Asia/Near East Bureau
U.S. Agency for International Development
1300 Pennsylvania Ave, NW
Washington, D.C. 20523-4101
Tel.: (202) 712-0270
Fax : (202) 216-3379
Internet : http://www.usaep.org

8. INDONESIAN EMBASSY AND CONSULATES IN THE UNITED STATES:

Embassy of the Republic of Indonesia
2020 Massachusetts Avenue, N.W.
Washington, D.C. 20046
Tel.: (202) 775-5200
Fax : (202) 775-5365
Internet: http://www.kbri.org

Consulate General Office-New York
5 East 68th St.
New York, NY 10021
Tel.: (212) 879-0600
Fax : (212) 570-6206

Consulate General Office-Los Angeles
3457 Wilshire Boulevard
Los Angeles, CA 90010
Tel.: (213) 383-5126
Fax : (213) 487-3971
E-mail : kabidpen@kjri-la.com
Internet : http://www.kjri-la.com

Consulate General Office-Houston
10900 Richmond Ave.
Houston, TX 77042
Tel.: (713) 785-1691
Fax : (713) 780-9644

Consulate General Office-Chicago
Illinois Center Suite 1422
233 North Michigan Ave

Chicago, IL 60601
Tel.: (312) 938-0101
Fax : (312) 938-3148

Consulate General Office-San Francisco
1111 Columbus Ave.
San Francisco, CA 94133
Tel.: (415) 474-9571
Fax : (415) 441-4320

9. MARKET RESEARCH, CONSULTANTS, AND LAWYERS

Performing market research in Indonesia is difficult because detailed statistics on production and consumption are often not available through published sources. External trade statistics, however, are fairly detailed and additional data can be obtained for a fee from the Central Bureau of Statistics (Biro Pusat Statistik):

BPS
Ir. Sutomo No. 8
P.0. Box 3
Jakarta Pusat
Tel.: (62-21) 384-1195, 384-2508, 381-0281-4
Fax : (62-21) 385-7046
E-mail : bpshq@bps.go.id
Internet : http://www.bps.go.id

Unrecorded trade may distort import statistics and trends. For example, BPS figures tend to understate import values, as these figures exclude duty-free imports, including duty-free imports for investment and certain other transactions. Although there is a growing number of Indonesian organizations active in market research, the number remains small and expertise varies. Branches of American banks will often conduct market surveys for their customers, and several U.S. consulting firms now have affiliates in Jakarta. A growing number of foreign law firms, including some from the United States, are also entering the Indonesian business community as business consultants. Members of INKINDO, the Association of Indonesian Consultants, are able to perform a wide range of research and consulting services. INKINDO was established by Indonesian consultants based in Jakarta. The contact information for this association is as follows:

Association of Indonesian Consultants (INKINDO)
Jl. Bendungan Hilir Raya, No. 29.
Jakarta 10210
Tel.: (62-21) 573-8577/78
Fax : (62-21) 573-3474.
E-mail : inkindo@pu.go.id
Contact: Ir. H. Muhayat, Chairman

PT. Data Consult publishes a biweekly newsletter entitled "Indonesian Commercial Newsletter." The newsletter contains a sectoral survey in each issue and other market information. The addresses of several market research firms in Jakarta are listed in the "Sources of Information" section of the Overseas Business Report. Information regarding firms that are capable of conducting market surveys, including the aforementioned ones, may be obtained from the

Foreign Commercial Service, U.S. Embassy in Jakarta, or in the following list of consultants and market research firms.

10. CONSULTANTS AND MARKET RESEARCH FIRMS

AC Nielsen Indonesia
15/F Wisma Bank Dharmala
Jl. Jendral Sudirman Kav. 28
Jakarta 12920
Tel.: (62-21) 521-2200
Fax : (62-21) 521-2203/2204
E-mail: acn@acnielsen.co.id
Internet : www.acnielsen.com
Expertise: Public relations consulting, media relations, crisis management, public relations planning, government consulting.
Contact: Mariana M.G. Warokka

Business Advisory Indonesia (PT. Laksana Tata Indonesia)
Wisma Bank Dharmala, 11th floor, Suite 1103
Jl. Jendral Sudirman Kav. 28
Jakarta 12920
Tel.: (62-21) 522-8613
Fax : (62-21) 522-8612
E-mail: bai@prima.net.id
Expertise: Management consulting, government and corporate research, official sworn-in English/Indonesia language translations of documentation's.
Contact: Mariana Warokka

Castle Group
Menara Batavia, 8th floor
Jl. K.H. Mas Mansyur Kav. 126
Jakarta 10220
Tel.: (62-21) 572-7321
Fax : (62-21) 572-7329
E-mail: castle@castleasia.com
Internet: http://www.castleasia.com
Expertise: Market entry strategy consulting, customized market and industry analysis, customized profiles of local business groups and potential, local regulations and business practices, syndicated sector reports, and business briefing program for senior managers.
Contact: James Castle

CIC Consulting Group
Jl. Raden Saleh No. 46
Jakarta 10330
Tel.: (62-21) 310-1081, 314-7433
Fax : (62-21) 310-1505
Cable: CISIRAYA-JAKARTA
E-mail: cisi-cic@idola.net.id
Expertise: Market and feasibility Studies (including pharmaceuticals, cosmetics, medical supplies, health equipment, food and beverages, hotels, golf course, resorts, and recreation facilities), periodical/business Reports, credit information services, partner seeking services, project reports, consumer research, business to business research, social research, and agricultural research.

Citra Duta Artistry (CDA International)
Niaga Tower, 25th Floor
Jl. Jendral Sudirman Kav.58
Jakarta 12190
Tel.: (62-21) 250-5346
Fax : (62-21) 250-5347
E-mail: cda@idola.net.id
Expertise: Office renovation, project management, architectural design, and interior design.

Consensus MBL
Division of the MBL Group Plc., an NFO Worldwide Company
Jl. Bangka Raya 18, Pela Mampang
Jakarta 12720
or
P.O. Box 4334
Jakarta 12043
Tel.: (62-21) 719-1858/9, 719-1861, 719-5355
Fax : (62-21) 799-0152, 719-9550
E-mail: cmblindo@dnet.net.id
Internet: www.mblasia.com
Contact Name: Gordon Guscott, Sjafril Djalal
Expertise: Market research and strategic planning and consultancy.

PT. Data Consult, Inc.
Maya Indah Building II
Jl. Kramat Raya No.5-L
Jakarta 13210
Tel.: (62-21) 390-4711, 390-4712, 390-1879
Fax : (62-21) 475-3227
Or Jl. Pulomas Raya 31
Jakarta 13210
Tel.: (62-21) 475-3302, 475-3304, 475-3226
Fax : (62-21) 475-3227
E-mail : datacon@idola.net.id
Internet : http://www.datacon.co.id
Expertise: Market Research.

Ganesha Aggies Jaya
Jl. Pertogogan II No. 22 A
Kebayron Baru
Jakarta 12160
Tel.: (62-21) 7279-3904
Fax : (62-21) 739-5049
E-mail: ganesha1@cbn.net.id
Expertise: Indonesian labor laws and practices, expatriate staffing, residence and work permits, company establishment, corporate and individual document processing, and human resource related activities and publishing Indonesian Labor Law Library CD-ROM.

Grant Thornton
Wisma Grant Thornton
Jl. Sisingamangaraja No. 3C
Jakarta Selantan 12120
Tel.: (62-21) 720-2605

Fax : (62-21) 720-2606
E-mail: gti@grant-thornton.co.id
Internet: http://www.grant-thornton.co.id
Expertise: Accounting and audit services, tax advice and compliance, government advisory, municipal finance, corporate recovery and reconstruction, merger and acquisition advisory, information technology, hospitality and leisure consulting, business establishment and maintenance, inbound investment services, corporate finance, valuation and business planning, employee compensation and benefit planning.

Harvest International Inc.
Wisma Metropolitan I, 10th floor
Jl. Jendral Sudirman, Kav. 29
Jakarta 12920
Tel.: (62-21) 525-1641, 570-1491
Fax : (62-21) 520-7789
E-mail: hgoldstein@harvest-international.com or
Expertise: Consulting in business development, investment, project development, and trade.

PT. IBIS Dharma Nusa
Fatmawati Mas Blok 1/113
Jl. R.S. Fatmawati No. 20
Jakarta 12430
Tel.: (62-21) 769-9757
Fax : (62-21) 765-4906
E-mail : henri@ibisworld.com
Expertise: Market research on industrial sectors.

Indonesia Executive Search (I.E.S.)
Graha Irama, 9th floor
Jl. H.R. Rasuna Said Kav. X-1 No. 1-2
Jakarta 12950
Tel.: (62-21) 526-1250
Fax : (62-21) 525-5529
E-mail: dansearch@attglobal.net
Contact Names: Dan Goldsmith, Managing Director
Expertise: Executive search services, human resource and management consultancy.

Penelitian Hukum Indonesia (PHI)
(PT Terataimas Indocitra)
Wisma Bank Dharmala, 11th floor, Suite 11-03
Jl. Jendral Sudirman Kav. 28
Jakarta 12920
Tel.: (62-21) 522-8613
Fax : (62-21) 522-8612
E-mail: hukum@rad.net.id
Expertise: CD-ROMs containing full text of Indonesian law in English and Indonesian, development of full text databases for business and industry, information systems consulting.

Plansearch Associates
Jl. Limau 1/28 A
Kebayoran Baru
Jakarta 12130
P.O. Box 83 JKSBA

Tel.: (62-21) 739-5017, 722-8052, 727-94117
Fax : (62-21) 739-5017
E-mail: plans@indo.net.id
Contact: Gunter J. Schwarze, Guido B. Schwarze, Ronald A. Schwarze.
Expertise: Intellectual Property, partner searches, financial investigations for money collections, market research, and environmental studies.

SOFRES FSA Jakarta (Taylor Nelson Sofres Group)
Menara Thamrin Suite 1401
Jl. M.H. Thamrin Kav. 3
Jakarta 10250
Tel.: (62-21) 230-2788
Fax : (62-21) 230-2794
E-mail: JakartaOffice@id.tnsofres.com
Internet: www.tnsofres.com
Contact Name: Hans Lang and Yanti Zen
Expertise: Quantitative and qualitative market research, customer satisfaction and awareness studies, advertising testing, test marketing, concept testing, brand tracking, trade, economic and industrial research.

12. LAW FIRMS AND ATTORNEYS

Ali Budiardjo, Nugroho, Reksodiputro
Graha Niaga, 24th Floor
Jl. Jendral Sudirman Kav. 58,
Jakarta 12190
Tel.: (62-21) 250-5125(11 lines), 250-5136
Fax : (62-21) 250-5121, 250-5122, 250-5392, 250-5001
E-mail: abnrco@abnr.co.id
Singapore Office:
50 Raffles Place
37-00 Singapore Land Tower
Singapore 048623
Tel.: (65) 320-8708
Fax : (65) 320-8709
Expertise: Commercial, corporate, and financing matters, including joint venture arrangements, licensing, banking, energy, mining, forestry, project finance, stock & bond issues, construction & engineering projects, maritime law, labor issues, patents, trademark, and other intellectual property matters.
Contact: T.M. Zahirsjah, Ferry P. Madian, Gregory Churchill

PT. CB Indonesia
16th Fl. Central Plaza
Jl. Jendral Sudirman Kav.47
Jakarta 12930
Tel.: (62-21) 525-1985, 570-1425, 525-3340
Fax : (62-21) 525-0734
E-mail: cbindon@attglobal.net.
Expertise: Joint ventures, insolvency and corporate reorganizations, finance and capital markets, infrastructure and property development, and commercial transactions and disputes.
Contact: Michael Horn

Dewi Soeharto & Rekan
Plaza Exim, 24th Fl.
Jl. Jendral Gatot Soebroto Kav.36-38
Jakarta 12190
Tel.: (62-21) 526-3473
Fax : (62-21) 526-3474
E-mail: dsrekan@indosat.net.id
Contact: Dewi Kamaratih Soeharto, Garry W. Christian
Expertise: Aviation, banking and finance, commercial, construction, corporate, energy and resources, entertainment industry contracts, environmental, foreign investment and joint ventures, government, intellectual property protection and enforcement, international trade, labor and employment, maritime, media and board casting, real property, securities, tax, telecommunications.

Frans Winarta & Partners
Kelapa Gading Boulevard TB 2/24
Kelapa Gading Permai
Jakarta Utara 14240
Tel.: (62-21) 453-3236, 453-2143
Fax : (62-21) 452-0083, 451-6605, 452-0933
E-mail: frans_winarta@hotmail.com
Contact: Frans H. Winarta
Expertise: Corporate law (cross-border acquisitions and mergers, investments, business, and matters regarding intellectual property), commercial laws and banking regulations, general international trade laws, employment and land laws, civil and administrative law, litigation and international commercial arbitration.

George Widjojo & Partners
Patents, Trademarks & Copyrights
Advocates & Solicitors
Jl. Kali Besar Barat No. 5
Jakarta 11230
Indonesia
P.O. Box 2102 / JKT
Jakarta 10021, Indonesia
Tel.: (62-21) 691-2226, 692-4533, 690-1707
Fax: (62-21) 692-3648, 693-0712
E-mail: gwidjojo@indosat.net.id
Contact person: Mr. George Widjojo
Expertise: Patents, Trademarks, Copyrights and Designs

Hadiputranto, Hadinoto & Partners
Bursa Efek Jakarta Tower II, 21st Floor
Jl. Jendral Sudirman Kav. 52-53
Jakarta Selatan
Tel.: (62-21) 515-5090, 515-5091, 515-5092
Fax : (62-21) 515-4840, 515-4845
Contact: Ms. Sri Indrastuti Hadiputranto
Expertise: International and general practice, corporate, commercial, foreign investment, tax: labor and employment law, banking and finance (including project finance), capital markets, intellectual property, construction, natural resources telecommunications, insurance, mergers and acquisitions, and environmental law.

Jusuf Indradewa & Partners-Legal Consultants
Bank Artha Graha Tower, 15th Floor
Lot 25, Sudirman Central Business District
Jl. Jendral Sudirman Kav. 52-53
Jakarta 12190
Tel.: (62-21) 515-2122
Fax : (62-21) 515-2382
E-mail: jusufind@uninet.net.id
Contact: Cecilia Sianawati (Managing Partner), Jusuf Indradewa (Senior Partner), Indra D. Santosa (Technical Advisor), Maya Pradjono (Partner)
Expertise: Legal matters relating to establishment of businesses, opening representative and branch offices, joint ventures, direct foreign investment companies, intellectual property rights, mergers and acquisitions, initial public offerings.

Karim Sani Law Firm
Wisma Danamon Aetna Life, 11th Floor
Jl. Jendral Sudirman Kav. 45-46
Jakarta 12930
Tel.: (62-21) 577-1177
Fax : (62-21) 577-1947, 577-1587
E-mail: kksm@indosat.net.id
Expertise: Investment, tax, energy, mining, information technology law, and arbitration/mediation.
Contact: Karen Mills (International Legal Advisor), Kitty Sugondo-Kramadibrata (Project Legal Structure & Commercial Citigation), Iswahjudi A. Karim (Banking & Finance), Asrul Sani (intellectual Property Rights & Commercial Litigation), Tio M. Manihuruk (Corp. Finance/Capital Markets & Property Investment)

Kusnandar & Co.
Aetna Danamon Tower II, 24th Fl.
Jl. Jendral Sudirman Kav. 45
Jakarta 12930
P.O. Box 2057, JKT 10001
Tel.: (62-21) 577-1435
Fax : (62-21) 577 1436
E-mail: kusnalaw@ub.net.id
Internet: http://www.kusnandar.co.id/
Expertise: Foreign and domestic investment, banking, multi finance, the capital market, securities, tax, natural resources, plantations civil, commercial & criminal trademark, patent & copyright litigation & enforcement trade secret, industrial design, liquidators & bankruptcy lawyers, merger, acquisition, consolidation & integrated circuit official receivers, administrators project finance, licensing, counterfeit domestic & overseas arbitration, admiralty, insurance trade, anti-monopoly company establishment in land, construction & conveyance, labor, unions & CLA, Indonesia or offshore tax review, maintenance accounting service, sworn translation.
Contact: Winita E. Kusnandar, John S. Beaumont

Lontoh & Kailimang
Jl. H.O.S. Cokroaminoto No. 47
Jakarta 10350
Tel.: (62-21) 392-3355
Fax : (62-21) 392-3366
E-mail: lonka@indo.net.id
Contact: Harry Ponto
Expertise: Civil law, including adoption and child custody, wills, collections, contracts,

corporations, government relations, foreign claims, insurance, labor, direct foreign investment, trademarks/copyrights, auto accidents, immigration, capital market, narcotics, customs, and criminal defense.

Lubis, Ganie, Surowidjojo
Menara Imperium, 30th Fl.
Jl. H.R. Rasuna Said Kav. 1
Jakarta 12480
Tel.: (62-21) 831-5005, 831-5025
Fax : (62-21) 831-5015, 831-5035
E-mail: lgslaw@rad.net.id
Contact: Lubis, Ganie, Surowidjojo
Expertise: Representation of foreign and Indonesian clients on commercial and corporate law matters, including acquisition, corporate reorganization, mergers, agency and distributorship, arbitration, banking, capital market, commercial litigation, construction, corporate finance and secured transactions, energy, foreign, and domestic investment, commercial litigation and arbitration, international trade, lease financing, maritime and shipping, mining, real estate transactions, tax, telecommunications, intellectual proprietary rights including trademark, copyrights and patents, venture capital, insurance and labor.

Makarim & Taira S
Summitmas I, 17th Fl. & 18th Fl.
Jl. Jendral Sudirman Kav. 61-62
Jakarta 12069
Tel.: (62-21) 252-1272, 252-2460
Fax : (62-21) 252-2750, 252-2751, 252-2234
E-mail: m_ts@pacific.net.id
Expertise: International and general practice. foreign investment, commercial, capital markets, banking and finance, constructions, energy and natural resources, intellectual property, commercial litigation, tax, mergers and acquisitions, property development.

Makes & Partner (in association with SKADDEN, ARPS, SLATE, MEAGHER & FLOM)
Menara Batavia, 7th Floor
Jl. K.H. Mas Mansyur Kav. 126
Jakarta 10220
Tel.: (62-21) 574-7181
Fax : (62-21) 574-7180
E-mail: makes@indosat.net.id
Contact: Iwan Setiawan
Expertise: Corporate and commercial law, restructuring and reorganizations, mergers and acquisitions (including tender offers), foreign and domestic capital investment (including joint ventures), banking and corporate finance (including bank financing, issuance of debt instruments and establishment of venture capital companies and local branches of international investment and commercial banks), capital markets (including debts and equity offerings by Indonesian companies in the Indonesian and International capital markets as well as listing on the Jakarta, Surabaya, Singapore, New York, London, and Luxemburg Stock Exchanges and Nasdaq), telecommunications, energy and infrastructure (including oil and gas contracts and project finance) and real property law.

Mochtar, Karuwin & Komar
Wisma Metropolitan II, 14th fl.
Jl. Jendral Sudirman, Kav 31
Jakarta 12920

Tel.: (62-21) 571-1130
Fax : (62-21) 571-1162, 570-1686
E-mail: mail@mkk.co.id
Contact: Emir Kusumaatmadja
Expertise: General corporate and commercial law, specializing in the legal aspects of international finance, foreign investment, infrastructure, and privatization.

Prof. Dr. Sudargo Gautama
Jl. Merdeka Timur 9
Jakarta 10110
Tel.: (62-21) 345-6529, 384-1358, 384-7165, 380-9488
Fax : (62-21) 384-6180, 381-3166
E-mail: sgautama@rad.net.id
Contact: Prof. Dr. Sudargo Gautama
Expertise: General, civil and criminal law, patents and trademarks, private international law, consulting, and litigation.

Rosetini Ibrahim & Associates
Wisma GKBI 33rd. Fl., Suite 3309
Jl. Jendral Sudirman #28
Jakarta 10210
Tel.: (62-21) 574-1225
Fax : (62-21) 574-1226
E-mail: rosetini@rosetini.com
Internet: www.rosetini.com
Contact: Rosetini Ibrahim, Richard Weiss, Dennie Rahmanto
Expertise: Corporate law, finance and foreign investments.

Soewito, Suhardiman, Eddymurthy & Kardono
Wisma Bank Dharmala, 14th Fl., Suite 1403
Jl. Jendral Sudirman Kav.28
Jakarta 12920
Tel.: (62-21) 521-2038
Fax : (62-21) 521-2039
E-mail: ssek@ssek.com
Internet: http://www.ssek.com
Contact: Darrell R. Johnson, Michael D. Twomey
Expertise: Corporate, commercial and financial law practice, energy and natural resources, maritime, banking, capital markets and securities law, insurance, intellectual property, investment, labor, franchising, real estate, construction and engineering, mergers and acquisitions, tax law, arbitration, hotel and tourist development, environmental law, international trade, government contracts, immigration, oil and gas law.

Taira & Suyudono
Menara Dea Suite 1104
Kawasan Mega Kuningan
Jakarta 12950, Indonesia
Tel.: (62-21) 576-3030 Fax: (62-21) 576-3033 E-mail: finlaw@taira.co.id
Contact: Frank Taira Supit, Benny Suyudono
Expertise: Corporate law, corporate finance, capital markets, infrastructure, financial litigation, financial transactions, complicated business

BASIC TITLES ON INDONESIA

Title	ISBN
Indonesia A "Spy" Guide - Strategic Information and Developments	1433023253
Indonesia A Spy" Guide"	1438723210
Indonesia Air Force Handbook	1433023261
Indonesia Air Force Handbook	1438723229
Indonesia Art Handicrafts, Children's Toys, and Paintings Export-Import and Business Opportunities Handbook	143302327X
Indonesia Art Handicrafts, Children's Toys, and Paintings Export-Import and Business Opportunities Handbook	1438723237
Indonesia Banking & Financial Market Handbook	1433023288
Indonesia Banking & Financial Market Handbook	1438723245
Indonesia Banks, Financial Companies Export-Import and Business Opportunities Handbook	1433023296
Indonesia Banks, Financial Companies Export-Import and Business Opportunities Handbook	1438723253
Indonesia Business and Investment Opportunities Yearbook	143302330X
Indonesia Business and Investment Opportunities Yearbook	1438723261
Indonesia Business and Investment Opportunities Yearbook Volume 1 Strategic Information and Opportunities	1438776942
Indonesia Business and Investment Opportunities Yearbook Volume 2 Leading Export-Import, Business, Investment Opportunities and Projects	1577519728
Indonesia Business Intelligence Report - Practical Information, Opportunities, Contacts	1433023318
Indonesia Business Intelligence Report - Practical Information, Opportunities, Contacts	143872327X
Indonesia Business Law Handbook - Strategic Information and Basic Laws	1438770073
Indonesia Business Law Handbook - Strategic Information and Basic Laws	1438770073
Indonesia Business Law Handbook - Strategic Information and Basic Laws	1433023326
Indonesia Business Law Handbook - Strategic Information and Basic Laws	1438723288
Indonesia Business Law Handbook Volume 2 Investment and Trade Laws Volume 2 Investment and Trade Laws	1577516478
Indonesia Chemical Industry Export-Import and Business Opportunities Handbook	1433023334
Indonesia Chemical Industry Export-Import and Business Opportunities Handbook	1438723296
Indonesia Clothing & Textile Industry Handbook	143872330X
Indonesia Clothing & Textile Industry Handbook	1433023342
Indonesia Clothing Manufacturing Export-Import and Business Opportunities Handbook	1433023350
Indonesia Clothing Manufacturing Export-Import and Business Opportunities Handbook	1438723318
Indonesia Company Laws and Regulations Handbook	1433069989
Indonesia Constitution and Citizenship Laws Handbook - Strategic Information and Basic Laws	1438779127
Indonesia Construction Industry Export-Import and Business Opportunities Handbook	1433023369

Title	ISBN
Indonesia Construction Industry Export-Import and Business Opportunities Handbook	1438723326
Indonesia Country Study Guide - Strategic Information and Developments	1433023377
Indonesia Country Study Guide - Strategic Information and Developments	1438723334
Indonesia Country Study Guide - Strategic Information and Developments Volume 1 Strategic Information and Developments	1438774613
Indonesia Customs, Trade Regulations and Procedures Handbook	1433023385
Indonesia Customs, Trade Regulations and Procedures Handbook	1438723342
Indonesia Diplomatic Handbook - Strategic Information and Developments	1433023393
Indonesia Diplomatic Handbook - Strategic Information and Developments	1438723350
Indonesia Ecology & Nature Protection Handbook	1433023407
Indonesia Ecology & Nature Protection Handbook	1438723369
Indonesia Ecology & Nature Protection Laws and Regulation Handbook	1433074001
Indonesia Economic & Development Strategy Handbook	1433023415
Indonesia Economic & Development Strategy Handbook	1438723377
Indonesia Education System and Policy Handbook	1433066246
Indonesia Electrical Machinery, Equipment, Apparatus Export-Import and Business Opportunities Handbook	1433023423
Indonesia Electrical Machinery, Equipment, Apparatus Export-Import and Business Opportunities Handbook	1438723385
Indonesia Electronic, Electrical, Communication Export-Import and Business Opportunities Handbook	1433023431
Indonesia Electronic, Electrical, Communication Export-Import and Business Opportunities Handbook	1438723393
Indonesia Energy Policy, Laws and Regulation Handbook	1433071762
Indonesia Energy Policy, Laws and Regulations Handbook	143302344X
Indonesia Energy Policy, Laws and Regulations Handbook	1438723407
Indonesia Export-Import Trade and Business Directory	1433023458
Indonesia Export-Import Trade and Business Directory	1438723415
Indonesia Food, Beverage and Tobacco Export-Import and Business Opportunities Handbook	1433023466
Indonesia Food, Beverage and Tobacco Export-Import and Business Opportunities Handbook	1438723423
Indonesia Footwear Manufacturing Export-Import and Business Opportunities Handbook	1433023474
Indonesia Footwear Manufacturing Export-Import and Business Opportunities Handbook	1438723431
Indonesia Foreign Policy and Government Guide	1433023482
Indonesia Foreign Policy and Government Guide	143872344X
Indonesia Government and Business Contacts Handbook	1433023490
Indonesia Government and Business Contacts Handbook	1438723458
Indonesia Health Care, Cosmetics, Pharmaceuticals Producers Handbook	1433023504
Indonesia Health Care, Cosmetics, Pharmaceuticals Producers Handbook	1438723466
Indonesia Healthcare Sector Organization, Management and Payment Systems Handbook - Strategic Information, Programs and Regulations	9781433085871
Indonesia Immigration Laws and Regulations Handbook - Strategic Information	1438782748

Title	ISBN
and Basic Laws	
Indonesia Industrial and Business Directory	1433023512
Indonesia Insolvency (Bankruptcy) Laws and Regulations Handbook - Strategic Information and Basic Laws	9781433085345
Indonesia Internet and E-Commerce Investment and Business Guide - Strategic and Practical Information: Regulations and Opportunities	1433023520
Indonesia Internet and E-Commerce Investment and Business Guide - Strategic and Practical Information: Regulations and Opportunities	1438723474
Indonesia Investment and Business Guide - Strategic and Practical Information	143876779X
Indonesia Investment and Business Guide - Strategic and Practical Information	143876779X
Indonesia Investment and Business Guide - Strategic and Practical Information	1433023539
Indonesia Investment and Business Guide - Strategic and Practical Information	1438723482
Indonesia Investment and Business Guide Volume 2 Business, Investment Opportunities and Incentives	1577518683
Indonesia Investment and Trade Laws and Regulations Handbook	1433075997
Indonesia Justice System and National Police Handbook	1433023547
Indonesia Justice System and National Police Handbook	1438723490
Indonesia Labor Laws and Regulations Handbook - Strategic Information and Basic Laws	143878094X
Indonesia Land Ownership and Agriculture Laws Handbook	1438759231
Indonesia Leather and Leather Product Manufacturing Export-Import and Business Opportunities Handbook	1433023555
Indonesia Leather and Leather Product Manufacturing Export-Import and Business Opportunities Handbook	1438723504
Indonesia Machinery & Equipment Export-Import and Business Opportunities Handbook	1433023563
Indonesia Machinery & Equipment Export-Import and Business Opportunities Handbook	1438723512
Indonesia Medical & Pharmaceutical Industry Handbook	1433023571
Indonesia Medical & Pharmaceutical Industry Handbook	1438723520
Indonesia Metals and Metal Products Export-Import and Business Opportunities Handbook	143302358X
Indonesia Metals and Metal Products Export-Import and Business Opportunities Handbook	1438723539
Indonesia Mineral & Mining Sector Investment and Business Guide - Strategic and Practical Information	1433023598
Indonesia Mineral & Mining Sector Investment and Business Guide - Strategic and Practical Information	1438723547
Indonesia Mining Laws and Regulations Handbook	1433077574
Indonesia Mining, Oil & Gas Industry Export-Import and Business Opportunities Handbook	1433023601
Indonesia Mining, Oil & Gas Industry Export-Import and Business Opportunities Handbook	1438723555
Indonesia Oil & Gas Sector Business & Investment Opportunities Yearbook	143302361X
Indonesia Oil & Gas Sector Business & Investment Opportunities Yearbook	1438723563
Indonesia Oil and Gas Exploration Laws and Regulation Handbook	1433078732

Title	ISBN
Indonesia Oil and Gas Industry Handbook	1433023628
Indonesia Oil and Gas Industry Handbook	1438723571
Indonesia Paper and Paper Product, Printing and Publishing Export-Import and Business Opportunities Handbook	1433023636
Indonesia Paper and Paper Product, Printing and Publishing Export-Import and Business Opportunities Handbook	143872358X
Indonesia Plastic Product Manufacturing Export-Import and Business Opportunities Handbook	1433023644
Indonesia Plastic Product Manufacturing Export-Import and Business Opportunities Handbook	1438723598
Indonesia Porcelain and Glass Manufacturing Export-Import and Business Opportunities Handbook	1433023652
Indonesia Porcelain and Glass Manufacturing Export-Import and Business Opportunities Handbook	1438723601
Indonesia Privatization Programs and Regulations Handbook	1433023660
Indonesia Privatization Programs and Regulations Handbook	143872361X
Indonesia Real Estate Companies Export-Import and Business Opportunities Handbook	1433023679
Indonesia Real Estate Companies Export-Import and Business Opportunities Handbook	1438723628
Indonesia Recent Economic and Political Developments Yearbook	1433063794
Indonesia Recent Economic and Political Developments Yearbook	1433063794
Indonesia Recent Economic and Political Developments Yearbook	1433063794
Indonesia Research & Development Policy Handbook	1433063166
Indonesia Research & Development Policy Handbook	1433063166
Indonesia Research & Development Policy Handbook	1433063166
Indonesia Rubber and Rubber Product Manufacturing Export-Import and Business Opportunities Handbook	1433023687
Indonesia Rubber and Rubber Product Manufacturing Export-Import and Business Opportunities Handbook	1438723636
Indonesia Starting Business (Incorporating) in Indonesia Guide	1433046997
Indonesia Starting Business (Incorporating) in....Guide	1433066254
Indonesia Stone, Marble, and Asbestos Manufacturing Export-Import and Business Opportunities Handbook	1433023695
Indonesia Stones, Marble, Granite and Asbestos Manufacturing Export-Import and Business Opportunities Handbook	1438723644
Indonesia Taxation Laws and Regulations Handbook	1433080028
Indonesia Technical Assistance Proposals 2006-2009 Vol 1 Project Assistance Proposals	1433066262
Indonesia Technical Assistance Proposals 2006-2009 Vol 2 Technical Assistance Proposals	1433066270
Indonesia Telecom Laws and Regulations Handbook	1433081911
Indonesia Telecommunication Industry Business Opportunities Handbook	1433023709
Indonesia Telecommunication Industry Business Opportunities Handbook	1438723652
Indonesia Textile, Clothing Products Export-Import and Business Opportunities Handbook	1433023717

Title	ISBN
Indonesia Textile, Clothing Products Export-Import and Business Opportunities Handbook	1438723660
Indonesia Transport Equipment and Ships Producers Handbook	1433023725
Indonesia Transport Equipment and Ships Producers Handbook	1438723679
Indonesia Transportation Policy and Regulations Handbook	1433066289
Indonesia Wood, Bamboo, Grass, Household Export-Import and Business Opportunities Handbook	1433023733
Indonesia Wood, Bamboo, Grass, Household Export-Import and Business Opportunities Handbook	1438723687
Indonesia: How to Invest, Start and Run Profitable Business in Indonesia Guide - Practical Information, Opportunities, Contacts	9781433083594

Title
Kuwait Oil & Gas Sector Business & Investment Opportunities Yearbook
Libya Oil & Gas Sector Business & Investment Opportunities Yearbook
Malaysia Oil & Gas Sector Business & Investment Opportunities Yearbook
Mexico Oil & Gas Sector Business & Investment Opportunities Yearbook
Morocco Oil & Gas Sector Business & Investment Opportunities Yearbook
Namibia Oil & Gas Sector Business & Investment Opportunities Yearbook
New Zealand Oil & Gas Sector Business & Investment Opportunities Yearbook
Nigeria Oil & Gas Sector Business & Investment Opportunities Yearbook
Norway Oil & Gas Sector Business & Investment Opportunities Yearbook
Oman Oil & Gas Sector Business & Investment Opportunities Yearbook
Pakistan Oil & Gas Sector Business & Investment Opportunities Yearbook
Papua New Guinea Oil & Gas Sector Business & Investment Opportunities Yearbook
Papua New Guinea Oil & Gas Sector Oil & Gas Sector Business & Investment Opportunities Yearbook
Peru Oil & Gas Sector Business & Investment Opportunities Yearbook
Philippines Oil & Gas Sector Business & Investment Opportunities Yearbook
Qatar Oil & Gas Sector Business & Investment Opportunities Yearbook
Sri Lanka Oil & Gas Sector Business & Investment Opportunities Yearbook
Romania Oil & Gas Sector Business & Investment Opportunities Yearbook
Russia Oil & Gas Sector Business & Investment Opportunities Yearbook
Saudi Arabia Oil & Gas Sector Business & Investment Opportunities Yearbook
Sudan Oil & Gas Sector Business & Investment Opportunities Yearbook
Suriname Oil & Gas Sector Business & Investment Opportunities Yearbook
Syria Oil & Gas Sector Business & Investment Opportunities Yearbook
Trinidad and Tobago Oil & Gas Sector Oil & Gas Sector Business & Investment Opportunities Yearbook
Tunisia Oil & Gas Sector Business & Investment Opportunities Yearbook
Turkey Oil & Gas Sector Business & Investment Opportunities Yearbook
Turkmenistan Oil & Gas Sector Business & Investment Opportunities Yearbook
Ukraine Oil & Gas Sector Oil & Gas Sector Business & Investment Opportunities Yearbook
United Arab Emirates Oil & Gas Sector Business & Investment Opportunities Yearbook
United Kingdom Oil & Gas Sector Business & Investment Opportunities Yearbook
United Kingdom Oil & Gas Sector Oil & Gas Sector Business & Investment Opportunities Yearbook
United States Oil & Gas Sector Business & Investment Opportunities Yearbook
Venezuela Oil & Gas Sector Business & Investment Opportunities Yearbook
Vietnam Investment Pojects and Joint Ventures Hnadbook
Vietnam Oil & Gas Sector Business & Investment Opportunities Yearbook
Yemen Oil & Gas Sector Business & Investment Opportunities Yearbook

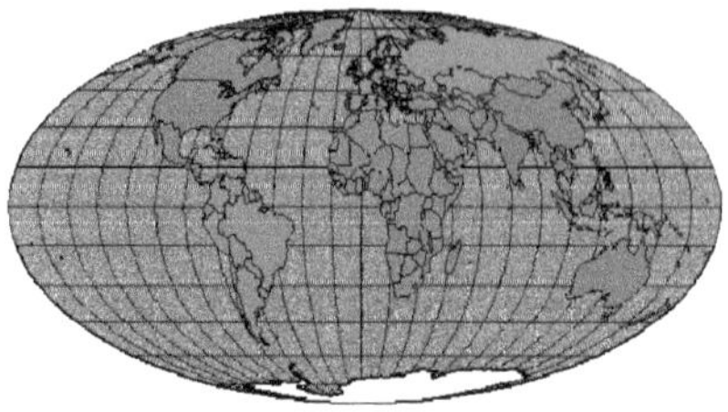

WORLD MINING LAWS AND REGULATIONS HANDBOOK LIBRARY

Price: $149.95 Each

1.	Afghanistan Mining Laws and Regulations Handbook
2.	Albania Mining Laws and Regulations Handbook
3.	Algeria Mining Laws and Regulations Handbook
4.	Angola Mining Laws and Regulations Handbook
5.	Argentina Mining Laws and Regulations Handbook
6.	Armenia Mining Laws and Regulations Handbook
7.	Australia Mining Laws and Regulations Handbook
8.	Austria Mining Laws and Regulations Handbook
9.	Azerbaijan Mining Laws and Regulations Handbook
10.	Bahrain Mining Laws and Regulations Handbook
11.	Bangladesh Mining Laws and Regulations Handbook
12.	Belarus Mining Laws and Regulations Handbook
13.	Belgium Mining Laws and Regulations Handbook
14.	Benin Mining Laws and Regulations Handbook
15.	Bolivia Mining Laws and Regulations Handbook
16.	Bosnia and Herzegovina Mining Laws and Regulations Handbook
17.	Botswana Mining Laws and Regulations Handbook
18.	Brazil Mining Laws and Regulations Handbook
19.	Brunei Mining Laws and Regulations Handbook
20.	Bulgaria Mining Laws and Regulations Handbook
21.	Burkina Faso Mining Laws and Regulations Handbook
22.	Burundi Mining Laws and Regulations Handbook
23.	Cambodia Mining Laws and Regulations Handbook
24.	Cameroon Mining Laws and Regulations Handbook
25.	Canada Mining Laws and Regulations Handbook
26.	Cape Verde Mining Laws and Regulations Handbook
27.	Cayman Islands Mining Laws and Regulations Handbook
28.	Central African Republic Mining Laws and Regulations Handbook
29.	Chad Mining Laws and Regulations Handbook
30.	Chile Mining Laws and Regulations Handbook
31.	China Mining Laws and Regulations Handbook
32.	Colombia Mining Laws and Regulations Handbook

33.	Comoros Mining Laws and Regulations Handbook
34.	Congo Mining Laws and Regulations Handbook
35.	Congo, Dem. Republic Mining Laws and Regulations Handbook
36.	Cook Islands Mining Laws and Regulations Handbook
37.	Costa Rica Mining Laws and Regulations Handbook
38.	Cote d'Ivoire Mining Laws and Regulations Handbook
39.	Croatia Mining Laws and Regulations Handbook
40.	Cuba Mining Laws and Regulations Handbook
41.	Czech Republic Mining Laws and Regulations Handbook
42.	Denmark Mining Laws and Regulations Handbook
43.	Djibouti Mining Laws and Regulations Handbook
44.	Dominican Republic Mining Laws and Regulations Handbook
45.	Dubai Mining Laws and Regulations Handbook
46.	Ecuador Mining Laws and Regulations Handbook
47.	Egypt Mining Laws and Regulations Handbook
48.	El Salvador Mining Laws and Regulations Handbook
49.	Equatorial Guinea Mining Laws and Regulations Handbook
50.	Eritrea Mining Laws and Regulations Handbook
51.	Estonia Mining Laws and Regulations Handbook
52.	Ethiopia Mining Laws and Regulations Handbook
53.	Fiji Mining Laws and Regulations Handbook
54.	Finland Mining Laws and Regulations Handbook
55.	France Mining Laws and Regulations Handbook
56.	Gabon Mining Laws and Regulations Handbook
57.	Gambia Mining Laws and Regulations Handbook
58.	Georgia Mining Laws and Regulations Handbook
59.	Germany Mining Laws and Regulations Handbook
60.	Ghana Mining Laws and Regulations Handbook
61.	Greece Mining Laws and Regulations Handbook
62.	Greenland Mining Laws and Regulations Handbook
63.	Guatemala Mining Laws and Regulations Handbook
64.	Guinea Mining Laws and Regulations Handbook
65.	Guinea-Bissau Mining Laws and Regulations Handbook
66.	Guyana Mining Laws and Regulations Handbook
67.	Haiti Mining Laws and Regulations Handbook
68.	Honduras Mining Laws and Regulations Handbook
69.	Hungary Mining Laws and Regulations Handbook
70.	Iceland Mining Laws and Regulations Handbook
71.	India Mining Laws and Regulations Handbook
72.	Indonesia Mining Laws and Regulations Handbook
73.	Iran Mining Laws and Regulations Handbook
74.	Iraq Mining Laws and Regulations Handbook
75.	Ireland Mining Laws and Regulations Handbook

76. Israel Mining Laws and Regulations Handbook
77. Italy Mining Laws and Regulations Handbook
78. Jamaica Mining Laws and Regulations Handbook
79. Japan Mining Laws and Regulations Handbook
80. Jordan Mining Laws and Regulations Handbook
81. Kazakhstan Mining Laws and Regulations Handbook
82. Kenya Mining Laws and Regulations Handbook
83. Korea, South Mining Laws and Regulations Handbook
84. Kuwait Mining Laws and Regulations Handbook
85. Kyrgyzstan Mining Laws and Regulations Handbook
86. Laos Mining Laws and Regulations Handbook
87. Latvia Mining Laws and Regulations Handbook
88. Lesotho Mining Laws and Regulations Handbook
89. Liberia Mining Laws and Regulations Handbook
90. Libya Mining Laws and Regulations Handbook
91. Lithuania Mining Laws and Regulations Handbook
92. Macedonia Republic Mining Laws and Regulations Handbook
93. Madagascar Mining Laws and Regulations Handbook
94. Malawi Mining Laws and Regulations Handbook
95. Malaysia Mining Laws and Regulations Handbook
96. Mali Mining Laws and Regulations Handbook
97. Mauritania Mining Laws and Regulations Handbook
98. Mauritius Mining Laws and Regulations Handbook
99. Mexico Mining Laws and Regulations Handbook
100. Moldova Mining Laws and Regulations Handbook
101. Mongolia Mining Laws and Regulations Handbook
102. Morocco Mining Laws and Regulations Handbook
103. Mozambique Mining Laws and Regulations Handbook
104. Myanmar Mining Laws and Regulations Handbook
105. Namibia Mining Laws and Regulations Handbook
106. Nepal Mining Laws and Regulations Handbook
107. Netherlands Mining Laws and Regulations Handbook
108. New Zealand Mining Laws and Regulations Handbook
109. Nicaragua Mining Laws and Regulations Handbook
110. Niger Mining Laws and Regulations Handbook
111. Nigeria Mining Laws and Regulations Handbook
112. Norway Mining Laws and Regulations Handbook
113. Oman Mining Laws and Regulations Handbook
114. Pakistan Mining Laws and Regulations Handbook
115. Papua New Guinea Mining Laws and Regulations Handbook
116. Paraguay Mining Laws and Regulations Handbook
117. Peru Mining Laws and Regulations Handbook
118. Philippines Mining Laws and Regulations Handbook

119. Poland Mining Laws and Regulations Handbook
120. Portugal Mining Laws and Regulations Handbook
121. Qatar Mining Laws and Regulations Handbook
122. Romania Mining Laws and Regulations Handbook
123. Russia Mining Laws and Regulations Handbook
124. Rwanda Mining Laws and Regulations Handbook
125. Sao Tome and Principe Mining Laws and Regulations Handbook
126. Saudi Arabia Mining Laws and Regulations Handbook
127. Senegal Mining Laws and Regulations Handbook
128. Serbia Mining Laws and Regulations Handbook
129. Sierra Leone Mining Laws and Regulations Handbook
130. Slovakia Mining Laws and Regulations Handbook
131. Slovenia Mining Laws and Regulations Handbook
132. Somalia Mining Laws and Regulations Handbook
133. South Africa Mining Laws and Regulations Handbook
134. Spain Mining Laws and Regulations Handbook
135. Sri Lanka Mining Laws and Regulations Handbook
136. Sudan Mining Laws and Regulations Handbook
137. Suriname Mining Laws and Regulations Handbook
138. Swaziland Mining Laws and Regulations Handbook
139. Sweden Mining Laws and Regulations Handbook
140. Syria Mining Laws and Regulations Handbook
141. Taiwan Mining Laws and Regulations Handbook
142. Tajikistan Mining Laws and Regulations Handbook
143. Tanzania Mining Laws and Regulations Handbook
144. Thailand Mining Laws and Regulations Handbook
145. Togo Mining Laws and Regulations Handbook
146. Trinidad and Tobago Mining Laws and Regulations Handbook
147. Tunisia Mining Laws and Regulations Handbook
148. Turkey Mining Laws and Regulations Handbook
149. Turkmenistan Mining Laws and Regulations Handbook
150. Uganda Mining Laws and Regulations Handbook
151. Ukraine Mining Laws and Regulations Handbook
152. United Arab Emirates Mining Laws and Regulations Handbook
153. United Kingdom Mining Laws and Regulations Handbook
154. United States Mining Laws and Regulations Handbook
155. Uruguay Mining Laws and Regulations Handbook
156. Uzbekistan Mining Laws and Regulations Handbook
157. Venezuela Mining Laws and Regulations Handbook
158. Vietnam Mining Laws and Regulations Handbook
159. Yemen Mining Laws and Regulations Handbook
160. Zambia Mining Laws and Regulations Handbook
161. Zimbabwe Mining Laws and Regulations Handbook

www.ingramcontent.com/pod-product-compliance
Ingram Content Group UK Ltd.
Pitfield, Milton Keynes, MK11 3LW, UK
UKHW051510290926
15471UKWH00008B/1530

9 781438 723556